SpringBoard®
English
Language Arts

STUDENT EDITION — GRADE 6

About The College Board

The College Board is a mission-driven not-for-profit organization that connects students to college success and opportunity. Founded in 1900, the College Board was created to expand access to higher education. Today, the membership association is made up of over 6,000 of the world's leading educational institutions and is dedicated to promoting excellence and equity in education. Each year, the College Board helps more than seven million students prepare for a successful transition to college through programs and services in college readiness and college success—including the SAT® and the Advanced Placement Program®. The organization also serves the education community through research and advocacy on behalf of students, educators, and schools. For further information, visit collegeboard.org.

ISBN: 978-1-4573-1292-2

4 5 6 7 8   22 23 24 25 26
Printed in the United States of America

Acknowledgements

The College Board gratefully acknowledges the outstanding work of the classroom teachers who have been integral to the development of this program. The end product is testimony to their expertise, understanding of student learning needs, and dedication to rigorous and accessible English Language Arts instruction.

Lance Balla
Everett School District
Everett, Washington

Christina Bartholet
Goodman Middle
School, Gig Harbor,
Washington

Carisa Barnes
San Diego Unified
School District
San Diego, California

Leia Bell
Hillsborough County
Public Schools
Tampa, Florida

Alysa Broussard
Lafayette Parish
School System
Lafayette, Louisiana

Robert J. Caughey
San Dieguito Union
High School District
San Diego, California

Susie Challancin
Bellevue School District 405
Bellevue, Washington

Amanda Connell
Lisle, Illinois

Paul De Maret
Poudre School District
Fort Collins, Colorado

Michael Gragert
Plano Independent
School District
Plano, Texas

Nancy Gray
Brevard County Schools
Viera, Florida

Charles F. Hall
Peninsula School District
Gig Harbor, Washington

Charise Hallberg
Bellevue School District 405
Bellevue, Washington

T.J. Hanify
Bellevue School District 405
Bellevue, Washington

Cheryl Harris
Hurst-Euless-Bedford
Independent School District
Bedford, Texas

Karen Kampschmidt
Fort Thomas Independent
School District
Fort Thomas, Kentucky

Kerstin Karlsoon
Hillsborough County
Public Schools
Tampa, Florida

LeAnn Klepzig
Bradley County Schools
Cleveland, Tennessee

Michelle Lewis
Spokane Public School
Spokane, Washington

Susie Lowry
Volusia County
School District
Deland, Florida

John Marshall
Mead School District
Mead, Washington

Kristie Messer
Burnet Consolidated
Independent School
District Burnet, Texas

Missy Miles
Carmel Christian School
Charlotte, North Carolina

Glenn Morgan
San Diego Unified
School District
San Diego, California

Amanda Olinger
Harrisburg School District
Harrisburg, South Dakota

Kristin Oliver
Rio Rancho Public
School District
Rio Rancho, New Mexico

Molly Olmstead
Peninsula School District
Gig Harbor, Washington

Julie Pennabaker
Quakertown Community
School District
Quakertown, Pennsylvania

Bryan Sandala
School District of
Palm Beach County
West Palm Beach, Florida

Amanda Shackelford
Lafayette Parish
School System
Lafayette, Louisiana

Angela Shuttles
Hillsborough County Public
Schools Tampa, Florida

Kimberlyn Slagle
Lafayette Parish
School System
Lafayette, Louisiana

Holly Talley
Hillsborough County
Public Schools
Ruskin, Florida

Maria Torres-Crosby
Hillsborough County
Public Schools
Tampa, Florida

Susan Van Doren
Zephyr Cove, Nevada

JoEllen Victoreen
San Jose Unified
School District
San Jose, California

Aimee Welshans
San Diego Unified
School District
San Diego, California

Rebecca Wenrich
Peninsula School District
Gig Harbor, Washington

Research and Planning Advisors

We also wish to thank the members of our SpringBoard Advisory Council and the many educators who gave generously of their time and their ideas as we conducted research for both the print and online programs. Your suggestions and reactions to ideas helped immeasurably as we created this edition. We gratefully acknowledge the teachers and administrators in the following districts.

ABC Unified School District
Cerritos, California

Allen Independent School
District
Allen, Texas

Bellevue, School District 405
Bellevue, Washington

Burnet Consolidated
Independent School District
Burnet, Texas

Community Unit School
District 308
Oswego, Illinois

Fresno Unified
School District
Fresno, California

Frisco Independent
School District
Frisco, Texas

Garland Independent
School District
Garland, Texas

Grapevine-Colleyville
Independent School District
Grapevine, Texas

Hamilton County Schools
Chattanooga, Tennessee

Hesperia Unified
School District
Hesperia, California

Hillsborough County Public
Schools
Tampa, Florida

ICEF Public Schools
Los Angeles, California
IDEA Public Schools
Weslaco, Texas

Irving Independent
School District
Irving, Texas

Keller Independent
School District
Keller, Texas

KIPP Houston
Houston, Texas

Lafayette Parish Schools
Lafayette Parish, Louisiana

Los Angeles Unified
School District
Los Angeles, California

Lubbock Independent
School District
Lubbock, Texas

Mansfield Independent
School District
Mansfield, Texas

Midland Independent
School District
Midland, Texas

Milwaukee Public Schools
Milwaukee, Wisconsin

New Haven School District
New Haven, Connecticut

Ogden School District
Ogden, Utah

Rio Rancho Public Schools
Rio Rancho, New Mexico

San José Unified
School District
San José, California

Scottsdale Unified
School District
Scottsdale, Arizona

Spokane Public Schools
Spokane, Washington

Tacoma Public Schools
Tacoma, Washington

SpringBoard English Language Arts

Lori O'Dea
Executive Director
Content Development

Natasha Vasavada
Executive Director
Pre-AP & SpringBoard

Doug Waugh
Vice President
SpringBoard & Pre-AP
Programs

Sarah Balistreri
Senior Director
ELA Content Development

Florencia Duran Wald
Senior Director
ELA Content Development

Julie Manley
Senior Director
Professional Learning

Joely Negedly
Senior Director
Pre-AP Humanities

Jessica Brockman
Product Manager
English Language Arts

Suzie Doss
Director
SpringBoard Implementation

Jennifer Duva
Director
English Language Arts

Spencer Gonçalves
Director
Digital Content
Development

Rebecca Grudzina
Senior Editor
English Language Arts

Georgia Scurletis
Senior Instructional Writer
Pre-AP English Language
Arts

Abigail Johnson
Editor
English Language Arts

Casseia Lewis
Assistant Editor
English Language Arts

Natalie Hansford
Editorial Assistant
English Language Arts

Table of Contents

ACTIVITY Unit 3: Changing Perspectives

Resources

Texts not included in these materials.

Introduction to SpringBoard English Language Arts

About SpringBoard ELA

SpringBoard was built around a simple belief: if you give students and teachers the best materials, engaging methods, and ongoing support, then student success will surely follow. Developed by teachers, SpringBoard brings your classroom to life with materials that help you practice the skills and learn the knowledge you need to excel in middle school, high school, and beyond. Read on to find out how SpringBoard will support your learning.

Instructional Materials

SpringBoard English Language Arts supplies a Student Edition and Teacher Edition, in print and digital form, for grades 6–12. In addition to using the English Language Arts curriculum, you can sharpen your reading, writing, and language skills with materials including Language Workshop, Close Reading Workshop, and Writing Workshop.

Design that Begins with the End in Mind

- Based on the Understanding by Design model, SpringBoard teaches the skills and knowledge that matter most to meet AP and college and career readiness standards.

- You will start each unit by unpacking the assessment, so you know where you're heading and why the skills you're developing matter.

- Each activity starts with clear, standards-aligned learning targets.

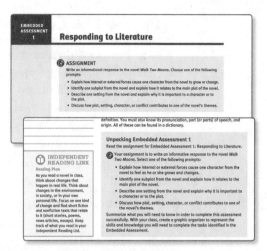

The Practice of Reading Closely

- SpringBoard puts a special focus on close reading, giving you strategies and structure for developing this key skill.

- You will encounter compelling texts—fiction, nonfiction, poetry, drama, visuals, and film.

A Living System of Learning

- SpringBoard puts you and your classmates in charge of your learning to create a more dynamic classroom experience.

- With a flexible design and rich library of tools and resources, SpringBoard helps your teacher personalize instruction for your class.

Bringing the Classroom to Life

When you enter a SpringBoard classroom you don't hear a teacher talking in the front of the room. You hear a buzz of excitement, with students working together and taking charge of how they learn. That's what the teachers who designed SpringBoard wanted for their classrooms, so they created a curriculum and materials that are focused on real classroom needs, encouraging teacher and student involvement.

SpringBoard translates the expectations of state standards into engaging daily lessons. We believe that reading, writing, speaking, and listening should all be learned together. You'll see examples of our integrated approach throughout our materials. And we put a special focus on close reading, giving you strategies and structure for developing this key skill.

Our Approach to Reading

In SpringBoard ELA, we move right into compelling texts—fiction, nonfiction, poetry, drama, visuals, and film—and offer the tools, supports, and approaches that will help you get the most out of every reading.

The Practice of Reading Closely

Texts take center stage in the SpringBoard ELA classroom, where you will prepare for close, critical reading of a wide range of materials. With guidance from your teacher, you will develop the habits of close reading that will serve you for a lifetime.

- **Setting a Purpose for Reading:** You ask questions, make predictions, observe genre characteristics and text structures, and prepare to annotate the text.

- **First Reading:** You read on your own, with a partner, in a group, or with the class. You annotate the text as you begin to uncover its meaning.

- **Making Observations:** Your teacher guides you to pause during or right after the first reading to observe the small details within a text in order to arrive at a deeper understanding of the whole.

- **Returning to the Text:** You continue to deepen your understanding of the text by responding to a series of text-dependent questions. You will use text evidence, speak with new vocabulary words, reflect on your classmates' ideas, and make connections among texts, ideas, and experiences.

- **Working from the Text:** You use the text as a source as you move from reading and analysis to productive work, including academic discussion and writing.

Reading Independently

As a SpringBoard student, you'll practice good reading habits in class so that you can read challenging texts in other classes and on your own. Independent reading is an integral part of every SpringBoard English Language Arts unit. At the beginning of the year, you will learn how to make a plan for independent reading. **Independent Reading Lists** for each unit give you a jump-start on selecting texts by offering a list of suggested titles, including a number of Spanish-language titles, that connect to the themes, genres, and concepts of the SpringBoard unit.

While you work your way through each unit, you will respond to **Independent Reading Links** that lead you to make connections between the reading you're doing on your own and the skills and knowledge you're developing in class. Twice per unit, **Independent Reading Checkpoints** give you a chance to reflect on and synthesize your independent reading in an informal writing assignment or discussion.

Reading to Build Knowledge

SpringBoard units are designed so that you can delve deeply into an overarching topic, theme, or idea. Each unit will pose essential questions that relate to the ideas and texts within the unit, and you will return to these questions again and again, each time refining your responses with new understanding and new evidence to support your point of view. You will also deepen your knowledge of key topics by conducting both on-the-spot and extended research, asking and answering questions, evaluating multiple sources, and synthesizing your findings.

Twice a unit you will go on a **Knowledge Quest**. Each Knowledge Quest begins with a Knowledge Question and supporting questions to focus your reading. After reading several texts that explore a topic, theme, or idea, you will get to return to the Knowledge Question and show your growing understanding of the topic by responding to a writing prompt or engaging in a discussion.

At the end of a Knowledge Quest, you will be encouraged to continue building your knowledge of the topic by going to **Zinc Reading Labs** and finding related texts to read. Zinc Reading Labs offers a variety of informational and literary texts that you can choose based on your interests. Vocabulary sets for each text let you learn new words and practice using them.

Your independent reading can also enhance your understanding of the topics you are studying in class if you want it to. SpringBoard's **Independent Reading Lists** include suggested books that relate to the topics and themes from each unit. By choosing those books you can see a different side of the topic, learn new words, and find other topics you want to learn more about.

Reading to Gain Perspectives

Gaining Perspectives features use a text as a jumping off point for examining an issue relevant to you. You will be asked to consider the perspectives of others and to empathize with others who have different points of view. You will also be asked to think about social and ethical norms and to recognize the family, school, and community resources available to you. Each Gaining Perspectives feature concludes with a writing task in which you will summarize the discussion you have with your classmates.

Our Approach to Writing

SpringBoard English Language Arts provides you with the support you need to write in all the major modes, emphasizing argumentative, informational, and narrative. You will write often, and you will learn to become a critical reviewer of your own and your peers' work through frequent opportunities for revision and editing. You will learn to plan with purpose, audience, topic, and context in mind; develop drafts with engaging ideas, examples, facts and commentary; revise for clarity, development, organization, style, and diction; and edit using the conventions of the English language.

The Craft of Writing

As you read texts by skilled authors, you will observe the many choices those authors make. You'll tune in to the ways authors purposefully use words, sentences, and structures to convey meaning. After analyzing and critiquing others' work, you will learn to apply your understanding of author's craft to your own writing. A few SpringBoard features help you do just that:

- **Writing prompts** lead up to the Embedded Assessments and give you practice with writing texts in multiple genres, including personal narratives, argumentative essays, letters, research papers, and more. Writing to Sources writing prompts drive you back to texts you have read or viewed to mine for evidence.

- **Focus on the Sentence** tasks help you process content while also practicing the craft of writing powerful sentences.

- **Grammar & Usage** features highlight interesting grammar or usage concepts that appear in a text, both to improve your reading comprehension and to help you attend to these concepts as you craft your own texts.

- **Language & Writer's Craft** features address topics in writing such as style, word choice, and sentence construction.

- **Language Checkpoints** offer in-depth practice with standard English conventions and guide you to develop an editor's checklist to use as a reference each time you check your own or a peer's written work.

Modes of Writing

SpringBoard helps you become a better academic writer by giving you authentic prompts that require you to use sources, and showing you how to work through the writing process. Over the course of the year you will have the chance to write narratives, arguments, and informational texts, and you will develop a wide range of writing skills:

- Consider task, audience, and purpose when structuring and organizing your writing.

- Incorporate details, reasons, and textual evidence to support your ideas.

- Generate research questions, evaluate sources, gather relevant evidence, and report and cite your findings accurately.

- Use research-based strategies that will guide you through the writing process.

Writing with a Focus on the Sentence

SpringBoard English Language Arts leverages sentence writing strategies that were developed by The Writing Revolution. These evidence-based strategies are part of the Hochman Method, the Writing Revolution's system for helping students learn to write across all content areas and grades. The Writing Revolution emphasizes the importance of embedding writing and grammar instruction into content. That's why SpringBoard's **Focus on the Sentence** tasks integrate sentence-level writing into the curriculum. These tasks not only help you learn and practice important grammar concepts and sentence forms, but they also provide a chance for you to process and demonstrate your understanding of texts, images, class discussions, and other content.

Our Approach to Vocabulary

Vocabulary is threaded throughout each unit and developed over the course of the SpringBoard English Language Arts year. You will have ample opportunities to read and hear new words, explore their meanings, origins, and connotations, and use them in written and oral responses.

- Important academic and literary terms that you will need to actively participate in classroom discussions are called out in your book.
- Challenging vocabulary terms found in reading passages are glossed at the point of use.
- Periodic Word Connections boxes guide you through the process of exploring a word with multiple meanings and nuances, an interesting etymology, a telling root or affix, a helpful Spanish cognate, a relationship to another word, or a connection to another content area.

Zinc Reading Labs

Zinc Reading Labs combines the best features of a typical vocabulary program with those of a typical reading program and makes reading and learning new words a game. Zinc offers a variety of nonfiction and fiction texts that you can choose from based on individual needs and interest. Each article has a corresponding vocabulary set that pre-teaches challenging words through spaced repetition, to help you genuinely learn and internalize the vocabulary. Additional vocabulary games focus on SAT/ACT power words and foundational words for English language learners.

Pre-AP Connections

SpringBoard shares Pre-AP's core principles and encourages you to build skills that you will use in high school and beyond. These principles are evident in every SpringBoard activity.

 ### Close Observation and Analysis
... to notice and consider

When reading, your teacher will guide you to pause to make observations and notice details in the text before analyzing or explaining. Only after you have noticed and enjoyed elements of the text do you then return to the text for deeper analysis and inferential thinking. This close reading sequence helps you interact and engage with the text in increasingly meaningful ways.

 ### Evidence-Based Writing
... with a focus on the sentence

SpringBoard challenges you to write increasingly complex, sophisticated, and precise sentences over the course of the year through regular practice with sentence-level writing. Instead of being isolated from reading, sentence-level grammar and writing exercises are integrated into the curriculum to enhance your comprehension and your ability to compose a variety of texts.

 ### Higher-Order Questioning
... to spark productive lingering

Each unit opens with two essential questions that relate to the topics, themes, and texts within that unit. You return to these questions throughout the unit and refine your answers as new evidence is presented. SpringBoard also encourages you to craft your own questions, and to dig deeply into the texts you read. After each reading passage, you evaluate the meaning of the text and examine the choices that the author made when writing it.

 ### Academic Conversations
... to support peer-to-peer dialogue

SpringBoard classrooms are places where students like you engage in collaborative learning. You will participate in discussion groups, writing groups, debates, Socratic seminars, literature circles, and oral interpretations and performances. These activities create an environment where you can share, compare, critique, debate, and build on others' ideas to advance your learning.

PSAT/SAT Connections

We want students to be rewarded for the hard work you do in your English Language Arts courses, including when you sit down to take important assessments. Therefore, SpringBoard English Language Arts focuses on the same essential knowledge and skills that are the center of the Evidence-Based Reading and Writing sections of the SAT Suite of Assessments (SAT, PSAT/NMSQT, PSAT™ 10, and PSAT™ 8/9). To be sure of our alignment, we conducted a research study, the results of which showed strong to exemplary alignment between the SpringBoard ELA courses and the corresponding SAT Suite tests. This means that you are getting ready for the SAT, PSAT/NMSQT, PSAT™ 10, and PSAT™ 8/9 in the classroom every day.

Tools and Supports

SpringBoard Digital

SpringBoard puts you in charge of what you learn and gives students and teachers the flexibility and support they need. SpringBoard Digital is an interactive program that provides always-available online content that's accessible from any device—desktop computer, laptop, tablet, or interactive whiteboard. The student edition allows you to interact with the text, respond to prompts, take assessments, and engage with a suite of tools, all in the digital space. Teachers get access to a correlations viewer that embeds correlations at point of use, a lesson planner, progress reports, grading, messaging, and more.

Zinc Reading Labs

All SpringBoard users have access to Zinc Reading Labs, where you can find a huge library of reading material chosen specifically to align with the SpringBoard English Language Arts curriculum.

Zinc offers:

- Fresh and engaging nonfiction and fiction content for independent reading.
- Interactive games, quizzes, and tasks that build skills and confidence.
- Freedom of choice: Zinc's massive and ever-growing library means that all students should find texts they want to read.

Turnitin Revision Assistant

When you develop drafts of an available Embedded Assessment through SpringBoard Digital, you can use a tool called Turnitin Revision Assistant. This online tool gives instant feedback to students as they write so they can polish their drafts and practice their revision skills. The feedback model Revision Assistant uses is based on scoring by SpringBoard teachers, and it's trained to assess the same rubric areas that they assess.

Revision Assistant offers:

- A template to help you create an outline.
- Actionable, instant feedback in specific areas such as structure, use of language, and ideas.
- Identification of strengths and weakness in your writing.

A Letter to the Student

Dear Student,

Welcome to the SpringBoard program! We created this program with you in mind: it puts you and your classmates at the center of your learning and equips you with the skills and knowledge you need to excel in middle school, high school, and beyond.

The energy and excitement you bring to class helps you and your classmates learn. You will explore compelling themes through readings, classroom discussions, and projects. You will dive into fascinating texts—some of which you'll choose on your own—from different genres including myths, poems, biographies, plays, and films. You will engage in lively discussions, debates, and performances so that you become confident sharing and presenting your ideas. You will write frequently to sharpen your ability to craft effective sentences, paragraphs, and longer texts. And you'll start each unit with a clear understanding of where you're headed by unpacking the skills and knowledge you'll need to do well on the assessment at the end.

SpringBoard helps you make connections between the concepts you're reading and writing about in class and the real world. Instead of just memorizing how to do things, you'll draw on your own and your classmates' experiences and knowledge to come to new and deeper understandings. When questions arise from the materials you're studying in class, you'll learn how to do both quick and longer-term research to find answers. Plus, you'll have access to tools and resources that are built right into the program, including powerful learning strategies, independent reading lists to help you select texts to read outside of class, and digital tools that you can access any time from any device—desktop computer, laptop, or tablet.

We want students to be rewarded for the hard work they do in their English Language Arts course. That's why the SpringBoard program focuses on the essential knowledge and skills that will prepare you for the challenging work you'll do in your high school classes, in AP courses, and in college.

Students from around the country are talking about how much they like the SpringBoard approach to learning. We hope you enjoy learning with SpringBoard, too.

Sincerely,

The SpringBoard Team

VISUAL PROMPT
A butterfly goes through several changes in its life. It starts as an egg, becomes a caterpillar and then a chrysalis, and finally emerges as a beautiful butterfly. In what ways do people change as they move through the stages of their lives?

STORIES OF CHANGE

What they don't understand about birthdays and what they never tell you is that when you're eleven, you're also ten, and nine, and eight, and seven, and six, and five, and four, and three, and two, and one. And when you wake up on your eleventh birthday you expect to feel eleven, but you don't. You open your eyes and everything's just like yesterday, only it's today.

–from "Eleven" by Sandra Cisneros

VOCABULARY

ACADEMIC
sequence
cause-effect
transitions
coherence

LITERARY
conflict (external/internal)
personal narrative
point of view
connotation
denotation
metaphor
simile
short story
theme
plot
foreshadowing
personification

ACTIVITY	CONTENTS	

ACTIVITY	CONTENTS	

Texts not included in these materials.

My Independent Reading List

Learning Strategies

Activating Prior Knowledge
Skimming/Scanning
QHT
Marking the Text
Summarizing/Paraphrasing
Graphic Organizer

Learning Targets

- Preview the big ideas, academic vocabulary, and literacy terms for the unit.
- Unpack the skills and knowledge needed to complete Embedded Assessment 1.

Preview

In this activity, you will think about the concept of change and preview the work you will do in this unit.

My Notes

Making Connections

When you think about change, what thoughts come to your mind? Have you perhaps changed schools? Have you made new friends? Has an old friend moved away? Change is a part of life. In this unit, you will analyze stories about change as well as write your own ideas and stories about change.

Essential Questions

Based on your current knowledge, how would you answer these questions?

1. How can change be significant?
2. What makes a good story?

Introducing the Strategy: QHT

QHT is a strategy for thinking about your own understanding of vocabulary words. The letters stand for questions, heard, and teach:

Q: words you may have seen but you are not sure about their meaning
H: words you have heard before but may not know them well
T: words you know so well you could teach them to someone else

To use **QHT**, think about how well you know each term and label each term with a letter.

Developing Vocabulary

Look at the Academic and Literary vocabulary on the Contents page. Apply the QHT strategy to see which words you already know and which you need to learn about.

Unpacking Embedded Assessment

Read the assignment for Embedded Assessment 1: Writing a Personal Narrative.

 Your assignment is to write a personal narrative that includes a well-told incident, a response to the incident, and a reflection about the significance of the incident.

In your own words, paraphrase the assignment and then summarize what you will need to know to complete this assessment successfully. With your class, create a graphic organizer to represent the skills and knowledge you will need to complete the tasks identified in the Embedded Assessment.

What Makes a Narrative?

Learning Targets

- Define the concept of change through the reading of a narrative and an article.
- Apply understanding of narrative elements to reading.
- Integrate ideas from multiple texts to build knowledge and vocabulary about migrant workers.

Preview

In this activity, you will begin to explore narrative texts and how they are related to real-life events.

Narratives

The story you will read in this activity, titled "The Circuit," is an example of a narrative. Narratives can be made up or based on real events. Generally, a narrative includes elements such as characters, dialogue, a setting, and the events or actions that lead to and follow a conflict. These events are often chronological. In "The Circuit," author Francisco Jiménez uses events from his own childhood to write about how change affects a boy and his family. As you work through the narrative and other supporting texts, think about how authors use the narrative form to write about changes in their lives, the lives of those around them, and the world.

Setting a Purpose for Reading

- As you read the story, underline details you learn about the main characters and mark places in the text where you see changes in their attitude or behavior.
- Circle unknown words and phrases. Use context clues to determine their meaning or use a dictionary. Some unfamiliar words in this story might be Spanish words.

Introducing the Strategy: Close Reading and Marking the Text

The Close Reading strategy involves reading a text word by word, sentence by sentence, and line by line to develop a complete understanding of it. Close Reading is characterized by marking the text as a way of reading actively. Marking the Text means making notes or writing questions that help you to understand the text.

Learning Strategies

Note-taking
Close Reading
Marking the Text
Diffusing
Visualizing

WORD CONNECTIONS

Roots and Affixes
The Greek root *chron* in **chronological** means "time." *Chronological* means "ordered by time." Other English words having to do with time also contain this root. Based on this new knowledge, determine the meaning of the words *chronicle, chronic, chronology,* and *synchronize.*

My Notes

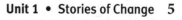

WORD CONNECTIONS

Content Connections

Bracero is a Spanish word that means "one who works with his arm." The word was used to describe Mexicans who were invited to come to the United States to work as laborers during World War II. With so many Americans overseas at war, workers were needed in industries such as agriculture and rail transportation. Braceros often worked under extreme conditions for low pay. The U.S. government Bracero program ended in 1964.

KNOWLEDGE QUEST

Knowledge Question:

What are some challenges that the children of migrant workers face, and how do these challenges affect the children's ability to get an education?

In Activity 1.2, you will read a text about a boy who travels across the United States with his family to follow seasonal work. You will use a photograph of field work to compare and contrast story elements. You will also read an article about how some children juggle school and work when a migrant season ends and a new one begins. While you read and build knowledge about the topic, think about your answer to the Knowledge Question.

About the Author

Francisco Jiménez (1943–) was born in Tlaquepaque, Mexico, and grew up in a family of migrant workers in California. He spent much of his childhood moving around California with no permanent home or regular schooling, yet he went on to have a distinguished academic career. A graduate of Santa Clara University, he also attended Harvard University and received both a master's degree and a PhD from Columbia University.

Short Story

The Circuit

by **Francisco Jiménez**

1   It was that time of year again. Ito, the strawberry sharecropper, did not smile. It was natural. The peak of the strawberry season was over and the last few days the workers, most of them *braceros*, were not picking as many boxes as they had during the months of June and July.

2   As the last days of August disappeared, so did the number of *braceros*. Sunday, only one—the best picker—came to work. I liked him. Sometimes we talked during our half-hour lunch break. That is how I found out he was from Jalisco, the same state in Mexico my family was from. That Sunday was the last time I saw him.

3   When the sun had tired and sunk behind the mountains, Ito signaled us that it was time to go home. "*Ya esora,*" he yelled in his broken Spanish. Those were the words I waited for twelve hours a day, every day, seven days a week, week after week. And the thought of not hearing them again saddened me.

4   As we drove home Papá did not say a word. With both hands on the wheel, he stared at the dirt road. My older brother, Roberto, was also silent. He leaned his head back and closed his eyes. Once in a while he cleared from his throat the dust that blew in from outside.

5   Yes, it was that time of year. When I opened the front door to the shack, I stopped. Everything we owned was neatly packed in cardboard boxes. Suddenly I felt even more the weight of hours, days, weeks, and months of work. I sat down on a box. The thought of having to move to Fresno and knowing what was in store for me there brought tears to my eyes.

6   That night I could not sleep. I lay in bed thinking about how much I hated this move.

7   A little before five o'clock in the morning, Papá woke everyone up. A few minutes later, the yelling and screaming of my little brothers and sisters, for whom the move was a great adventure, broke the silence of dawn. Shortly, the barking of the dogs accompanied them.

8   While we packed the breakfast dishes, Papá went outside to start the "*Carcanchita*." That was the name Papá gave his old '38 black Plymouth. He bought it in a used-car lot in Santa Rosa in the winter of 1949. Papá was very proud of his little **jalopy**. He had a right to be proud of it. He spent a lot of time looking at other cars before buying this one. When he finally chose the *Carcanchita*, he checked it thoroughly before driving it out of the car lot. He examined every inch of the car. He listened to the motor, tilting his head from side to side like a parrot, trying to detect any noises that spelled car trouble. After being satisfied with the looks and sounds of the car, Papá then insisted on knowing who the original owner was. He never did find out from the car salesman, but he bought the car anyway. Papá figured the original owner must have been an important man because behind the rear seat of the car he found a blue necktie.

9   Papá parked the car out in front and left the motor running. "*Listo*," he yelled. Without saying a word, Roberto and I began to carry the boxes out to the car. Roberto carried the two big boxes and I carried the two smaller ones. Papá then threw the mattress on top of the car roof and tied it with ropes to the front and rear bumpers.

10   Everything was packed except Mamá's pot. It was an old large galvanized pot she had picked up at an army surplus store in Santa María the year I was born. The pot had many dents and nicks, and the more dents and nicks it acquired the more Mamá liked it. "*Mi olla*," she used to say proudly.

11   I held the front door open as Mamá carefully carried out her pot by both handles, making sure not to spill the cooked beans. When she got to the car, Papá reached out to help her with it. Roberto opened the rear car door and Papá gently placed it on the floor behind the front seat. All of us then climbed in. Papá sighed, wiped the sweat off his forehead with his sleeve, and said wearily: "*Es todo*."

12   As we drove away, I felt a lump in my throat. I turned around and looked at our little shack for the last time.

13   At sunset we drove into a labor camp[1] near Fresno. Since Papá did not speak English, Mamá asked the camp foreman if he needed any more workers. "We don't need no more," said the foreman, scratching his head. "Check with Sullivan down the road. Can't miss him. He lives in a big white house with a fence around it."

14   When we got there, Mamá walked up to the house. She went through a white gate, past a row of rose bushes, up the stairs to the front door. She rang the doorbell. The porch light went on and a tall husky man came out. They exchanged a few words. After the man went in, Mamá clasped her hands and hurried back to the car. "We have work! Mr. Sullivan said we can stay there the whole season," she said, **gasping** and pointing to an old garage near the stables.

[1] housing for migrants near the fields where they work

© 2021 College Board. All rights reserved.

WORD CONNECTIONS

Cognates
Many words are similar in English and Spanish. These words are cognates. Some cognates from this story are: *adventura* (adventure), *Mamá* (mother, mama), *Papá* (father, papa), and *motor* (motor).

My Notes

jalopy: an old car worn down by use

gasping: speaking with deep, difficult breaths

My Notes

15 The garage was worn out by the years. It had no windows. The walls, eaten by termites, **strained** to support the roof full of holes. The dirt floor, populated by earth worms, looked like a gray road map.

16 That night, by the light of a kerosene lamp, we unpacked and cleaned our new home. Roberto swept away the loose dirt, leaving the hard ground. Papá plugged the holes in the walls with old newspapers and tin can tops. Mamá fed my little brothers and sisters. Papá and Roberto then brought in the mattress and placed it on the far corner of the garage. "Mamá, you and the little ones sleep on the mattress. Roberto, Panchito, and I will sleep outside under the trees," Papá said.

17 Early next morning Mr. Sullivan showed us where his crop was, and after breakfast, Papá, Roberto, and I headed for the vineyard to pick.

18 Around nine o'clock the temperature had risen to almost one hundred degrees. I was completely soaked in sweat and my mouth felt as if I had been chewing on a handkerchief. I walked over to the end of the row, picked up the jug of water we had brought, and began drinking. "Don't drink too much; you'll get sick," Roberto shouted. No sooner had he said that than I felt sick to my stomach. I dropped to my knees and let the jug roll off my hands. I remained motionless with my eyes glued on the hot sandy ground. All I could hear was the drone of insects. Slowly I began to recover. I poured water over my face and neck and watched the dirty water run down my arms to the ground.

19 I still felt a little dizzy when we took a break to eat lunch. It was past two o'clock and we sat underneath a large walnut tree that was on the side of the road. While we ate, Papá jotted down the number of boxes we had picked. Roberto drew designs on the ground with a stick. Suddenly I noticed Papá's face turn pale as he looked down the road. "Here comes the school bus," he whispered loudly in alarm. Instinctively, Roberto and I ran and hid in the vineyards. We did not want to get in trouble for not going to school. The neatly dressed boys about my age got off. They carried books under their arms. After they crossed the street, the bus drove away. Roberto and I came out from hiding and joined Papá. "*Tienen que tener cuidado,*" he warned us.

20 After lunch we went back to work. The sun kept beating down. The buzzing insects, the wet sweat, and the hot dry dust made the afternoon seem to last forever. Finally the mountains around the valley reached out and swallowed the sun. Within an hour it was too dark to continue picking. The vines blanketed the grapes, making it difficult to see the bunches. "*Vámonos,*" said Papá, signaling to us that it was time to quit work. Papá then took out a pencil and began to figure out how much we had earned our first day. He wrote down numbers, crossed some out, wrote down some more. "*Quince,*" he **murmured**.

21 When we arrived home, we took a cold shower underneath a water-hose. We then sat down to eat dinner around some wooden crates that served as a table. Mamá had cooked a special meal for us. We had rice and tortillas with *carne con chile*, my favorite dish.

strained: pulled or stretched by force

murmured: spoke softly or quietly

22 The next morning I could hardly move. My body ached all over. I felt little control over my arms and legs. This feeling went on every morning for days until my muscles finally got used to the work.

23 It was Monday, the first week of November. The grape season was over and I could now go to school. I woke up early that morning and lay in bed, looking at the stars and **savoring** the thought of not going to work and of starting sixth grade for the first time that year. Since I could not sleep, I decided to get up and join Papá and Roberto at breakfast. I sat at the table across from Roberto, but I kept my head down. I did not want to look up and face him. I knew he was sad. He was not going to school today. He was not going tomorrow, or next week, or next month. He would not go until the cotton season was over, and that was sometime in February. I rubbed my hands together and watched the dry, acid stained skin fall to the floor in little rolls.

24 When Papá and Roberto left for work, I felt relief. I walked to the top of a small grade next to the shack and watched the "Carcanchita" disappear in the distance in a cloud of dust.

25 Two hours later, around eight o'clock, I stood by the side of the road waiting for school bus number twenty. When it arrived I climbed in. Everyone was busy either talking or yelling. I sat in an empty seat in the back.

26 When the bus stopped in front of the school, I felt very nervous. I looked out the bus window and saw boys and girls carrying books under their arms. I put my hands in my pant pockets and walked to the principal's office. When I entered I heard a woman's voice say: "May I help you?" I was startled. I had not heard English for months. For a few seconds I remained speechless. I looked at the lady who waited for an answer. My first instinct was to answer her in Spanish, but I held back. Finally, after struggling for English words, I managed to tell her that I wanted to enroll in the sixth grade. After answering many questions, I was led to the classroom.

27 Mr. Lema, the sixth grade teacher, greeted me and assigned me a desk. He then introduced me to the class. I was so nervous and scared at that moment when everyone's eyes were on me that I wished I were with Papá and Roberto picking cotton. After taking roll, Mr. Lema gave the class the assignment for the first hour. "The first thing we have to do this morning is finish reading the story we began yesterday," he said enthusiastically. He walked up to me, handed me an English book, and asked me to read. "We are on page 125," he said politely. When I heard this, I felt my blood rush to my head; I felt dizzy. "Would you like to read?" he asked hesitantly. I opened the book to page 125. My mouth was dry. My eyes began to water. I could not begin. "You can read later," Mr. Lema said understandingly.

28 For the rest of the reading **period** I kept getting angrier and angrier with myself. I should have read, I thought to myself.

My Notes

savoring: enjoying something and making it last

period: a specific length of time

My Notes

29 During recess I went into the restroom and opened my English book to page 125. I began to read in a low voice, pretending I was in class. There were many words I did not know. I closed the book and headed back to the classroom.

30 Mr. Lema was sitting at his desk correcting papers. When I entered he looked up at me and smiled. I felt better. I walked up to him and asked if he could help me with the new words. "Gladly," he said.

31 The rest of the month I spent my lunch hours working on English with Mr. Lema, my best friend at school.

32 One Friday during lunch hour Mr. Lema asked me to take a walk with him to the music room. "Do you like music?" he asked me as we entered the building.

33 "Yes, I like *corridos*," I answered. He then picked up a trumpet, blew on it, and handed it to me. The sound gave me goose bumps. I knew that sound. I had heard it in many *corridos*. "How would you like to learn how to play it?" he asked. He must have read my face because before I could answer, he added: "I'll teach you how to play it during our lunch hours."

34 That day I could hardly wait to get home to tell Papá and Mamá the great news. As I got off the bus, my little brothers and sisters ran up to meet me. They were yelling and screaming. I thought they were happy to see me, but when I opened the door to our shack, I saw that everything we owned was neatly packed in cardboard boxes.

Knowledge Quest

- What do the characters and events remind you of?
- What inference can you make about the narrator's emotions at the end of the story?

Returning to the Text

- Return to the text as you respond to the following questions. Use text evidence to support your responses.
- Write any additional questions you have about the story in your Reader/Writer Notebook.

1. **KQ** Determine the meaning of *sharecropper* by using the word's structure and the context of the first paragraph. Then confirm its meaning in a dictionary. What is Ito's role as a strawberry sharecropper?

_____

_____

_____

_____

2. Based on the figurative phrase "lump in my throat" in paragraph 12, how does Panchito feel about the move? Cite other evidence from the story to support your answer.

_____

_____

_____

_____

3. Revisit paragraphs 14 and 16. How does Mamá feel about having to stay in a garage for the whole season? What actions do the family members take to make the garage a comfortable but temporary home? Cite text evidence to support your answer.

_____

_____

_____

_____

4. **KQ** What changes does the family continually face throughout the story? How do the family members' actions in paragraph 21 show the way they face change?

_____

_____

_____

_____

ACADEMIC

To **sequence** something is to put things in an order, so a sequence of events is a set of events that follows one after another in a sequential or orderly presentation of steps or events.

LITERARY

In an **external conflict,** the character struggles with an outside force. In an **internal conflict,** the character struggles with his or her own needs or emotions. Both kinds of conflict can cause the character to have an internal response expressed as thoughts or feelings and/ or an external response, expressed through words or actions.

5. Starting with paragraph 23, Panchito gets ready for school. What kinds of feelings does he have about leaving the family's work and going to school? Highlight text that helps you answer the question.

_____

_____

_____

_____

6. Reread paragraphs 26–33. What word in paragraph 27 does the author use to describe how Mr. Lema speaks to Panchito? Why is Mr. Lema an important person in Panchito's life?

_____

_____

_____

_____

7. **KQ** What does the ending of this story say about the life of migrant workers? How does the ending relate to the title of the story? Cite evidence from the text to support your answer.

_____

_____

_____

_____

 Gaining Perspectives

The narrator does not have the typical life of a child. He must deal with physical exertion and fatigue because he goes to work early in the morning while everyone else goes to school. Role-play with a partner the jobs the narrator and his father do. Think of different ways that the narrator could take care of himself while working long hours and how choices about self-care could affect him at home and school. When you are finished, summarize the ideas that you and your partner came up with in your Reader/Writer Notebook.

Working from the Text

8. Return to the story and review the words and phrases that you underlined. Use these annotations to work with your class to create a **sequence** of events.

9. Use the following table to organize details about the setting, characters, and their **internal** and **external responses** to conflict.

Change the Narrator and His Family Face	Description of Setting	Internal and External Responses to Conflict	Textual Evidence Including Dialogue
In the beginning of the story,			
Then			
Next,			

Change the Narrator and His Family Face	Description of Setting	Internal and External Responses to Conflict	Textual Evidence Including Dialogue
Finally,			

10. What conclusion can you draw about the narrator's attitude toward change? Provide evidence from the story that supports your conclusion.

☑ Check Your Understanding

Think of a story you know well. Describe the story to your partner using the vocabulary you learned in this activity: characters, dialogue, setting, sequence of events, and conflict.

Setting a Purpose for Reading

- As you read the article, use the My Notes section to describe any similarities you see between it and the narrative you just read by Francisco Jiménez.
- Circle unknown words and phrases. Try to determine the meaning of the words by using context clues, word parts, or a dictionary.

About the Author

Peter Balonon-Rosen is an associate producer and reporter. He creates original feature stories for radio programs such as *Marketplace, All Things Considered,* and NPR's *Morning Edition*. Balonon-Rosen is a graduate of Tufts University, where he studied American studies and film studies. His work in journalism emphasizes equity issues, such as for students with disabilities, choices in education, labor and housing, and services for migrant workers.

Article

Schools Hustle to Reach Kids Who Move with the Harvest, Not the School Year

by **Peter Balonon-Rosen**

KNOWLEDGE QUEST

Knowledge Question:

What are some challenges that the children of migrant workers face, and how do these challenges affect the children's ability to get an education?

1   If you found yourself carving a jack-o-lantern this Halloween, did you take a second to think about who picked that pumpkin?

2   Maybe it was Anayeli Camacho, one of the country's estimated 3 million migrant farm workers, and mother of two. For part of the year she rents a trailer on farmland in Oaktown, Ind., where she works in the fields, harvesting pumpkins and other crops.

3   But as the fall harvest comes to a close, she and her family will head back down south for the winter, following seasonal work. This is what Camacho has done for the last decade, traveling north and south, from Florida to Indiana, bringing her family, which now includes 4-year-old Ximena, along with her.

4   Ximena is young, but her education is arguably **vital** right now. Often children living this lifestyle face interrupted schooling, cultural and **language barriers**, and **social isolation** — all factors that **inhibit** a child's ability to do well in school.

5   Her preschool, a public school for migrant children ages 2 to 5, is working on that.

6   "Because their parents move around a lot, they don't have the stability of being in one location for very long where they might be able to take advantage of other preschool services," says Debbie Gries, education coordinator for the Indiana Migrant Regional Center.

7   "Our goal, when they're 5, is to have them ready for kindergarten," wherever that may be.

For migrant families, barriers to school services

8   The children of migrant workers are some of the country's poorest, most undereducated and hardest to track down.

9   But tracking them down is exactly what a preschool for migrant children needs to do.

10   "Staff go into fields trying to find and talk to these families and see if they want to enroll their kids in the program," says Ray Melecio, assistant director for ESCORT, an assistance center for migrant education program. "Sometimes, these families don't want to be found."

My Notes

vital: important

language barriers: blockers to communication due to a difference in languages spoken between two people

social isolation: the condition of being separated from other people

inhibit: stop

11 And timing is a big issue. Families move with planting and harvest schedules, not the school year.

12 In 2015, the U.S. Department of Education spent about $365 million to fund migrant education programs in 47 states so that children can pick up school again wherever their families land.

13 The programs across the country take different shapes. Some work through nearby district services. Tutors can visit children at home in rural areas with few families. Or, when there's a cluster of migrant children, a preschool center like Ximena's.

14 We wondered what a day looks like for these children, so we asked if we could come along.

Getting to school

15 For starters, the day begins early. At 6:30 a.m. there's a knock on the door at the Camacho family trailer.

16 Inside, 4-year-old Ximena has been sprinting back and forth for nearly 30 minutes.

17 Outside, Ximena's bus to preschool sits rumbling, in the dark, on the gravel road. On board, a teacher buckles her into a car seat.

18 Soon, almost all of the children fall asleep. It's still dark outside. The ride is an hour, weaving through farms to pick up more children on the way.

19 "We run our morning route really early because most of the parents, they are starting when it's light outside," says Gries, the education coordinator.

At school

20 The sun is just rising when Ximena and classmates arrive. At school the focus is learning, not just childcare, in both English and Spanish.

21 Teachers lead children in songs full of English vocabulary—like animals and parts of the body. Children dance, jump and sing.

22 And then math: learning to count.

23 "One, two, three, four, five!" Ximena says, excitedly. "Uno, dos, tres, quatro, cinco!"

24 There's preschool geometry, too. Sarah Ross, who teaches here, reaches into a bin of brightly-colored shapes.

25 "What shape is this?" Ross asks, pulling one out.

26 "Circle!" the group yells back.

27 Outside, in the preschool's lush green yard, children practice dribbling a soccer ball.

Wrapping up and heading home

My Notes

28 Back inside, Mirna Sandoval reads to students. She used to be a migrant worker. Now, she's these children's teacher, reading *The Lion King* in Spanish. *El Rey León.*

29 As Sandoval and students repeat "Hakuna Matata" in singsong voices, children can't contain fits of laughter.

30 Soon, they pile back onto the bus where teachers, once again, buckle them into car seats. Now, heading home.

31 As the bus speeds past fields where many parents work, children sing, "The Wheels on the Bus Go Round and Round." Then, a verse about piggies who go "oink, oink, oink."

32 Christine Vaughn, a teacher, pauses.

33 "Wait a minute, why's there a piggy on our bus?" she asks.

34 "Because it has to go to school!" one girl yells.

"Farmers in fear of losing migrant labor" from the *Arkansas Democrat-Gazette*.

Ⓦ Knowledge Quest

- What questions do you have about the first few paragraphs?
- What do you notice in the article that someone skimming over it might miss?

Returning to the Text

- Return to the texts and photograph as you respond to the following questions. Use text evidence to support your responses.
- Write any additional questions you have about the texts or photograph in your Reader/ Writer Notebook.

11. **KQ** Reread paragraphs 1–3. Why do migrant families, such as the one described in the article, need to move around so much?

_____

_____

_____

_____

12. **KQ** According to paragraph 4, what *inhibits* a migrant child's ability to do well in school? What happens when a child's ability to succeed in school is *inhibited*?

_____

_____

_____

_____

13. Reread paragraphs 25 and 26 of "The Circuit." What problems does Panchito have after working in the fields for months without going to school? Now reread paragraph 4 of the article by Balonon-Rosen. Do Panchito's problems sound like ones that other children of migrant workers might face? Explain your answer.

_____

_____

_____

_____

14. **KQ** Read Debbie Gries's explanation in paragraph 6 for some migrant families not taking advantage of special services. What is the *stability* that migrant families lack? Based on the information in this paragraph, what do you think *stability* means?

_____

_____

_____

_____

15. According to paragraph 10 of the article, some migrant working families don't want to be found by staff members of the migrant education program who want to help enroll their children. Based on what you read in paragraph 19 of "The Circuit," why might this be?

_____

_____

_____

_____

_____

16. KQ What modifications or changes might a school make to address the challenges of children who come to school seasonally? Use information from both the article and "The Circuit" to help you answer this question.

_____

_____

_____

_____

_____

_____

⊘ Knowledge Quest

After reading "The Circuit" and this article and viewing the photo of modern-day migrant workers that accompanies the article, discuss with a partner the challenges that children of migrant workers face. How do these unique challenges affect the wants and needs of those children and their families?

⬛ INDEPENDENT READING LINK

You can continue to build your knowledge about moving and change by reading related articles at ZINC Reading Labs. Search for keywords such as *moving home* or *immigrants*.

🍂 ZINC

Working from the Text

17. Return to the narrative, "The Circuit," and the photograph of migrant workers, and compare and contrast them with how the article describes children in migrant-worker families. What are the similarities and differences in the way people view these children, and why do you think people have these views? Review the words and phrases that you underlined throughout the texts. Use these annotations as you work with your class to compare and contrast the narrative's ideas with the real-life ideas in the article and photograph.

18. Use the table to organize what you learn about housing, money, time spent, and education for students with jobs like that of Panchito in "The Circuit." Compare and contrast the information you learn from the narrative, article, and photograph.

	Housing	Money	Time Each Day	Education
What the narrative says:				
What the article says:				
What the photograph shows:				

19. What conclusions can you draw about how education can change to accommodate special circumstances? Provide text evidence to support your conclusion.

 **Check Your Understanding**

Think of an article or a story you have read about school or education. With a partner, discuss barriers that the characters or people in the text faced. Then think about how the author of the text describes the educational setting.

Planning for Independent Reading

Learning Targets

- Examine ways to choose a literary text for independent reading.
- Set goals in an independent reading plan.

Preview

In this activity, you will go through the process of choosing a book that interests you and planning for your independent reading.

Learning Strategies

Activating Prior Knowledge
Discussion Groups
Previewing

My Notes

Planning Independent Reading

Reading varied genres of fiction and nonfiction narratives—a novel, a memoir, a graphic novel, a biography, or a personal narrative or essay—will help you see how writers create narratives. Think about these questions to help you choose books to read outside of class.

1. What have you enjoyed reading in the past? What is your favorite book or favorite type of book? Who is your favorite author?

2. Preview the book you have selected. What do the front and back covers show you? What types of visuals are shown? What features does the book have (review blurbs, acknowledgments, a foreword, a preface)? What can you learn about the book or its author by reading these features?

3. Read the first few pages. How does the author try to hook you to keep reading? What can you tell about the characters and setting so far? Does the book seem too hard, too easy, or just right? Do you feel a connection to it in some way?

Choosing a Book

Your teacher will guide you in a book pass. Practice previewing each book, looking at the covers, and reading the first few pages.

4. In your Reader/Writer Notebook, record each book's title and author, something from your previewing that stands out to you, and your rating of the book.

5. After previewing each book and thinking about the goals of this unit, do you want to continue reading the book you brought to the group or choose something else? Write the title of the first book you will read in the My Independent Reading list on the Contents pages of this unit.

6. Create an Independent Reading Plan to help you set personal reading goals. Keep this plan in your Reader/Writer Notebook.

I have chosen to read _____

by (author) _____

because (reason from previewing) _____

I will set aside time to read at (time, place) _____

I should finish this text by (date) _____

7. Record your daily reading pace in your Independent Reading Log. Write a brief daily report in your log responding to what you have read.

Personal Narrative: Incident-Response-Reflection

Learning Strategies

Predicting
Close Reading
Marking the Text
Graphic Organizer
Visualizing

VOCABULARY

LITERARY

A **personal narrative** is a story based on one's own life and told in the first person.

Point of view is the perspective from which a story or poem is told. In first-person point of view, the narrator is a character in the story using first-person pronouns such as *I* and *we* to tell what he or she sees and knows. In third-person point of view, the narrator is someone outside the story using third-person pronouns such as *he*, *she*, and *they* to tell the story.

Third-person narrators can be *omniscient* or *limited*. Omniscient narrators show what all of the characters are thinking and doing. Limited narrators show the action of the story through the eyes of one character.

Learning Targets

- Analyze how the response in a personal narrative contributes to the development of the story.
- Identify an organizational structure to develop ideas and events in a personal narrative.

Preview

In this activity, you will read a personal narrative and examine the central action, the narrator's response, and the significance of the incident.

Genre Study: Personal Narrative

A **personal narrative** is a first-person **point of view** autobiographical story. Personal narratives often include a significant incident, the writer's response to the incident, and a reflection on the meaning of the incident.

- The **incident** is the central piece of action that is the focus of the narrative.
- The **response** is the immediate emotions and actions associated with the incident.
- The **reflection** is a description that explores the significance of the incident.

Setting a Purpose for Reading

- While you read, underline places in the text where you learn details about the narrator and notice changes in attitude or behavior.
- Circle unknown words and phrases. Try to determine the meaning of the words by using context clues, word parts, or a dictionary.

About the Author

Dan Greenburg (1936–) is a novelist, journalist, screenwriter, playwright, and humorist who has also done stand-up comedy. He has written for both adults and children. His successful series *The Zack Files* was inspired by his own son Zack. Greenburg wanted to write books that his son would like to read.

My Notes

_____

_____

_____

_____

_____

_____

_____

_____

_____

_____

Personal Narrative

My Superpowers

by **Dan Greenburg**

1   Do you ever wish you had superpowers?

2   When I was a kid, growing up on the North Side of Chicago and being picked on by bullies, I prayed for superpowers. Like Superman, I wanted to be able to fly faster than speeding bullets, to be more powerful than **locomotives**, to leap tall buildings at a single bound. Mainly, I wanted to punch bullies in the stomach so hard that my fist came out of their backs.

3   Winters in Chicago are so cold that frost forms leafy patterns on your bedroom window and stays there for months. The wind howls off Lake Michigan, and a thick shell of pitted black ice covers the streets and sidewalks from December to April. To keep warm in winter, I wore a heavy wool coat, a wool muffler, wool mittens, furry earmuffs and—one of my most treasured possessions—a Chicago Cubs baseball cap autographed by a player named Big Bill Nicholson.

4   On the coldest days of winter, three bullies waited for me after school, just for the fun of **terrorizing** me. The biggest one was a fat ugly kid named Vernon Manteuffel. Vernon and his two buddies would pull off my Cubs cap and tease me with it. They'd pretend to give it back, then toss it around in a game of keep-away.

5   One day in February when the temperature was so low I felt my eyeballs cracking, Vernon and his friends caught up with me on my way home. As usual, they tore off my Cubs cap and started playing catch with it. What made it worse than usual was that on this particular day I happened to be walking home with a pretty girl named Ann Cohn, who lived across the street from me. Ann Cohn had green eyes and shiny black hair and I had a goofy crush on her. As if it wasn't bad enough that these guys humiliated me when I was alone, now they were doing it in front of Ann Cohn.

6   I was so embarrassed, I began to cry. Crying in front of Ann Cohn made me even more embarrassed. I was speechless with shame and anger. Driven by rage, I did what only an insane person would do: I attacked Vernon Manteuffel. I punched him in the chest and grabbed back my Cubs cap.

7   Vernon saw that I had become a madman. People don't know what to do with madmen. Vernon looked shocked and even a little afraid. He backed away from me. I attacked the second boy, who also backed away from me. Encouraged by their backing away, I ran after them, screaming, punching, flailing at them with both fists. I chased them for two blocks before they finally pulled ahead and disappeared. Breathing hard, tears streaming down my face, I felt I had regained my honor, at least temporarily.

GRAMMAR & USAGE

Hyperbole

Writers use hyperbole to add humor to a text. In paragraph 2, the author says, "I wanted to punch bullies in the stomach so hard that my fist came out their backs." This is an example of hyperbole because it is a wild exaggeration. Hyperbole is different from ordinary exaggeration. It is an exaggeration that couldn't actually happen.

The use of hyperbole adds humor to a difficult subject. It also helps show the author's voice and personality. Without the use of hyperbole, writing about this topic would have a much different tone.

locomotives: engine cars that power trains
terrorizing: frightening someone

My Notes

WORD CONNECTIONS

Word Relationships
In paragraph 10, the author uses the phrase *real-life adventures* to categorize the experiences he wrote about in national magazines. When writers categorize pieces of information, they use a single word or phrase to label the pieces so that readers understand how all the pieces relate to each other.

8   That weekend, perhaps made braver by my triumph over the three bullies, I kissed Ann Cohn on her sofa. I can't tell you exactly why I did that. Maybe because it was a cold, cloudy Saturday and there was nothing else to do. Maybe because we both wondered what it would feel like. In any case, I could now brag that, at age eight, I had personally kissed an actual girl who wasn't related to me.

9   I never did get those superpowers. Not as a kid, at least.

10   When I grew up, I became a writer. I discovered a particular pleasure in going on risky adventures. I wrote about my real-life adventures for national magazines: I spent four months riding with New York firefighters and running into burning buildings with them. I spent six months riding with New York homicide cops as they chased and captured drug dealers and murderers. I flew upside-down over the Pacific Ocean with a stunt pilot in an open-cockpit airplane. I took part in dangerous **voodoo** ceremonies in Haiti. I spent time on a tiger ranch in Texas and learned to tame two-hundred-pound tigers by yelling "*No!*" and smacking them hard on the nose. I found that tigers were not much different from the bullies of my childhood in Chicago.

11   I also wrote fiction. I created entire worlds and filled them with people I wanted to put in there. I made these people do and say whatever it pleased me to have them do and say. In the worlds I made up, I was all-powerful—I *had superpowers*.

12   I began writing a series of children's books called *The Zack Files*, about a boy named Zack who keeps stumbling into the supernatural. In many of these books I gave Zack temporary powers—to read minds, to travel outside his body, to travel back into the past, to triumph over ghosts and monsters. I created another series called *Maximum Boy*, about a boy named Max who accidentally touches **radioactive** rocks that just came back from outer space and who suddenly develops superpowers. Maximum Boy is me as a kid in Chicago, but with superpowers.

13   Oh yeah, I almost forgot. In *The Zack Files*, I created a fat, stupid kid who sweats a lot and thinks he's cool, but who everyone laughs at behind his back. You know what I named this fool? Vernon Manteuffel. I do hope the real Vernon knows.

Making Observations
- What images catch your attention?
- What is one detail that sticks with you?

voodoo: religious practices involving spells and spirits
radioactive: full of dangerous radiation

Returning to the Text

- Return to the text as you respond to the following questions. Use text evidence to support your responses.
- Write any additional questions you have about the narrative in your Reader/Writer Notebook.

1. Why does the author start the narrative with a question? How does the question contribute to the author's voice?

_____

_____

_____

2. How did the author's experience with a bully change him? Cite evidence from the narrative in your answer.

_____

_____

_____

_____

3. What is the author's message in this personal narrative?

_____

_____

_____

_____

Working from the Text

4. During the class discussion, use a graphic organizer like the one below to take notes on the key parts of "My Superpowers." The incident in a personal narrative is like the **cause**, and the response is like an **effect**. Use your annotations to help locate textual evidence that supports your ideas.

Incident (Cause)	Response (Effect)	Reflection (The lessons the narrator learned from this experience)

☑ Check Your Understanding

Using the information from your class discussion and the graphic organizer, briefly summarize what the narrator learns from the incident in the story. Use specific details from the text in your summary.

INDEPENDENT READING LINK

Read and Discuss

How is the concept of change present in the book you are reading on your own? What is happening to the characters (or subjects) that is causing them to change, or what can you predict will happen? With a small group of your peers, compare how the theme of change is playing out in each of your independent reading books. Add your notes to an Independent Reading section of your Reader/Writer Notebook.

He Said, She Said: Characterization

Learning Strategies

Collaborative Discussion
Predicting
Close Reading
Marking the Text
Graphic Organizer
Visualizing
Note-taking

My Notes

Learning Targets

- Make inferences about a character and provide textual evidence in a short, written response.
- Explain how an author develops the point of view of characters.
- Practice the use and conventions of pronouns and dialogue.

Preview

In this activity, you will read an excerpt from a novel, analyze different characters' points of view, and write about how people can have different attitudes about an incident.

Setting a Purpose for Reading

- Use the My Notes section to describe any connections you have with the characters and how they behave and change over the course of the story.
- Circle unknown words and phrases. Try to determine the meaning of the words by using context clues, word parts, or a dictionary.

About the Author

Wendelin Van Draanen (1965–) started writing for adults but discovered that she much preferred writing for children. She has had much success with her Sammy Keyes mystery series, several of which have won the Edgar Allan Poe Award for best children's mystery. She lives with her family in California.

GRAMMAR & USAGE

Italics

Writers use **italics** to emphasize words or phrases. In paragraph 2, Van Draanen puts the word *eighth* in italics to emphasize the narrator's feeling about how much time has passed since second grade. Apparently, the narrator feels like it has been a really long six years!

When reading a word in italics, place a special emphasis on the word to ensure that you read it the way the author intended.

Novel Excerpt

from  Flipped

by Wendelin Van Draanen

from the chapter "Diving Under"

1   All I've ever wanted is for Juli Baker to leave me alone. For her to back off—you know, just give me some *space*.

2   It all started the summer before second grade when our moving van pulled into her neighborhood. And since we're now about done with the *eighth* grade, that, my friend, makes more than half a decade of strategic avoidance and social discomfort.

3   She didn't just barge into my life. She barged and shoved and wedged her way into my life. Did we invite her to get into our moving van and start

climbing all over boxes? No! But that's exactly what she did, taking over and showing off like only Juli Baker can.

4 My dad tried to stop her. "Hey!" he says as she's **catapulting** herself on board. "What are you doing? You're getting mud everywhere!" So true, too. Her shoes were, like, caked with the stuff.

5 She didn't hop out, though. Instead, she planted her rear end on the floor and started pushing a big box with her feet. "Don't you want some help?" She glanced my way. "It sure looks like you *need* it."

6 I didn't like the **implication**. And even though my dad had been tossing me the same sort of look all week, I could tell—he didn't like this girl either. "Hey! Don't do that," he warned her. "There are some really valuable things in that box."

7 "Oh. Well, how about this one?" She scoots over to a box labeled LENOX and looks my way again. "We should push it together!"

8 "No, no, no!" my dad says, then pulls her up by the arm. "Why don't you run along home? Your mother's probably wondering where you are."

9 This was the beginning of my soon-to-become-acute awareness that the girl cannot take a hint. Of any kind. Does she zip on home like a kid should when they've been invited to leave? No. She says, "Oh, my mom knows where I am. She said it was fine." Then she points across the street and says, "We just live right over there."

10 My father looks to where she's pointing and mutters, "Oh boy." Then he looks at me and winks as he says, "Bryce, isn't it time for you to go inside and help your mother?"

11 I knew right off that this was a ditch play. And I didn't think about it until later, but ditch wasn't a play I'd run with my dad before. Face it, pulling a ditch is not something discussed with dads. It's like, against parental law to tell your kid it's okay to ditch someone, no matter how annoying or *muddy* they might be.

12 But there he was, putting the play in motion, and man, he didn't have to wink twice. I smiled and said, "Sure thing!" then jumped off the liftgate and headed for my new front door.

13 I heard her coming after me but I couldn't believe it. Maybe it just sounded like she was chasing me; maybe she was really going the other way. But before I got up the nerve to look, she blasted right past me, grabbing my arm yanking me along.

14 This was too much. I planted myself and was about to tell her to get lost when the weirdest thing happened. I was making this big windmill motion to break away from her, but somehow on the downswing my hand wound up tangling into hers. I couldn't believe it. There I was, holding the mud monkey's hand!

GRAMMAR & USAGE

Reflexive and Intensive Pronouns

The words *myself*, *yourself*, *himself*, *herself*, *itself*, *ourselves*, *yourselves*, and *themselves* can be used as reflexive or intensive pronouns depending on how they are used in a sentence.

A **reflexive pronoun** is the object of a sentence; it refers back to the subject of the sentence. Look at paragraph 14. In the phrase "I planted myself," *myself* is a reflexive pronoun that refers back to *I*, the subject of the sentence.

An **intensive pronoun** adds emphasis to a noun in the sentence. For example, in the sentence "I was holding hands with Juli herself," the word *herself* emphasizes the noun *Juli*. Notice that the intensive pronoun can be removed without changing the meaning of the sentence: *I was holding hands with Juli.*

When you encounter one of these pronouns in your reading, look to see how the word is used in the sentence. Then you can tell if the pronoun is used as a reflexive or an intensive pronoun.

Revisit the list of reflexive and intensive pronouns provided above. Then write two sentences, one using a reflexive pronoun and one using an intensive pronoun. Model your sentences after the example sentences from *Flipped*.

catapulting: throwing
implication: idea her comment suggested

My Notes

15 I tried to shake her off, but she just clamped on tight and yanked me along, saying, "C'mon!"

16 My mom came out of the house and **immediately** got the world's sappiest look on her face. "Well, hello," she says to Juli.

17 "Hi!"

18 I'm still trying to pull free, but the girl's got me in a death grip. My mom's grinning, looking at our hands and my fiery red face. "And what's your name, honey?"

19 "Julianna Baker. I live right over there," she says, pointing with her unoccupied hand.

20 "Well, I see you've met my son," she says, still grinning away.

21 "Uh-huh!"

22 Finally I break free and do the only manly thing available when you're seven years old—I dive behind my mother.

23 Mom puts her arm around me and says, "Bryce, honey, why don't you show Julianna around the house?"

24 I flash her help and warning signals with every part of my body, but she's not receiving. Then *she* shakes *me* off and says, "Go on."

25 Juli would've tramped right in if my mother hadn't noticed her shoes and told her to take them off. And after those were off, my mom told her that her dirty socks had to go, too. Juli wasn't embarrassed. Not a bit. She just peeled them off and left them in a crusty heap on our porch.

26 I didn't exactly give her a tour. I locked myself in the bathroom instead. And after about ten minutes of yelling back at her that no, I wasn't coming out anytime soon, things got quiet out in the hall. Another ten minutes went by before I got the nerve to peek out the door.

27 No Juli.

28 I snuck out and looked around, and yes! She was gone.

29 Not a very sophisticated ditch, but hey, I was only seven.

30 My troubles were far from over, though. Every day she came back, over and over again. "Can Bryce play?" I could hear her asking from my hiding place behind the couch. "Is he ready yet?" One time she even cut across the yard and looked through my window. I spotted her in the nick of time and dove under my bed, but man, that right there tells you something about Juli Baker. She's got no concept of personal space. No respect for privacy. The world is her playground, and watch out below—Juli's on the slide!

immediately: right away

from the chapter "Flipped"

31 The first day I met Bryce Loski, I flipped. Honestly, one look at him and I became a lunatic. It's his eyes. Something in his eyes. They're blue, and framed in the blackness of his lashes, they're dazzling. **Absolutely** breathtaking.

32 It's been over six years now, and I learned long ago to hide my feelings, but oh, those first days. Those first years! I thought I would die for wanting to be with him.

33 Two days before the second grade is when it started, although the anticipation began weeks before—ever since my mother had told me that there was a family with a boy my age moving into the new house right across the street.

34 Soccer camp had ended, and I'd been so bored because there was nobody, absolutely nobody, in the neighborhood to play with. Oh, there were kids, but every one of them was older. That was dandy for my brothers, but what it left me was home alone.

35 My mother was there, but she had better things to do than kick a soccer ball around. So she said, anyway. At the time I didn't think there was anything better than kicking a soccer ball around, especially not the likes of laundry or dishes or vacuuming, but my mother didn't agree. And the danger of being home alone with her was that she'd recruit me to help her wash or dust or vacuum, and she wouldn't tolerate the dribbling of a soccer ball around the house as I moved from chore to chore.

36 To play it safe, I waited outside for weeks, just in case the new neighbors moved in early. **Literally**, it was *weeks*. I entertained myself by playing soccer with our dog, Champ. Mostly he'd just block because a dog can't exactly kick and score, but once in a while he'd dribble with his nose. The scent of a ball must overwhelm a dog, though, because Champ would eventually try to chomp it, then lose the ball to me.

37 When the Loskis' moving van finally arrived, everyone in my family was happy. "Little Julianna" was finally going to have a playmate.

38 My mother, being the truly sensible adult that she is, made me wait more than an *hour* before going over to meet him. "Give them a chance to stretch their legs, Julianna," she said. "They'll want some time to adjust." She wouldn't even let me watch from the yard. "I know you, sweetheart. Somehow that ball will wind up in their yard and you'll just *have* to go retrieve it."

39 So I watched from the window, and every few minutes I'd ask, "Now?" and she'd say, "Give them a little while longer, would you?"

GRAMMAR & USAGE

Sentences and Fragments
In narrative writing, authors often use simple sentences or fragments in dialogue.

A **simple sentence** contains one independent clause with a single subject and a verb. "I know you, sweetheart" in paragraph 38 is an example of a simple sentence used in dialogue. The effect is that an entire thought is expressed by the speaker.

A **fragment** is not a complete sentence; it is missing either a subject or a verb. "Sure thing!" in paragraph 12 of "Diving Under" is an example of a fragment. Authors may use fragments intentionally in dialogue and for stylistic reasons. Fragments can make dialogue more realistic because people often use fragments when speaking.

---

absolutely: completely
literally: without exaggeration

My Notes

40 Then the phone rang. And the minute I was sure she was good and preoccupied, I tugged on her sleeve and asked, "Now?"

41 She nodded and whispered, "Okay, but take it easy! I'll be over there in a minute."

42 I was too excited not to charge across the street, but I did try very hard to be **civilized** once I got to the moving van. I stood outside looking in for a record-breaking length of time, which was hard because there he was! About halfway back! My new sure-to-be best friend, Bryce Loski.

43 Bryce wasn't really doing much of anything. He was more hanging back, watching his father move boxes onto the liftgate. I remember feeling sorry for Mr. Loski because he looked worn out, moving boxes all by himself. I also remember that he and Bryce were wearing matching turquoise polo shirts, which I thought was really cute. Really *nice*.

44 When I couldn't stand it any longer, I called, "Hi!" into the van, which made Bryce jump, and then quick as a cricket, he started pushing a box like he'd been working all along.

45 I could tell from the way Bryce was acting so guilty that he was supposed to be moving boxes, but he was sick of it. He'd probably been moving things for days! It was easy to see that he needed a rest. He needed some juice! Something.

46 It was also easy to see that Mr. Loski wasn't about to let him quit. He was going to keep on moving boxes around until he collapsed, and by then Bryce might be dead. Dead before he'd had the chance to move in!

47 The tragedy of it catapulted me into the moving van. I had to help! I had to save him!

48 When I got to his side to help him shove a box forward, the poor boy was so exhausted that he just moved aside and let me take over. Mr. Loski didn't want me to help, but at least I saved Bryce. I'd been in the moving van all of three minutes when his dad sent him off to help his mother unpack things inside the house.

49 I chased Bryce up the walkway, and that's when everything changed. You see, I caught up to him and grabbed his arm, trying to stop him so maybe we could play a little before he got trapped inside, and the next thing I know he's holding my hand, looking right into my eyes.

50 My heart stopped. It just stopped beating. And for the first time in my life, I had that feeling. You know, like the world is moving all around you, all beneath you, all *inside* you, and you're floating. Floating in midair. And the only thing keeping you from drifting away is the other person's eyes. They're

civilized: polite

connected to yours by some invisible physical force, and they hold you fast while the rest of the world swirls and twirls and falls completely away.

51 I almost got my first kiss that day. I'm sure of it. But then his mother came out the front door and he was so embarrassed that his cheeks turned completely red, and the next thing you know he's hiding in the bathroom.

52 I was waiting for him to come out when his sister, Lynetta, saw me in the hallway. She seemed big and mature to me, and since she wanted to know what was going on, I told her a little bit about it. I shouldn't have, though, because she wiggled the bathroom doorknob and started teasing Bryce something fierce. "Hey, baby brother!" she called through the door. "There's a hot chick out here waiting for you! Whatsa matter? Afraid she's got cooties?"

53 It was so embarrassing! I yanked on her arm and told her to stop it, but she wouldn't, so finally I just left.

54 I found my mother outside talking to Mrs. Loski. Mom had given her the beautiful lemon Bundt cake that was supposed to be our dessert that night. The powdered sugar looked soft and white, and the cake was still warm, sending sweet lemon smells into the air.

55 My mouth was watering just looking at it! But it was in Mrs. Loski's hands, and I knew there was no getting it back. All I could do was try to eat up the smells while I listened to the two of them discuss grocery stores and the weather forecast.

56 After that Mom and I went home. It was very strange. I hadn't gotten to play with Bryce at all. All I knew was that his eyes were a dizzying blue, that he had a sister who was not to be trusted, and that he'd almost kissed me.

Making Observations
- Can you identify with the feelings of the characters at different points?
- What made this story funny?
- What's the main difference between the first chapter and the second?

☑ Focus on the Sentence

Use information from *Flipped* to change each of the fragments below into a complete sentence. Write the sentences with correct capitalization and punctuation.

when bryce first meets juli

_____

likes bryce because

_____

Returning to the Text

- Return to the text as you respond to the following questions. Use text evidence to support your responses. Be sure to respond with appropriate register, vocabulary, tone, and voice.
- Write any additional questions you have about the story in your Reader/Writer Notebook.

1. Describe the first meeting between Juli and Bryce from Bryce's point of view. How does Bryce feel about meeting Juli? Use details from the story to support your answer.

_____

_____

_____

_____

2. What changes in paragraph 31?

_____

_____

_____

_____

3. Find the part of the story that both Bryce and Juli describe. How are Juli's words different from Bryce's? How do the words show Juli's feelings about what is happening?

_____

_____

_____

_____

4. Why does the author use different chapters to represent each character? How does this structure contribute to the development of the plot?

_____

_____

_____

_____

Working from the Text

5. Writers often use a word's **connotation**, along with its **denotation**, to create an effect or meaning. For example, what do the verbs *barged, shoved*, and *wedged* say about how a character is moving? What image of the character do you get based on these words? In paragraph 17, notice that Juli uses the verbs *charge* and *catapult* to describe how she moves. These verbs mean more than simply "to walk or run"; they have strong connotations. How does the connotative effect of these words describe Juli's attitude toward her friendship with Bryce?

As you continue to work on the characterization of Juli and Bryce in the following questions, use additional examples of connotation to support your responses.

6. Record the textual evidence of the author's characterization in the following graphic organizer.

What Bryce/Juli says:	What Bryce/Juli does:
What others say about Bryce/Juli:	**How Bryce/Juli appears:**

7. Make an inference about the characters' attitudes in *Flipped*. To support your thinking, include textual evidence about what the characters say and do.

I know Bryce thinks Juli is _____ because he says,

I know Juli thinks Bryce is _____ because she says,

LITERARY

Connotation refers to the suggested or implied meaning or emotion associated with a word. In contrast, **denotation** refers to the literal meaning, or dictionary definition, of a word.

8. To fill out the following chart, use evidence from the text to show the differences in Bryce's and Juli's perspectives about an incident and how each character responded to it.

	Bryce's Point of View	Juli's Point of View
Incident		
Response		

LANGUAGE & WRITER'S CRAFT: Punctuating Dialogue

Writers use **dialogue** to give characters voices and to advance the plot of a narrative. Using dialogue requires a special set of punctuation rules. Look at how the writer uses dialogue in paragraphs 16–21 of *Flipped*.

My mom came out of the house and immediately got the world's sappiest look on her face. "Well, hello," she says to Juli.

"Hi!"

I'm still trying to pull free, but the girl's got me in a death grip. My mom's grinning, looking at our hands and my fiery red face. "And what's your name, honey?"

"Julianna Baker. I live right over there," she says, pointing with her unoccupied hand.

"Well, I see you've met my son," she says, still grinning away.

"Uh-huh!"

What do you notice about the use of quotation marks? How does the writer indicate who is speaking?

When writing dialogue, remember these points:

- Place a character's spoken words inside quotation marks (beginning and ending).
- Place the comma, exclamation mark, or question mark inside the ending quotation mark. If the quote is the end of the sentence, put the period inside the ending quotation mark, too.
- Capitalize the first word of dialogue.
- Start a new paragraph when a different character speaks.

PRACTICE Edit the following text. Rewrite the text following the punctuation rules for dialogue.

Hello, I said to the new family next door. My name is Janell. Hi, said the boy awkwardly. I'm Lavar. He seemed nervous. I tried to ease his nerves by saying, it must be weird moving to a new state. "Yeah, it is, he responded.

My Notes

9. **Collaborative Discussion:** Describe a time when you and another person (a friend, an adult, a teacher, a sibling) saw the same incident differently. Explain both how you saw the incident and how the other person viewed it.

10. Use the graphic organizer to prewrite about the incident you shared during the collaborative discussion.

I Say ...	_____ Says ...
Reflection: What did you learn, or how did you grow?	Reflection: What would _____ say you learned or how you grew?

INDEPENDENT READING LINK

Read and Connect

Record in your Reader/Writer Notebook how the author of the book you are reading independently is developing character. Analyze the plot elements of your book. Compare these elements to the elements used in *Flipped* (such as multiple points of view and dialogue). How are the texts similar? How are they different?

Narrative Writing Prompt

Write about the incident for which you completed the prewrite in a way that shows the differing attitudes about what happened. Be sure to:

- Establish the incident (setting, conflict, character) and describe the response to the incident.
- Create dialogue that incorporates the characters' feelings and punctuate it correctly.
- Use descriptive language such as connotative diction and vivid verbs.
- Use proper names and pronouns appropriately and punctuate your narrative correctly.

Return to the text of *Flipped* as a model of how to incorporate these elements in your writing.

Language Checkpoint: Punctuating Complete Sentences

> **Learning Targets**
> * Understand the difference between complete sentences and fragments.
> * Revise writing to use fragments appropriately for effect.

Punctuating Complete Sentences

Knowing the difference between complete sentences and sentence fragments is an important part of becoming a strong writer and self-editor. A sentence is considered complete when it includes a subject and a verb and expresses a complete idea. Look at the paragraph below from the novel *Flipped*, by Wendelin Van Draanen. Which sentence seems complete, and which seems like a fragment?

> All I've ever wanted is for Juli Baker to leave me alone. For her to back off—you know, just give me some space.

1. **Quickwrite:** Writers sometimes "break the rules" of grammar when they are trying to produce a specific effect in their writing. What are some reasons an author might break the rules by using sentence fragments?

2. Read the following excerpts from Flipped. Mark the fragments in the excerpts.

Excerpt 1

> I tried to shake her off, but she just clamped on tight and yanked me along, saying, "C'mon!"
>
> My mom came out of the house and immediately got the world's sappiest look on her face. "Well, hello," she says to Juli.
>
> "Hi!"
>
> I'm still trying to pull free, but the girl's got me in a death grip. My mom's grinning, looking at our hands and my fiery red face. "And what's your name, honey?"
>
> "Julianna Baker. I live right over there," she says, pointing with her unoccupied hand.

Excerpt 2

> The first day I met Bryce Loski, I flipped. Honestly, one look at him and I became a lunatic. It's his eyes. Something in his eyes. They're blue, and framed in the blackness of his lashes, they're dazzling. Absolutely breathtaking.
>
> It's been over six years now, and I learned long ago to hide my feelings, but oh, those first days. Those first years! I thought I would die for wanting to be with him.

3. **Think-Pair-Share** with a partner about the difference between the fragments in the excerpts above. How do the fragments enhance the story? Write your responses below.

Fragments Versus Complete Sentences

Writers choose different ways to use language depending on their audience and what they are writing. For example, writers typically do not use fragments in academic, business, or professional writing, but they may use fragments in fiction to create an informal—even humorous—tone. Using fragments can enhance your writing in the right situations; however, you must be careful not to use fragments accidentally or when you are writing formal, academic texts. In these situations, using fragments can hurt your credibility.

4. Decide whether each selection of text is a fragment (F) or a sentence (S). Circle the corresponding letter.

a. All I've ever wanted is for Juli Baker to leave me alone.   F / S

b. For her to back off—you know, just give me some space.   F / S

c. Juli wasn't embarrassed.   F / S

d. Not a bit.   F / S

e. He needed some juice!   F / S

f. Something.   F / S

g. Dead before he'd had the chance to move in!   F / S

Revising

Correct the accidental fragments in the paragraph below and add intentional fragments for a stylistic effect.

It was my team against Marcos's team, and there was so much tension between us it was like a rubber band being stretched to the breaking point. The game was going well. It was one to three. My team was winning, of course. It was my turn at bat, and a friend of mine named Rocko was pitching. He threw the first ball. It was a strike. He threw the second ball. It was a strike. I took a deep breath, and he lined up for the pitch. I knew he was going to throw a fastball. Because of his eyes. I waited for the pitch. I hit the ball so fast it was on fire, but I didn't hit it high enough. SMASH! It hit Mr. Thompson's window. I looked so scared. Because not only did I break the grumpiest man's window in the neighborhood. My mom has sonic ears. I know she heard that smash of his window.

☑ Check Your Understanding

What questions can you ask yourself when editing your work to check for sentence fragments? How can you be sure they are appropriate? Add the questions to your Editor's Checklist.

Practice

Reread the narrative you wrote in Activity 1.5. Work with a partner to:

• Highlight any place you used dialogue or wrote fragments.

• Add a fragment to dialogue to create a more casual tone if none is present.

• Add a fragment to help convey the narrator's voice.

• Check for accidental fragments that take away from the text and correct the fragments as needed.

Analyzing Narratives

Learning Targets
- Analyze the author's use of descriptive language in a personal narrative and its effect on the reader.

Preview
In this activity, you will read a personal narrative and analyze how the author uses simile and metaphor.

Descriptive Language
Writers use descriptive language, such as figurative language (including **metaphor** and **simile**), vivid verbs, and sensory language, to add interest, detail, and voice to their writing. If you are unsure about the meaning of these terms, look them up in the glossary of this book or in a dictionary.

Setting a Purpose for Reading
- Underline words and phrases that describe the narrator's feelings. Then use the My Notes section to describe any time you have felt similar emotions.
- Circle unknown words and phrases. Try to determine the meaning of the words by using context clues, word parts, or a dictionary.

Learning Strategies
Paraphrasing
Close Reading
Marking the Text
Graphic Organizer
Note-taking

VOCABULARY
LITERARY
The most common examples of figurative language are **metaphor** and **simile**. A simile compares two unlike things using words such as *like* or *as*. *His music is like a fast trip on a roller coaster.* A metaphor compares two unlike things without using the words *like* or *as*. Often a form of *to be* is used. *Her music is a trip to the streets of Memphis.*

About the Author

Gary Soto (1952–) grew up in Fresno, California. In many of his stories, Soto writes about the experiences of growing up as a Mexican American in the barrio, a Spanish-speaking neighborhood. While his stories draw on his own experiences and cultural heritage, the themes of his stories often relate to the experiences many young people face. His poems, short stories, and novels have won numerous awards and prizes.

My Notes

_____
_____
_____
_____
_____
_____
_____
_____
_____
_____
_____
_____
_____
_____
_____

Personal Narrative

The Jacket

by **Gary Soto**

1   My clothes have failed me. I remember the green coat that I wore in fifth and sixth grades when you either danced like a champ or pressed yourself against a greasy wall, bitter as a penny toward the happy couples.

2   When I needed a new jacket and my mother asked what kind I wanted, I described something like bikers wear: black leather and silver studs, with enough belts to hold down a small town. We were in the kitchen, steam on the

© 2021 College Board. All rights reserved.

My Notes

windows from her cooking. She listened so long while stirring dinner that I thought she understood for sure the kind I wanted. The next day when I got home from school, I discovered draped on my bedpost a jacket the color of day-old guacamole. I threw my books on the bed and approached the jacket slowly, as if it were a stranger whose hand I had to shake. I touched the **vinyl** sleeve, the collar, and peeked at the mustard-colored lining.

3   From the kitchen mother yelled that my jacket was in the closet. I closed the door to her voice and pulled at the rack of clothes in the closet, hoping the jacket on the bedpost wasn't for me but my mean brother. No luck. I gave up. From my bed, I stared at the jacket. I wanted to cry because it was so ugly and so big that I knew I'd have to wear it a long time. I was a small kid, thin as a young tree, and it would be years before I'd have a new one. I stared at the jacket, like an enemy, thinking bad things before I took off my old jacket, whose sleeves climbed halfway to my elbow.

4   I put the big jacket on. I zipped it up and down several times, and rolled the cuffs up so they didn't cover my hands. I put my hands in the pockets and flapped the jacket like a bird's wings. I stood in front of the mirror, full face, then profile, and then looked over my shoulder as if someone had called me. I sat on the bed, stood against the bed, and combed my hair to see what I would look like doing something natural. I looked ugly. I threw it on my brother's bed and looked at it for a long time before I slipped it on and went out to the backyard, smiling a "thank you" to my mom as I passed her in the kitchen. With my hands in my pockets I kicked a ball against the fence, and then climbed it to sit looking into the alley. I hurled orange peels at the mouth of an open garbage can, and when the peels were gone I watched the white puffs of my breath thin to nothing.

5   I jumped down, hands in my pockets, and in the backyard, on my knees, I teased my dog, Brownie, by swooping my arms while making birdcalls. He jumped at me and missed. He jumped again and again, until a tooth sunk deep, ripping an L-shaped tear on my left sleeve. I pushed Brownie away to study the tear as I would a cut on my arm. There was no blood, only a few loose pieces of fuzz. Damn dog, I thought, and pushed him away hard when he tried to bite again. I got up from my knees and went to my bedroom to sit with my jacket on my lap, with the lights out.

6   That was the first afternoon with my new jacket. The next day I wore it to sixth grade and got a D on a math quiz. During the morning recess Frankie T., the playground terrorist, pushed me to the ground and told me to stay there until recess was over. My best friend, Steve Negrete, ate an apple while looking at me, and the girls turned away to whisper on the monkey bars. The teachers were no help: they looked my way and talked about how foolish I looked in my new jacket. I saw their heads bob with laughter, their hands half covering their mouths.

vinyl: a type of plastic

7 Even though it was cold, I took off the jacket during lunch and played kickball in a thin shirt, my arms feeling like **braille** from goose bumps. But when I returned to class I slipped the jacket on and shivered until I was warm. I sat on my hands, heating them up, while my teeth chattered like a cup of crooked dice. Finally warm, I slid out of the jacket but put it back on a few minutes later when the fire bell rang. We paraded out into the yard where we, the sixth graders, walked past all the other grades to stand against the back fence. Everybody saw me. Although they didn't say out loud, "Man, that's ugly," I heard the buzz-buzz of gossip and even laughter that I knew was meant for me.

8 And so I went, in my guacamole-colored jacket. So embarrassed, so hurt, I couldn't even do my homework. I received C's on quizzes and forgot the state capitals and the rivers of South America, our friendly neighbor. Even the girls who had been friendly blew away like loose flowers to follow the boys in neat jackets.

9 I wore that thing for three years until the sleeves grew short and my forearms stuck out like the necks of turtles. All during that time no love came to me—no little dark girl in a Sunday dress she wore on Monday. At lunchtime I stayed with the ugly boys who leaned against the chainlink fence and looked around with **propellers** of grass spinning in our mouths. We saw girls walk by alone, saw couples, hand in hand, their heads like bookends pressing air together. We saw them and spun our propellers so fast our faces were blurs.

10 I blame that jacket for those bad years. I blame my mother for her bad taste and her cheap ways. It was a sad time for the heart. With a friend I spent my sixth-grade year in a tree in the alley, waiting for something good to happen to me in that jacket, which had become the ugly brother who tagged along wherever I went. And it was about that time that I began to grow. My chest puffed up with muscle and, strangely, a few more ribs. Even my hands, those fleshy hammers, showed bravely through the cuffs, the fingers already hardening for the coming fights. But that L-shaped rip on the left sleeve got bigger; bits of stuffing coughed out from its wound after a hard day of play. I finally Scotch-taped it closed, but in rain or cold weather the tape peeled off like a scab and more stuffing fell out until that sleeve shriveled into a **palsied** arm. That winter the elbows began to crack and whole chunks of green began to fall off. I showed the cracks to my mother, who always seemed to be at the stove with steamed-up glasses, and she said that there were children in Mexico who would love that jacket. I told her that this was America and yelled that Debbie, my sister, didn't have a jacket like mine. I ran outside, ready to cry, and climbed the tree by the alley to think bad thoughts and watch my breath puff white and disappear.

11 But whole pieces still casually flew off my jacket when I played hard, read quietly, or took **vicious** spelling tests at school. When it became so spotted that my brother began to call me "camouflage," I flung it over the fence into the alley. Later, however, I swiped the jacket off the ground and went inside to drape it across my lap and **mope**.

braille: a system of writing for blind people that uses raised dots

propellers: fanlike objects with turning blades

palsied: shaking uncontrollably because of an illness

vicious: cruel and dangerous

mope: feel aimless and unhappy

12   I was called to dinner: steam silvered my mother's glasses as she said grace; my brother and sister with their heads bowed made ugly faces at their glasses of powdered milk. I gagged too, but eagerly ate big rips of buttered tortilla that held scooped-up beans. Finished, I went outside with my jacket across my arm. It was a cold sky. The faces of clouds were piled up, hurting. I climbed the fence, jumping down with a grunt. I started up the alley and soon slipped into my jacket, that green ugly brother who breathed over my shoulder that day and ever since.

Making Observations

- What do you notice about the setting of the story?
- Which details about the jacket are important?
- What feelings does the narrator have about the jacket?

Returning to the Text

- Return to the text as you respond to the following questions. Use text evidence to support your responses.
- Write any additional questions you have about the story in your Reader/Writer Notebook.

1. What mood does the first sentence set up?

   _____

   _____

   _____

   _____

2. What is the point of view of this text? How does writing the story from this point of view help develop the plot?

   _____

   _____

   _____

   _____

3. What is one example of personification in the story? What is the mood it creates?

   _____

   _____

   _____

   _____

4. Why does the narrator use hyperbole to describe Frankie T. in paragraph 6?

_____

_____

_____

5. How does the narrator respond to the jacket? How does that response drive the plot?

_____

_____

_____

6. Paragraphs 7, 8, and 9 have vivid similes that describe how the narrator is feeling. Underline examples. Choose one that struck you, rewrite it, and explain its effect.

_____

_____

_____

_____

7. In the final paragraph of the narrative, Soto uses the following metaphor to describe his jacket: "... my jacket, that green ugly brother who breathed over my shoulder that day and every day since." Based on this line, what can you conclude about the significance of the jacket in Soto's life?

_____

_____

_____

_____

LANGUAGE & WRITER'S CRAFT: Vivid Verbs

Verbs show action, existence, or occurrence. Verb choice in writing can help build a specific mood for a story. Vivid verbs describe action in ways that help readers create mental images.

Each word in the examples below is related to the word *walked*, but each vivid verb indicates a more exact meaning than *walked*, thereby creating a different mood.

Example: They **marched** to school. (creates serious mood)
They **scrambled** to school. (creates panicked mood)
They **sauntered** to school. (creates relaxed mood)
They **skipped** to school. (creates gleeful mood)

Look at paragraph 4 of "The Jacket." Create mental images for the vivid verbs *zipped*, *rolled*, *flapped*, *combed*, *slipped*, *kicked*, and *hurled*. What mood is created by these specific verb choices?

PRACTICE Reread paragraph 5 of "The Jacket" and underline the vivid verbs. Choose two of them and describe the mood they create. Then rewrite those two sentences using different verbs. Tell how the new verbs change the mood.

Working from the Text

8. In addition to figurative language and vivid verbs, writers use sensory details to enhance their writing. Revise the following paragraph to include sensory details that appeal to any of the five senses.

   June and her friends were playing baseball in her yard. Billy was up at the plate. When June pitched the ball, Billy hit the ball high into the air. June watched the ball fly into her attic window. The glass shattered. June and Billy looked at each other and ran out of the yard.

9. Skim through "The Jacket," looking for examples of descriptive language. Write four examples in the table. Then analyze each example to understand the effect the author is trying to create. Finally, evaluate the example for its effectiveness.

Type of Descriptive Language	Example of Descriptive Language	Analyze the Effect	Evaluate How Effective It Is

10. With your group, choose one of the narratives you have read and make a poster that demonstrates your analysis of the story by creatively incorporating the following:

- Title and author of text
- An ending to this sentence: *This narrative is effective because ...*
- Examples of textual evidence that support the sentence
- Pictures/symbols/color that illustrate the elements of a narrative

As you complete your poster, think about the answer to the Essential Question: What makes a good story?

☑ Check Your Understanding

Select a short passage in the text that includes vivid description of a person, place, or situation. Describe the effect of this passage on you as a reader. How does the description make you feel? What does the passage help you understand about the story?

> ### ✍ Writing to Sources: Informational Text
>
> Describe the writer's use of descriptive language, including similes, metaphors, vivid verbs, and sensory language. How does the use of descriptive language help express the narrator's response to the incident? Be sure to:
>
> - Start the paragraph with a topic sentence that directly addresses the prompt.
> - Support your answer by referencing textual evidence from the narrative.
> - Punctuate complete sentences.

Learning Strategies

Drafting
Brainstorming
Graphic Organizer
Mapping
Note-taking

Learning Targets

- Brainstorm a personal incident about change to develop a narrative.
- Establish a sequence of events and use organization to plan the details for a narrative.
- Write dialogue and commentary to help establish the context of an incident.

Preview

In this activity, you will start to think about a memorable incident in your own life and begin drafting your own personal narrative.

The Writing Process

In creating your personal narrative, you will use the following writing process:

Planning and Prewriting: brainstorm ideas and plan your writing using the incident-response-reflection structure

Drafting: write your narrative with an effective beginning, middle, and end, including interesting details, descriptive language, and transitions

Revising: add words, phrases, sentences, and ideas to enhance your writing

Editing: check for correct grammar and spelling

1. **Prewriting:** Write about changes that have happened in your life and changes that could occur in the future.

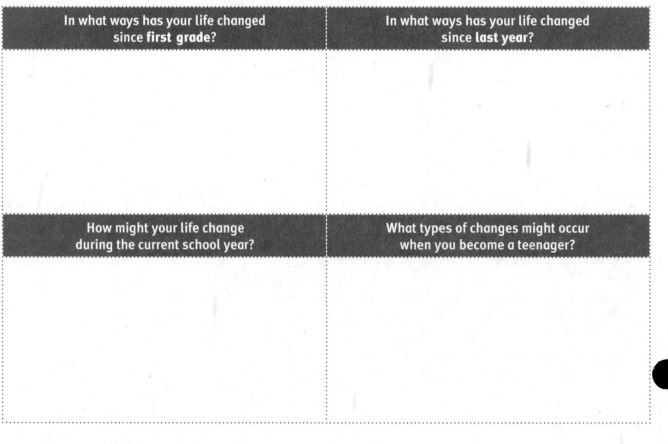

In what ways has your life changed since **first grade**?	In what ways has your life changed since **last year**?
How might your life change during the current school year?	What types of changes might occur when you become a teenager?

2. What words, phrases, and images show the kinds of changes you and your classmates have faced? Interview your classmates and make a list for each of the five areas shown below.

Hobbies	Beliefs	Appearance	School	Responsibilities

3. Think about the narratives you have read and how the writers created a story around an incident. List some of the incidents that resulted in some kind of change to your life. An example might be events that happened when changing from elementary school to middle school.

4. Choose one memorable incident that you would be willing to share as a visual memory map. Think back to that incident and determine what happened at the beginning, in the middle, and at the end. Try to come up with nine or ten events for the entire incident, at least three for each part. Use the graphic organizer to list the events of the incident.

My Incident:

Events at the Beginning	Events in the Middle	Events at the End

5. Next, brainstorm details of the events. Record descriptive language (connotative diction, sensory details, vivid verbs) and dialogue. Use the questions in the boxes to guide your thoughts.

Structure of a Personal Narrative

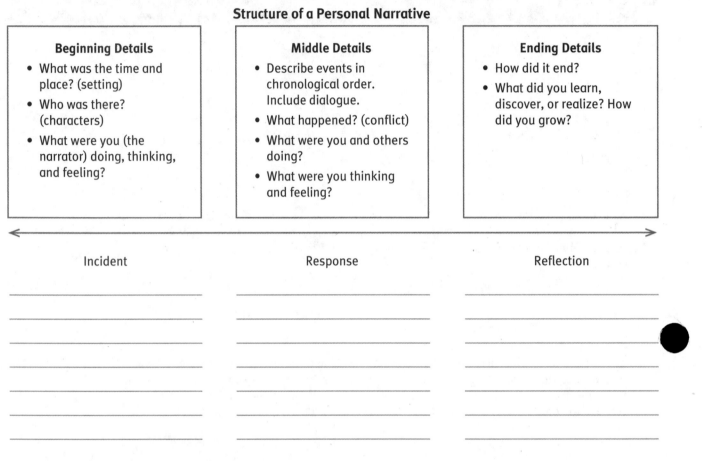

Beginning Details	**Middle Details**	**Ending Details**
• What was the time and place? (setting) • Who was there? (characters) • What were you (the narrator) doing, thinking, and feeling?	• Describe events in chronological order. Include dialogue. • What happened? (conflict) • What were you and others doing? • What were you thinking and feeling?	• How did it end? • What did you learn, discover, or realize? How did you grow?

Incident   Response   Reflection

Creating a Memory Map

For each event you have listed, you will create one panel or page and include the following:

• Write a sentence that gives specific details about the event. Then write commentary using a different-colored pen. Your **commentary** should explain the importance of the event or explain your feelings and emotions at the time.

• Using a third color, provide one sentence of dialogue for the scene.

• Create a drawing or graphic representation for each event.

• Give your Memory Map a title that will intrigue the reader and represent the narrative.

• Be prepared to present your Memory Map, telling your story to either a small group or the whole class.

You will use your Memory Map in the next activities as you write a narrative.

Creating a Narrative: Prewriting and Drafting

Learning Targets
- Apply the writing process while drafting a personal narrative.
- Use a variety of transition words, phrases, and clauses to create coherence in a narrative.
- Craft an opening sentence that hooks the reader and establishes the narrative.

Preview
In this activity, you will start organizing your personal narrative.

Learning Strategies
Generating Questions
Brainstorming
Summarizing
Graphic Organizer

My Notes

Planning a Narrative

1. **Prewriting:** Using the topic from your Memory Map or another topic of your choice, think about whether there are additional questions you might ask. Use the reporter's questions (*who, what, when, where, why,* and *how*) to fill in details of the narrative plan.

2. **Planning:** Organize the answers to your questions in a graphic organizer such as the one below (see the Resources section for a full-page version).

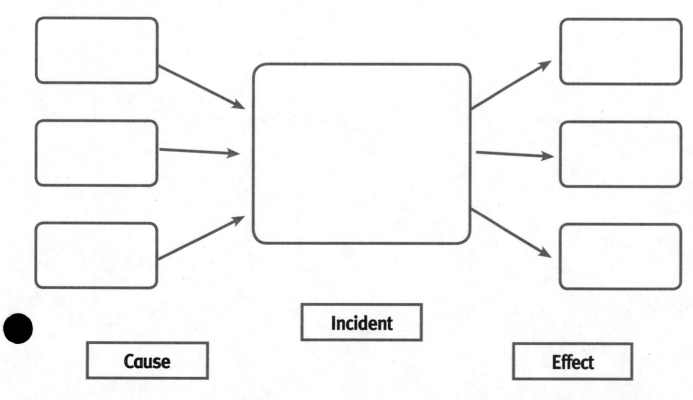

Incident

Cause

Effect

3. **Characterization:** Plan the characters by deciding what they say and do.

What the Character Says:	What Others Say:
What the Character Does:	**Descriptions of the Character's Appearance:**
What the Character Thinks:	**Language Techniques:**

LANGUAGE & WRITER'S CRAFT: Transitions

Transitions are words that link two ideas, sentences, or paragraphs by showing their relationship. Transitions create coherence within and across paragraphs. Without effective transitions, a text can seem choppy and hard to read.

One group of transition words is **subordinating conjunctions**. Writers use subordinating conjunctions to form complex sentences by combining two sentences and making one a dependent clause. Using complex sentences helps make writing more varied to readers. Varying sentence types helps make writing more appealing to readers.

Examples of Subordinating Conjunctions: *after, because, although, if*

- **Although** we had a great time at the street fair, I was very tired the next day.
- We can go to the museum tomorrow **if** you clean your room before going to bed.
- I received a good grade on my test **because** I studied for days before.
- **After** we ran out of milk, we had to change our plans for making dessert.

Notice that subordinating conjunctions can be at the beginning or in the middle of sentences. You might also notice that when subordinating conjunctions are used at the beginning of a sentence, a comma follows the dependent clause.

PRACTICE The following paragraph is choppy. Revise it by creating complex sentences with subordinating conjunctions.

My writing process is easy to follow. I read the source text closely. I study the prompt to make sure I understand it. I read the source text one more time with the prompt in mind. It takes some time to do. I make an outline that addresses the prompt. I write my rough draft based on the outline. I finish by editing and proofreading.

Writing the Beginning

How have you seen authors interest, or "hook," their audiences? What types of beginnings do you enjoy? Narratives must begin in a way that grabs the reader's attention and interests him or her enough to continue reading.

Some authors use the AQQS strategy to hook their readers. AQQS is an acronym for:

Anecdote: a short sketch or account of a biographical incident
Question: a question that focuses the reader's attention on the subject of the writing
Quote: a line of dialogue or a famous quotation that points to the idea of the narrative

> **ACADEMIC**
>
> When you use **transitions** to connect ideas, you are helping to create **coherence**. Coherence is the clear and orderly presentation of ideas in your writing and speaking. This ability to make your thinking cohere, or stick together, is an important skill in writing and thinking about any subject.

VOCABULARY

Statement of intrigue: a statement designed to capture the reader's interest and compel him or her to read more

4. Reread the openings of the narratives in Activities 1.2, 1.4, 1.5, and 1.6. In the last column of the graphic organizer, describe the type of hook each author uses.

	Text	What choice did the author make to hook the reader? (Which AQQS Strategy does the author use?)
"The Circuit"	"It was that time of year again. Ito, the sharecropper, did not smile. It was natural. The peak of strawberry season was over and the last few days the workers, most of them *braceros*, were not picking as many boxes as they had during the months of June and July."	
"My Superpowers"	"Do you ever wish you had superpowers?"	
Flipped From the chapter "Diving Under"	"All I've ever wanted is for Juli Baker to leave me alone. For her to back off—you know, just give me some space."	
"The Jacket"	"My clothes have failed me. I remember the green coat that I wore in fifth and sixth grades when you either danced like a champ or pressed yourself against a greasy wall, bitter as a penny toward the happy couples."	

☑ Check Your Understanding

Which narrative opening do you believe is most effective? Why?

Writing an Ending

5. Reread the endings in the narratives in Activities 1.2, 1.4, 1.5, and 1.6. Then complete the graphic organizer.

Title of Text	Describe how the narrator ends the story.	Summarize how the narrator changes because of the incident. Consider what the narrator learns and how he or she has grown as a person.
"The Circuit"	Jiménez explains	The ending shows that

Title of Text	Describe how the narrator ends the story.	Summarize how the narrator changes because of the incident. Consider what the narrator learns and how he or she has grown as a person.
"My Superpowers"	Greenburg explains	The ending shows that
Flipped from the chapter "Diving Under"	Van Draanen explains	The ending shows that
"The Jacket"	Soto explains	The ending shows that

☑ Check Your Understanding

Look back at your notes and other writing you've done. Which transition words do you use most frequently? Which words can you try to use in your personal narrative, and why do you choose those words?

📝 Drafting the Embedded Assessment

Write a draft of your narrative about a change that is significant to you. Remember to refer to your Memory Map, questions and answers about details, and characterization graphic organizer to help guide you as you write. Be sure to:

- Write from the first-person point of view and include vivid details of the characters' feelings using dialogue and descriptive language.
- Establish the incident (setting, conflict, character) and include a narrative hook.
- Describe the response (events).
- Include a reflection.
- Use at least two subordinating conjunctions to create complex sentences with correct use of commas.

Learning Strategies

Adding
Drafting
Sharing and Responding
Writer's Checklist
Self-editing

My Notes

Learning Targets

- Examine and use revision strategies to enhance narrative writing.
- Add dialogue and incorporate transitions and sensory details into a final draft.

Preview

No one ever creates a perfect piece of writing with just one try. Revision gives you the chance to look at your writing critically and decide how to improve it. In this activity, you will use the editing strategies you have been learning to revise the draft of your personal narrative.

Introducing the Strategy: Adding

The **adding** strategy is a revision strategy. With this strategy, you make conscious choices to enhance a piece of your writing by adding words, phrases, sentences, or ideas. For example, characters and incidents should be fully developed in narrative writing. Adding details as you revise can make a character come alive for the reader or make the story more appealing.

Adding Dialogue

Adding dialogue is one way to enhance narrative writing. When adding dialogue, it is important to vary your use of dialogue tags. *Dialogue tags* are phrases used to explain who is speaking. For example, look at this line from *Flipped*:

"No, no, no!" my dad says, then pulls her up by the arm.

The dialogue tag is the phrase "my dad says."

1. Brainstorm words other than *says* that you could use in dialogue tags, categorizing them by beginning letter. These verbs should be vivid and more descriptive than *said*.

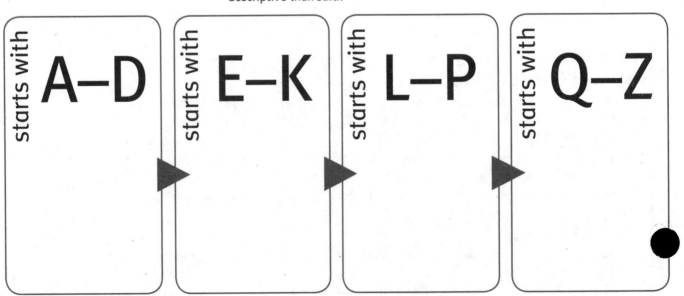

starts with **A–D** starts with **E–K** starts with **L–P** starts with **Q–Z**

2. Your teacher will share with you a sample of a comic strip, or you might bring in one of your favorite comic strips. Mark the text with different colors for each character in the comic strip. Then transform the conversation in the comic strip into written dialogue in paragraph form. Remember to punctuate the dialogue correctly and use a variety of dialogue tags.

3. Share your dialogue with a partner and compare how you each wrote the words of the characters in the comic strip. How were your paragraphs alike? How were they different?

4. Create a Writer's Checklist for using dialogue.

☑ Check Your Understanding

Use the checklist to revise your narrative to include dialogue.

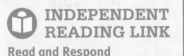

INDEPENDENT READING LINK

Read and Respond

Create an outline that shows the structure of how your independent reading book is organized. Show how the author has used the structure to develop the plot.

My Notes

Revision Practice

5. The following student narrative does not include any transitional words or phrases. It also lacks details to help the reader imagine the scene. Highlight each place where a transition might fit. Underline sentences that would benefit from sensory details and vivid verbs. Circle or draw a box around the pronouns.

When the author Gary Soto was in sixth grade, he needed a new jacket. His mother bought him a green jacket that he did not like at all. It was ugly. It was bad luck for him at school. He did poorly on tests and his friends didn't pay any attention to him. He thought his teachers and classmates all made fun of him and his jacket. The author's luck didn't change over time. No girls came his way. He tried to show his mother how bad his jacket looked. Her glasses were always steamed up. The author blames those bad times on his green jacket.

6. Rewrite the paragraph above, adding transitions, sensory details, and vivid verbs.

Revising Your Opening

7. Reread the opening of your narrative. Does it have a hook that grabs the reader's attention? Are you using a compound or complex sentence that establishes the narrative? Review the AQQS strategy. If needed, revise your narrative opening to use one of these techniques.

Revising Your Ending

8. Reread your ending. Does it have a reflection on the incident, following the incident-response-reflection pattern? How can you make your ending stronger? Do you need to add sensory language or transitions? Revise the ending to your narrative.

Creating a Finished Document

9. Among the steps to finishing your narrative is writing a title. To find ideas for the title:

   - Skim the narrative for a word or phrase that captures the big idea or theme of the narrative. Use interesting, descriptive words for your title.

   - State the change the narrator experienced, in a clever way.

   - Make your title unique; an effective title is not just a labeling of the genre or type of text (e.g., Personal Narrative).

10. The last step to creating a final draft is to check that it is correct and as good as you can make it. To prepare your document for publication, do the following:

   - Remember to use spelling strategies and ask for help with spelling words correctly. You can proofread your draft by having someone else read for spelling mistakes or by using the spell-check feature on word-processing software.

   - Check that you have used correct grammar and punctuation.

   - Use available resources before, during, and after your writing. Resources such as a dictionary and thesaurus will help you prepare your narrative for publication.

Independent Reading Checkpoint

Write a summary about how the theme of change is presented in your independent reading book. Explain the significance of these changes using text evidence to support your explanations. Tell how the theme of change in your book compares to the theme of change in at least one of the assigned texts you read.

Writing a Personal Narrative

ASSIGNMENT

Your assignment is to write a personal narrative that includes a well-told incident, a response to the incident, and a reflection about the significance of the incident.

Planning and Prewriting: Take time to make a plan for your personal narrative.	■ What activities have you completed or ideas have you brainstormed that will help you as you think of an appropriate incident to write about? ■ How will you make sure you understand all that needs to be part of your personal narrative? ■ What prewriting strategies can you use to help you create ideas? Will you work from your Memory Map?
Drafting: Determine the structure of your personal narrative.	■ What will you include in the beginning, the middle, and the end of your narrative? ■ How will you introduce your incident? ■ How will you be sure to write about the significance of the incident in a way that conveys importance?
Evaluating and Revising the Draft: Create opportunities to review and revise in order to make your work the best it can be.	■ During the process of writing, have you paused at points to share and respond with others how well you are following the structure of a narrative? ■ Are you considering revising your draft to add transitions and additional details to the incident? Once you get suggestions, are you creating a plan to include revision ideas in your draft? ■ Have you used the Scoring Guide to help you evaluate how well your draft included the requirements of the assignment?
Checking and Editing for Publication: Confirm that your final draft is ready for publication.	■ How will you check for grammatical and technical accuracy? ■ How will you make sure that everything is spelled correctly?

Reflection

After completing this Embedded Assessment, think about how you went about accomplishing this assignment and answer the questions below:

- How did the activities leading up to this Embedded Assessment help you to be successful?
- What activities were especially helpful, and why?

SCORING GUIDE

Scoring Criteria	Exemplary	Proficient	Emerging	Incomplete
Ideas	The narrative • presents a clearly focused and significant incident. • develops experiences, events, and/or characters through thorough and effective use of dialogue, pacing, and descriptive details.	The narrative • presents a focused and significant incident. • develops experiences, events, and/or characters through techniques such as dialogue, pacing, and descriptive details.	The narrative • presents an inconsistently focused incident. • begins to develop experiences, events, and/or characters through some use of dialogue, pacing, and/or descriptive details.	The narrative • presents an unfocused or unclear incident. • fails to develop experiences, events, and/or characters; minimal use of elaborative techniques.
Structure	The narrative • engages and orients the reader in an introduction. • sequences events in the incident and response logically and naturally. • uses a variety of transitional strategies effectively. • provides an insightful reflective conclusion.	The narrative • orients the reader with an adequate introduction. • sequences events in the incident and response logically. • uses transitional words, phrases, and clauses to link events and signal shifts. • provides a reflective conclusion.	The narrative • provides a weak or unrelated introduction. • sequences events unevenly. • uses inconsistent, repetitive, or basic transitional words, phrases, and clauses. • provides a weak or disconnected conclusion.	The narrative • lacks an introduction. • sequences events illogically. • uses few or no transitional strategies. • lacks a conclusion.
Use of Language	The narrative • uses precise words and sensory language effectively to convey the experience. • demonstrates command of the conventions of standard English capitalization, punctuation, spelling, grammar, and usage (including pronoun use, sentence variety, dialogue tags, and punctuation).	The narrative • uses generally precise words and sensory language to convey the experience. • demonstrates adequate command of the conventions of standard English capitalization, punctuation, spelling, grammar, and usage (including pronoun use, sentence variety, dialogue tags, and punctuation).	The narrative • uses few precise words and little sensory language. • demonstrates partial or inconsistent command of the conventions of standard English capitalization, punctuation, spelling, grammar, and usage (including pronoun use, sentence variety, dialogue tags, and punctuation).	The narrative • uses limited, vague, and unclear words and language. • lacks command of the conventions of standard English capitalization, punctuation, spelling, grammar, and usage; frequent errors obscure meaning.

Unpacking Embedded Assessment 2

Learning Strategies

Adding
Drafting
Sharing and Responding
Writer's Checklist
Self-editing

INDEPENDENT READING LINK

Reading Plan

During this half of the unit, find some other short stories that interest you. Consider reading many stories by one author or stories on the same topic by many authors. Short stories come in many genres, including mystery and fantasy. Find ones that you like, and keep track of your reading in the My Independent Reading section on the unit Contents page.

My Notes

Learning Targets

- Reflect on prior learning and identify the skills and knowledge necessary to complete Embedded Assessment 2 successfully.
- Reassess knowledge of academic vocabulary and literary terms in the unit.

Preview

In this activity, you will unpack Embedded Assessment 2 and preview the next half of the unit.

Making Connections

In the first part of this unit, you thought about changes in your life and learned how to write a personal narrative. In the second part of the unit, you will expand on your writing skills by learning to write a short story that will appeal to an audience.

Essential Questions

1. Do you have new ideas about how change can be significant?

2. Have your ideas about what makes a good story changed?

Developing Vocabulary

Create a graphic organizer with three columns, one each for Q, H, and T. Re-sort the following words from the first half of the unit using the QHT strategy. Compare this sort with your original sort. Where has it changed most? Where has it changed least?

Literary Terms		Academic Vocabulary
conflict (internal/external)	personal narrative	sequence
connotation		cause-effect
denotation		transitions
simile		coherence
metaphor		

Unpacking Embedded Assessment 2

Closely read the assignment for Embedded Assessment 2: Writing a Short Story.

 Write a story using dialogue, vivid verbs, and figurative language that captures a real or imagined experience and includes characters, conflict, and a plot with exposition, climax, and resolution.

Also read the Scoring Guide for Embedded Assessment 2 on page 101. With your class, create a graphic organizer to use as a visual reminder of the required knowledge (what you need to know) and skills (what you need to do). Copy the graphic organizer for future reference. After each activity, use this graphic to guide reflection about what you have learned and what you still need to learn in order to be successful on the Embedded Assessment.

Personal Narrative vs. Short Story: Comparing Genres

Learning Strategies

Graphic Organizer
Paraphrasing

Learning Targets

- Analyze and compare story elements across genres.
- Make connections between literary elements across genres.

Preview

In this activity, you will learn about the short story genre and compare it to the genre of personal narrative.

Genre Study: Narrative

1. Based on your current understanding, how do you think writing a personal narrative and writing a short story are similar? How are they different? Fill in the chart below with your ideas for each genre.

	Personal Narrative	Short Story
Topics		
Setting		
Plot		
Characters		
Dialogue		

2. With a group, discuss your ideas about how personal narratives and short stories may be similar or different. Write down the conclusions you can draw based on your discussion.

3. What do these similarities and differences mean for you as a writer? Do you think writing a short story will be more or less challenging than writing a personal narrative?

Check Your Understanding

Look back over the notes in your chart. How can you apply your knowledge of the way literary elements are used in personal narrative to add realistic details to your short story?

What's in a Short Story?

Collaborative Discussion
Note-taking
Predicting
Rereading
Graphic Organizer
Drafting

VOCABULARY

LITERARY

A **short story** is a fictional narrative that presents a sequence of events, or plot, that include a conflict. Short stories come in all genres, including realistic fiction, science fiction, historical fiction, mystery, adventure, and humor.

Learning Targets

- Identify the theme of a short story by analyzing narrative elements.
- Use narrative writing to develop a character and transform a story from third-person into first-person point of view.
- Integrate ideas from multiple texts to build knowledge and vocabulary about the concept of positive responses.

Preview

In this activity, you will read a **short story** and view a related historical photograph to make connections. Then you will rewrite a scene from the short story from the first-person point of view of the story's main character.

Setting a Purpose for Reading

- As you read the short story, circle words that introduce characters, underline descriptions of the setting, and use the My Notes section to summarize important events.
- Circle unknown words and phrases. Try to determine the meaning of the words by using context clues, word parts, or a dictionary.

About the Author

Langston Hughes (1902–1967) began his writing career early. By eighth grade, he was named the class poet. He regularly wrote verse for his high school magazine. Hughes entered Columbia University in 1921 and discovered the arts scene in Harlem. He became a prominent figure in the Harlem Renaissance. His poetry, plays, and stories frequently focus on the African American experience, particularly on the struggles and feelings of people in a segregated society. His poetry was especially informed by the jazz and blues rhythms of African American music.

My Notes

Short Story

Thank You, M'am

by **Langston Hughes**

1   She was a large woman with a large purse that had everything in it but hammer and nails. It had a long strap, and she carried it slung across her shoulder. It was about eleven o'clock at night, and she was walking alone, when a boy ran up behind her and tried to snatch her purse. The strap broke with the single tug the boy gave it from behind. But the boy's weight and the weight of the purse combined caused him to lose his balance so, instead of taking off full blast as he had hoped, the boy fell on his back on the sidewalk, and his legs flew up. The large woman simply turned around and kicked him right square in his blue-jeaned sitter. Then she reached down, picked the boy up by his shirt front, and shook him until his teeth rattled.

2   After that the woman said, "Pick up my pocketbook, boy, and give it here."

3   She still held him. But she bent down enough to permit him to **stoop** and pick up her purse. Then she said, "Now ain't you **ashamed** of yourself?"

4   Firmly gripped by his shirt front, the boy said, "Yes'm."

5   The woman said, "What did you want to do it for?"

6   The boy said, "I didn't aim to."

7   She said, "You a lie!"

8   By that time two or three people passed, stopped, turned to look, and some stood watching.

9   "If I turn you loose, will you run?" asked the woman.

10   "Yes'm," said the boy.

11   "Then I won't turn you loose," said the woman. She did not release him.

12   "I'm very sorry, lady, I'm sorry," whispered the boy.

13   "Um-hum! And your face is dirty. I got a great mind to wash your face for you. Ain't you got nobody home to tell you to wash your face?"

14   "No'm," said the boy.

15   "Then it will get washed this evening," said the large woman starting up the street, dragging the frightened boy behind her.

16   He looked as if he were fourteen or fifteen, frail and **willow**-wild, in tennis shoes and blue jeans.

17   The woman said, "You ought to be my son. I would teach you right from wrong. Least I can do right now is to wash your face. Are you hungry?"

18   "No'm," said the being-dragged boy. "I just want you to turn me loose."

KNOWLEDGE QUEST

Knowledge Question:

When times are difficult, how does a positive response from someone help us to change our actions and outlook?

In Activity 1.12, you will read a text about a boy who experiences change after making a mistake. You will use a picture taken in 1938 to compare and contrast story elements. While you read and build knowledge about the theme, think about your answer to the Knowledge Question.

WORD CONNECTIONS

Etymology

The term **nelson** is derived from *full nelson*, which dates back to the early 19th century. It is supposedly named after the British war hero Admiral Horatio Nelson, who used strategies based on surrounding the opponent to win the Battle of the Nile and the Battle of Trafalgar.

stoop: bend forward and down

ashamed: feeling shame or guilt

willow: long and thin, like a willow tree branch

My Notes

19 "Was I bothering *you* when I turned that corner?" asked the woman.

20 "No'm."

21 "But you put yourself in contact with me," said the woman. "If you think that that contact is not going to last awhile, you got another thought coming. When I get through with you, sir, you are going to remember Mrs. Luella Bates Washington Jones."

22 Sweat popped out on the boy's face and he began to struggle. Mrs. Jones stopped, jerked him around in front of her, put a half-nelson about his neck, and continued to drag him up the street. When she got to her door, she dragged the boy inside, down a hall, and into a large kitchenette-furnished room at the rear of the house. She switched on the light and left the door open. The boy could hear other roomers laughing and talking in the large house. Some of their doors were open, too, so he knew he and the woman were not alone. The woman still had him by the neck in the middle of her room.

23 She said, "What is your name?"

24 "Roger," answered the boy.

25 "Then, Roger, you go to that sink and wash your face," said the woman, whereupon she turned him loose–at last. Roger looked at the door—looked at the woman—looked at the door—*and went to the sink*.

26 "Let the water run until it gets warm," she said. "Here's a clean towel."

27 "You gonna take me to jail?" asked the boy, bending over the sink.

28 "Not with that face, I would not take you nowhere," said the woman. "Here I am trying to get home to cook me a bite to eat and you snatch my pocketbook! Maybe, you ain't been to your supper either, late as it be. Have you?"

29 "There's nobody home at my house," said the boy.

30 "Then we'll eat," said the woman, "I believe you're hungry—or been hungry—to try to snatch my pocketbook."

31 "I wanted a pair of blue suede shoes," said the boy.

32 "Well, you didn't have to snatch my pocketbook to get some suede shoes," said Mrs. Luella Bates Washington Jones. "You could of asked me."

33 "M'am?"

34 The water dripping from his face, the boy looked at her. There was a long pause. A very long pause. After he had dried his face and not knowing what else to do, dried it again, the boy turned around, wondering what next. The door was open. He could make a dash for it down the hall. He could run, run, run, run, *run!*

35 The woman was sitting on the day-bed. After a while she said, "I were young once and I wanted things I could not get."

36 There was another long pause. The boy's mouth opened. Then he frowned, but not knowing he frowned.

My Notes

37 The woman said, "Um-hum! You thought I was going to say *but*, didn't you? You thought I was going to say, *but I didn't snatch people's pocketbooks.* Well, I wasn't going to say that." Pause. Silence. "I have done things, too, which I would not tell you, son—neither tell God, if he didn't already know. So you set down while I fix us something to eat. You might run that comb through your hair so you will look presentable.

38 In another corner of the room behind a screen was a gas plate and an **icebox**. Mrs. Jones got up and went behind the screen. The woman did not watch the boy to see if he was going to run now, nor did she watch her purse which she left behind her on the day-bed. But the boy took care to sit on the far side of the room where he thought she could easily see him out of the corner of her eye, if she wanted to. He did not trust the woman not to trust him. And he did not want to be mistrusted now.

39 "Do you need somebody to go to the store," asked the boy, "maybe to get some milk or something?"

40 "Don't believe I do," said the woman, "unless you just want sweet milk yourself. I was going to make cocoa out of this canned milk I got here."

41 "That will be fine," said the boy.

42 She heated some lima beans and ham she had in the icebox, made the cocoa, and set the table. The woman did not ask the boy anything about where he lived, or his folks, or anything else that would embarrass him. Instead, as they ate, she told him about her job in a hotel beauty-shop that stayed open late, what the work was like, and how all kinds of women came in and out, blondes, red-heads, and Spanish. Then she cut him a half of her ten-cent cake.

43 "Eat some more, son," she said.

44 When they were finished eating she got up and said, "Now, here, take this ten dollars and buy yourself some blue suede shoes. And next time, do not make the mistake of latching onto *my* pocketbook *nor nobody else's*—because shoes come by devilish like that will burn your feet. I got to get my rest now. But I wish you would behave yourself, son, from here on in."

45 She led him down the hall to the front door and opened it. "Goodnight! Behave yourself, boy!" she said, looking out into the street.

46 The boy wanted to say something else other than "Thank you, m'am" to Mrs. Luella Bates Washington Jones, but he couldn't do so as he turned at the barren stoop and looked back at the large woman in the door. He barely managed to say "Thank you" before she shut the door. And he never saw her again.

Ⓥ Knowledge Quest

- Which parts of the story appeal to your emotions?
- What ideas about positive changes do you have while reading the story?

icebox: refrigerator

This photograph of a street in Harlem was taken in 1938 by Berenice Abbott. Langston Hughes was a prominent member of the Harlem Renaissance and may have used the sights and sounds of this time in American history as inspiration for his story. What setting did you envision as you read the story?

Returning to the Text

- Return to the text as you respond to the following questions. Use text evidence to support your responses. Be sure to respond with appropriate register, vocabulary, tone, and voice.
- Write any additional questions you have about the story in your Reader/Writer Notebook.

1. How do the details of setting and character in the first paragraph set up the conflict of this story?

_____

_____

_____

_____

2. In paragraph 25, Mrs. Jones finally turns Roger loose: "Roger looked at the door—looked at the woman—looked at the door—*and went to the sink*." Why did the author choose to italicize this part of the text?

_____

_____

_____

_____

3. How does the dialogue between Roger and Mrs. Luella Bates Washington Jones differ from standard English? Use the examples in paragraphs 28 and 32 to explain why the author would not want to use standard English in these instances.

_____

_____

_____

_____

4. How do Roger's internal thoughts in paragraph 34 develop the plot?

_____

_____

_____

_____

5. **KQ** What is the meaning of _trust_ in paragraph 38? Use context clues and a dictionary to help you find out. Then tell what trust has to do with the change you see in Roger's actions and outlook.

_____

_____

_____

_____

6. How does the photograph of Harlem in 1938 help you understand the story's setting? Compare and contrast what you learn about life in Harlem from the text and the photograph.

_____

_____

_____

_____

7. **KQ** Even though Roger never sees Mrs. Jones again after their interaction in the story, what evidence supports Mrs. Jones's promise in paragraph 21, "When I get through with you, sir, you are going to remember Mrs. Luella Bates Washington Jones"?

_____

_____

_____

INDEPENDENT READING LINK

You can continue to build your knowledge about positive responses by reading related articles at ZINC Learning Labs. Search for keywords such as *difficult times* and *overcoming challenges*.

ZINC

Knowledge Quest

After reading the text and viewing the photo, tell a partner about your understanding of how a positive response can help a person change his or her actions and outlook. Go back through the text to find an example of a positive response. Then think of one of your own.

Working from the Text

8. Use the following table to organize your annotations from the first read:

Provide evidence, including visual information from the historical photograph, to describe the setting of the short story.	**List the main characters.**
Summarize the incident of the story.	
Provide evidence, including dialogue from the text, to describe each character's response to the incident.	
Summarize the ending of the story.	

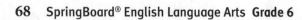

9. Look at the first two sentences of the story. How do the sensory details help you picture the woman and her purse?

Find another sentence that includes sensory details. Describe how the sensory details help you picture the characters or setting.

VOCABULARY

LITERARY

Theme is the central idea, message, topic, or purpose of a literary work. Most works have more than one theme, some expressed more explicitly than others. Identifying themes in a text requires reading carefully and making inferences.

10. Look around your classroom and choose an object. How does it look? How does it feel when you touch it or hold it? Does it have a smell? Write a sentence that uses sensory details to describe the object.

☑ Check Your Understanding

What is one of the story's **themes**? Describe what the reader learns about life through the interaction between Roger and Mrs. Luella Bates Washington Jones. Use evidence from the text to support your idea.

My Notes

_____

_____

_____

_____

_____

_____

_____

_____

_____

_____

_____

_____

_____

_____

_____

_____

_____

_____

_____

_____

_____

_____

_____

_____

✍ Narrative Writing Prompt

This story is told from the third-person point of view. Choose a scene or plot event and imagine Roger's thoughts and feelings about what is happening. Draft a first-person narrative of his thinking at that point in the story. Be sure to:

• Use first-person point of view.

• Maintain the character of Roger as the author presents him.

• Include a sentence with sensory details that describe characters or setting.

• Use a variety of first-person pronouns (subjective, objective, intensive, and possessive) and ensure that they are in the correct case.

Save this writing response so that you can revisit it when generating ideas for the original short story you will create for Embedded Assessment 2.

Learning Strategies

Guided Reading
Note-taking
Graphic Organizer
SIFT
Manipulatives
Drafting

Learning Targets

- Explain how a character responds to change.
- Describe how a well-structured story plot develops.

Preview

In this activity, you will learn how stories are structured and start to plan a short story of your own.

VOCABULARY

LITERARY

Plot is the sequence of related events that make up a story. Plot often unfolds in a linear cause-and-effect structure: something happens, and then something else happens in response. Sometimes plot develops in a nonlinear way through literary devices like flashbacks, parallel story lines, and dreams.

WORD CONNECTIONS

Multiple-Meaning Words

A single word sometimes has several meanings. For example, the word **exposition** refers to the plot of a short story. It also describes a type of writing. It may also describe a fair or public exhibit.

WORD CONNECTIONS

Roots and Affixes

Resolution is a noun form of *resolve*. The root *sol* or *solve* means "to set loose or free." This root occurs in *solution*, *absolution*, and *resolute*.

The Latin prefix *re-* means "back" or "again."

Elements of Storytelling

Storytellers use the following elements of **plot** to develop and organize ideas.

Exposition: the events that give the reader background information needed to understand the story. The introduction to the story usually reveals the setting, the major characters, and the conflict.

Rising Action: the major events that develop the plot and lead to the climax.

Climax: the event that is the turning point in the story, at which the conflict could be resolved in different ways.

Falling Action: the events that begin to conclude the story and lead to the ending.

Resolution: the events that conclude the story and reveal the theme.

Types of Conflict

You learned in the first part of the unit that conflict is an important part of a story. Writers reveal conflict through the dialogue and events of a story. Conflict is used to move the action forward, reveal information about characters, and create a decision or change.

The two main types of conflict are internal conflict and external conflict.

- *Internal conflict* occurs when a character struggles with his or her own needs, desires, or emotions.
- *External conflict* occurs when a character struggles with an outside force, such as another character or something in nature.

Reviewing and Analyzing a Fairy Tale

Fairy tales apply familiar story ideas—such as a quest toward a goal or a rags-to-riches character arc—to the plot elements of storytelling. A rags-to-riches fairy tale involves a poor, struggling person who finds fortune or success. *Cinderella* is a classic example. A quest fairy tale is about a hero on a journey of adventure who achieves something important. *The Lord of the Rings* is a kind of quest fairy tale.

1. After your teacher reads a fairy tale aloud, summarize the story. Make sure your summary maintains the meaning of the story and is sequenced by plot elements.

2. Write the events you have listed from the fairy tale in the appropriate places on the plot diagram.

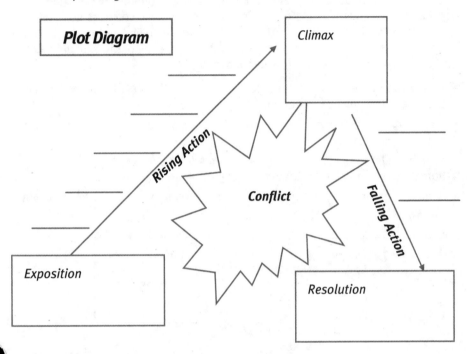

Plot Diagram

Climax

Rising Action

Conflict

Falling Action

Exposition

Resolution

3. After analyzing plot, character, conflict, and setting, what would you conclude is the theme of this fairy tale?

☑ Check Your Understanding

Recall a well-known story, such as a fairy tale or fable. Then identify the rising action, climax, conflict, falling action, and resolution in that story. Write a summary that maintains the meaning of the tale in your Reader/Writer Notebook.

My Notes

Applying Your Understanding of Plot

Create a plot for a story of your own that follows a rags-to-riches or hero quest plot line. The setting for your story can be any time or place and does not need to use typical fairy tale fantasy characters or magic. Make up and write at least seven events on the provided plot diagram. You might choose one of the following plot outlines and imagine how the story might develop.

- An unhappy young boy with three terrible older brothers is told he can become the eldest if he can outsmart them.
- A poor country girl saves a wealthy woman's life, and then their lives turn in the opposite direction.
- A sixth grader faces difficult choices when a story he writes about his hometown is made into a successful Hollywood movie.
- A musical group who can't come up with a good song roams the city searching for inspiration.

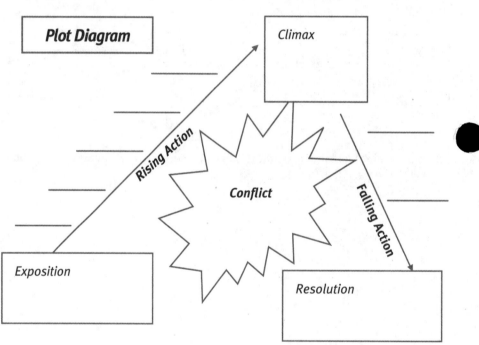

In the Beginning

Learning Targets

- Identify the elements of the exposition of a story by accurately recording textual evidence that supports interpretation.
- Identify and utilize varied sentence patterns in writing.

Preview

In this activity, you will explore foreshadowing and other common elements of myths.

Genre Study: Myth

Myths are traditional stories that have been passed down from long, long ago. They usually explain something about the natural world and include gods and goddesses that take human forms, possess supernatural powers, and interfere with people's lives. Strange, made-up creatures often play a role in myths as well. Myths have been retold or referenced in storybooks, movies, graphic novels, and comic books.

1. **Quickwrite:** What are some myths you have read about, seen in movies, or been told? What do the stories have in common? What cultures did they come from?

Setting a Purpose for Reading

- Use the My Notes section to identify any characteristics of myths you notice.
- Circle unknown words and phrases. Try to determine the meaning of the words by using context clues, word parts, or a dictionary.

Myth

Orpheus
and Eurydice

by **Bob Blaisdell**

1   Now let us hear the story of the great musician and singer Orpheus. A sad fate awaited this poet of the Argo[1]. We know that when Orpheus sang to the tunes he played on his **lyre** even the muddy stones on the side of the road sat up and listened. The trees swayed in time to his music. He gave spirit to those things which have none and joy to those which have. If a man or beast felt hot, eager anger, Orpheus's songs would soon soothe him.

---

[1] The ship Jason and the Argonauts used on their quest for the Golden Fleece; built by Argus with instructions from Athena

Learning Strategies

Marking the Text
Metacognitive Markers
Graphic Organizer
Rereading
Skimming/Scanning
Visualizing

WORD CONNECTIONS

Roots and Affixes
The study of **myths** is called *mythology*. The suffix *-logy* is from Greek and means "the study of." This much-used word part appears in many words in English, such as *biology*, *psychology*, *criminology*, and *ecology*.

My Notes

_____
_____
_____
_____
_____
_____
_____
_____
_____
_____
_____
_____

lyre: a small, stringed instrument

Cerberus by William Blake, 1824–27

My Notes

_____

_____

_____

_____

_____

_____

_____

_____

_____

_____

_____

_____

_____

_____

_____

_____

fleet-footed: quick

faintest: barely able to be heard

proceeded: began or continued

dreary: sad or hopeless

2 Orpheus fell in love with Eurydice. They trembled with delight in each other's presence and their love gave Orpheus the joy that his music gave others. They were soon married.

3 It was during their honeymoon that a son of Apollo, Aristaeus, desiring Eurydice for his own, chased her. She, dashing away from the path to escape him, stepped on a snake, which bit her. She tumbled to the ground and cried for help. Aristaeus was frightened and ran away. Orpheus was terrified at her desperate call and came running to her.

4 But it was too late.

5 Orpheus cried. His beloved was dead! He wandered away, tears in his eyes. Even in his grief, however, Orpheus's lyre still played beautifully and his voice still melted the hearts of stones, as well as men's soft hearts, and his songs of sorrow made the gods weep. Zeus asked **fleet-footed** Hermes to go to the mortal. "Escort him alive down to Hades," commanded Zeus through his tears. "See if my brother Hades, lord of the dead, will return Eurydice to him."

6 Hermes took Orpheus by the hand and led the way across the seas to the secret entrance of the underworld. The terrible three-headed watchdog, Cerberus, hearing Orpheus's sweet music, lay down and sighed, and, without the **faintest** bark, allowed the god and his mortal guest to go past.

7 Orpheus sang his mournful song to the lord and queen of the underworld, Hades and Persephone. Perhaps remembering her own sweet life above ground, Persephone had pity for Orpheus and persuaded her husband to return Eurydice's soul to the upper world, where she could live again with her beloved.

8 "Very well," said Hades. "You go on your way, back the way you came, and Eurydice will follow. But you must not look at her until she has passed out of the underworld. If you do, she will stay here with me. You may look at her all you like when you get her above."

9 Orpheus promised not to look. As the singer **proceeded** through the dark, **dreary** caves of the underworld, followed by Eurydice, he wanted to turn and see his wonderful wife. He resisted and resisted, but the way out was so long and so winding that he feared she might get lost.

10 Finally, he was so afraid that she had not been able to follow him that he slowly turned his head around to look. His eyes grew wide, and there he saw her, his dear Eurydice. He reached for her, to take her by the hand—and she

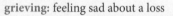

began to fade and disappeared, leaving Orpheus with only the memory of her loving expression.

11   He cried out, for he was now back at the entrance to the underworld. Cerberus shoved him along, out of the way, with three snarling snouts. Orpheus turned again, hoping to be allowed to return and beg for Eurydice, but Hermes held him back, and Cerberus snarled.

12   Hermes led the **grieving** man home. Poor Orpheus's heart for music was gone, and thereafter he lived and died alone.

Making Observations
- What emotions did you experience while you read?
- What happens in the myth?

grieving: feeling sad about a loss

Orpheus and Eurydice by Edward Poynter, 1862

Returning to the Text

- Return to the text as you respond to the following questions. Use text evidence to support your responses.
- Write any additional questions you have about the myth in your Reader/Writer Notebook.

2. What point of view is the myth told from? What tone does the narrator set for the story in the first paragraph?

_____

_____

_____

_____

3. What trait must Orpheus show in order to bring Eurydice back? Why does he struggle? Cite evidence from the text to support your answer.

_____

_____

_____

_____

4. What elements in the story are characteristic of a myth?

_____

_____

_____

_____

5. How does the author's language in the final paragraph set a mood for the resolution?

_____

_____

_____

_____

6. How do the details in the painting help you better understand an element of the myth? Make a statement about the details and then connect them to the text.

_____

_____

_____

_____

Working from the Text

7. Use the graphic organizer to analyze the beginning of the story—its exposition. The exposition of a story introduces the setting, characters, and conflict. In addition, skim the story to find examples of **foreshadowing**.

Exposition	Details from the Text	Graphic Representation	What is foreshadowed?
Setting			
Character(s)			
Conflict			

☑ Focus on the Sentence

Myths often try to explain natural phenomena (such as earthquakes and volcanos) or teach a lesson (such as "respect your elders"). Below are three lessons from "Orpheus and Eurydice." Identify whether each statement is a complete sentence or fragment.

_____ Don't let fear and distrust win.

_____ Lack of self-control can have dire consequences.

_____ The affect of music.

> **LITERARY**
> **Foreshadowing** refers to clues or hints signaling events that will occur later in the plot of a story. Authors use foreshadowing to add suspense and expectation about what will happen in a story.

VOCABULARY

LANGUAGE & WRITER'S CRAFT: Varied Sentence Patterns

Writers vary sentence patterns in order to add interest for the reader and to give life and rhythm to their writing. Too many sentences with the same structure and length can become boring for readers. Writers also use sentence patterns to develop their own distinctive style.

Example: Paragraphs 2 and 3 of "Orpheus and Eurydice" include varied sentence patterns that engage the reader.

> Orpheus fell in love with Eurydice. They trembled with delight in each other's presence and their love gave Orpheus the joy that his music gave others. They were soon married.

> It was during their honeymoon that a son of Apollo, Aristaeus, desiring Eurydice for his own, chased her. She, dashing away from the path to escape him, stepped on a snake, which bit her. She tumbled to the ground and cried for help. Aristaeus was frightened and ran away. Orpheus was terrified at her desperate call and came running to her.

By varying sentence structure, writers can accomplish specific goals. Longer sentences are used to provide a lot of information. Using transitions and coordinating conjunctions such as *and, but, or, for,* and *nor* creates longer sentences. Shorter sentences are used to emphasize a particular fact or idea. Dialogue also tends to include short sentences because people rarely speak using very long sentences.

Return to the myth of "Orpheus and Eurydice." Choose a section of the text to reread and examine the sentences.

- Highlight a short sentence. What was the effect of the sentence length or pattern?
- Underline a long sentence and note when the coordinating conjunction *and* is used. What is the effect of the sentence length or pattern?
- Identify a sentence that stands out to you. Is it long or short, and what is its effect?

PRACTICE Revise the following paragraph to include varied sentence patterns.

> I love baseball. I love summer. Baseball is a summer sport. I love to feel like part of a team. Baseball is a team sport. I am good at baseball. I can catch. I can throw. I can hit the ball. I love baseball when my team wins. Winning is not everything. I love baseball when my team loses. Baseball is my favorite sport.

🖋 Narrative Writing Prompt

Write a great new opening paragraph for this myth. Be sure to:

- Establish the story's context by introducing the setting, characters, and conflict of the story.
- Choose a voice that engages the reader.
- Use figurative language.
- Use a variety of sentence lengths and patterns.

A Day of Change: Developing the Story

Learning Targets

- Analyze how conflicts in a story advance the plot's rising action and climax.

Preview

In this activity, you will read another short story and imagine a new scene for a story you've analyzed.

Learning Strategies

Group Discussion
Previewing
Predicting
Metacognitive Markers
Rereading
Graphic Organizer

Setting a Purpose for Reading

- As you read the story, underline details you learn about the main character and mark places in the text where you see changes in her behavior or attitude.
- Circle unknown words and phrases. Try to determine the meaning of the words by using context clues, word parts, or a dictionary.

About the Author

Sandra Cisneros (1954–) is best known for writing *The House on Mango Street*, a novel that explores the life of a young girl growing up in the Latin American section of Cisneros's hometown, Chicago. Cisneros says she creates stories from things that have touched her deeply: "… in real life a story doesn't have shape, and it's the writer that gives it a beginning, a middle, and an end." She has won several awards, including the Texas Medal of the Arts and a MacArthur Fellowship.

GRAMMAR & USAGE

Indefinite Pronouns
Indefinite pronouns refer to nonspecific persons or things. In this passage, the author uses the indefinite pronouns *everything* in paragraph 1 and *something* in paragraph 2 to refer to nonspecific things. In paragraph 3, the author uses the word *somebody* to refer to a person who is not specifically named. Authors often use indefinite pronouns when they want to be vague or open-ended. As you read, notice when the author uses nonspecific pronouns and how their use affects your understanding of the text.

Short Story

Eleven

from *Woman Hollering Creek and Other Stories,* **by Sandra Cisneros**

1   What they don't understand about birthdays and what they never tell you is that when you're eleven, you're also ten, and nine, and eight, and seven, and six, and five, and four, and three, and two, and one. And when you wake up on your eleventh birthday you expect to feel eleven, but you don't. You open your eyes and everything's just like yesterday, only it's today. And you don't feel eleven at all. You feel like you're still ten. And you are—underneath the year that makes you eleven.

2   Like some days you might say something stupid, and that's the part of you that's still ten. Or maybe some days you might need to sit on your mama's lap

My Notes

_____

_____

_____

_____

_____

_____

_____

_____

_____

_____

_____

_____

_____

_____

_____

because you're scared, and that's the part of you that's five. And maybe one day when you're all grown up maybe you will need to cry like if you're three, and that's okay. That's what I tell Mama when she's sad and needs to cry. Maybe she's feeling three.

3   Because the way you grow old is kind of like an onion or like the rings inside a tree trunk or like my little wooden dolls that fit one inside the other, each year inside the next one. That's how being eleven years old is.

4   You don't feel eleven. Not right away. It takes a few days, weeks even, sometimes even months before you say Eleven when they ask you. And you don't feel smart eleven, not until you're almost twelve. That's the way it is.

5   Only today I wish I didn't have only eleven years rattling inside me like pennies in a tin Band-Aid box. Today I wish I was one hundred and two instead of eleven because if I was one hundred and two I'd have known what to say when Mrs. Price put the red sweater on my desk. I would've known how to tell her it wasn't mine instead of just sitting there with that look on my face and nothing coming out of my mouth.

6   "Whose is this?" Mrs. Price says, and she holds the red sweater up in the air for all the class to see. "Whose? It's been sitting in the coatroom for a month."

7   "Not mine," says everybody. "Not me."

8   "It has to belong to somebody," Mrs. Price keeps saying, but nobody can remember. It's an ugly sweater with red plastic buttons and a collar and sleeves all stretched out like you could use it for a jump rope. It's maybe a thousand years old and even if it belonged to me I wouldn't say so.

9   Maybe because I'm skinny, maybe because she doesn't like me, that stupid Sylvia Saldívar says, "I think it belongs to Rachel." An ugly sweater like that, all **raggedy** and old, but Mrs. Price believes her. Mrs. Price takes the sweater and puts it right on my desk, but when I open my mouth nothing comes out.

10   "That's not, I don't, you're not . . . Not mine," I finally say in a little voice that was maybe me when I was four.

11   "Of course it's yours," Mrs. Price says. "I remember you wearing it once." Because she's older and the teacher, she's right and I'm not.

12   Not mine, not mine, not mine, but Mrs. Price is already turning to page thirty-two, and math problem number four. I don't know why but all of a sudden I'm feeling sick inside, like the part of me that's three wants to come out of my eyes, only I squeeze them shut tight and bite down on my teeth real hard and try to remember today I am eleven, eleven. Mama is making a cake for me for tonight, and when Papa comes home everybody will sing Happy birthday, happy birthday to you.

13   But when the sick feeling goes away and I open my eyes, the red sweater's still sitting there like a big red mountain. I move the red sweater to the corner of my desk with my ruler. I move my pencil and books and eraser as far from it as possible. I even move my chair a little to the right. Not mine, not mine, not mine.

raggedy: worn out and tattered

14   In my head I'm thinking how long till lunchtime, how long till I can take the red sweater and throw it over the schoolyard fence, or leave it hanging on a **parking meter**, or bunch it up into a little ball and toss it in the alley. Except when math period ends, Mrs. Price says loud and in front of everybody, "Now, Rachel, that's enough," because she sees I've shoved the red sweater to the tippy-tip corner of my desk and it's hanging all over the edge like a waterfall, but I don't care.

15   "Rachel," Mrs. Price says. She says it like she's getting mad. "You put that sweater on right now and no more nonsense."

16   "But it's not—"

17   "Now!" Mrs. Price says.

18   This is when I wish I wasn't eleven, because all the years inside of me—ten, nine, eight, seven, six, five, four, three, two, and one—are pushing at the back of my eyes when I put one arm through one sleeve of the sweater that smells like cottage cheese, and then the other arm through the other and stand there with my arms apart like if the sweater hurts me and it does, all itchy and full of germs that aren't even mine.

19   That's when everything I've been holding in since this morning, since when Mrs. Price put the sweater on my desk, finally lets go, and all of a sudden I'm crying in front of everybody. I wish I was invisible but I'm not. I'm eleven and it's my birthday today and I'm crying like I'm three in front of everybody. I put my head down on the desk and bury my face in my stupid clown-sweater arms. My face all hot and spit coming out of my mouth because I can't stop the little animal noises from coming out of me, until there aren't any more tears left in my eyes, and it's just my body shaking like when you have the **hiccups**, and my whole head hurts like when you drink milk too fast.

20   But the worst part is right before the bell rings for lunch. That stupid Phyllis Lopez, who is even dumber than Sylvia Saldívar, says she remembers the red sweater is hers! I take it off right away and give it to her, only Mrs. Price pretends like everything's okay.

21   Today I'm eleven. There's a cake Mama's making for tonight, and when Papa comes home from work we'll eat it. There'll be candles and presents, and everybody will sing Happy birthday, happy birthday to you, Rachel, only it's too late.

22   I'm eleven today. I'm eleven, ten, nine, eight, seven, six, five, four, three, two, and one, but I wish I was one hundred and two. I wish I was anything but eleven, because I want today to be far away already, far away like a runaway balloon, like a tiny o in the sky, so tiny-tiny you have to close your eyes to see it.

Retrato de Muchacha/Portrait of a Girl by Frida Kahlo, 1931

parking meter: machine that collects payment for parking

hiccups: gasping sounds one makes due to an uncontrolled muscle spasm

Making Observations
- What details about the main character stand out to you?
- What happens in the story?

Returning to the Text

- Return to the text as you respond to the following questions. Use text evidence to support your responses.
- Write any additional questions you have about the story in your Reader/Writer Notebook.

1. What can you infer about the conflict of the story? How is it both internal and external?

_____

_____

_____

_____

2. How does Cisneros show the transition from one event to another?

_____

_____

_____

3. What is the effect of a phrase that repeats, such as "Not mine, not mine, not mine"? How does this sentence type help develop the story?

_____

_____

_____

_____

4. What words in the story convey a mood? What mood does Cisneros want to convey?

_____

_____

_____

_____

5. What can you infer about Rachel's teacher, Mrs. Price, based on her dialogue with Rachel?

_____

_____

_____

_____

6. How is the conflict resolved? How does the resolution affect Rachel?

_____

_____

_____

_____

☑ Focus on the Sentence

Use details from the story to complete the following sentences.

The sweater is ugly because _____

The sweater is ugly, but _____

The sweater is ugly, so _____

Working from the Text

7. Use the graphic organizer below to list the conflicts Rachel faces in "Eleven." Be sure to consider both Rachel's external and internal conflicts.

Conflicts (problems) Rachel faces	Is the conflict resolved?

WORD CONNECTIONS

Roots and Affixes

Internal and **external** derive from the Latin _interus_ ("placed on the inside") and _exterus_ ("placed on the outside"). The word part _inter-_, meaning "in between," is found in such words as _interior_, _interface_, and _intermission_. The word part _exter-_ (also spelled _extra-_ and _extro-_) means "outside" or "beyond." It appears in words such as _extreme_, _extrovert_, _extracurricular_, and _extract_.

My Notes

8. Summarize a theme of this story.

_____

_____

_____

_____

9. Focusing on the rising action and climax of the story, list events in the appropriate places on the plot diagram.

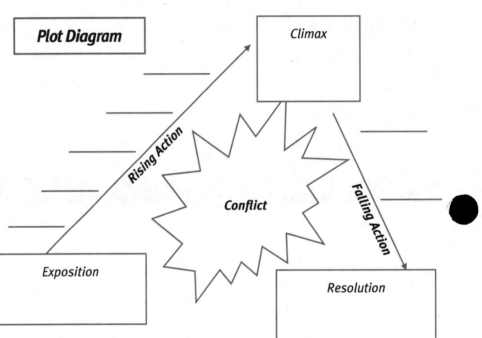

Plot Diagram

Climax

Rising Action

Conflict

Falling Action

Exposition

Resolution

✒️ Narrative Writing Prompt

Make up a brief dialogue between Rachel and another person in the story, focusing on one conflict from the text. Use the same exposition but change the rising action and climax. Consider having Rachel talk to her teacher about the misunderstanding or having Rachel confront Phyllis about not claiming the red sweater. Be sure to:

- Sequence events logically to focus on a conflict to develop the rising action and climax.
- Use dialogue and dialogue tags.
- Use figurative language and varied syntax.

Save this writing prompt response so that you can revisit it when generating ideas for the original short story you will create for Embedded Assessment 2.

Learning Targets

- Analyze the resolution to a story and transform it to create a different resolution.
- Create a thematic statement about a short story, using textual evidence.
- Identify types of figurative language and how they can be used to create mental images.

Preview

In this activity, you will read a short story and think about how a theme develops.

Setting a Purpose for Reading

- Underline figurative language the author uses (such as similes, metaphors, and **personification**). Use this figurative language to create a mental image of the scene and characters.
- Circle unknown words and phrases. Try to determine the meaning of the words by using context clues, word parts, or a dictionary.

About the Author

Walter Dean Myers (1937–2014) wrote many books for children and young adults, two of which—*Scorpions* and *Somewhere in the Darkness*—received Newbery Honors. His stories focus on the challenges and triumphs of growing up in a difficult environment. His memoir, *Bad Boy*, reveals how he overcame racial challenges and his own shortcomings to become a successful author. Of his writing method, Myers said he liked to cut out pictures of his characters before he began. He also claimed to enjoy revision more than writing a first draft of a story.

Short Story

The Treasure of Lemon Brown

by **Walter Dean Myers**

1   The dark sky, filled with angry, swirling clouds, reflected Greg Ridley's **mood** as he sat on the **stoop** of his building. His father's voice came to him again, first reading the letter the principal had sent to the house, then lecturing endlessly about his poor efforts in math.

Learning Strategies

Activating Prior Knowledge
Graphic Organizer
Previewing
Predicting
Marking the Text

VOCABULARY

LITERARY

Personification is figurative language that gives human characteristics to an animal, idea, or nonliving object. For example, *The beam of the flashlight danced crazily*. Authors use personification to help readers visualize and relate to the elements of the story.

My Notes

_____
_____
_____
_____
_____
_____
_____
_____
_____
_____
_____

mood: a person's overall state of mind; the way a person is feeling at a given time

stoop: stairway entrance outside a residence

GRAMMAR & USAGE

Possessive Pronouns

Pronouns replace nouns in a text, referring to a person or thing previously mentioned. For example, in the second sentence of paragraph 3, He refers to (and replaces) Greg.

Like nouns, pronouns can show possession. The possessive pronouns include mine, hers, his, theirs, ours, and its. Find the phrase father's *brows* in paragraph 4. The noun father's shows possession; the brows belong to the father. The phrase father's brows can be replaced by *his brows*. His is a possessive pronoun.

When you read a sentence with a possessive pronoun, you may need to reread to determine the noun to which the pronoun refers. Find the phrase his jeans in paragraph 6. Ask yourself, "Whose jeans are being described?"

Paying attention to pronouns is one way you can monitor your own understanding as you read.

2   "I had to leave school when I was thirteen," his father had said, "that's a year younger than you are now. If I'd had half the chances you have, I'd . . ."

3   Greg sat in the small, pale green kitchen listening, knowing the lecture would end with his father saying he couldn't play ball with the Scorpions. He had asked his father the week before, and his father had said it depended on his next report card. It wasn't often the Scorpions took on new players, especially fourteen-year-olds, and this was a chance of a lifetime for Greg. He hadn't been allowed to play high school ball, which he had really wanted to do, but playing for the Community Center team was the next best thing. Report cards were due in a week, and Greg had been hoping for the best. But the principal had ended the **suspense** early when she sent the letter saying Greg would probably fail math if he didn't spend more time studying.

4   "And you want to play *basketball*?" His father's brows knitted over deep brown eyes. "That must be some kind of a joke. Now you just get into your room and hit those books."

5   That had been two nights before. His father's words, like the distant thunder that now echoed through the streets of Harlem, still rumbled softly in his ears.

6   It was beginning to cool. Gusts of wind made bits of paper dance between the parked cars. There was a flash of nearby lightning, and soon large drops of rain splashed onto his jeans. He stood to go upstairs, thought of the lecture that probably **awaited** him if he did anything except shut himself in his room with his math book, and started walking down the street instead. Down the block there was an old **tenement** that had been abandoned for some months. Some of the guys had held an impromptu checker tournament there the week before, and Greg had noticed that the door, once boarded over, had been slightly ajar.

suspense: a feeling of nervous uncertainty before something happens

awaited: waited for

tenement: a set of rooms that form a living space

7   Pulling his collar up as high as he could, he checked for traffic and made a dash across the street. He reached the house just as another flash of lightning changed the night to day for an instant, then returned the graffiti-scarred building to the grim shadows. He vaulted over the outer stairs and pushed tentatively on the door. It was open, and he let himself in.

8   The inside of the building was dark except for the dim light that filtered through the dirty windows from the streetlamps. There was a room a few feet from the door, and from where he stood in the entrance, Greg could see a squarish patch of light on the floor. He entered the room, frowning at the musty smell. It was a large room that might have been someone's parlor at one time. **Squinting**, Greg could see an old table on its side against one wall, what looked like a pile of rags or a torn mattress in the corner, and a couch, with one side broken, in front of the window.

9   He went to the couch. The side that wasn't broken was comfortable enough, though a little creaky. From the spot he could see the blinking neon sign over the bodega on the corner. He sat awhile, watching the sign blink first green then red, allowing his mind to drift to the Scorpions, then to his father. His father had been a postal worker for all Greg's life, and was proud of it, often telling Greg how hard he had worked to pass the test. Greg had heard the story too many times to be interested now.

10   For a moment Greg thought he heard something that sounded like a scraping against the wall. He listened carefully, but it was gone.

11   Outside the wind had picked up, sending the rain against the window with a force that shook the glass in its frame. A car passed, its tires hissing over the wet street and its red taillights glowing in the darkness.

12   Greg thought he heard the noise again. His stomach tightened as he held himself still and listened intently. There weren't any more scraping noises, but he was sure he had heard something in the darkness—something breathing!

13   He tried to figure out just where the breathing was coming from; he knew it was in the room with him. Slowly he stood, tensing. As he turned, a flash of lightning lit up the room, frightening him with its sudden brilliance. He saw nothing, just the overturned table, the pile of rags and an old newspaper on the floor. Could he have been imagining the sounds? He continued listening, but heard nothing and thought that it might have just been rats. Still, he thought, as soon as the rain let up he would leave. He went to the window and was about to look when he heard a voice behind him.

14   "Don't try nothin' 'cause I got a razor sharp enough to cut a week into nine days!"

15   Greg, except for an involuntary tremor in his knees, stood stock still. The voice was high and brittle, like dry twigs being broken, surely not one he had ever heard before. There was a shuffling sound as the person who had been speaking moved a step closer. Greg turned, holding his breath, his eyes straining to see in the dark room.

squinting: partially closing one's eyes

My Notes

16 The upper part of the figure before him was still in darkness. The lower half was in the dim rectangle of light that fell unevenly from the window. There were two feet, in cracked, dirty shoes from which rose legs that were wrapped in rags.

17 "Who are you?" Greg hardly recognized his own voice.

18 "I'm Lemon Brown," came the answer. "Who're you?"

19 "Greg Ridley."

20 "What you doing here?" The figure shuffled forward again, and Greg took a small step backward.

21 "It's raining," Greg said.

22 "I can see that," the figure said.

23 The person who called himself Lemon Brown **peered** forward, and Greg could see him clearly. He was an old man. His black, heavily wrinkled face was surrounded by a halo of crinkly white hair and whiskers that seemed to separate his head from the layers of dirty coats piled on his smallish frame. His pants were bagged to the knee, where they were met with rags that went down to the old shoes. The rags were held on with strings, and there was a rope around his middle. Greg relaxed. He had seen the man before, picking through the trash on the corner and pulling clothes out of a Salvation Army box. There was no sign of a razor that could "cut a week into nine days."

24 "What are you doing here?" Greg asked.

25 "This is where I'm staying," Lemon Brown said. "What you here for?" "Told you it was raining out," Greg said, leaning against the back of the couch until he felt it give slightly.

26 "Ain't you got no home?"

27 "I got a home," Greg answered.

28 "You ain't one of them bad boys looking for my treasure, is you?" Lemon Brown cocked his head to one side and squinted one eye. "Because I told you I got me a razor."

29 "I'm not looking for your treasure," Greg answered, smiling. "*If* you have one."

30 "What you mean, *if* I have one." Lemon Brown said. "Every man got a treasure. You don't know that, you must be a fool!"

31 "Sure," Greg said as he sat on the sofa and put one leg over the back. "What do you have, gold coins?"

32 "Don't worry none about what I got," Lemon Brown said. "You know who I am?"

33 "You told me your name was orange or lemon or something like that."

34 "Lemon Brown," the old man said, pulling back his shoulders as he did so, "they used to call me Sweet Lemon Brown."

peered: looked curiously or carefully

35 "Sweet Lemon?" Greg asked.

36 "Yessir. Sweet Lemon Brown. They used to say I sung the blues so sweet that if I sang at a funeral, the dead would **commence** to rocking with the beat. Used to travel all over Mississippi and as far as Monroe, Louisiana, and east on over to Macon, Georgia. You mean you ain't never heard of Sweet Lemon Brown?"

37 "Afraid not," Greg said. "What . . . happened to you?"

38 "Hard times, boy. Hard times always after a poor man. One day I got tired, sat down to rest a spell and felt a tap on my shoulder. Hard times caught up with me."

39 "Sorry about that."

40 "What you doing here? How come you don't go in home when the rain come? Rain don't bother you young folks none."

41 "Just didn't." Greg looked away.

42 "I used to have a knotty-headed boy just like you." Lemon Brown had half walked, half shuffled back to the corner and sat down against the wall. "Had them big eyes like you got. I used to call them moon eyes. Look into them moon eyes and see anything you want."

43 "How come you gave up singing the blues?" Greg asked.

44 "Didn't give it up," Lemon Brown said. "You don't give up the blues; they give you up. After a while you do good for yourself, and it ain't nothing but foolishness singing about how hard you got it. Ain't that right?"

45 "I guess so."

46 "What's that noise?" Lemon Brown asked, suddenly sitting upright. Greg listened, and he heard a noise outside. He looked at Lemon Brown and saw the old man pointing toward the window.

47 Greg went to the window and saw three men, neighborhood thugs, on the stoop. One was carrying a length of pipe. Greg looked back toward Lemon Brown, who moved quietly across the room to the window. The old man looked out, then beckoned frantically for Greg to follow him. For a moment Greg couldn't move.

48 Then he found himself following Lemon Brown into the hallway and up the darkened stairs. Greg followed as closely as he could. They reached the top of the stairs, and Greg felt Lemon Brown's hand first lying on his shoulder, then probing down his arm until he took Greg's hand into his own as they crouched in the darkness.

49 "They's bad men," Lemon Brown whispered. His breath was warm against Greg's skin.

50 "Hey! Rag man!" A voice called. "We know you in here. What you got up under them rags? You got any money?"

51 Silence.

commence: begin, start

My Notes

52 "We don't want to have to come in and hurt you, old man, but we don't mind if we have to."

53 Lemon Brown squeezed Greg's hand in his own hard, gnarled fist. There was a banging downstairs and a light as the men entered.

54 They banged around noisily, calling for the rag man.

55 "We heard you talking about your treasure." The voice was slurred. "We just want to see it, that's all."

56 "You sure he's here?" One voice seemed to come from the room with the sofa.

57 "Yeah, he stays here every night."

58 "There's another room over there; I'm going to take a look. You got that flashlight?"

59 "Yeah, here, take the pipe too."

60 Greg opened his mouth to quiet the sound of his breath as he sucked it in uneasily. A beam of light hit the wall a few feet opposite him, then went out.

61 "Ain't nobody in that room," a voice said. "You think he gone or something?"

62 "I don't know," came the answer. "All I know is that I heard him talking about some kind of treasure. You know they found that shopping bag lady with that load of money in her bags."

63 "Yeah. You think he's upstairs?"

64 "HEY, OLD MAN, ARE YOU UP THERE?" Silence.

65 "Watch my back. I'm going up."

66 There was a footstep on the stairs, and the beam from the flashlight danced crazily along the peeling wallpaper. Greg held his breath. There was another step and a loud crashing noise as the man banged the pipe against the wooden banister. Greg could feel his temples throb as the man slowly neared them. Greg thought about the pipe, wondering what he would do when the man reached them—what he could do.

67 Then Lemon Brown released his hand and moved toward the top of the stairs. Greg looked around and saw stairs going up to the next floor. He tried waving to Lemon Brown, hoping the old man would see him in the dim light and follow him to the next floor. Maybe, Greg thought, the men wouldn't follow them up there. Suddenly, though, Lemon Brown stood at the top of the stairs, both arms raised high above his head.

68 "There he is!" A voice cried from below.

69 "Throw down your money, old man, so I won't have to **bash** your head in!"

70 Lemon Brown didn't move. Greg felt himself near panic. The steps came closer, and still Lemon Brown didn't move. He was an eerie sight, a bundle of rags standing at the top of the stairs, his shadow on the wall looming over him. Maybe, the thought came to Greg, the scene could be even eerier.

bash: smash or hit with force

My Notes

71 Greg wet his lips, put his hands to his mouth and tried to make a sound. Nothing came out. He swallowed hard, wet his lips once more and howled as evenly as he could.

72 "What's that?"

73 As Greg howled, the light moved away from Lemon Brown, but not before Greg saw him hurl his body down the stairs at the men who had come to take his treasure. There was a crashing noise, and then footsteps. A rush of warm air came in as the downstairs door opened, then there was only an **ominous** silence. Greg stood on the landing. He listened, and after a while there was another sound on the staircase.

74 "Mr. Brown?" he called.

75 "Yeah, it's me," came the answer. "I got their flashlight."

76 Greg exhaled in relief as Lemon Brown made his way slowly back up the stairs.

77 "You OK?"

78 "Few bumps and bruises," Lemon Brown said.

79 "I think I'd better be going," Greg said, his breath returning to normal. "You'd better leave, too, before they come back."

80 "They may hang around for a while," Lemon Brown said, "but they ain't getting their nerve up to come in here again. Not with crazy rag men and howling spooks. Best you stay a while till the coast is clear. I'm heading out west tomorrow, out to East St. Louis."

81 "They were talking about treasures," Greg said. "You really have a treasure?"

82 "What I tell you? Didn't I tell you every man got a treasure?" Lemon Brown said. "You want to see mine?"

83 "If you want to show it to me," Greg shrugged.

84 "Let's look out the window first, see what them scoundrels be doing," Lemon Brown said.

85 They followed the oval beam of the flashlight into one of the rooms and looked out the window. They saw the men who had tried to take the treasure sitting on the **curb** near the corner. One of them had his pants leg up, looking at his knee.

86 "You sure you're not hurt?" Greg asked Lemon Brown.

87 "Nothing that ain't been hurt before," Lemon Brown said. "When you get as old as me all you say when something hurts is, 'Howdy, Mr. Pain, sees you back again.' Then when Mr. Pain see he can't worry you none, he go on mess with somebody else."

88 Greg smiled.

ominous: implying that something bad will happen

curb: raised cement border at the edge of the street

WORD CONNECTIONS

Multiple-Meaning Words
The word blue can mean a kind of color. It can also mean feeling depressed, gloomy, or sad. *Blues* music is a genre of music created by African Americans in the southern United States that is often about depressing or sad subjects.

My Notes

_____

_____

_____

_____

_____

_____

_____

_____

_____

_____

_____

_____

89 "Here, you hold this." Lemon Brown gave Greg the flashlight.

90 He sat on the floor near Greg and carefully untied the strings that held the rags on his right leg. When he took the rags away, Greg saw a piece of plastic. The old man carefully took off the plastic and unfolded it. He revealed some yellowed newspaper clippings and a battered harmonica.

91 "There it be," he said, nodding his head. "There it be."

92 Greg looked at the old man, saw the distant look in his eye, then turned to the clippings. They told of Sweet Lemon Brown, a blues singer and harmonica player who was appearing at different theaters in the South. One of the clippings said he had been the hit of the show, although not the headliner. All of the clippings were reviews of shows Lemon Brown had been in more than fifty years ago. Greg looked at the harmonica. It was dented badly on one side, with the reed holes on one end nearly closed.

93 "I used to travel around and make money to feed my wife and Jesse—that's my boy's name. Used to feed them good, too. Then his mama died, and he stayed with his mama's sister. He growed up to be a man, and when the war come he saw fit to go off and fight in it. I didn't have nothing to give him except these things that told him who I was, and what he come from. If you know your pappy did something, you know you can do something too.

94 "Anyway, he went off to war, and I went off still playing and singing. 'Course by then I wasn't as much as I used to be, not without somebody to make it worth the while. You know what I mean?"

95 "Yeah." Greg nodded, not quite really knowing.

96 "I traveled around, and one time I come home, and there was this letter saying Jesse got killed in the war. Broke my heart, it truly did.

97 "They sent back what he had with him over there, and what it was is this old mouth fiddle and these clippings. Him carrying it around with him like that told me it meant something to him. That was my treasure, and when I give it to him he treated it just like that, a treasure. Ain't that something?"

98 "Yeah, I guess so," Greg said.

99 "You guess so?" Lemon Brown's voice rose an octave as he started to put his treasure back into the plastic. "Well, you got to guess 'cause you sure don't know nothing. Don't know enough to get home when it's raining."

100 "I *guess* . . . I mean, you're right."

101 "You OK for a youngster," the old man said as he tied the strings around his leg, "better than those scalawags what come here looking for my treasure. That's for sure."

102 "You really think that treasure of yours was worth fighting for?" Greg asked. "Against a pipe?"

103 "What else a man got 'cepting what he can pass on to his son, or his daughter, if she be his oldest?" Lemon Brown said. "For a big-headed boy you sure do ask the foolishest questions."

104 Lemon Brown got up after patting his rags in place and looked out the window again. "Looks like they're gone. You get on out of here and get yourself home. I'll be watching from the window so you'll be all right."

105 Lemon Brown went down the stairs behind Greg. When they reached the front door the old man looked out first, saw the street was clear and told Greg to scoot on home.

106 "You sure you'll be OK?" Greg asked.

107 "Now didn't I tell you I was going to East St. Louis in the morning?" Lemon Brown asked. "Don't that sound OK to you?"

108 "Sure it does," Greg said. "Sure it does. And you take care of that treasure of yours."

109 "That I'll do," Lemon said, the wrinkles around his eyes suggesting a smile. "That I'll do."

110 The night had warmed and the rain had stopped, leaving puddles at the curbs. Greg didn't even want to think how late it was. He thought ahead of what his father would say and wondered if he should tell him about Lemon Brown. He thought about it until he reached his stoop, and decided against it. Lemon Brown would be OK, Greg thought, with his memories and his treasure.

111 Greg pushed the button over the bell marked Ridley, thought of the lecture he knew his father would give him, and smiled.

Making Observations
- What about the language in this story stands out to you?
- What images stuck with you?

☑ Focus on the Sentence

Use details from the story to complete the following sentences.

Lemon Brown has a treasure, but

_____

Lemon Brown has a treasure, so

_____

Returning to the Text

- Return to the text as you respond to the following questions. Use text evidence to support your responses.
- Write any additional questions you have about the story in your Reader/Writer Notebook.

1. Explain how the author uses language to create a mood during the first half of the story.

_____

_____

_____

_____

2. What sensory details can you find in paragraphs 8–11? Try to name one for each sense: taste, smell, touch, sight, and hearing. How do these details help a reader predict that something ominous is coming?

_____

_____

_____

_____

3. The author distinguishes Greg from Lemon by giving each person a unique voice. How would you describe Lemon Brown's voice based on the language he uses? How would you describe Greg's voice?

_____

_____

_____

_____

4. How do Greg and Lemon's external reactions to the "scalawags" or "bad men" develop the plot?

_____

_____

_____

_____

5. Literally, what is Lemon Brown's treasure? Why does it mean so much to him?

_____

_____

_____

_____

6. From whose point of view is the story told? How does the author's chosen point of view help achieve a purpose? What is the purpose?

_____

_____

_____

Working from the Text

7. What are your initial reactions to the ending of this story? Were you surprised? If so, what surprised you?

8. Reread the text and mark it for the following:

   - Exposition
   - Rising action
   - Climax
   - Falling action
   - Resolution

   Share your marked passages with a partner. With your partner, create a story board to demonstrate your understanding of the text. For each panel, include a drawing that symbolizes a key moment for that part in the plot and include textual evidence to support the drawing.

9. Provide an example of a simile, a metaphor, and the use of personification in the story. How do these examples of figurative language enhance the story? What purpose does this figurative language serve?

_____

_____

_____

_____

10. The story is told from a limited third-person point of view—the narrator is a third person but sees everything, including Lemon, from Greg's perspective. What purpose does this point of view achieve?

_____

_____

_____

_____

11. What are the themes of "The Treasure of Lemon Brown"? You should give evidence from the story to support your responses. Complete this sentence with three themes: "The Treasure of Lemon Brown" is a story about ...

_____

_____

_____

_____

INDEPENDENT READING LINK

Read and Discuss

Make a list of the themes present in your independent reading book. As a class, take turns discussing the themes you've discovered. Try to match similarly themed texts and discuss whether the texts also share a genre, a plot type, or other features.

12. Write theme statements, no more than one sentence each, using the themes you described.

_____

_____

_____

_____

13. Now, transform one theme statement into a question to use in a collaborative discussion.

_____

_____

_____

_____

_____

14. What is the portion of the story that makes up the falling action and resolution?

_____

_____

_____

_____

15. Think about the stories you have read in this unit. Each one has a setting that includes a historical and cultural context. What are some cultural and historical settings you have read about in this unit? How are they similar? How are they different? What influence does each setting have on the story's plot and characters?

_____

_____

_____

_____

_____

☑ Check Your Understanding

Quickwrite: What is another way this story could have ended? How could some of the story's conflicts have been resolved differently?

Sparking Ideas

Learning Targets

- Analyze picture books for images that spark writing ideas.
- Write a short story with characters, conflict, plot, dialogue, and sensory details.

Preview

In this activity, you will read mystery picture books and write the first draft of a story.

Learning Strategies

Previewing
Visual Prompt
Graphic Organizer
Brainstorming
Mapping
Prewriting

INDEPENDENT READING LINK

Read and Respond

Investigate how the author of your independent reading book uses sensory details. Record your favorite sensory words, phrases, and sentences from this book in your Reader/Writer Notebook.

Genre Study: Mystery

1. When you hear the word *mystery*, what do you think of? What do you think makes a good mystery?

2. Chris Van Allsburg has written several books that are mysteries. Some include multiple story lines and episodes in a series as well as descriptive imagery. Among Allsburg's best-known books are the following:

   - *The Polar Express*
   - *The Mysteries of Harris Burdick*
   - *The Wreck of the Zephyr*
   - *Jumanji*
   - *The Stranger*
   - *The Garden of Abdul Gasazi*

   Find copies of these or other picture books and write questions about particular pictures that intrigue you. Using one or more of the images as your inspiration, write freely to draft a story in a genre of your choice, such as realistic fiction, mystery, or adventure.

3. Select one of your freewrites to develop further. Before you continue to draft, plan your story, taking its genre into account. Who will your audience be? What is your purpose for writing? Then think about your main character, such as a name, age, favorite hobby, behaviors and actions, and accomplishments. Use a graphic organizer such as the one below to plan your characters.

Characterization	
Describe your main character's appearance.	**What does this appearance say about your character?**

Characterization	
Describe some of your main character's actions.	**What do these actions say about your character?**
Other characters	**Details about these characters**

4. What words or phrases could you include from each sense (taste, touch, sight, smell, hearing) in your story? What vivid verbs and connotative diction help show that sense? What figurative language could you use?

5. Consider your plot. What is the main conflict or problem? How will it be solved? How can you add a twist? How will you introduce the setting and characters? How can you build to the climax?

✍ Drafting the Embedded Assessment

Draft a short story, adding the elements you've brainstormed as you write. Be sure to:

- Sequence events logically using elements of plot.
- Use characterization and dialogue to develop conflict.
- Use language purposefully (e.g., figurative and/or sensory details and a variety of sentences).
- Consider your genre, purpose for writing, and intended audience as you make choices.

Return to any of the texts in the unit to reinforce these elements in your writing.

Save this writing prompt response so that you can revisit it when generating ideas for the original short story you will create for Embedded Assessment 2.

📦 Independent Reading Checkpoint

Prepare a short oral presentation about a connection you can make between your independent reading and a text you read in class. It could be a thematic connection, a cultural or historical connection, or a plot connection. In addition, describe any personal connections you felt to your independent reading and in-class reading. Were the connections similar, or did each text evoke a different memory or feeling? Provide a brief, logical summary of your independent reading so your classmates can understand what you are talking about. Present evidence from each text that supports your connection. When giving your presentation, be sure to:

- Maintain good eye contact with your audience.
- Speak at an appropriate rate and volume, and enunciate well enough to be understood and taken seriously.
- Use natural gestures to engage your audience and convey information.
- Use language conventions appropriate for a formal presentation in front of your peers.

Writing a Short Story

ASSIGNMENT

Write a story using dialogue, vivid verbs, and figurative language that captures a real or imagined experience and includes characters, conflict, and a plot with exposition, climax, and resolution.

Planning and Prewriting: Take time to make a plan for your short story.	▪ Review the unit activities and your Reader/Writer Notebook for ideas. What activities have you completed that will help you as you create a short story with the required elements?
	▪ What would you like your short story to be about? Who will be your audience? What genre would you like to write? What prewriting strategies can you use to help you create ideas?
Drafting: Decide the structure of your story and how you will incorporate the elements of a short story.	▪ How will you make use of the story starters in the unit to help you create and develop a short story?
	▪ Will you work from a plot diagram or an outline of a story idea? Is there another way you can create a structure that develops the characters and plot of your story?
Evaluating and Revising: Create opportunities to review and revise in order to make your work the best it can be.	▪ During the process of drafting, have you paused at points to share and respond with others to learn how well you are integrating the necessary narrative techniques into your short story?
	▪ Is your story developing as you want it to? Are you willing to change your story if you must? Once you get suggestions, are you creating a plan to include revision ideas in your draft?
	▪ Have you used the Scoring Guide to help you evaluate how well your draft includes the requirements of the assignment?
Checking and Editing for Publication: Confirm your final draft is ready for publication.	▪ How will you check for grammatical and technical accuracy?
	▪ Have you verified spelling using online dictionaries, thesauruses, or other resources?

Reflection

After completing this Embedded Assessment, think about how you went about accomplishing this assignment and answer this question: How did you make sure your final draft was the best it could be in terms of spelling, vocabulary use, and conventions for punctuating and writing dialogue?

SCORING GUIDE

Scoring Criteria	Exemplary	Proficient	Emerging	Incomplete
Ideas	The short story • develops a focused and compelling conflict. • establishes an interesting setting, character(s), and point of view. • uses a variety of narrative techniques to effectively advance the plot.	The short story • presents and develops a focused conflict. • establishes a setting, character(s), and point of view. • uses sufficient narrative techniques to advance the plot, such as dialogue and descriptive detail.	The short story • presents an undeveloped or unclear conflict. • establishes setting, character(s), and point of view unevenly. • uses partial or weak narrative techniques to advance the plot.	The short story • lacks a conflict. • does not establish setting, character(s), and/or point of view. • uses minimal narrative techniques.
Structure	The short story • engages and orients the reader with exposition. • sequences events in the plot logically and naturally to add interest or suspense. • uses a variety of transitional strategies effectively and purposefully. • provides a thoughtful resolution.	The short story • orients the reader with adequate exposition. • sequences events in the plot logically (rising action, climax, falling action). • uses transitional words, phrases, and clauses to link events and signal shifts. • provides a logical resolution.	The short story • provides weak or vague exposition. • sequences events in the plot unevenly. • uses inconsistent, repetitive, or basic transitional words, phrases, and clauses. • provides a weak or disconnected resolution.	The short story • lacks exposition. • sequences events in the plot illogically or incompletely. • uses few or no transitional strategies. • lacks a resolution.
Use of Language	The short story • uses connotative diction, vivid verbs, figurative language, and sensory language effectively. • demonstrates command of the conventions of standard English capitalization, punctuation, spelling, grammar, and usage (including pronouns, sentence patterns, and dialogue).	The short story • uses adequate connotative diction, vivid verbs, figurative language, and sensory language. • demonstrates adequate command of the conventions of standard English capitalization, punctuation, spelling, grammar, and usage (including pronouns, sentence patterns, and dialogue).	The short story • uses weak or inconsistent diction, verbs, figurative language, and sensory language. • demonstrates partial or inconsistent command of the conventions of standard English capitalization, punctuation, spelling, grammar, and usage (including pronouns, sentence patterns, and dialogue).	The short story • uses limited, vague, and unclear diction and language. • lacks command of the conventions of standard English capitalization, punctuation, spelling, grammar, and usage; frequent errors interfere with meaning.

VISUAL PROMPT
Plants change from one season to another and often grow in unexpected places. What trait does this plant show that you might use in your own goals for change?

THE POWER TO CHANGE

I wanted everything to be like it *was*. I wanted to be back in Bybanks, Kentucky, in the hills and the trees, near the cows and chickens and pigs. I wanted to run down the hill from the barn and through the kitchen door that banged behind me and see my mother and my father sitting at the table peeling apples.

—from *Walk Two Moons* by Sharon Creech

VOCABULARY

ACADEMIC
compare
contrast
inference
prediction
communicate
synthesize

LITERARY
topic sentence
commentary
novel
subplot
introduction
hook
thesis statement
conclusion
biography
autobiography

CONTENTS

ACTIVITY

Texts not included in these materials.

My Independent Reading List

Learning Strategies

QHT
Marking the Text
Skimming/Scanning
Graphic Organizer

My Notes

Learning Targets
- Preview the big ideas and vocabulary for the unit.
- Identify and analyze the skills and knowledge needed to complete Embedded Assessment 1 successfully.

Preview

In this activity, you will think about growth and change and preview the first Embedded Assessment of this unit.

Making Connections

In the last unit, you explored change in your own life. As part of that exploration, you learned to write narratives—both a personal narrative and a short story. In this unit, you will continue to explore change, but now you will broaden your exploration to look at change in the world around you.

Essential Questions

Based on your current knowledge, how would you respond to these questions?
1. How can talking and working with others help one analyze a novel?
2. How do external forces affect a person's emotions and influence internal forces toward change?

Developing Vocabulary

Look at the Academic Vocabulary and Literary Terms on the Contents page. Use the QHT strategy to analyze which terms you may know and which terms you may need to learn more deeply. Use print or digital resources to learn more about the terms. Keep in mind that there is more to knowing a new word than just the definition. You must also know its pronunciation, part (or parts) of speech, and origin. All of these can be found in a dictionary.

INDEPENDENT READING LINK

Reading Plan

As you read a novel in class, think about changes that happen in real life. Think about changes in the environment, in society, or in your own personal life. Focus on one kind of change and find short fiction and nonfiction texts that relate to it (short stories, poems, news articles, essays). Keep track of what you read in your Independent Reading List.

Unpacking Embedded Assessment 1

Read the assignment for Embedded Assessment 1: Responding to Literature.

 Your assignment is to write an informative response to the novel *Walk Two Moons*. Select one of the following prompts:

- Explain how internal or external forces cause one character from the novel to feel as he or she grows and changes.
- Identify one subplot from the novel and explain how it relates to the main plot of the novel.
- Describe one setting from the novel and explain why it is important to a character or to the plot.
- Discuss how plot, setting, character, or conflict contributes to one of the novel's themes.

Summarize what you will need to know in order to complete this assessment successfully. With your class, create a graphic organizer to represent the skills and knowledge you will need to complete the tasks identified in the Embedded Assessment.

Forces of Change

Learning Targets

- Analyze the effect of internal and external forces on a character in a film.
- Respond to an informative writing prompt using clear organization and details from a film to support the topic.

Preview

In this activity, you will view parts of a film and analyze the effects of internal and external forces on a character.

Learning Strategies

Graphic Organizer
Think Aloud
Marking the Text
Drafting
Self-Editing/Peer-Editing

Film Study

1. You will watch film clips from the movie *Up*. As you watch each clip, use the graphic organizer to take notes on the internal and external changes in Carl Fredricksen's life, how he responds to them, and how they advance the plot of the film.

Scene	What changes does Carl Fredricksen experience?	External Forces: events or other people that cause change	Internal Forces: Carl's own decisions or emotions that cause change
Meeting Ellie			
Scenes from Their Lives			
Construction			
Up and Away			

VOCABULARY

LITERARY

A **topic sentence** states the main ideas of a paragraph. **Commentary** is the writer's statements about the meaning and importance of the details and examples.

Introduction to Writing Informative Text

In the last unit, you learned about narrative writing, which can be based on true incidents or made-up stories. Another form of writing is informative writing, which explains, defines, clarifies, or gives information about a topic.

2. Following is a sample informative paragraph that explains how Carl Fredricksen's life changes due to external forces in the film *Up*. Mark the paragraph as follows:

- Circle the **topic sentence**.
- Underline details and examples from the film.
- Highlight **commentary** about how external forces cause Carl to change.
- Put an asterisk (*) next to each transition word.

In the film *Up*, Carl Fredricksen's life changes due to several external forces. Ellie is one of the first external forces he encounters. She makes Carl a member of her club without giving him any choice about it. She also pushes him to walk the plank to get his balloon, which is how he breaks his arm. These events may seem like bad things, but they aren't because they add adventure to Carl's life.

3. Good topic sentences establish the who, what, when, why, or how of the paragraph. Now identify the parts of the sample paragraph's topic sentence. What information does it establish?

Who:

What:

When:

Why:

How:

4. When writing informative texts, good writers use a formal writing style. How is formal writing different from informal writing? Why might it be important to use a formal writing style in informative texts?

_____

_____

_____

✏️ Writing to Sources: Informative Text

Work with your class to write a paragraph explaining how Carl Fredricksen's life changes due to internal forces in the film *Up*. Be sure to:

- Include a topic sentence that states the main idea.
- Use supporting details and examples from your graphic organizer.
- Add commentary about how internal forces cause Carl to change. Use an academic tone and voice, and include academic vocabulary.
- Maintain a formal writing style throughout your paragraph.

_____

_____

_____

_____

_____

_____

_____

_____

_____

LANGUAGE & WRITER'S CRAFT: Verb Tenses

One way writers show the passage of time in their writing is by using different verb tenses. Verb tenses can show action happening in the past, present, or future. Good writers use verb tenses consistently within sentences. Inconsistent use of verb tenses can be confusing to readers.

Examples

Present: She *sings* in the chorus.

Past: She *sang* in the chorus.

Future: She *will sing* in the chorus.

Consistent: She *sings* in the chorus, and he *plays* in the band.

Inconsistent: She *sings* in the chorus, and he *played* in the band. (mixes present and past)

Problems most often occur in verb tenses that include auxiliary verbs. An auxiliary verb is a word, such as *can, do, may, must, ought, shall, will, has, have, had, am, are, is, was,* or *were,* that is added before the main verb of the sentence.

Examples

Present Perfect: She *has sung* in the chorus.

Past Perfect: She *had sung* in the chorus.

Future Perfect: She *will have sung* in the chorus.

Consistent: I was *talking* to Sarah, and I *said*, "Will you be at the party?"

Inconsistent: I was *talking* to Sarah, and I *say*, "Will you be at the party?"

PRACTICE When writing about literature and film, use the present tense. For example, "In *Up*, Carl Fredricksen *attaches* balloons to his house." Edit the following paragraph about the film to use consistent verb tense.

> *Up* is the story of Carl Fredricksen, who finally decided to follow his dreams. But rather than jump in the car or took a plane, he will attach thousands of balloons to his house and floats away. "So long, boys!" he called to some men below.

☑ Check Your Understanding

Circle the verbs in the paragraph you wrote for the previous prompt. Revise them as needed to use the correct verb tense.

Beginning the Journey

Learning Targets

- Preview the class novel and take notes in a graphic organizer.
- Record textual evidence in a double-entry journal and add original commentary.

Preview

In this activity, you will preview the mystery novel *Walk Two Moons* and learn how to take notes in a double-entry journal.

Learning Strategies

Graphic Organizer
Previewing
Note-taking
Quickwrite
Double-Entry Journal

VOCABULARY

ACADEMIC

A **novel** is a type of literary text that tells a fictional story. It reveals its plot through the actions, speech, and thoughts of its characters. Novels come in many genres, including mystery, science fiction, fantasy, realistic fiction, and historical fiction.

Novel Study

Now you will begin reading Sharon Creech's **novel** *Walk Two Moons*. Just like a short story, a novel is a work of fiction. Short stories tend to be written about a few characters with one major conflict. In contrast, novels tend to include more characters and more conflicts.

1. **Quickwrite:** This novel is a mystery. What do you already know about the literary genre of mystery? What are some characteristics that mysteries share?

_____

_____

_____

2. Whenever you pick up a new book to read, it is a good idea to preview it. Begin with the front and back covers and the first few pages just inside the front cover. Then answer the questions in the following graphic organizer.

Title	Why do you think the novel is called *Walk Two Moons*? Describe the lettering used for the title (color, size, style). Does the title look interesting to you?
Author	What do you know about the author? Have you ever read any other works by this author?
Pictures	Do you see any pictures or illustrations? If so, describe what you see. Why do you think these images were selected?
Words	Is a description of the book provided? If so, summarize it in one or two sentences. Has the novel or its author won any awards? If so, what were they for?
Epigraph	What does the epigraph say? How could that quote relate to a theme?
Contents	Pick one chapter title and predict what that chapter might be about.

My Notes

_____

_____

_____

_____

_____

_____

_____

_____

_____

_____

_____

_____

_____

_____

_____

_____

Introducing the Strategy: Double-Entry Journal

A **double-entry journal** is a chart in which a passage is written on the left side (textual evidence) and a response to the passage is written on the right side (commentary). Responses might involve asking questions of the text, forming personal opinions about the text, interpreting the text, or reflecting on the process of making meaning of the text.

3. As you read *Walk Two Moons*, you will take notes in a double-entry journal to record thoughts and questions in response to your reading. You may respond in these ways:

- Write about an experience in your own life that relates to what is happening in the novel.
- Write your opinions about what is happening in the novel.
- Write your questions about what is happening in the novel.
- Make predictions about things that might happen based on your understanding of mysteries. Confirm and revise your predictions as you read.
- Make inferences or draw conclusions based on what is happening in the novel. Track changes you have to make to these responses as you get more information.
- Record information that helps deepen your understanding of the novel.
- Record the definitions for tough or interesting vocabulary that you come across in your reading. Look these words up in a dictionary to see how they are pronounced and where they came from.
- Record interesting figurative language and literary devices the author uses.

Draw a horizontal line under each entry. Complete this example as you read Chapter 1 of *Walk Two Moons*.

Passage from Text	Page	Personal Response/Commentary
"Just over a year ago, my father plucked me up like a weed and took me and all our belongings (no, that is not true—he did not bring the chestnut tree, the willow, the maple, the hayloft, or the swimming hole, which all belonged to me) and we drove three hundred miles straight north and stopped in front of a house in Euclid, Ohio."	1	This passage reminds me of when I had to move away from my old house in the city. I was really angry that we couldn't bring the playground with us. It sounds like she really likes trees and being outdoors and that she will have to give up those things in her new home. Why is she moving, and where is her mother?

If you are having trouble thinking of what to write, use these response starters:

- I really like (or dislike) this part because ...
- I wonder why ...
- I predict that ...
- I think that the character should ...
- This reminds me of the time when I ...
- This reminds me of a book I read (movie I watched) ...

4. Following is an example of a blank double-entry journal form to use for the next few chapters. Copy this form into your Reader/Writer Notebook. You may need several pages for writing your thoughts while you are reading the rest of *Walk Two Moons*.

Title of Novel:
Author:

Passage from Text	Page	Personal Response/Commentary

☑ **Focus on the Sentence**

Complete this sentence so that it describes how to use a double-entry journal.

After quoting a passage from a text _____

Language Checkpoint:
Understanding Verb Tense

Preview

In this activity, you will learn how to identify the uses of different verb tenses and how to avoid verb tense shifts that can confuse your readers.

Understanding Verb Tense

The most basic sentence contains two parts: a subject and a verb. A **verb** describes the action of the subject, and the **verb tense** describes when the action takes place. By using verb tenses, writers can "control time"—they can move from the past to the present and beyond.

1. Sharon Creech begins *Walk Two Moons* with the following sentence. Identify the verbs.

   Gramps says that I am a country girl at heart, and that is true.

2. With a partner, decide whether the verbs are in past, present, or future tense. present tense

3. **Quickwrite:** Why do you think Sharon Creech begins the novel with this tense?

4. Later in the paragraph, the tense shifts. Identify the verbs in the following sentence.

   Just over a year ago, my father plucked me up like a weed and took me and all our belongings […] and we drove three hundred miles straight north and stopped in front of a house in Euclid, Ohio.

5. Discuss the following questions with a partner: Which tense or tenses are these verbs in? Are they all in the same tense, or are the tenses different? Why does Creech use those tenses?

Verb Tense Shifts

Usually writers stay in one tense throughout a sentence or paragraph. Sometimes, however, it is necessary to shift between tenses.

6. Read the following sentences from the novel and identify the verbs and verb tenses used.

   I am as ornery and stubborn as an old donkey. My father says I lean on broken reeds and will get a face full of swamp mud one day.

7. Why does the tense shift in these sentences? Is the shift clear?

8. Now read the following sentences about *Walk Two Moons*. They all have inappropriate shifts in verb tense. Change the underlined verbs' tenses to create a coherent sentence.

   a. Salamanca first sees Phoebe on the day she moved to Euclid, Ohio.
   b. Her father finds a hidden fireplace behind the brick wall while he was working on the house.

   c. Salamanca is nervous as she left on a long car trip with her grandparents.

Editing

Read the following reading responses from a sample double-entry journal and circle the verbs. Then work with a partner to smooth out the tense shifts in the responses. Remember to use the present tense when writing about literature.

Salamanca was a girl with a unique name. She was 13 and lives in Kentucky with her dad. She does not like the woman that her dad was seeing. Because of this, she judged this woman in her narrative descriptions.

_____

_____

_____

_____

_____

_____

Salamanca drove from Kentucky to Ohio with her grandparents. She had to go on the trip because her grandparents cannot be trusted to go alone. There were many reasons to go on the trip, and some are to see Salamanca's mom and leave Salamanca's dad alone with his girlfriend.

_____

_____

_____

_____

_____

_____

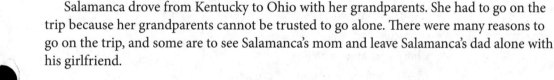 Check Your Understanding

Imagine you are editing a classmate's writing and you notice inappropriate shifts in the use of verbs. In your own words, write an explanation to help your classmate understand the mistakes being made and how to revise the draft for clarity. Then add an item to your Editor's Checklist to help you remember how to catch verb tense errors in your own writing.

_____

_____

_____

_____

Practice

Return to the informative text you wrote in Activity 2.2. Circle the verbs you used and identify which tense they are in. Are they consistent? If necessary, revise your work to be clearer for a reader.

Planting the Seeds of Character Analysis

Learning Strategies

Graphic Organizer
Rereading
Note-taking
Skimming/Scanning
Drafting

My Notes

Learning Targets

- Use knowledge of characterization to write informative literary analysis paragraphs that compare and contrast characters.
- Record textual evidence about characters in a novel and use the evidence to write commentary that explains or analyzes the characters.

Preview

In this activity, you will use details from *Walk Two Moons* to compare and contrast characters from the story.

Novel Study

1. Skim and scan Chapters 1–4 of *Walk Two Moons* to find details about the characters and add them to the graphic organizer that follows. Your double-entry journal may help you locate passages, since you have been noting page numbers. Remember that authors use the following techniques to develop a character:

   - character's appearance
   - character's actions
   - what the character says
   - what others say about the character

Name	Details about Character
Sal	
Phoebe	

2. Take a closer look at the two main characters in *Walk Two Moons* by using the following graphic organizer to note all the ways the author uses characterization. You will use these notes to **compare** and **contrast** the characters.

Characterization Notes		
	Salamanca Tree Hiddle	**Phoebe Winterbottom**
What does the character look like?		
What does the character do?		
What does the character say?		
What do others say about them?		

3. An appositive is a noun, a noun phrase, or a noun clause that is used to rename or explain another noun. For example, *Sharon Creech, <u>the author of our class novel</u>, won a John Newbery Medal.* When writing about literature, writers often use appositives to describe characters.

Mark the appositives in the following sentences.

- Sal, the new girl in town, misses her mother dearly.

- Phoebe and Sal, the main characters in the novel *Walk Two Moons*, are different in many ways.

☑ **Focus on the Sentence**

Add an appositive to the following sentence. Be sure your appositive adds information that is relevant to the sentence.

Sal, _____, carries a black spider to the window and sets it free.

VOCABULARY

ACADEMIC

To **compare** and **contrast** is to identify similarities and differences. Exploring ideas or objects by comparing and contrasting them is an effective way to analyze ideas. Comparing and contrasting works best when the two things are part of a similar category.

🎁 **INDEPENDENT READING LINK**

Read and Connect

Find a topic that you can compare and contrast in your independent reading. You can compare people, objects, situations, or themes. The topics can be in two different texts you've read independently, or one independent text and *Walk Two Moons*. Write a paragraph that explains the similarities and differences between the texts.

LANGUAGE & WRITER'S CRAFT: Transitions for Comparing and Contrasting

Good writers use transition words and phrases to help guide readers through the comparisons and contrasts they include in their writing.

Examples

Transitions of comparison: *in the same way, likewise, as, also, similarly*

Transitions of contrast: *but, although, however, yet, nevertheless, on the other hand*

When writing sentences with these transitions, be sure to include the appropriate punctuation marks.

Examples

<u>Period, new sentence, comma:</u> Mikayla is courageous and daring. *Similarly*, Andreas loves to test himself with new challenges.

<u>Semicolon with comma:</u> Raquel is a great dancer; *however*, Jameel is a great singer.

<u>Comma:</u> Brooklynn has long hair, *but* Addison has short hair.

PRACTICE Edit the following draft by inserting transition words that signal comparisons and contrasts. Make sure the revised sentences use the appropriate punctuation and capitalization.

Melissa likes to run. Alexis likes to run. Melissa is a good long-distance runner. Alexis is a better sprinter. Alexis would win a race of 400 meters or less. Melissa would win a race of 800 meters or longer.

✍ Writing to Sources: Informational Text

Write a paragraph that compares and contrasts the two main characters in *Walk Two Moons*. Include examples from the text that show different types of characterization: appearance, actions, words, and the reactions of others. Be sure to:

- Use a topic sentence.
- Include supporting details and commentary, using an academic tone and voice.
- Use transition words and appositives with correct punctuation.
- Use present-tense verbs.
- Maintain a formal writing style.

☑ Check Your Understanding

Revisit the informative paragraph you wrote comparing and contrasting characters. Highlight all of the transition words and phrases you used. Check that you used the correct punctuation and capitalization with these transitions. Revise as needed to add transitions and correct punctuation and capitalization.

Language Checkpoint: Using Noun Agreement

Learning Targets
- Understand how to create noun agreement in sentences.
- Edit writing to create noun agreement.

Preview
In this activity, you will practice using proper noun agreement when writing complex sentences.

Using Noun Agreement

As you begin writing more complex sentences, you should keep in mind that the many parts of the sentence will need to agree in order for your reader to understand you. For instance, nouns need to agree. Look at this sentence from *Walk Two Moons* by Sharon Creech.

> My grandparents Hiddle are my father's parents, and they are full up to the tops of their heads with goodness and sweetness, and mixed in with all that goodness and sweetness is a large dash of peculiarity.

In this sentence, Sal refers to her two grandparents, each of which has a head. Because the noun *grandparents* is plural, the noun phrase *tops of their heads* is also plural. In other words, the nouns agree in number.

1. **Quickwrite:** What would the sentence "My grandparents Hiddle are my father's parents, and they are full up to the top of their head with goodness and sweetness" imply? Why is noun agreement important?

2. Look at the following sentences and identify the noun agreement mistakes. How would you change each sentence to correct the mistake?

Noun Agreement	
Before	**After**
I don't enjoy any of the chores I have to do, but cleaning the toilet is the most disgusting tasks.	I don't enjoy any of the chores I have to do, but cleaning the toilet is the most disgusting task.
All three of my siblings were a scholarship winner in high school.	
Alyssa asked all her friends to become a member of the new intramural volleyball team, even though some of them were not a good athlete.	
They shook their head with disbelief when they saw the mess on the floor.	
They had a headache after the loud concert.	

Editing

Read the student writing that follows. Correct any errors in noun agreement within the paragraph.

Sal and Phoebe are important to each other in the story. Phoebe is Sal's first friend in her new school, and even though they are a good friend, they are very different from one another. Phoebe and Sal are different in how they look, act, and talk. Salamanca, Sal, has dark hair that is long and black and that everyone wants to touch. On the other hand, Phoebe has "the most pleasant round face, her hair curled in short ringlets as yellow as a crow's foot" and "sky-blue eyes" (p. 13). Their appearance is not the only ways they are different. Phoebe thinks that Sal is "ever so brave" because she carried a spider to the window instead of running away from it. Phoebe is quiet and seems shy, so she thinks that Sal is brave for touching the spider. The girls also have a different way of talking. Sal tells a lie about blackberries because she doesn't want to talk about her mother. Phoebe has a "wild imagination" because she says that Ms. Cadaver's "sticking-out red hair is spooky." Sal says, "This was Phoebe's power." Phoebe can imagine all sorts of things that are wild and interesting. All of the differences are the reason they are such good friends. Although Sal and Phoebe may look, act, and talk in different ways, Phoebe and Sal like each other for their difference.

☑ Check Your Understanding

Create a sentence that uses noun agreement. Share it with a partner and discuss why noun agreement is needed in the sentence. Then write a question for your Editor's Checklist that reminds you to check for noun agreement in your writing.

Practice

Reread the informative paragraph you wrote in Activity 2.4, comparing and contrasting Sal and Phoebe. Check for noun agreement. Be sure to:

- Verify that nouns that refer to the same thing agree in number.
- Correct any confusing references.
- Clarify to whom and what you are referring when you are comparing or contrasting information.

Mapping the Journey: Plot and Subplot

Learning Targets

- Evaluate how characters change as the plot moves toward a resolution.
- Apply understanding of plot and subplot to a discussion of the novel *Walk Two Moons*.

Preview

In this activity, you evaluate how the plot of *Walk Two Moons* evolves and affects the characters.

Learning Strategies

Graphic Organizer
Predicting
Note-taking
Quickwrite
Think-Pair-Share

VOCABULARY

ACADEMIC

An **episode** is one event in a series of events. Stories are made up of many episodes that unfold over time and lead to the resolution of the story's main conflict.

A story's **resolution** is the point at which its main conflict is resolved, or its main problem is solved.

Novel Study

1. **Quickwrite:** How can going on a physical (external) journey change your emotional (internal) self?

2. Events in a novel's or film's various **episodes** often contribute to a character's growth or change. Sometimes the changes are immediate; other times, you do not realize how the character has changed until the story's **resolution**. Use the following graphic organizer to record episodes that lead to character changes in *Walk Two Moons*.

Episodes	How the Characters Respond to the Changes

3. There are two kinds of journeys in *Walk Two Moons*.

   • Brainstorm or illustrate events from the *physical* (external) journey that Sal takes with her grandparents.

   • Brainstorm or illustrate events from the *emotional* (internal) journeys that Phoebe and Sal experience.

Events from physical journey:

Events from emotional journey:

LITERARY

VOCABULARY

Subplot is a secondary plot that occurs along with a main plot. Subplots often involve secondary characters in separate settings at points in time that are different from the main plot (like flashbacks).

4. Novels often have both a main plot and one or more **subplots**. The main plot focuses on a main character and has the greatest impact on the story. The subplot usually involves other characters and intersects with the main plot in some way. Which journey in *Walk Two Moons* is the main plot of the novel? What are the subplots? How are the subplots related to the main plot in terms of time? Why are the plots structured in this way? Explain your reasoning.

☑ Check Your Understanding

Discuss the plot and subplots of the book you are reading with a partner. You could also choose another book, a television show, or a movie you know well or have recently read or viewed. Be sure to express your ideas about the plot and subplot clearly. Build on your partner's ideas during the discussion.

🕮 INDEPENDENT READING LINK

Read and Discuss

Think about the events (real or fictional) that have taken place in the text you are reading independently. Summarize a key event and how a character in the story changes in response to the plot's evolution. Talk to a partner about your ideas and be sure to summarize the events leading up to this point.

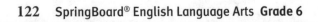

A Tree of One's Own: Setting

Learning Strategies

Graphic Organizer
Visualizing
Sketching

Learning Targets

- Write about how the setting of a novel relates to its theme or central idea.
- Revise writing to include compound sentences.

Preview

In this activity, you will visualize the details of the setting of *Walk Two Moons* and connect those details to the story's theme.

Novel Study

1. Read Sal's description of the singing tree in Chapter 16. Fill in the columns in the graphic organizer, noting how she feels when she is at the singing tree and what setting details help create that feeling or mood in her.

Place	Time	Feeling or Mood	Details

2. Think of the singing tree on Sal's farm in Kentucky. What do the details about the tree tell you about the theme or central idea of the novel? Fill in the left column in the chart with evidence from the text about the singing tree. Fill in the right column by making inferences about how each detail relates to the theme or central idea of the novel. Then discuss with a partner how making inferences, based on text evidence, can strengthen literary analysis.

Details about Singing Tree	How Details Relate to Theme or Central Idea

3. On a separate piece of paper, sketch the setting of Sal's singing tree. Include details from your graphic organizer that relate to the theme or central idea of the novel. Label the important details on your sketch.

✍ Writing to Sources: Informational Text

Write a paragraph about how Sal's singing tree relates to the theme or central idea of the novel. Explain how the external setting affects Sal's internal feelings. Be sure to:

- Use a topic sentence and supporting details from the novel.
- Relate each detail to the theme or central idea.
- Include commentary about how the setting makes Sal feel.
- Use transition words and correct noun agreement. Also, demonstrate correct verb tense and pronoun usage.

LANGUAGE & WRITER'S CRAFT: Sentence Variety

Good writers use a variety of sentence types and sentence structures to keep readers engaged. One way to improve the sentence variety in your writing is to combine short, simple sentences to create compound sentences.

A **compound sentence** is two or more independent clauses linked by a semicolon or by a comma and a **coordinating conjunction**. The most common coordinating conjunctions are *and*, *but*, and *or*.

Examples

Independent clauses linked by a semicolon: *It was not a call; it was a true birdsong, with trills and warbles.*

Independent clauses linked by a comma and a coordinating conjunction: *I had pleaded to go along, but my father said he didn't think I should have to go through that.*

When revising their writing, good writers identify when they have used one type of sentence too often. Then they change their sentences to add variety that will maintain reader interest.

Examples

Too many short sentences: *It was a sunny day. I went to the park. Some kids wanted to play basketball. They were short one player for a full game. I said I'd play.*

Revised for variety: *It was a sunny day, so I went to the park. Some kids wanted to play basketball, but they were short one player for a full game. I said I'd play.*

PRACTICE Revise the sentences by combining independent clauses to create at least two new compound sentences.

I went hiking with my friends. I reached the top of the mountain first. I saw a beautiful stream rushing down into the valley. I felt the cold breeze on my neck. The sun was warm on my face.

☑ Check Your Understanding

Revisit the response you wrote to the writing prompt in this activity. Find places where you can combine simple sentences to create compound sentences. Rewrite the sentences to improve your writing.

Questions and Discussions

Learning Strategies

Discussion Groups
Questioning the Text
Fishbowl

My Notes

_____

_____

_____

_____

_____

_____

_____

_____

_____

_____

_____

_____

_____

_____

_____

_____

_____

_____

_____

WORD CONNECTIONS

Roots and Affixes

The word **universal** comes from a Latin word. The first part of universal contains the Latin prefix *uni-*, meaning "one." The middle part comes from the Latin root *ver*, meaning "turn." The ending of the word contains the suffix *-al*, which indicates an adjective. Keep these common word parts in mind as you read and encounter new vocabulary.

Learning Targets

- Use verbal and nonverbal communication when posing and responding to literal, interpretive, and universal questions about *Walk Two Moons*.
- Identify and implement effective discussion techniques.

Preview

In this activity, you will join a discussion group to collaboratively question and analyze *Walk Two Moons*.

Literary Analysis

For Embedded Assessment 1, you will write an essay responding to a prompt based on the novel *Walk Two Moons*. In the past few activities, you began your reading and analysis of the novel by identifying plot and subplot, analyzing characterization, and identifying narrative elements such as setting.

In the next few activities, you will learn additional skills and strategies for a deeper literary analysis: skills that you will use in writing your response to literature.

Introducing the Strategy: Questioning the Text

A strategy for thinking actively and interpretively about your reading is questioning the text. As you read or reread any text, you can ask questions that aid your understanding with different levels of ideas. **Questioning** helps you experience a text in depth.

- **Literal questions** (Level 1): These are questions you can answer by looking directly to the text. They often begin with *who, what, where,* or *when*.

  Example: *What did Ellie pin onto Carl's shirt when she made him a member of her club?*

- **Interpretive questions** (Level 2): These are questions you cannot answer by looking directly to the text; however, textual evidence points to and supports your answers.

  Example: *Why do you think Carl didn't want to move into the retirement home?*

- **Universal questions** (Level 3): These are questions that go beyond the text. They require you to think about the larger issues or ideas raised by the text.

  Example: *Why do people dream of traveling to strange and faraway lands?*

1. In your own words, describe each type of question.

2. Write examples of the three levels of questions based on your reading so far of *Walk Two Moons.*

Literal:

Interpretive:

Universal:

3. Your teacher will assign a section of the novel for your small group to study. As a group, prepare for your discussion by creating at least two questions for each level of questioning.

Literal:

Interpretive:

Universal:

My Notes

Communicating in Discussion Groups

You have participated in discussions in the past. Think about your past discussion group experiences. What made them effective? What did not work so well?

A discussion group should work together to consider a topic, text, or question. All members of a discussion group need to **communicate** effectively to help the group work smoothly and achieve its goals. Group members should allow opportunities for everyone to participate. With your class, create a list of guidelines to help ensure good communication.

4. Think about the communication process from the speaker's viewpoint as well as the listener's viewpoint.

As a speaker:

INDEPENDENT READING LINK

Read and Discuss

Compose a universal question that relates to your independent reading. Discuss this question with a small group. Can you apply one another's universal questions to your own reading? Do you agree with one another's responses? Discuss the themes you have in common as well as the differences.

As a listener:

5. All discussion groups need a process or a strategy to help them accomplish their goals. It also helps to have formal or informal roles in discussion groups. What are some of the roles that people might have, and what would they do?

6. Follow your teacher's directions to form a new group of students who wrote levels of questions on different sections of *Walk Two Moons*. As your new group discusses these different questions, use the graphic organizer that follows to record key ideas. Remember to follow the communication norms for speakers and listeners as well as the discussion roles you identified with your class in questions 4 and 5. Give one another feedback on which questions were the most effective at encouraging interesting discussions and bringing out new ideas about meaning in the novel.

My Notes

_____
_____
_____
_____
_____
_____
_____
_____
_____
_____
_____
_____
_____
_____
_____
_____
_____
_____
_____
_____
_____
_____

An Interesting Point Made by a Member of My Group	Evidence the Person Provided	My Thoughts

☑ Check Your Understanding

- What were your strengths as a discussion group? What were your challenges, and how did you overcome them?

_____

_____

_____

_____

_____

- Revisit the Essential Question: How can talking and working with others help one understand a novel?

_____

_____

_____

_____

_____

Diction Detectives and "Evidence"

Learning Strategies

Graphic Organizer
Close Reading
Skimming/Scanning
Self-Editing/Peer-Editing

Learning Targets

- Closely read text to analyze how an author uses diction to portray a character.
- Use context to determine the meaning of words and phrases.

Preview

In this activity, you will analyze Sharon Creech's diction in *Walk Two Moons* and learn how to add figurative language to your own writing.

My Notes

_____
_____
_____
_____
_____
_____
_____
_____
_____
_____

Novel Study

1. In Unit 1, you learned that diction refers to an author's word choice, which is one way an author can develop character. Skim/scan the chapters of *Walk Two Moons* that you have read and list some of the words Sharon Creech chooses that give Sal, Phoebe, Gram, Gramps, and the other characters their unique voices.

2. Chapter 22 is titled "Evidence" because Phoebe and Sal are both looking for clues about why their mothers went missing. With a partner or small group, read the chapter closely, looking for interesting word choices and thinking about what the author was trying to show or achieve with them. Search for words, phrases, or passages that are especially descriptive, interesting, or confusing. Record and analyze them in the graphic organizer that follows.

Page	Word, Phrase, or Passage	Why did you choose this word, phrase, or passage?	Why do you think the author used this word, phrase, or passage?
	Word:		
	Phrase:		
	Passage:		

3. The words and sentences around a word are called its *context*. You may find clues in the context to help you determine the meaning of unfamiliar words. When Phoebe asks her father about the word *malinger*, he has her look it up in the dictionary. Read the following passage and underline context clues that could have helped Phoebe understand this word.

   Her father placed his hand on her forehead, looked deep into her eyes and said, "I'm afraid you have to go to school."

   "I'm sick. Honest," she said. "It might be cancer."

   "Phoebe, I know you're worried, but there's nothing we can do but wait. We have to go on with things. We can't malinger."

4. Skim/scan the paragraphs following this passage and try to find context clues that help you define the words *frenzy, cardigan, skittish*, and *sullen*. Use a dictionary to verify words' meanings.

5. In Unit 1, you learned about how figurative language can enhance your own writing by forming an image in your reader's mind that will create a specific emotion or emphasize an important idea.

   Look closely at the diction in Sharon Creech's figurative language. Try to walk around in her shoes (metaphorically) and deduce the reasoning behind her choices. Record examples in the graphic organizer.

Page	Word, Phrase, or Passage	Why did you choose this word, phrase, or passage?	Why do you think the author used this word, phrase, or passage?

WORD CONNECTIONS

Roots and Affixes

The word **metaphor** comes from the Greek roots *meta*, meaning "after" or "beyond," and *phor*, meaning "to carry."

Meta appears in *metacognitive*, *metamorphosis*, and *metabolism*.

The root *phor* occurs in the words *euphoria* and *phosphorescent*.

Personification has the Latin root *person*, from *persona*, referring to the masks representing characters in ancient *dramas*.

LANGUAGE & WRITER'S CRAFT: Figurative Language

Using figurative language in your writing is one way to make your writing more interesting to readers. The way that you use figurative language is part of your own style, or voice. Three types of figurative language that you can use are **similes, metaphors,** and **personification**.

A **simile** is a creative comparison between two unlike things using the word *like* or *as*.

A **metaphor** is a creative comparison between two unlike things where one thing becomes another.

Personification is a kind of metaphor that gives objects or abstract ideas human characteristics.

Examples:

The moon was bright on the cold, dark night.

Revised using a **simile:** *The moon was as bright as a flashlight on the cold, dark night.*

Revised using a **metaphor:** *The moon was a flashlight on the cold, dark night.*

Revised using **personification:** *The moon flashed its smile down on the cold, dark night.*

PRACTICE Write three sentences: one that uses a simile, one that uses a metaphor, and one that uses personification. Label the sentences appropriately. If needed, use the examples of Sharon Creech's figurative language that you recorded in the chart on the previous page as a guide.

INDEPENDENT READING LINK

Read and Connect

What are some examples of figurative language in the texts you are independently reading? In your Reader/ Writer Notebook, record some of your favorite uses of figurative language. Tell what the figurative language is describing. Describe a way you could use a similar style of figurative language in your own writing.

☑ Focus on the Sentence

The following vivid phrases are either complete sentences or fragments. Copy the complete sentences on the line, adding correct capitalization and punctuation. Turn the fragments into complete sentences with capitalization and punctuation by using details from the text.

fumbled around like ducks in a fit _____

_____

she wore a wrinkled blouse and skirt _____

_____

had nearly chomped their heads off _____

_____

those are fishes in the air _____

_____

Moving Away

Learning Targets

- Compare and contrast characters from a poem and novel that have similar themes.
- Identify figurative language and how it is used to create mental images.
- Create a thematic statement that links a poem and a novel.
- Integrate ideas from multiple texts to build knowledge and vocabulary about how a person might act and feel when a friend moves away.

Preview

In this activity, you will read a poem to gain further insight into the character of Sal from the novel *Walk Two Moons*.

Setting a Purpose for Reading

- As you read, underline figurative language the author uses, such as **similes**, **metaphors**, and **hyperboles**.
- Circle unknown words and phrases. Try to determine the meaning of the words by using context clues, word parts, or a dictionary.

About the Author

Judith Viorst (1931–) is a journalist and an author who writes fiction and nonfiction for both adults and children. Her well-known and loved children's classic *Alexander and the Terrible, Horrible, No Good, Very Bad Day* and its sequels are based on the (mis)adventures of her own three sons.

Poetry

Since Hanna Moved Away

by **Judith Viorst**

> The tires on my bike are flat.
>
> The sky is grouchy gray.
>
> At least it sure feels like that
>
> Since Hanna moved away.
>
> 5 Chocolate ice cream tastes like prunes.
>
> December's come to stay.
>
> They've taken back the Mays and Junes
>
> Since Hanna moved away.

VOCABULARY

LITERARY

Remember that a **simile** uses the word *like* or *as* to compare two things that are mostly unalike. (For example: *Flowers smell like halibut.*) A **metaphor** compares two unlike things without using the word *like* or *as*. (For example: *Every handsome dog's a mutt.*) **Hyperboles** are exaggerated or unbelievable statements. (For example: *December's come to stay.* The author uses this sentence to show that, to the speaker, every day without Hanna seems cold and dreary.)

 KNOWLEDGE QUEST

Knowledge Question:
How might a person act and feel when a friend moves away?
In Activity 2.9, you will read a poem and view a photograph on the theme of how moving can impact a person's life. While you read and build knowledge about the theme, think about your answer to the Knowledge Question.

It is common to lament some of life's changes, especially a friend moving away.

Flowers smell like **halibut**.

10 Velvet feels like hay.

Every handsome dog's a mutt

Since Hanna moved away.

Nothing's fun to laugh about.

Nothing's fun to play.

15 They call me, but I won't come out

Since Hanna moved away.

⊘ Knowledge Quest

* What does the poem make you think about the person who is speaking?
* What imagery could you picture in your mind?

My Notes

Returning to the Text

* Return to the poem as you respond to the following questions. Use text evidence to support your responses.
* Write any additional questions you have about the poem in your Reader/Writer Notebook.

1. What does the author mean by "December's here to stay" and "They've taken back the Mays and Junes"? How does this figurative language affect the mood of the poem?

_____

_____

_____

_____

2. **KQ** What is the speaker's perspective on moving in "Since Hanna Moved Away"? How does this perspective help you understand Sal's perspective on moving in the first half of *Walk Two Moons*?

_____

_____

_____

_____

halibut: a very large saltwater flatfish

3. How does the title of the poem relate to the poem's theme, and what is the effect of its repetition throughout the stanzas of the poem?

_____

_____

_____

_____

_____

4. **KQ** Look at the photo included with "Since Hanna Moved Away." The person in this photo laments about a move, as does the poem's speaker and Sal from *Walk Two Moons*. What does it mean to *lament*? List examples of times when a person might lament.

_____

_____

_____

_____

_____

5. **KQ** What theme is developed in both "Since Hanna Moved Away" and *Walk Two Moons*? How is this theme developed differently in each text?

_____

_____

_____

_____

_____

Ⓢ Knowledge Quest

Discuss with a partner how "Since Hanna Moved Away" and *Walk Two Moons* have shaped your perspective on how a person might act and feel when a friend moves away. Be sure to:

- Explain your answer to your partner, be specific, and give details.
- When your partner explains his or her answer, ask for clarification by posing follow-up questions as needed.
- Record the ideas you talked about in your Reader/Writer Notebook.

INDEPENDENT READING LINK

You can continue to build your knowledge about this theme by reading related fiction and poetry at ZINC Reading Labs. Select the **fiction** and **poetry** filters, and type keywords such as *friendship* or *moving away* in the **Search all ZINC articles** field.

ZINC

Working from the Text

6. Read the following sentences from *Walk Two Moons*. What do they say about Sal's perspective on moving?

   - "I had been praying that a miracle would happen and my mother would come back and we would return to Bybanks and everything would be exactly as it used to be."
   - "After driving for so long through the hot South Dakota prairie, it was a shock to come upon the Badlands."
   - "They were strangers to each other when they got on that bus, but, by the time they got off, six days later, they were friends."

7. Skim the poem "Since Hanna Moved Away" to find examples of how the speaker feels about moving. How are Sal's feelings the same? How are they different?

8. Draw a Venn diagram in your Reader/Writer Notebook. Label one circle "Sal" and the other circle "Speaker." Then note similarities between the two characters in the overlap between the circles and feelings or experiences that belong to just one character in that character's circle.

9. Write a thematic statement about change. To find your thematic statement, ask yourself the following questions about "Since Hanna Moved Away" and *Walk Two Moons*:

   - How are the characters the same and different?
   - What lesson(s) did the characters learn?
   - How does the theme of each text link to this unit's Essential Question, *How do internal and external forces help people grow?*

☑ Focus on the Sentence

Use one of the sentence frames that follow to write a thematic statement about the nature of change based on what you learned from "Since Hanna Moved Away" and *Walk Two Moons*.

- Sometimes, _____.
- Life is full of changes, but _____.
- Change happens when _____.

Reporting from Paradise Falls

Learning Targets

- Learn the skill of summarizing and apply it to a film.
- Determine the theme of a film or story by analyzing details such as setting, plot, and character.

Preview

In this activity, you will view parts of a film and discuss its theme.

Film Study

Earlier in this unit, you analyzed setting, plot, and character within the context of literature, film, and your own life. Look back at those analyses and then write a brief definition for each of the following literary terms in your own words.

Setting (Activity 2.6):

Plot (Activity 2.5):

Character (Activity 2.4):

1. You will next watch some film clips. Working with a small group, divide the work so that one person is taking notes on each literary element as you watch the clips. Especially note changes in each element.

Learning Strategies

Graphic Organizer
Summarizing
Note-taking

My Notes

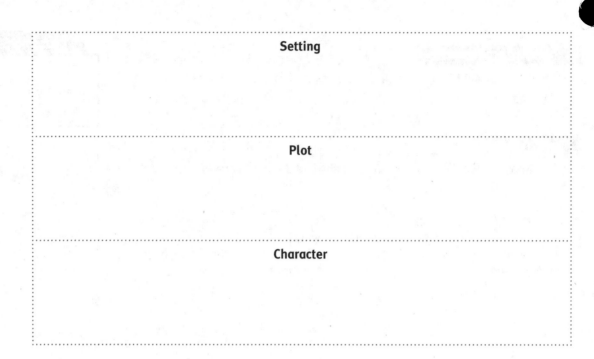

Setting

Plot

Character

Working from the Film

Summarizing involves reading text or listening to a speaker and then restating the main ideas in your own words. It is important to make sure that your summary is accurate and logically ordered and that it maintains the meaning of the text you read or heard.

2. Write a brief summary of your notes on setting, plot, or character.

_____

_____

_____

_____

3. Share your notes with your group and take notes in the preceding chart on what other group numbers report about setting, plot, or characters.

4. With your class, identify possible themes, or central messages, for the film *Up*. Remember that a theme should be a message, not just a topic. If *Up* is about the topic of adventure, the theme is the message the film communicates about adventure. Use evidence from the film to support your ideas.

_____

_____

_____

_____

☑ Check Your Understanding

Write a short, accurate summary of the film clips from *Up*. Be sure to include details about its setting, plot, and characters and order the details logically.

Making Connections and Visualizing Art

Learning Targets

- Analyze internal and external conflicts and how characters respond to conflict in a text.
- Make connections within a text, between texts, between a text and self, and between a text and the broader world.
- Synthesize the literary elements of *Walk Two Moons* in order to create a collaborative visual representation.

Preview

In this activity, you will explore literary conflict and create a visual representation of conflicts in *Walk Two Moons*.

Learning Strategies

Visualizing
Graphic Organizer
Think Aloud
Predicting
Rereading
Quickwrite
Think-Pair-Share

Internal and External Conflicts

1. As you viewed clips from the film *Up*, you analyzed many internal and external forces that cause Carl Fredricksen to change. Whenever the main character struggles against internal and external forces, there is a *conflict* in the story.

   List one internal conflict that Carl Fredricksen struggles with, such as a difficult decision or emotion.

   List one external conflict that Carl Fredricksen struggles against, such as a force of nature or another character.

2. On a separate piece of paper, draw two circles: one labeled "Sal" and one labeled "Phoebe." Review the notes you've been taking in your double-entry journal for *Walk Two Moons* and find one example of an internal conflict that each girl is facing as well as one example of an external conflict. Inside each circle, draw an illustration that represents the internal conflict its character faces. Then draw an illustration that represents the external conflict outside both circles.

3. In a collaborative group, compare and contrast your illustrations for Sal's and Phoebe's internal and external conflicts. Based on your analysis, discuss who is struggling more with internal conflict and who is struggling more with external conflict.

My Notes

My Notes

Making Connections

4. An important element of literary analysis is recognizing that the events and conflicts in a text are similar to events and conflicts in other texts and in real life. Connecting a text you are reading to other texts you have read and to experiences from your own life helps you not only understand the text but also understand the life lessons it may teach. Make connections within and between *Walk Two Moons* and other texts, yourself, and the world. Record your connections in the graphic organizer.

Event from Book	Type of Connection	Explain Connection
	Text to Same Text Make a connection to another event in the same novel.	
	Text to Different Text Make a connection to an event in a different novel or text.	
	Text to Self Make a connection to an event in your own life.	
	Text to World Make a connection to an event in history or society.	

5. Making text connections also involves reflecting on what has happened in the book up to this point and predicting what will happen next. Use the following graphic organizer to connect the past to the future in *Walk Two Moons*.

What has happened previously?	What do you predict will happen as the book continues?

☑ Check Your Understanding

In your Reader/Writer notebook, make a connection between a character in the film *Up* and a character in *Walk Two Moons*. Explain that connection.

Visualizing the Text

6. Reread the section from Chapter 30, in which Sal talks about the power of visualization. Mark the text by highlighting or underlining every time Sal uses any form of the word *visualize*.

Once, before she left, my mother said that if you visualize something happening, you can make it happen. For example, if you are about to run a race, you visualize yourself running the race and crossing the finish line, and presto! When the time comes, it really happens. The only thing I did not understand was what if everyone visualized himself winning the race?

Still, when she left, this is what I did. I visualized her reaching for the phone. Then I visualized her dialing the phone. I visualized our phone number clicking through the wires. I visualized the phone ringing.

It did not ring.

I visualized her riding the bus back to Bybanks. I visualized her walking up the driveway. I visualized her opening the door.

It did not happen.

7. **Quickwrite:** Do you think it is possible to affect the future by picturing something happening? Explain your reasoning in the My Notes space.

8. On a separate piece of paper, use the following prompts to create the outline of a tree. As you read or review a chapter of *Walk Two Moons*, use the tree to take notes on different literary elements.

   - Write the *chapter title* as the trunk.
   - Describe or draw images on the tree's branches to represent *events*.
   - Draw birds or animals in the tree to represent the *characters* and label them with names.
   - Describe the *setting(s)* with words or images as the ground at the base of the tree.
   - Create roots that describe *events that happened earlier* in the book.
   - In the sky above the tree, make *predictions* about what will happen next. Confirm or revise them as you read.
   - Add leaves to the tree with interesting *diction* from the chapter.

9. **Collaborative Group:** Share your sketches and then collaborate to create a new tree outline on poster board that **synthesizes** all of your ideas into one project. Assign a different color to each person and provide a key so that you can see which details came from each group member.

☑ Check Your Understanding

How did sketching the tree help you understand the chapter better? What did you contribute to the tree that you created in your small group? What were the challenges of working with the group, and how did you deal with them?

ACADEMIC

To **synthesize** is to combine parts or elements into a single or unified piece. Synthesizing requires thinking about all of the information you have, deciding what is important, choosing a structure to present it in, and putting it in a logical order.

VOCABULARY

Learning Strategies

Literature Circles
Discussion Groups
Double-Entry Journal
Graphic Organizer
Note-taking
Fishbowl

My Notes

Learning Targets

- Analyze elements of the structure and content of a text using text evidence with a Literature Circle.
- Evaluate Literature Circles as a strategy to facilitate close reading and collaborative discussion of meaning in a text.

Preview

In this activity, you will learn how to actively participate in a Literature Circle discussion to share ideas about *Walk Two Moons*.

Introducing the Strategy: Literature Circles

A **Literature Circle** is made up of a group that all reads the same text and then participates in a discussion of that text. Each person in the group takes on a different role, with the roles rotating to each group member. The roles are Discussion Leader, Diction Detective, Bridge Builder, Reporter, and Artist.

Literature Circle Roles

Each role within a Literature Circle group has specific responsibilities, but all roles must listen actively and respond appropriately. Performance of the roles rotates so that each person in the group has an opportunity to serve in each role. Everyone in the group should listen to identify points where group members agree and disagree. Areas in which you disagree could be good topics for discussion and reflection.

Discussion Leader: Your job is to develop a list of questions you think your group should discuss about the assigned section of the book. Use your knowledge of Levels of Questions to create thought-provoking interpretive and universal

My Notes

questions. Try to create questions that encourage your group to consider many ideas. Help your group explore these important ideas and share their reactions. You will be in charge of leading the day's discussion. You will listen actively to group members' responses and ask clarifying questions when you need to.

Diction Detective: Your job is to carefully examine the diction (word choice) in the assigned section. Search for words, phrases, and passages that are especially descriptive, powerful, funny, thought-provoking, surprising, or even confusing. List the words or phrases and explain why you selected them. Then write your thoughts about why the author might have selected these words or phrases. What is the author trying to say? How does the diction help the author achieve his or her purpose? What tone do the words indicate?

Bridge Builder: Your job is to build bridges between the events of the book and other people, places, or events in school, the community, or your own life. Look for connections between the text, yourself, other texts, and the world. Also, ask other group members questions to help you make connections between what has happened already and what might happen as the narrative continues. Look for the characters' internal and external conflicts and the ways in which they respond to these conflicts internally, through thoughts and feelings, and externally, through words and actions.

Reporter: Your job is to identify and report on the key points of the reading assignment. Ask questions to help clarify the assignment. Make a list or write a summary that describes how the setting, plot, and characters are developed in this section of the book. Consider characters' interactions, major events that occur, and shifts in the setting or the mood that seem significant. Share your report at the beginning of the group meeting to help your group focus on the key ideas presented in the reading. Like that of a newspaper reporter, your report must be concise yet thorough.

Artist: Your job is to create an illustration related to the reading. It can be a sketch, cartoon, diagram, flowchart, or other image. It can be of a scene, an idea, a symbol, or a character. Show your illustration to the group without any explanation. Ask each group member to respond either by making comments or by asking clarifying questions. Listen closely while everyone responds. Then explain your picture and respond appropriately by answering any questions that have not been answered.

Preparing for Discussion

1. Your teacher will assign roles and put you in Literature Circle groups to practice close reading and discussion of texts with a classic fairy tale. Review some literary terms you should use in discussion and the directions for your role. Also, review the skills you learned in the following activities, where you were actually practicing the skills needed for each role:

   Discussion Leader (Activity 2.7)

   Diction Detective (Activity 2.8)

   Reporter (Activity 2.10)

   Bridge Builder (Activity 2.11)

   Artist (Activity 2.11)

   Create a place card to use during the meeting. Include the role title and a symbolic visual on the front. On the back, write a brief description of your role.

My Notes

_____
_____
_____
_____
_____
_____
_____
_____
_____
_____
_____
_____
_____
_____
_____
_____
_____
_____
_____
_____
_____
_____
_____

Discussion Instructions

2. Keep a double-entry journal with notes that will help you prepare for your role. Remember to copy or summarize important passages on the left side of your journal. On the right-hand side:

   - Discussion Leader: Keep track of questions to ask.
   - Diction Detective: Record interesting words and phrases, especially figurative language.
   - Reporter: Take notes on the setting, plot, and characters, especially shifts or changes.
   - Bridge Builder: Take notes on predictions, connections (text to self, text to text, and text to world), and conflict.
   - Artist: Take notes on how to create a visual representation.

3. Meet with the other students who are also preparing for the role you have been given. Share the notes you took and discuss how you can use them in your Literature Circle meetings. Make a copy of the Discussion Note-taking Graphic Organizer that is large enough to keep notes in.

4. When your role is prepared, go back to your Literature Circle group. Review the guidelines for communicating in discussion groups, which you made in Activity 2.7.

Participating in a Discussion

5. At your teacher's direction, team up with another group to use the fishbowl strategy. While the inner circle is discussing the text, the outer circle will take notes on the Discussion Group Note-taking graphic organizer. After the first discussion, switch places so that the inner circle becomes the outer circle for the second discussion.

Discussion Note-taking Graphic Organizer

An Interesting Point Made by a Member of the Discussion Group	Support the Person Provided	Support the Person Provided

6. Give each circle (inner and outer) a chance to respond to the discussion, commenting on the strengths and challenges that each group had in its analysis of the text. Fill out the Group Meeting Reflection Chart. Reflect on what you can improve during your Literature Circle meeting for the upcoming Embedded Assessment.

Group Meeting Reflection Chart		
	Challenges	Goals
Speaking		
Listening		
Understanding the Text		

INDEPENDENT READING LINK

Read and Discuss

What kind of changes are present in your independent reading? Discuss what the changes are with your Literature Circle group. Listen as other members of the group share how change is present in their texts. Compare and contrast how change is present in all of the texts.

☑ Check Your Understanding

Reflect on your discussion group experiences. How did Literature Circle discussions contribute to your close reading of the novel? How did they support your ability to analyze meaning and make connections to ideas within and outside the novel?

_____

_____

_____

_____

Circling the Moon: Literature Circle Discussion

Learning Strategies

Literature Circles
Graphic Organizer
Discussion
Note-taking

Learning Targets

- Analyze a novel's literary elements through close reading and collaborative discussion.
- Collaboratively create a poster representing the synthesis of ideas from close reading and analysis.

Preview

In this activity, you will have another Literature Circle discussion where you will share ideas and interpret the meaning of *Walk Two Moons*.

Preparing for Discussion

1. Work with your teacher to learn your group assignment and the role you will play in the group analysis and discussions of the final reading of *Walk Two Moons*. Then record information about your role and your group goals. Use the graphic organizer that follows for your group discussions.

My Role:

_____

My Goal: During the Literature Circle discussion, I will be sure to

_____

_____

_____

My Group Members:_____

_____

_____

Discussion Note-taking Graphic Organizer

An Interesting Point Made by a Member of the Discussion Group	Support the Person Provided	My Thoughts

Creating a Synthesis Poster

2. Work collaboratively with your Literature Circle group to synthesize the analysis from your meeting(s) into a creative poster. You should include elements of each Literature Circle role as follows:

   - interesting and thought-provoking questions from the Discussion Leader
   - insightful connections or predictions made by the Bridge Builder
   - images and/or graphic organizers created by the Artist
   - key quotes identified and interpreted by the Diction Detective
   - summary statements written by the Reporter
   - a title for your poster based on a theme of the novel *Walk Two Moons*

3. After observing other posters, record an important idea that stands out to you from *Walk Two Moons* for each literary element.

An important idea about a **character(s)** is ...	An important idea about a **conflict** is ...	An important idea about the **plot** or **subplot** is ...
An important idea about the **setting** is ...	An important idea about a **theme** is ...	Other thoughts I have ...

✍ Informative Writing Prompt

Think about your collaborative group experiences during this unit and your personal response to the experience. Write a paragraph explaining how communication and collaboration with your Literature Circle group helped you to understand, appreciate, and analyze the novel. Use the scoring guide for Embedded Assessment 1 and your knowledge of the structure of Informative texts to write your own "be sure to" suggestions.

-
-
-
-
-

📖 Independent Reading Checkpoint

Look back at your independent reading notes and summarize what you learned about changes from your reading.

Responding to Literature

ASSIGNMENT

Write an informative response to the novel *Walk Two Moons*. Choose one of the following prompts:

- Explain how internal or external forces cause one character from the novel to grow or change.
- Identify one subplot from the novel and explain how it relates to the main plot of the novel.
- Describe one setting from the novel and explain why it is important to a character or to the plot.
- Discuss how plot, setting, character, or conflict contributes to one of the novel's themes.

Planning and Prewriting: Take time to choose and make a plan for your Informative response.	■ Which prompt do you feel best prepared to respond to in writing? ■ How have the activities in this unit and the Literature Circle roles helped prepare you for this prompt? ■ How can notes from your Literature Circle discussions and the synthesis posters support your response?
Drafting: Determine the key ideas to include.	■ How can your response demonstrate your understanding of literary terms such as plot/subplot, setting, character, conflict, or theme? ■ What elements of an effective informative essay will you use to organize your response? ■ Which details from the novel will you use to support your ideas?
Evaluating and Revising the Draft: Create opportunities to review and revise your work.	■ During the process of writing, when can you pause to share and respond with others? What digital tools can you use to do this? ■ What is your plan to include suggestions and revision ideas into your draft? ■ How can you revise your draft to use transitions and a variety of sentence structures? ■ How can the Scoring Guide help you evaluate how well your draft meets the requirements of the assignment?
Checking and Editing for Publication: Confirm that your final draft is ready for publication.	■ How will you check for grammatical and technical accuracy, such as proper spelling and punctuation?

Reflection

After completing this Embedded Assessment, think about how you went about accomplishing this task and respond to the following:

- How would you adjust or change the Literature Circle experience to help you better analyze text?

SCORING GUIDE

Scoring Criteria	Exemplary	Proficient	Emerging	Incomplete
Ideas	The response • conveys original ideas by analyzing a work of literature and explaining thoroughly how one or more literary elements contribute to the overall text. • develops ideas with relevant supporting details and examples.	The response • conveys focused ideas by analyzing a work of literature and explaining how one or more literary elements contribute to the overall text. • develops ideas with supporting details and examples.	The response • conveys ideas unevenly or partially explains how one or more literary elements contribute to the overall text. • develops ideas with insufficient or irrelevant supporting details and examples.	The response • lacks analysis or explanation of how literary elements contribute to an overall text. • uses minimal supporting details and examples.
Structure	The response • introduces the main idea in an engaging manner. • uses a well-chosen organizational structure that progresses smoothly to connect ideas. • uses a variety of effective transitions purposefully. • provides a satisfying conclusion.	The response • introduces the main idea clearly. • uses an organizational structure that progresses logically to connect ideas. • uses appropriate transitions to clarify the relationships among ideas. • provides a logical conclusion.	The response • provides a weak or unclear introduction. • uses a flawed or inconsistent organizational structure. • uses inconsistent, repetitive, or basic transitions. • provides a weak or disconnected conclusion.	The response • lacks an introduction. • has little or no organizational structure. • uses few or no transitions. • lacks a conclusion.
Use of Language	The response • uses literary terms such as plot/subplot, setting, character, conflict, or theme in an insightful manner. • demonstrates command of the conventions of standard English capitalization, punctuation, spelling, grammar, and usage (including pronoun agreement, sentence variety, and verb tense).	The response • uses literary terms such as plot/subplot, setting, character, conflict, or theme correctly. • demonstrates adequate command of the conventions of standard English capitalization, punctuation, spelling, grammar, and usage (including pronoun agreement, sentence variety, and verb tense).	The response • uses literary terms incorrectly or insufficiently. • demonstrates partial or inconsistent command of the conventions of standard English capitalization, punctuation, spelling, grammar, and usage (including pronoun agreement, sentence variety, and verb tense).	The response • fails to use literary terms. • lacks command of the conventions of standard English capitalization, punctuation, spelling, grammar, and usage; frequent errors obscure meaning.

Learning Strategies

Graphic Organizer
Marking the Text
Think-Pair-Share

My Notes

Learning Targets

- Analyze and summarize the components of Embedded Assessment 2.

Preview

In this activity, you will unpack Embedded Assessment 2 and preview the next half of the unit.

Making Connections

In the first half of the unit, you saw how people sometimes turn to nature for comfort when going through a significant change in life, just as Sal relied on a tree for comfort in *Walk Two Moons*. Similarly, in this half of the unit, you will discover how animals, a part of nature, can play a significant role in creating positive change in a person's everyday life.

Essential Questions

Now that you have participated in a Literature Circle, would you change your answer to the first Essential Question on how talking and working with others can help one analyze a novel? If so, how would you change your answer? If not, why not?

Developing Vocabulary

Look in your Reader/Writer Notebook at the new Academic Vocabulary words and Literary Terms you learned in the first half of this unit. Which words do you now know well, and which do you still need to learn more about?

INDEPENDENT READING LINK

Reading Plan

For this half of the unit, find a book to read in which humans interact with animals. It could be a novel, a memoir, a biography, or an autobiography. Check the glossary of this book for descriptions of these genres. Set a reading schedule for yourself so you will finish the book by the time you've finished the unit.

Unpacking Embedded Assessment 2

Read the assignment for Embedded Assessment 2: Writing an Informative Essay.

Write a multiparagraph essay explaining how people can enhance their lives through observing and interacting with animals. What can human beings learn from animals? In what ways can they help us? In your essay, give examples from your own life, from texts you have studied in this unit, from your independent reading, or from society that help support your explanation.

In your own words, summarize what you will need to know to complete this assessment successfully. With your class, create a graphic organizer to represent the skills and knowledge you will need to complete the tasks identified in the Embedded Assessment.

Explaining and Interpreting Change

Learning Targets

- Explore the positive and negative connotations of the word *change* and write an organized paragraph about different types of change.
- Develop an introductory paragraph that includes a thesis statement, details, and transitions.

Preview

In this activity, you will explore the topic of change and compose a strong introductory paragraph.

Learning Strategies

Graphic Organizer
Drafting
Marking the Text
Word Sort

Thinking About Change

1. The word *change* can have positive or negative connotations. Brainstorm the feelings you associate with a variety of changes. As you fill in the graphic organizer that follows, use three different colors: one for positive changes, one for negative changes, and one for neutral changes.

   - In the inner circle, list words and images to represent changes that have happened in **your life**.

   - In the outer circle, list words and images to represent changes that characters have experienced in **texts you have read**.

   - Between the lines of the box and the edge of the outer circle, list words and images to represent changes that you have observed in **society**. Think about changes in science, technology, entertainment, your country, or your local community.

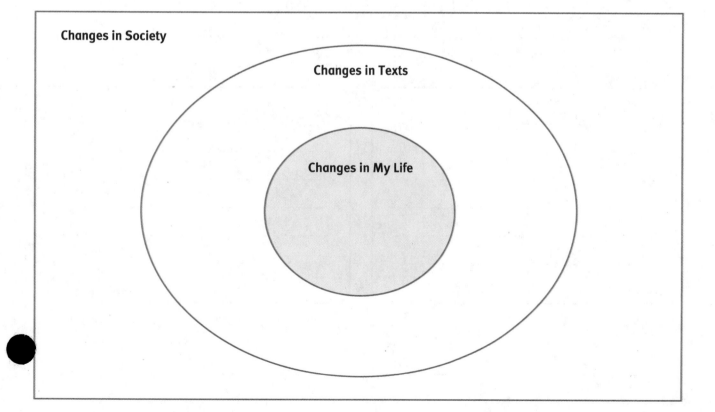

2. Now focus on the changes you listed in the center of the circle: changes in your own life. Try to categorize them as changes in responsibility, family relationships, friends, interests, school, fears, or physical appearance.

3. In the following graphic organizer, write a different category of change on the top line of each box. Then list specific changes from your life that fit within each category. Finally, on the lines below each box, write a topic sentence that you could use for a paragraph about the changes you wrote in that box. Remember that a topic sentence *controls the content of a paragraph, contains a subject, and reveals an opinion.*

Changes in Me

T.S.: _____

T.S.: _____

T.S.: _____

T.S.: _____

My Notes

4. Read the following informative paragraph and mark the text as follows:

- Underline the topic sentence.
- Scan the paragraph and put a star next to the writer's two new responsibilities.
- Circle the transition words and phrases.
- Put an asterisk in front of the sentences that develop each of the writer's new responsibilities with commentary.

Sample Informative Paragraph

I have always had chores to do around the house, but this year I have more to do than ever before. The first thing that happened was that I got my first pet! Jeff, the gerbil, was a gift from my aunt, whose pet gerbil, Fluffy, had babies. I got Jeff in April, and since then I have had total responsibility for his feeding and care. I have to be sure he has water and food every day. I also have to clean his cage every week and shred newspapers for the bottom of his cage. But the best part of this job is that I have to play with him every day so that he gets plenty of exercise. My mom also expects me to take care of my little brother for a little while every day. Mainly, this means going into his room and playing with him for 30 minutes just before dinner. My mom asked me to do this so she can fix dinner without having to worry about Patrick. Patrick is only three, so I play kids' games with him like Memory, or I read a book to him, or sometimes we watch a video. During this time, I'm the only one who takes care of him. Sometimes, I have to feed him or take him to the bathroom. I like taking care of my brother, and my mom really appreciates it. Taking care of Jeff and Patrick is making me more responsible.

> ### Informative Writing Prompt
> Draft a paragraph explaining an area of change in your life. Choose one of the areas of change from your graphic organizer. Be sure to:
> - Write a topic sentence.
> - Include supporting details and commentary.
> - Use transition words and phrases and a variety of sentence structures.

My Notes

5. In the spaces, mark "A" if you agree and "D" if you disagree with the statement about change.

_____ Change cannot be avoided.

_____ Change can be a good thing.

_____ People never really change.

_____ Change can ruin a friendship.

_____ Without change, a person cannot grow.

_____ Change is hard work.

_____ It's possible for one person to change the world.

_____ Change is usually uncomfortable.

_____ You should not try to change other people.

_____ Nothing ever really changes.

6. Choose one of the statements you strongly agree with and explain why.

7. Read the following sample **introduction** to an essay about change. Mark the text as follows:

- Underline the **hook**.
- Highlight the **thesis statement**.
- Circle or use a different color highlighter for the word that you think best describes the topic of the essay.

Sample Introduction

Benjamin Franklin once said, "When you're finished changing, you're finished." This means that in order to be truly alive, one must be changing and growing. I agree because every new experience can make a person change. Sometimes the change is positive, and other times it is negative. Either way, there is no avoiding change.

8. Fill out the graphic organizer that follows by interpreting each quote, deciding whether you agree or disagree, and explaining why.

VOCABULARY

LITERARY

An **introduction** is the opening part of an essay, which should get the reader's attention and indicate the topic.

The **hook** in the introduction is a compelling idea or statement designed to get the reader's attention.

A **thesis statement** is a sentence in the introduction of an essay that states the writer's position or opinion on the topic of the essay.

Quotation	Interpretation: What does it mean?	Agree or Disagree?	Reason: Why do you agree or disagree?
"When you're finished changing, you're finished." *Benjamin Franklin*			
"There's nothing wrong with change, if it is in the right direction." *Winston Churchill*			
"If you don't like something, change it. If you can't change it, change your attitude." *Maya Angelou*			
"Time is a dressmaker specializing in alterations." *Faith Baldwin*			
"Not everything that is faced can be changed. But nothing can be changed until it is faced." *James Baldwin*			
"They always say time changes things, but you actually have to change them yourself." *Andy Warhol*			

📝 Informative Writing Prompt

Choose a quote from the graphic organizer and use it as you draft an introductory paragraph on the topic of change. Be sure to:

- Include a hook.
- Write a statement about the quote.
- Include a thesis that states an opinion about your agreement with the quote.

Writing and Changing Together

Learning Strategies

Drafting
Collaborating
Adding
Outlining
Replacing

Learning Targets

- Draft the body and conclusion of an informative essay.
- Revise writing to include parallel structure.

Preview

In this activity, you will draft and revise an essay about change.

My Notes

Composing Body Paragraphs Together

1. You have already written an introduction for an informative essay and an informative paragraph about a change in your life. Work together with your class to draft a body paragraph about a change in a character from a book or story you have read together. Be sure to include these elements:

   - **Topic sentence:** a sentence that includes a subject and an opinion that works directly to support the thesis
   - **Transitions:** words used to connect ideas (for example, *for instance*)
   - **Supporting information:** specific examples, details, evidence, and facts
   - **Commentary:** sentences that explain how the information is relevant to the thesis/topic sentence and bring a sense of closure to the paragraph

2. On a separate page, work with a partner or small group to draft an additional informative paragraph about a change in the world. Begin by revisiting the graphic organizer you completed in the previous activity. Agree on a change that has taken place in society, science/technology, entertainment, the economy, your country, or your community. Make sure you include all the elements of a body paragraph listed previously.

Finishing the Essay

3. With your class and your writing group, discuss the elements of an effective **conclusion**. What questions should a conclusion answer?

LITERARY
A **conclusion** is one or more paragraphs that bring the essay to a close and leave an impression with the reader. Good conclusions are satisfying, showing thoughtful synthesis of ideas and information.

VOCABULARY

4. Read through your introduction and body paragraph on the topic of change. Then write sentences about the literal, interpretative, and universal elements of change that you discussed in these paragraphs. Your sentence about the literal elements of change should sum up how you defined change in your paragraphs. Your sentence about the interpretative elements of change should explain what you think change means for you, other people, and the world. Your sentence about the universal elements of change should explain why you think change matters. Together, these sentences will form the conclusion of your essay.

Literal:

Interpretive:

Universal:

My Notes

5. You have now constructed all of the elements of an informational essay about change. Organize the paragraphs using the following outline and then follow your teacher's instructions to prepare a focused, structured, and cohesive draft before revising.

I. Introduction (previous activity)

II. Support paragraph about a change in yourself (previous activity)

III. Support paragraph about a change from a text (this activity)

IV. Support paragraph about a change from society (this activity)

V. Conclusion (this activity)

My Notes

Introducing the Strategy: Replacing

When you revise by **replacing**, you focus on your word choice to create meaning and effect. Replacing bland words with more specific words helps make your writing clearer and more varied. Begin by circling words that are meaningless, boring, or awkwardly placed. For each circled word, select two new words and write them above the original word or in the margin. Use a variety of resources to find new words, including a dictionary or thesaurus, your Reader/Writer Notebook, and the Word Wall. Read your sentence twice, each time with a different replacement word. Decide which word most precisely conveys your intended meaning and cross out the other.

6. Revise the conclusion, using the replacing strategy. Circle three words to replace, and write them on the lines. Use your vocabulary resources to select two replacement words for each circled word. Read the sentence(s) twice, each time with a different word. Circle the best option.

Change is good. Some people try not to change, but they are just wasting their time. I like change because it keeps me from being bored all the time. Try not to think about bad changes because that will just make you sad. Instead think about the good things that have happened to you, and you will realize that those are changes too.

Word 1: _____ Replacement Options: 1. _____ 2. _____

Word 2: _____ Replacement Options: 1. _____ 2. _____

Word 3: _____ Replacement Options: 1. _____ 2. _____

7. Practice: Look at your own informative essay on change. Circle three words to replace, and use your vocabulary resources to select two replacement words for each circled word. Record your work on the lines. Read the sentence(s) twice, each time with a different word. Circle the best option. Finally, explain how your revisions strengthen the text.

Word 1: _____ Replacement Options: 1. _____ 2. _____

Word 2: _____ Replacement Options: 1. _____ 2. _____

Word 3: _____ Replacement Options: 1. _____ 2. _____

Explanation:

_____

_____

_____

LANGUAGE & WRITER'S CRAFT: Parallel Structure

Parallel structure involves using the same grammatical structure for all words or phrases that name items in a series. Remember to use **commas** to separate the words or phrases in a series, as shown in the examples.

Examples

- *Carrie loved swimming, running, and playing tennis.*
- *His eyes were swollen shut, his face was red and puffy, and his nose was lopsided.*
- *Every day John walked in the door, threw his backpack on the chair, and opened the refrigerator.*
- *You may sit in the back, you may sit in the front, or you may sit anywhere in between.*

PRACTICE Combine the ideas in the following sentence using parallel structure. The sentence is taken from the article "Saying Farewell to a Faithful Pal," which you will read in the next activity.

Marley chewed couches. He slashed screens. He also was a slinger of drool and a tipper of trash cans.

8. Reread your informative essay about change. Apply the revision strategies that you have learned in this unit to improve your writing.

- Combine ideas by using parallel structure or compound sentences.
- Add details, commentary, and figurative language.
- Replace words to make your language more precise, interesting, and original.

☑ Check Your Understanding

Reflect on the changes you made to your essay and how these changes improved your writing. What will you be sure to do when you write your next informative essay?

Reflecting on Marley: Textual Evidence

Learning Strategies

Diffusing
Marking the Text
Graphic Organizer

My Notes

Learning Targets

- Identify and interpret textual evidence.
- Write a response to a prompt, using textual evidence to support a thesis.
- Integrate ideas from multiple texts to build knowledge and vocabulary about the roles dogs play in the lives of humans.

Preview

In this activity, you will read a memoir about a beloved family dog and write about the purpose of pets.

Setting a Purpose for Reading

- As you read, mark the text by underlining words, phrases, and sentences that tell why Grogan loved his dog.
- Circle unknown words and phrases. Try to determine the meaning of the words by using context clues, word parts, or a dictionary.

Introducing the Strategy: Diffusing

With this strategy, you use context clues to help find the meaning of unknown words. When **diffusing**, underline words that are unfamiliar. Think of two possible substitutions (synonyms) and confirm your definition. You can confirm your definition by checking reference sources such as a dictionary or a thesaurus.

About the Author

John Grogan (1957–) is a newspaper columnist and the author of the best-selling memoir *Marley and Me*, a book based on the ideas in the article you are about to read. *Marley and Me* has been adapted into a young reader's edition, several children's books, and a major motion picture. Grogan says that he began writing in school because he "was so bad at everything else." In addition to *Marley and Me*, he has written articles for numerous magazines and newspapers.

Memoir

Saying Farewell to a Faithful Pal

by **John Grogan**

1   In the gray of dawn, I found the shovel in the garage and walked down the hill to where the lawn meets the woods. There, beneath a wild cherry tree, I began to dig.

2   The earth was loose and blessedly unfrozen, and the work went fast. It was odd being out in the backyard without Marley, the Labrador retriever who for 13 years made it his business to be tight by my side for every excursion out the door, whether to pick a tomato, pull a weed, or fetch the mail. And now here I was alone, digging him this hole.

3   "There will never be another dog like Marley," my father said when I told him the news, that I finally had to put the old guy down. It was as close to a compliment as our pet ever received.

4   No one ever called him a great dog—or even a good dog. He was as wild as a banshee and as strong as a bull. He crashed joyously through life with a gusto most often associated with natural disasters.

5   He's the only dog I've ever known to get expelled from obedience school.

6   Marley was a chewer of couches, a slasher of screens, a slinger of drool, a tipper of trash cans. He was so big he could eat off the kitchen table with all four paws planted on the floor—and did so whenever we weren't looking.

7   Marley shredded more mattresses and dug through more drywall than I care to remember, almost always out of sheer terror brought on by his mortal enemy, thunder.

Cute but Dumb

8   He was a majestic animal, nearly 100 pounds of quivering muscle wrapped in a luxurious fur coat the color of straw. As for brains, let me just say he chased his tail till the day he died, apparently convinced he was on the verge of a major canine breakthrough.

9   That tail could clear a coffee table in one swipe. We lost track of the things he swallowed, including my wife's gold necklace, which we eventually recovered, shinier than ever. We took him with us once to a chi-chi outdoor café and tied him to the heavy wrought-iron table. Big mistake. Marley spotted a cute poodle and off he **bounded**, table in tow.

10   But his heart was pure.

© 2021 College Board. All rights reserved.

KNOWLEDGE QUEST

Knowledge Question:

What roles do dogs play in the lives of humans?

Across Activities 2.17 and 2.18, you will read three texts about the ways dogs assist people with day-to-day tasks. While you read and build knowledge about the topic, think about your answer to the Knowledge Question.

My Notes

bounded: leaped or jumped with great energy

WORD CONNECTIONS

Roots and Affixes
The prefix *mis-* is from Old English and means "bad" or "wrong." This prefix is commonly used in English (**mistake, miscarriage, mischievous**) to indicate that something is incorrect or not as desired or planned.

My Notes

_____
_____
_____
_____
_____
_____
_____
_____
_____
_____
_____
_____
_____
_____
_____
_____
_____
_____
_____
_____
_____

despite: in spite of
optimism: seeing the positive in all things
lug: an awkward, clumsy fellow
devotion: dedication

11   When I brought my wife home from the doctor after our first pregnancy ended in a miscarriage, that wild beast gently rested his blocky head in her lap and just whimpered. And when babies finally arrived, he somehow understood they were something special and let them climb all over him, tugging his ears and pulling out little fistfuls of fur. One day when a stranger tried to hold one of the children, our jolly giant showed a ferocity we never imagined was inside him.

12   As the years passed, Marley mellowed, and sleeping became his favorite pastime. By the end, his hearing was shot, his teeth were gone, his hips so riddled with arthritis he barely could stand. **Despite** the infirmities, he greeted each day with the mischievous glee that was his hallmark. Just days before his death, I caught him with his head stuck in the garbage pail.

Life Lessons Learned

13   A person can learn a lot from a dog, even a loopy one like ours.

14   Marley taught me about living each day with unbridled exuberance and joy, about seizing the moment and following your heart. He taught me to appreciate the simple things—a walk in the woods, a fresh snowfall, a nap in a shaft of winter sunlight. And as he grew old and achy, he taught me about **optimism** in the face of adversity.

15   Mostly, he taught me about friendship and selflessness and, above all else, unwavering loyalty.

16   When his time came last week, I knelt beside him on the floor of the animal hospital, rubbing his gray snout as the veterinarian discussed cremation with me. No, I told her, I would be taking him home with me.

17   The next morning, our family would stand over the hole I had dug and say goodbye. The kids would tuck drawings in beside him. My wife would speak for us all when she'd say: "God, I'm going to miss that big, dumb **lug**."

18   But now I had a few minutes with him before the doctor returned. I thought back over his 13 years—the destroyed furniture and goofy antics; the sloppy kisses and utter **devotion**. All in all, not a bad run.

19   I didn't want him to leave this world believing all his bad press. I rested my forehead against his and said: "Marley, you are a great dog."

Knowledge Quest
- What emotions did you feel while reading the memoir?
- What details about Marley stand out to you?

Returning to the Text

- Return to the text as you respond to the following questions. Use text evidence to support your responses.
- Write any additional questions you have about the memoir in your Reader/Writer Notebook.

1. How do the first two sentences of the memoir contribute to the text? What is the effect of these sentences on the reader?

_____

_____

_____

_____

2. How does the author structure positive and negative details to show how Marley was both challenging and good for his family? List specific details and explain how their order in the story affects the reader's opinion.

_____

_____

_____

_____

3. **KQ** In paragraph 8, the author describes a time when Marley thought he was "on the verge of a major canine breakthrough." What does *canine* mean? Use a dictionary to find out. Then give some examples of canine qualities Marley possessed that made him a good companion to his owner.

_____

_____

_____

_____

4. What was the author's purpose for writing the memoir? How is the author's purpose conveyed in the text?

_____

_____

_____

_____

5. **KQ** What are things the text shows that people can learn from dogs? What does the author learn from Marley?

_____

_____

_____

_____

Working from the Text

6. Find sentences from the story that show why Grogan loved his dog. Copy them into the Textual Evidence column of the following graphic organizer along with your thoughts on what these sentences tell about Grogran's feelings. Then use the notes in your graphic organizer to help you write a summary of the story that is logically organized, clear, and true to the meaning of the story.

Textual Evidence	Importance: What does the evidence tell you about Grogan's feelings for his dog?

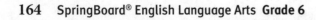

INDEPENDENT READING LINK

Read and Discuss

How is the value of human and animal interaction demonstrated in the book you are reading on your own? Are the themes present in your independent reading similar to those present in "Saying Farewell to a Faithful Pal"? With a small group, discuss various animal-related themes found in your independent reading. Compare and contrast these themes with the story you have just read.

Writing to Sources: Informational Text

Why do people have pets? Using John Grogan and Marley as examples, explain what human beings love about and learn from their pets. Be sure to:

- Write a thesis statement including the topic and your opinion.
- Use textual evidence and supporting details from the newspaper column.
- Add personal commentary while maintaining a formal style. Use the replacing strategy to make your vocabulary academic.

Making Connections Through Research

Learning Strategies

KWHL
Predicting
Paraphrasing
Generating Questions

Learning Targets

- Closely read and analyze an autobiographical text about how animals can help people, citing text evidence to support analysis and inferences.
- Closely read an informational text about service dogs and cite text evidence for analysis and inferences.
- Conduct research to answer questions about how animals help people.
- Integrate ideas from multiple texts to build knowledge and vocabulary about the roles dogs play in the lives of humans.

Preview

In this activity, you will read about animal intelligence and do some research into how animals can help people.

Setting a Purpose for Reading

- Use the My Notes section to write a prediction about the author's main point. As you read, underline details that might connect to the main idea. Revise your predictions as you read.
- Circle unknown words and phrases. Try to determine the meaning of the words by using context clues, word parts, or a dictionary.

About the Author

Temple Grandin (1947–) was born in Boston, Massachusetts. She is an American doctor of animal science, a professor at Colorado State University, a best-selling author, and a consultant to the livestock industry on animal behavior. As a person with high-functioning autism, Grandin is also widely noted for her work in autism advocacy. Autism is a brain-based disorder characterized by social-communication challenges and restricted repetitive behaviors, activities, and interests.

Autobiography

Dogs Make Us Human

from **Animals in Translation**

by **Temple Grandin and Catherine Johnson**

1   The aborigines have a saying: "Dogs make us human." Now we know that's probably **literally** true. People wouldn't have become who we are today if we hadn't **co-evolved** with dogs.

My Notes

KNOWLEDGE QUEST

Knowledge Question:
What roles do dogs play in the lives of humans?

literally: actually, without exaggeration
co-evolved: evolved at the same time together

My Notes

2   I think it's also true, though in a different way, that all animals make us human. That's why I hope we will start to think more respectfully about animal intelligence and talent. That would be good for people, because there are a lot of things we can't do that animals can. We could use their help.

3   But it would be good for animals, too. Dogs first started living with people because people needed dogs and dogs needed people. Now dogs still need people, but people have forgotten how much they need dogs for anything besides love and companionship. That's probably okay for a dog who's been bred to be a companion animal, but a lot of the bigger breeds and **practically** all of the mix breeds were built for work. Having a job to do is a part of their nature; it's who they are. The sad thing is, now that hardly anyone makes his living herding sheep, most dogs are out of a job.

4   It doesn't have to be that way. I read a little story on the Web site for the American Veterinary Medical Association that shows the incredible things animals are capable of doing, and would do if we gave them a chance. It was about a dog named Max who had trained himself to monitor his mistress's blood sugar levels even while she was asleep. No one knows how Max was doing this, but my guess is people must smell slightly different when their blood sugar is low, and Max had figured that out. The lady who owned him was a severe diabetic, and if her blood sugar levels got low during the night Max would wake up her husband and bug him until he got up and took care of her.

5   You have to think about that story for only five seconds to realize how much dogs have to offer. Dogs and a lot of other animals.

For many years, dogs have been trained to rescue people caught in avalanches. One dog on a search-and-rescue team can cover more ground more thoroughly than 20 people searching on foot.

practically: almost, nearly

Knowledge Quest

- What questions do you have after reading the excerpt?
- What details about dogs and humans stand out to you?

Returning to the Text

- Return to the text as you respond to the following questions. Use text evidence to support your responses.
- Write any additional questions you have about the autobiography excerpt in your Reader/ Writer Notebook.

1. What can you tell about Grandin's message from the first two paragraphs?

_____

_____

_____

_____

2. Paraphrase the evidence Grandin gives to support the idea that animals helping humans can be good for the animals, too. Make sure to order the evidence logically.

_____

_____

_____

_____

3. KQ In paragraph 3, the author says that some dogs are *bred* to be companion animals, while others are *bred* for work. *Bred* is the past tense form of the verb *breed*. What does *breed* mean in this context? Use a dictionary to find out. Then tell how the characteristics companion dogs are *bred* for might be different from those of service dogs.

_____

_____

_____

_____

4. What is the main idea of this text? Which details support this?

_____

_____

_____

_____

My Notes

5. **KQ** Think about Marley in "Saying Farewell to a Faithful Pal." In what ways did Marley help Grogan to be human? How might Grandin have characterized Marley?

Working from the Text

6. What questions do you have about dogs as pets after reading this text? What else would you like to know?

Setting a Purpose for Reading

- During reading, underline examples you encounter of how service dogs help humans.
- Circle unknown words and phrases. Try to determine the meaning of the words by using context clues, word parts, or a dictionary.

About the Author

Morieka Johnson is a pet blogger and broadcast host for Mother Nature Network and SoulPup.com. Her works cover everything from dog behavior and care to distinct characteristics of dog breeds. Johnson is a graduate of Emory University and Northwestern University, where she studied journalism and creative writing. Her articles and experiences shed light on many important jobs that dogs can do to help humans.

Article

5 things you don't know about service dogs

by **Morieka Johnson**

1　Service dogs accomplish pretty amazing **feats** on a daily basis. Bethe Bennett's miniature schnauzer nudged her back to consciousness after a fall. The trained service dog also retrieved an emergency phone list so Bennett could call neighbors for assistance. A pooch named Mr. Gibbs totes Alida

KNOWLEDGE QUEST

Knowledge Question:
What roles do dogs play in the lives of humans?

feats: difficult or triumphant achievements

Knobloch's oxygen tank so the 2-year-old can dash around with other children. Mr. Gibbs even braves playground slides with Alida.

2 Sandra Leavitt also relies on a service dog to help battle her rare seizure disorder. Nikki, a 4-year-old pit bull, was trained to detect scent changes in Leavitt's blood and provide warning signs up to two hours before seizures occur.

3 "We are starting to realize what a dog's nose means to human beings," says Jennifer Arnold, founder of Canine Assistants, a nonprofit organization that trains service dogs for people with disabilities or special needs. "There are so many applications for dogs in our society that benefit mankind. They already do; they just haven't gotten the credit they deserve."

4 While some of these heroics are known, here are five things you probably didn't know about these working dogs.

Service dogs are not pets

5 The Americans With Disabilities Act (ADA) defines service animals as dogs individually trained to do work or perform tasks for a person with a disability. Tasks can range from calming a veteran with post-traumatic stress disorder to retrieving keys from a hook on the wall—but just don't call them pets.

6 "Keep the word 'pet' out of there," says Paul Bowskill, general manager of Service Dogs America, a company that sells harnesses, vests and wallet cards that help identify dogs as service animals. "They are an extension of the person who has the disability."

7 This also serves as another reason to ask before you pet a dog. It may be on the job.

Preparing a service dog can be costly, time-consuming

8 Getting a dog to routinely perform specialized tasks can take months— even years—of preparation. Canine Assistants places dogs through a labor-intensive, 18-month program that begins with **neuromuscular** stimulation exercises when puppies are only 2 days old. These exercises, originally used to prepare military dogs, prepare the animals to handle potentially stressful situations. Professional trainers also teach dogs to retrieve items for individuals with mobility issues, and a network of volunteers places them in social situations, such as navigating an office or taking public transportation. Arnold estimates that Canine Assistants spends about $24,500 on training as well as lifetime care for each service animal.

9 When dogs are ready, the organization uses extensive personality tests to identify 12 to 14 individuals from a waiting list of more than 1,600 people. During a two-week training camp, dogs interact with families and then make their selection.

10 "Until you see it, you just don't believe it," Arnold says. "They crawl up on their person like, 'Where have you been?'"

My Notes

neuromuscular: nerve and muscle

My Notes

Any breed can do it, but retrievers were born for it

11 Arnold and her team primarily work with golden retrievers and Lab mixes, noting attributes that go beyond breed characteristics.

12 "They love to retrieve because they love to use their mouths," she says. "Public **perception** also is important for us because we want the dog to be a social icebreaker."

13 According to the ADA, any breed can work as a service dog. But breed-specific bans have presented challenges for individuals who use pit bulls as service dogs. A retired police officer named Jim Sak gained national recognition after he won a temporary **injunction** reuniting him and his pit bull service dog, despite a city ban on the breed. Leavitt also has taken **preemptive** measures to fight breed bans, attending a city council meeting with her pit bull.

14 "The council tried to kick me out until I showed them the service dog card," Leavitt told the Utah Standard-Examiner. "I couldn't have her as a service dog if I had to [mark] her as dangerous."

Those service dog vests are optional

15 With a few exceptions, service dogs can accompany human partners anywhere that's open to the public, including airports or restaurants. Dogs must wear a leash or tether, unless it interferes with accomplishing a task. But the ADA does not require gear identifying them as working dogs, and business owners can only make limited inquiries when it is not obvious what service the animal provides.

16 Organizations such as the United States Service Dog Registry sell identification gear and recommend that individuals with disabilities clearly display patches or "working dog" vests to help educate the public and facilitate access to public areas.

17 "Travel through O'Hare [airport] at 4:30 or 5 p.m. with a service dog that doesn't have a vest on; it's like going through a mine field," Bowskill says. "They'll still stop you, but it's easier with a vest."

Service dogs require care, too. But the rewards are priceless

18 Dogs get sick, they get injured and they require daily care. Arnold tells prospective clients that caring for a service dog is a long-term **proposition** that delivers big **dividends**. Quest Magazine, produced by the Muscular Dystrophy Association, captures a few fun and funny stories on its website. With a service dog by their side, many people with disabilities are able to work and reach new levels of independence.

19 "It's a huge commitment," she says. "But the fact that it's a huge commitment is a huge benefit for folks who had never been responsible for something in their lives."

perception: way of seeing or believing something

injunction: warning or order

preemptive: preventative

proposition: official statement of an idea

dividends: incentives or money that is paid out on a regular basis

⊘ Knowledge Quest

- What are your first thoughts after reading the article?
- What surprising fact did you learn about service dogs?

Returning to the Text

- Return to the poem as you respond to the following questions. Use text evidence to support your responses.
- Write any additional questions you have about the poem in your Reader/Writer Notebook.

7. **KQ** How do the dogs described in this article support the point that Grandin makes in "How Dogs Make Us Human"?

_____

_____

_____

8. Morieka Johnson chooses five details about service dogs to focus on in the article. Why are these particular details important for Johnson to point out?

_____

_____

_____

9. **KQ** In paragraph 13, the author tells readers about _breed-specific_ bans. What does _breed-specific_ mean? Use a dictionary to find out. Then explain why _breed-specific_ bans are sometimes unfair.

_____

_____

_____

_____

10. Johnson mentions that caring for a service dog is "a long-term proposition that delivers big dividends." How is caring for a service dog a long-term commitment? What do you infer are the "big dividends" awarded to people who care for service dogs?

_____

_____

_____

_____

INDEPENDENT READING LINK

You can continue to build your knowledge about dogs and other animals by reading related articles at ZINC Reading Labs. Search for keywords such as *dogs or animal behavior.*

My Notes

Knowledge Quest

Think about the knowledge you've gained by reading "Saying Farewell to a Faithful Pal," "Dogs Make Us Human," and "5 things you don't know about service dogs." Then discuss with a partner how your view has changed about the roles dogs play in the lives of humans. Be sure to:

- Explain your answer to your partner, be specific, and use as many details as possible.
- When your partner explains his or her answer, ask for clarification by posing follow-up questions as needed.
- After the discussion, write down the ideas you talked about.

Conducting Research

Informative writing provides information about a topic, which often means researching the topic to learn more about it and to find evidence for your writing.

11. What do you know about conducting research? What experience do you have with it? Number the lines 1 to 6 to show a logical order for the research process.

_____ Write questions that can be answered through research.

_____ Evaluate sources.

_____ Identify the topic, issue, or problem.

_____ Communicate findings.

_____ Draw conclusions.

_____ Gather evidence and refocus or refine the major research question when necessary.

12. Use a KWHL graphic organizer to guide your research on the topic of animals helping people. First, fill out the first two columns.

K: What do you **know** about the ways that animals help people? Try to think of at least three ways that animals can help people live better lives.

W: What do you **want** to know about the ways that animals help people?

13. Now, fill in the "**H**" column with the title and author of the text you just read.

Topic: Animals Helping People			
K Thinking about what you already KNOW helps you focus on your topic.	**W** Thinking about what you WANT to know helps you create questions to guide your research.	**H** Thinking about HOW and where you will find information helps you identify possible resources that match your questions.	**L** Thinking about what you LEARNED helps you draw conclusions in order to communicate your findings.

14. In the **L** column, add information about what you learned from reading "Dogs Make Us Human." What did you learn about animals helping people?

15. In the W column, add new questions that you have. In the H column, brainstorm how and where you will conduct research to answer your questions. When brainstorming, consider conducting research that will lead to both primary sources (sources written by the subject, or at the time of the event) and secondary sources (sources written about the subject by someone else). Keep notes indicating which type each resource will be.

16. Follow your teacher's instructions on how to gather more research about animals helping people. As you do, complete the KWHL chart.

☑ Check Your Understanding

After doing additional research and reading, summarize the research process you used and describe how it helped you answer the questions you wrote in your KWHL chart.

📦 **INDEPENDENT READING LINK**

Read and Connect

Is there anything related to the research topic in your independent reading? Add the information to your KWHL chart. Be sure to note any similarities and differences between the information in your research and the information in your independent reading. Keep track of which source information is coming from. You will need to cite your sources later.

Synthesizing Temple's Story

Learning Strategies

Graphic Organizer
Marking the Text
Double-Entry Journal

VOCABULARY

LITERARY

A **biography** is an informative text that tells the story of a person's life but is written by someone other than that person.

An **autobiography** is an informative text that tells the story of a person's life and is written by that person.

Learning Targets

- Analyze and summarize the main ideas in a text.
- Apply reading strategies to an autobiography and use textual evidence to respond to a writing prompt.

Preview

In this activity, you will watch a film and read excerpts from an autobiography and biography in order to write an informative text about Temple Grandin.

Genre Study: Biography and Autobiography

Two of the most popular genres are **biography** and **autobiography**. Many people enjoy reading books and watching films about the lives of others. Both genres use a narrative text structure, but they are presented from different points of view. Biographies are written by someone other than the subject, and autobiographies are written by the subjects themselves. You have already read a part of Temple Grandin's autobiography, and now you will read another part of it and compare it to an excerpt from a biography written about her.

Setting a Purpose for Viewing

- As you view clips, use the following double-entry journal to take notes. Record descriptions, events, and observations on the left side. Add your questions, connections, predictions, responses, and commentary on the right side.
- Record unfamiliar words or phrases in your My Notes section.

Biographical Film *Temple Grandin*	My Personal Commentary

My Notes

Working from the Film

1. Summarize the film *Temple Grandin*. Be sure to organize your summary logically.

2. Write a thesis statement about the film *Temple Grandin*. Be sure to include the topic and an opinion.

Reading Strategies Review

3. You have used a variety of reading strategies in this unit. Rate your understanding of each strategy in the following chart. Then add one or two additional reading strategies that you are ready to use on your own. Consult the Reading Strategies section in the Resources at the end of this book for a complete list and description of all the reading strategies.

Reading Strategy	I'm still getting familiar with this strategy.	I am comfortable using this strategy with a little help.	I am ready to use this strategy on my own.
Chunking the Text			
Using Context Clues (Diffusing)			
Marking the Text			
Questioning the Text			
Graphic Organizer			
Summarizing			
Double-Entry Journal			

4. Choose two of these strategies to help you make meaning of the text you will read next.

Strategy 1: _____

Strategy 2: _____

Setting a Purpose for Reading

- Underline words or phrases that help you create an image in your mind of the setting the author describes.

- Circle unknown words and phrases. Try to determine the meaning of the words by using context clues, word parts, or a dictionary.

My Notes

_____

_____

_____

_____

_____

_____

_____

_____

_____

_____

_____

_____

_____

_____

_____

_____

_____

_____

_____

_____

_____

_____

_____

_____

_____

_____

_____

_____

_____

_____

_____

amplified: made larger, greater, or stronger

psychological: pertaining to the mind

Autobiography

My Story

from **Animals in Translation**

_by_ **Temple Grandin and Catherine Johnson**

1   People who aren't autistic always ask me about the moment I realized I could understand the way animals think. They think I must have had an epiphany.

2   But it wasn't like that. It took me a long time to figure out that I see things about animals other people don't. And it wasn't until I was in my forties that I finally realized I had one big advantage over the feedlot owners who were hiring me to manage their animals: being autistic. Autism made school and social life hard, but it made animals easy.

3   I started to fall in love with animals in high school when my mother sent me to a special boarding school for gifted children with emotional problems. Back then they called everything "emotional problems." Mother had to find a place for me because I got kicked out of high school for fighting. I got in fights because kids teased me. They'd call me names, like "Retard," or "Tape recorder."

4   They called me Tape Recorder because I'd stored up a lot of phrases in my memory and I used them over and over again in every conversation. Plus there were only a few conversations I like to have, so that **amplified** the effect. I especially like to talk about the rotor ride at the carnival. I would go up to somebody and say, "I went to Nantasket Park and I went on the rotor and I really liked the way it pushed me up against the wall." Then I say stuff like, "How did you like it?" and they'd say how they liked it, and then I'd tell the story all over again, start to finish. It was like a loop inside my head, it just ran over and over again. So the other kids called me Tape Recorder.

5   Teasing hurts. The kids would tease me, so I'd get mad and smack 'em. That simple. They always started it, they liked to see me react.

6   My new school solved that problem. The school had a stable and horses for the kids to ride, and the teachers took away horseback riding privileges if I smacked somebody. After I lost privileges enough times I learned just to cry when somebody did something bad to me. I'd cry, and that would take away the aggression. I still cry when people are mean to me.

7   Nothing ever happened to the kids who were teasing.

8   The funny thing about the school was, the horses had emotional problems, too. They had emotional problems because in order to save money the headmaster was buying cheap horses. They'd been marked down because they had gigantic behavior problems. They were pretty, their legs were fine, but emotionally they were a mess. The school had nine horses altogether, and two of them couldn't be ridden at all. Half of the horses in that barn had serious **psychological** problems. But I didn't understand that as a fourteen-year-old.

9   So there we all were up at boarding school, a bunch of emotionally disturbed teenagers living with a bunch of emotionally disturbed animals. There was one horse, Lady, who was a good horse when you rode her in the ring, but on the trail she would go berserk. She would rear, and constantly jump around *and* prance; you had to hold her back with the bridle or she'd bolt to the barn.

10   Then there was Beauty. You could ride Beauty, but he had very nasty habits like kicking and biting while you were in the saddle. He would swing his foot up and kick you in the leg or foot, or turn his head around and bite your knee. You had to watch out. Whenever you tried to mount Beauty he kicked and bit—you had both ends coming at you at the same time. …

11   All the horses at the school had been abused. Beauty had been kept locked in a dairy stanchion all day long. I don't know why. These were badly abused animals; they were very, very messed up.

12   But I had no understanding of this as a girl. I was never mean to the horses at the school (the other kids were sometimes), but I wasn't any horse-whispering autistic **savant**, either. I just loved the horses. I was so wrapped up in them that I spent every spare moment working the barns. I was dedicated to keeping the barn clean, making sure the horses were groomed. One of the high points of my high school career was the day my mom bought me a really nice English bridle and saddle. …

13   Boy did I take care of that saddle. I loved it so much I didn't even leave it in the tack room where it belonged. I brought it up to my **dorm** every day and kept it with me. I bought special saddle soap and leather conditioner from the saddle shop, and I spent hours washing and polishing it. …

14   Animals kept me going. I spent every waking minute that I didn't have to be studying or going to school with those horses. I even rode Lady at a show. It's hard to imagine today, a school keeping a stable of emotionally disturbed and dangerous horses for its underaged students to ride. These days you can't even play dodgeball in gym class because somebody might get hurt. But that's the way it was. A lot of us got nipped or stepped on or thrown at that school, but no one was ever seriously hurt, at least not while I was there. So it worked out.

15   I wish more kids could ride horses today. People and animals are supposed to be together. We spent quite a long time evolving together, and we used to be partners. Now people are cut off from animals unless they have a dog or a cat.

My Notes

Temple Grandin in Fort Collins, Colorado, 2005.

savant: person with extensive knowledge or capability in one subject

dorm: building where students live

Making Observations
- How would you describe Temple Grandin?
- What questions do you have after reading the text?
- What is a detail you noticed that someone else might have missed?

Returning to the Text

- Return to the text as you respond to the following questions. Use text evidence to support your responses.
- Write any additional questions you have about the autobiography excerpt in your Reader/Writer Notebook.

5. How does the information in paragraph 2 help you understand a key point of the text?

_____

_____

_____

_____

6. How does Grandin change as a result of her new school? How is this change explained in the text?

_____

_____

_____

_____

7. How does Grandin feel about the saddle her mom gave her? What evidence from the text supports your understanding?

_____

_____

_____

_____

8. What does Grandin mean when she says, "Animals kept me going"? What evidence from the text helps support your inference?

_____

_____

_____

_____

My Notes

About the Author

Sy Montgomery is an animal lover who writes books for children and adults. She researches her writing firsthand, getting up close and personal with wild animals to learn all about them. Her award-winning nonfiction can be found around the world, and so can she as she travels to talk about her work.

Biography

excerpt from

Hampshire School for Wayward Wizards

Chapter 6 from Temple Grandin: How the Girl Who Loved Cows Embraced Autism and Changed the World

by **Sy Montgomery**

1   … But the memories she treasures most from high school are of the horses. All these years later, she remembers each of them by name. Bay Lady was the horse she rode most of the time: great in the ring—but halfway on the trail she'd prance and plunge. Otherwise she was the "perfect lady." Star couldn't compete in horse shows because she had ankle problems. Circus, a big, gentle horse, died of colic, a **digestive** disease brought on by eating oat straw. Beauty was gorgeous, but he bit and kicked. Teddy was gentle enough for the littlest kids. King was an old gray horse, so well-mannered that just about anyone could ride him: then you could graduate to riding someone like Flash or Silver. Lady was hot-tempered, and her eyes were wild. "Nobody could ride that horse," Tina Henegar, another schoolmate, remembered. "But Temple could—and beautifully. She was the best."

2   Temple loved them all and could ride better than anyone.

3   It's no wonder. Horses, like autistic people, are very sensitive to detail and don't like change. That's why a horse might be frightened by a new white hat, but not a familiar black one—or might panic at the sight of a common object like a wheelbarrow in an unusual place or seen from a different angle. Temple could tell when a horse was starting to get nervous: a fearful horse swishes his tail, and the swishing becomes more rapid with **mounting** fear. But because Temple also noticed the same details the horses did—like a bale of hay slightly out of place—she could make small changes to calm the animal's fear before it turned to panic.

4   Temple spent much of her time in the horse barn. She cleaned the stalls. She refilled the feed bins. She cleaned the leather bridles and saddles and other equipment, making repairs if needed. When the farrier came to hammer new shoes onto the horses' hooves, she held the reins and kept the horses calm.

digestive: relating to food being broken down in the body
mounting: increasing

My Notes

5 Back at home, Temple's mother wished her daughter would study harder and get better grades instead of riding horses and mending bridles. But Temple was proud that she now had an important, responsible job in the barn. The **welfare** of nine horses depended largely on her care. To Temple, her academic classes didn't seem to matter half as much. They were "boring, boring, boring."

6 Soon she began to find it impossible to concentrate on schoolwork anyway. Now in high school, she felt that something new and terrible was happening to her. Her body was changing. The rush of new chemicals her body was producing to change her into a young woman threw Temple's unusual brain into overdrive. She started having panic attacks.

Making Observations
- What stands out most to you about this text?
- What questions does this text help you answer?

welfare: health and happiness

Returning to the Text

- Return to the text as you respond to the following questions. Use text evidence to support your responses.
- Write any additional questions you have about the biography in your Reader/Writer Notebook.

9. What is the author's point of view about Grandin's autism? How is the point of view conveyed in the text?

_____

_____

_____

_____

10. How is the concept of autism being an advantage for Grandin treated differently in the two texts? What might explain this difference?

_____

_____

_____

11. You read excerpts from Grandin's autobiography and a biography written about her. What unique type of information does each genre offer?

_____

_____

_____

_____

12. What details in this text help you understand the previous text better?

_____

_____

_____

_____

My Notes

_____

_____

_____

_____

_____

_____

_____

_____

_____

_____

_____

_____

_____

_____

_____

_____

_____

_____

_____

_____

_____

_____

_____

_____

_____

_____

_____

_____

_____

_____

_____

_____

☑ Check Your Understanding

Write three sentences about Temple Grandin, one in the form of a statement, one in the form of a question, and one in the form of an exclamation. Be sure to use correct capitalization and punctuation.

Statement _____

_____

Question _____

_____

Exclamation _____

_____

Gaining Perspectives

Imagine that Temple Grandin is a new student at your school, and you want to make her feel welcome. In a small group, investigate places you can find reliable information about the ways Temple learns. Try reading from resources on the Internet, watching a video, or listening to an audiobook. Then, based on what you learn, use decision-making skills to plan three activities that Temple might take part in during her first week at school. When you are finished planning, list your activities in your Reader/Writer Notebook.

✍ Writing to Sources: Informational Text

How did animals help Temple Grandin deal with the challenges of autism? Be sure to:

- Write a thesis statement, including the topic and your opinion.
- Use textual evidence and supporting details from all three sources.
- Add personal commentary while maintaining a formal style.
- Spell correctly.

⬡ Independent Reading Checkpoint

Review your independent reading notes. Use those notes to write a summary of the text. Swap summaries with a partner who has not read the text to see if your summary maintained the meaning of the text and is logical.

Writing an Informative Essay

ASSIGNMENT

Read the following quotation by John Muir, an American naturalist and writer:

"Any glimpse into the life of an animal quickens our own and makes it so much the larger and better in every way."

Write a multiparagraph essay explaining how people can improve their lives through observing and interacting with animals. In your essay, give examples from your own life, from texts you have studied in this unit, from your independent reading, or from society that help support your explanation.

Planning and Prewriting: Take time to make a plan for your informative essay.	■ Which prewriting strategies and graphic organizers could help you brainstorm a variety of examples from literature, experience, and research? ■ Which two or three examples would be the best selections for your essay? ■ How can you summarize your response to the prompt in a thesis statement?
Drafting: Determine the structure of your essay.	■ How can you restate and interpret the quote in the prompt in order to introduce your thesis? ■ What elements of effective support paragraphs will you use to organize your response? ■ How can you conclude your essay in a way that answers the question "So what?"
Evaluating and Revising the Draft: Create opportunities to review and revise your work.	■ During the process of writing, when can you pause to share and respond with others? ■ What is your plan to include suggestions and revision ideas in your draft? ■ How can you use strategies such as adding and replacing to revise your draft? ■ How can the Scoring Guide help you evaluate how well your draft meets the requirements of the assignment?
Checking and Editing for Publication: Confirm that your final draft is ready for publication.	■ How will you check for grammatical and technical accuracy, such as proper spelling and punctuation?

Reflection

After completing this Embedded Assessment, think about how you went about accomplishing this task and respond to the following:

- How did you use a variety of examples from literature, experience, and research to support your response to the prompt?

SCORING GUIDE

Scoring Criteria	Exemplary	Proficient	Emerging	Incomplete
Ideas	The essay • responds to the prompt with a clearly focused and well-sustained main idea. • integrates relevant evidence from various sources (e.g., literature, nonfiction, personal experience, research) with detail and commentary.	The essay • responds to the prompt with a focused and sustained main idea. • integrates evidence from multiple sources (e.g., literature, nonfiction, personal experience, research) with commentary.	The essay • responds to the prompt with an unfocused or inconsistently sustained main idea. • uses irrelevant or insufficient evidence; may lack multiple sources or provide weak commentary.	The essay • does not respond to the prompt; response is vague or confusing. • uses minimal evidence and commentary.
Structure	The essay • introduces the main idea in an engaging hook and clear thesis. • uses an effective multiparagraph organizational structure. • uses a variety of transitions and topic sentences to create coherence and integrate ideas. • provides an insightful conclusion.	The essay • introduces the main idea with a hook and thesis. • uses an appropriate multiparagraph organizational structure. • uses transitions and topic sentences to create coherence. • provides a conclusion that connects to larger ideas.	The essay • introduces the main idea with a weak hook or thesis. • uses a flawed or inconsistent organizational structure. • uses transitions and topic sentences ineffectively or inconsistently. • provides a weak, illogical, or repetitive conclusion.	The essay • does not include an introduction. • has little or no obvious organizational structure. • uses few or no transitions and topic sentences. • lacks a conclusion.
Use of Language	The essay • uses precise and accurate diction to illustrate the topic. • demonstrates command of the conventions of standard English capitalization, punctuation, spelling, grammar, and usage (including parallel structure, commas in a series, and semicolons).	The essay • uses diction that is appropriate to the topic and purpose. • demonstrates adequate command of the conventions of standard English capitalization, punctuation, spelling, grammar, and usage (including parallel structure, commas in a series, and semicolons).	The essay • uses basic diction inappropriate to the topic or purpose. • demonstrates partial or inconsistent command of the conventions of standard English capitalization, punctuation, spelling, grammar, and usage (including parallel structure, commas in a series, and semicolons).	The essay • uses diction that is vague or confusing. • lacks command of the conventions of standard English capitalization, punctuation, spelling, grammar, and usage; frequent errors obscure meaning.

VISUAL PROMPT
How can your perspective change when you look at a picture? What details do you notice in this image?

CHANGING PERSPECTIVES

We ask only that our story be told in fairness. We do not ask you to overlook what we did, but we do ask you to understand it.

–from "The First Americans" by Scott H. Peters

CONTENTS

My Independent
Reading List

ACTIVITY	CONTENTS	

© 2021 College Board. All rights reserved.

Learning Strategies

Activating Prior Knowledge
Skimming/Scanning
QHT
Marking the Text

VOCABULARY

ACADEMIC

A **controversy** is a public debate or dispute concerning a matter of opinion. A controversial issue is debatable, or an issue about which there can be disagreement.

 INDEPENDENT READING LINK

Reading Plan

Think about a controversial topic in your school or community that interests you. It could be a topic that you already have an opinion about or you could be undecided about it. Find a collection of news articles, opinion pieces, editorials, letters to the editor, and other texts that discuss the controversy. Keep track of them in the My Independent Reading section of the table of contents.

Learning Targets

- Preview the big ideas and vocabulary for the unit.
- Gain specific understanding of the academic vocabulary word *controversy* and its relevance in the unit.
- Identify and analyze the skills and knowledge needed to complete Embedded Assessment 1 successfully.

Preview

In this activity, you will think about what you already know about controversy and debates.

Making Connections

In the last unit, you read a novel and other texts about the changes that occur throughout people's lives. You also looked at change from different perspectives: changes in your own life, changes in your community, and changes in the broader world. In this unit, you will examine arguments and how writers try to persuade others to agree with their opinions on issues that cause **controversy**.

Essential Questions

Based on your current knowledge, how would you answer these questions? Write your responses in your Reader/Writer Notebook.

1. Why do we have controversy in society?
2. How do we communicate in order to convince others?

Developing Vocabulary

Mark the Academic Vocabulary and Literary Terms using the QHT strategy.

Unpacking Embedded Assessment 1

Read the assignment for Embedded Assessment 1: Researching and Debating a Controversy.

Work collaboratively to research one side of a controversy that is affecting your school, your community, or society. Then participate in a modified debate in which you argue your position and incorporate a visual display with appropriate headings and labels and/or multimedia for support.

Mark the text for what you will need to know in order to complete this assessment successfully. With your class, create a graphic organizer to represent the skills and knowledge you will need to complete the tasks identified in the Embedded Assessment.

It Is Time to Argue and Convince

Learning Targets
- Infer the meanings and explain the denotations and connotations of key vocabulary terms.
- Practice paraphrasing to support reading, listening, and writing skills.
- Generate a controversial topic of interest.

Preview
In this activity, you will explore the term *argument* and think about controversies your class might debate over the course of this unit's activities.

Learning Strategies
Think-Pair-Share
Close Reading
Marking the Text
Paraphrasing
Brainstorming
Quickwrite
Freewriting

ACADEMIC
In formal speech or writing, an **argument** is a set of reasons given to support an opinion, often with the aim of persuading others that an action or idea is right or wrong. **Argumentation** is the act of formally engaging in an argument about a debatable issue.

VOCABULARY

Introducing Argument

1. **Quickwrite:** Have you ever tried to change the mind of someone in your family? Were you successful, and if so, how did you convince the person?

   _____

   _____

   _____

   _____

2. Brainstorm all the meanings you know for the word **argument**. The concept of **argumentation** will become important during this unit.

3. Compare your brainstorm to dictionary and thesaurus entries for the word *argument*. What other definitions for *argument* can you find? What other words are associated with *argument?* Also, what other words have similar meanings to *argument,* and how are their connotations different?

4. What comes to mind when you hear the word *controversy*? Complete the Word Map graphic organizer to develop understanding of the word.

Definition in Own Words	Personal Associations/Connotations
Visual Representation	**Examples from Texts, Society, or History**

Introducing the Strategy: Paraphrasing

Paraphrasing is putting a passage of text in your own words while maintaining its meaning. Often, paraphrased text is shorter than the original passage, but not always. When paraphrasing a text, remember to order its information logically. Use paraphrasing during reading to help you check your understanding of a text. Use it while taking notes on something a speaker is saying. Also, use it to support claims in your writing.

5. When you communicate your own argument about a controversy or an issue, it is essential to be able to paraphrase information. To practice paraphrasing, read and paraphrase the following quotes on controversy.

Original	My Paraphrasing
"If it matters, it produces controversy." —Jay Greene, retired NASA engineer	
"A wise man has well reminded us, that 'in any controversy, the instant we feel angry, we have already ceased striving for Truth, and begun striving for Ourselves.'" —Thomas Carlyle	
"When a thing ceases to be a subject of controversy, it ceases to be a subject of interest." —William Hazlitt	

6. **Quickwrite:** Do you agree or disagree with any of the quotes? Explain.

7. Read the following list of claims relating to controversies from society today and place a check mark to indicate whether you agree or disagree with each one. When you are done filling out the Anticipation Guide, turn and talk to your neighbor about the two or three topics that you are most interested in. During your discussion, remember to ask and answer specific questions about the topic under discussion.

Anticipation Guide: Exploring Hot Topics	Agree	Disagree
Social networking should be banned at school.		
Cell phones and other electronic devices should be banned at school.		
Banning homework would hurt a student's education.		
Certain books should be banned from school.		
Junk food should be banned from schools.		
Schools should ban peanut butter.		
Kids should be banned from appearing on reality television.		
Plastic bags should be banned.		
Plastic water bottles should be banned.		
Skateboarding should be banned in public places.		
Dangerous sports such as motor racing and boxing should be banned.		
Pit bulls should be banned as pets.		
Exotic animals should be banned as pets.		
Football should be banned in middle school.		
Teenagers should be banned from playing violent video games.		

8. **Freewrite:** A controversial topic I feel strongly about is _____

_____

☑ Check Your Understanding

Write your ideas about the following in your Reader/Writer Notebook:

- three things you have learned about an argument
- two hot topics that interest you and why
- one thing you learned about paraphrasing

Learning Strategies

Graphic Organizer
Close Reading
Marking the Text
Paraphrasing
Quickwrite

VOCABULARY

ACADEMIC

In argumentation, a writer makes a claim stating a position or opinion about a topic. To claim is to assert or maintain as a fact. A claim is the overall thesis describing the author's position on an issue.

KNOWLEDGE QUEST

Knowledge Question:

What are some intended goals of homework, and how can homework policy be changed to better align with these goals?

Across Activities 3.3 and 3.4, you will read three texts about the pros and cons of homework. While you read and build knowledge about the topic, think about your answer to the Knowledge Question.

professional: expert

Learning Targets

- Identify a writer's claim and explain the reasons presented for or against a topic.
- Write a debatable claim stating a position or opinion about a topic.
- Integrate ideas from multiple texts to build knowledge and vocabulary about the intended goals of homework.

Preview

In this activity, you will read an editorial about homework, paraphrase the claim made in the article, and explain why you agree or disagree with it.

What Is a Claim?

In argumentative writing, the author's position is known as a **claim**. The claim functions like a thesis statement. Identifying the author's claim helps you understand the author's opinion or point of view on a topic.

Often, an author's claim appears in the opening paragraph. Sometimes the claim is in the middle of the text or even at the end. To identify a writer's claim, look for a statement of position or opinion that reflects what the author is trying to say about a controversial topic. A claim will be a statement that is not fact, so the author should provide reasons that support the claim.

Setting a Purpose for Reading

- Highlight the sentence in the first paragraph where the author states her claim.
- Underline facts and details that support the author's claim.
- Circle unknown words and phrases. Try to determine the meaning of the words by using context clues, word parts, or a dictionary.

Opinion Piece

A Teacher's Defense of Homework

by **Andrea Townsend**, *The Atlantic*, **Sept. 25, 2013**

1   I am a parent, and I struggle daily with making sure my daughter does her homework. I can certainly identify with the anxiety Karl Taro Greenfeld describes in his essay "My Daughter's Homework Is Killing Me" (published in *The Atlantic's* October 2013 issue). Here, however, I'd like to speak as a teacher rather than a parent. I'd like to explain why, in my **professional** opinion, American kids need homework.

2   I teach biology at the Charles School, a five-year early-college high school in Columbus, Ohio. I believe that my job is to prepare my students for college. In order to do that, I teach a wide variety of topics including cells, genetics, evolution, and ecology, using the National Science Standards. I teach each topic in depth so that the students understand and appreciate the information.

I teach them about the scientific method, lab **procedures**, and scientific writing, all skills they will need in college. It's a lot to fit into one short year, and my class requires a lot of effort from my students.

3 I require my students to read one chapter out of their textbook each week, and to complete a short take-home quiz on the material. It helps to supplement the notes I give in class, so that I can spend more class time on labs and other hands-on activities. I learned in college that hands-on work is the best way for students to learn, and that's certainly true. However, it's definitely not the most *efficient* way. So, if I'm going to offer interactive activities in class, I need students to put in some time and effort studying outside of class as well.

4 A few times a year, I require students to write a scientific paper. We spend a significant amount of time on these assignments at school, but effort outside of class is required as well. And I think that's great. Schoolwork prepares students for work-related tasks, **financial** planning, and any project that ends with the feeling of a job well done. Long-term planning, projects, and deadlines are a key part of adulthood.

5 Nevertheless, some parents think their kids are getting too much work. One argument, which Greenfeld uses, is to compare American students with those in other countries. In his article, Greenfeld cites the fact that students in many overseas countries are scoring higher than American children, while being assigned less homework. He uses Japan as an example. In 2011, Japan was ranked fourth in science scores in the Trends in International Mathematics and Science Study. But according to a study cited in Greenfeld's article, Japanese students are actually assigned less homework by their teachers. Why, then, do they achieve more? The answer comes when you look at the differences in our cultures and our views on education. Japanese teachers may not be assigning much homework, *but it turns out that Japanese kids are doing plenty of homework anyway.*

> **procedures:** lists of steps in an experiment
> **financial:** related to money

My Notes

6   I spoke with Chris Spackman, who is the English as a Second Language coordinator at my school. Chris taught for 13 years in Japan, and served on the Board of Education in the city of Kanazawa. I asked him why Japanese kids are scoring so high on achievement tests despite having relatively little homework. "Because Japanese kids go to *juku*," he answered. He went on to explain that *juku* is a common after-school program that prepares Japanese kids for achievement testing. In Japan, senior high school is not required or guaranteed. Instead, students compete for spots at **prestigious** high schools by scoring high on achievement tests. "Some schools are for art, or college prep," says Chris. "You have to study hard in junior high to get into the high school that you want." In high school, Japanese kids continue to go to *juku* so that they can get into the college they want as well. So, Japanese kids do academic work outside of school, just not necessarily work assigned by their classroom teacher.

7   There is room for compromise on the homework debate. In their book *Reforming Homework*, Richard Walker and Mike Horsley state that while homework isn't very beneficial for younger kids, it's still beneficial for older students. I agree. I've learned, while preparing my students to start college early, that study skills become much more important than they were in primary school. It's also important for teachers to assign work that's high in quality, instead of quantity. The **vast** majority of teachers I know are careful to only assign work that's important for student success. Remember, teachers have to grade all of these assignments—we wouldn't want to spend extra time grading papers that have no value.

8   In the comments on Greenfeld's article, some readers assume that teachers don't have our students' best interests at heart. But usually, teachers who aren't incredibly devoted to their students don't last in the profession. The teachers who do stay are committed to giving the best education to their students. We wouldn't be assigning that homework, giving that test, or reading that book if we didn't truly believe it was worthwhile. All we ask is that you trust us, just a little.

⊘ Knowledge Quest

- What ideas about the need for homework stood out to you?
- What questions do you have about homework after reading this opinion piece?

prestigious: well-regarded
vast: large

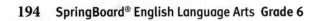

Returning to the Text

- Return to the text as you respond to the following questions. Use text evidence to support your responses.
- Write any additional questions you have about the editorial in your Reader/Writer Notebook.

1. Who is the intended audience of the article? Why did the author write the article?

_____

_____

_____

_____

2. **KQ** In paragraph 3, the author says she uses homework to "supplement" the notes she gives in class. What does *supplement* mean in this opinion piece? Use context clues and a dictionary to help you decide. Then tell why the author thinks it is necessary to *supplement* her notes with homework.

_____

_____

_____

_____

3. How does the author strengthen her argument in paragraphs 5 and 6?

_____

_____

_____

_____

4. Why does the author say there is room for compromise in paragraph 7?

_____

_____

_____

_____

5. **KQ** At what age does the author say homework becomes more important, and how does she provide evidence to support her claim?

_____

_____

_____

My Notes

Working from the Text

6. Which of these statements from the article is the **best** example of a claim?

   A. I struggle daily with making sure my daughter does her homework.

   B. American kids need homework.

   C. I teach each topic in depth so that students understand and appreciate the information.

7. Explain the claim.

_____

_____

_____

_____

8. Explain why you agree or disagree with the claim. Then share your position with one or more classmates. Listen as your partner states his or her position and note whether you agree or disagree. Have a short discussion to determine how strongly you disagree and why. Practice speaking clearly and refer to reasons and evidence from the text to support your position.

_____

_____

_____

_____

Claims Are Debatable

A claim must be something that people could reasonably have differing opinions on. If your claim is something that is generally agreed upon or accepted as fact, then there is no reason to try to convince people.

Example of a non-debatable claim: *Air pollution is bad for the environment.* This claim is not debatable. First, the word *pollution* means that something is bad or negative in some way. Further, all studies agree that air pollution has a negative impact; they simply disagree on the specific impact it will have or the scope of the problem. No one could reasonably argue that air pollution is good.

Example of a debatable claim: *At least 25 percent of the federal budget should be spent on limiting air pollution.* This claim is debatable because reasonable people could disagree with it. Some people might think that this is how we should spend the nation's money. Others might believe that this amount is too much to spend to limit air pollution. Still others could argue that corporations, not the government, should be paying to limit air pollution.

☑ Check Your Understanding

Quickwrite: Briefly state a claim a writer could make to support the idea that students should not be assigned homework. Tell whether the claim is debatable and why.

🞅 INDEPENDENT READING LINK

Read and Respond

Find a claim stated in one of the texts you are reading independently. Decide whether it is debatable and write the opposing claim if it is debatable.

Creating Support with Reasons and Evidence

Learning Targets

- Identify reasons and evidence in a text and analyze how they support claims.
- Participate in an effective debate by using evidence from texts, contributing ideas clearly, and responding to others' ideas.
- Integrate ideas from multiple texts to build knowledge and vocabulary about the intended goals of homework.

Preview

In this activity, you will learn how to identify the ways reasons and evidence support claims in argumentative texts. You will also take sides in the homework argument after reading additional articles about the topic.

Learning Strategies

Graphic Organizer
Marking the Text
Rereading

VOCABULARY

ACADEMIC

Reasons are the points that explain why the author is making a certain claim.

Evidence is the facts, details, and information that support the reasons for the claim. Strong arguments have clear reasons with strong evidence.

Reasons and Evidence

A claim should be backed up with support. A writer can support his or her viewpoint with **reasons** and **evidence**. Reasons are the points or opinions the writer gives to show why his or her claim should be accepted. In writing, each reason often acts as the topic sentence of a paragraph.

Evidence is a more specific type of support. Different kinds of evidence, such as facts, statistics, examples, observations, quotations, and expert opinions, can be used to support reasons. Sometimes people believe that their reasons should be sufficient to win an argument, but arguments without evidence are just personal opinions. Argumentative speakers and writers should attempt to use both reasons and evidence to be most effective.

Introducing the Strategy: Rereading

Good readers often reread a text to help them make sense of it and find information they did not notice during the first reading. Rereading a text two or three times is sometimes needed for full understanding.

Revisiting an Argument

1. You will now go back and reread the editorial in Activity 3.3 to find reasons and evidence that support the author's position. Use the Side A column in the following graphic organizer to identify the components of the argument.

Side A	Side B
Claim:	Claim:
Reason:	Reason:
Evidence:	Evidence:
Type of evidence:	Type of evidence:

Setting a Purpose for Reading

- As you read, underline reasons and evidence that the author uses to support her claim.
- Highlight words and phrases that indicate a formal tone.
- Circle unknown words and phrases. Try to determine the meaning of the words by using context clues, word parts, or a dictionary.

About the Author

Amedee Marchand Martella (1993–) is a graduate student in the Department of Psychology at Carnegie Mellon University (CMU) and a fellow in CMU's Program in Interdisciplinary Education Research (PIER). She graduated from the University of Colorado Boulder with a double major in ecology & evolutionary biology and psychology. Her research interests center on improving K–16 student performance in STEM areas through the use of effective teaching practices.

Opinion Piece

A High School Student's Perspective on Homework

by **Amedee Martella, ASCD Website**

KNOWLEDGE QUEST

Knowledge Question:
What are some intended goals of homework, and how can homework policy be changed to better align with these goals?

1 For years I have never fully understood my parents' celebrations of or concerns about my education. They have strong opinions about everything from the curricula used in my classes to how instruction is provided. My parents are both professors in the educational psychology and special education fields, so I have heard their views on education all my life.

2 One area that has prompted much discussion in our household surrounds the use of homework, particularly since I entered high school. Based on my own experiences, listening to my parents in their classes, and my research, I have come to the conclusion that homework could use some serious modification.

3 First, mastery can only be achieved by correct practice over time. My parents are advocates of explicit instruction; that is, teachers should show us what to do, give us opportunities to do it, and then give us a chance to show that we can do it on our own. Homework was designed to build on skills covered extensively in class. I should be able to complete an assignment with little to no confusion at home as long as it involves previously learned skills. I read Harris Cooper's 1989 article "Synthesis of Research on Homework," published in *Educational*

Leadership, which is cited by many of the researchers who have studied homework and its effects. Two recommendations stood out for me:

- "Homework will not be used to teach complex skills. It will generally focus on simple skills and material or on the integration of skills already possessed by the student." (p. 90)

- "Parents will rarely be asked to play a formal instructional role in homework. Instead, they should be asked to create a home environment that facilitates student self-study." (p. 90)

4 Many of the homework assignments I have received throughout my years of schooling have involved activities not previously practiced. When a teacher assigns homework incorporating information that was just recently taught or not taught at all, it puts a tremendous amount of stress on students. Worse yet, I think, it puts a great deal of stress on our parents. We rely on our parents to help us be successful. Our parents have to figure out how to do the assignment and then teach it to us. Many of the projects and activities are too difficult to be done without our parents' help. Students who have no help at home, therefore, are at a total disadvantage and their grades might falter because of this lack of assistance…

5 Second, homework should not exceed two hours per night. Again, Cooper provides recommendations about the length of homework. He says the following (p. 90):

- Grades 1–3: 1–3 assignments a week, each lasting no more than 15 minutes.

- Grades 4–6: 2–4 assignments a week, each lasting 15–45 minutes.

- Grades 7–9: 3–5 assignments a week, each lasting 45–75 minutes.

- Grades 10–12: 4–5 assignments a week, each lasting 75–120 minutes.

Many high school students, like these Kingwood High School football players in Houston, Texas, have obligations after school that limit their homework time.

My Notes

6 If we assume that we know how to do the homework we are assigned, we should be able to complete it in a reasonable amount of time. But consider the schedules of many high school students: we often wake up early in the morning; some of us have long bus rides; and many of us have sports practices, jobs, or other extracurricular activities before or after school. We have to make time to eat dinner and complete our chores. Now add on three or more hours of homework a night and you have instant stress, not only for students but also for their families. I have known my peers to stay up until midnight trying to finish their homework on top of everything else they have to do in their busy lives. These students are not always procrastinators—they just simply cannot do it all…

7 In summary, I enjoy school and appreciate the time my teachers take in providing feedback on homework assignments and in reviewing them in class. If teachers take the time to assign homework we can actually do within a reasonable amount of time, we will enjoy the experience much more, be less stressed, and have more time to spend with our families each evening.

Reference

Cooper, H. (1989, November). Synthesis of research on homework. *Educational Leadership, 47*(3), 85–91.

⊘ Knowledge Quest

- What stands out most for you about the information on homework in this piece?
- What is your first reaction to the author's opinion on homework: Do you agree or disagree with it?

☑ Focus on the Sentence

Write a question for each of the following answers based on the article.

Question: _____

_____

Answer: a maximum of two hours per night

Question _____

_____

Answer: to practice and build on skills learned in class

Returning to the Text

- Return to the text as you respond to the following questions. Use text evidence to support your responses.
- Write any additional questions you have about the text in your Reader/Writer Notebook.

2. What is the author's claim in this article? Who is the author's intended audience? How do you know?

_____

_____

_____

_____

3. What makes the author an authority figure on homework?

_____

_____

_____

_____

4. KQ In paragraph 3, the author cites information from an article by Harold Cooper that says homework should "'focus on simple skills or on the integration of skills already possessed by the student.'" What does *integration* mean in this context? Use a dictionary to help you decide. Then tell what you think a homework assignment that involves an *integration* of students' current skills might involve and whether you think this kind of assignment is something students could do independently.

_____

_____

_____

_____

5. In paragraphs 3 and 5, why does the author use bullet points? How does this structure contribute to her purpose?

_____

_____

_____

_____

6. KQ The following claim is made in "A Teacher's Defense of Homework:" "Homework isn't very beneficial for younger kids." How does "A High School Student's Perspective on Homework" support this claim?

_____

_____

_____

_____

7. **KQ** How does the author address the opposing viewpoint that students only have to stay up late doing homework because they are procrastinators?

_____

_____

_____

_____

Setting a Purpose for Reading

- As you read the news article, underline reasons and evidence that the subjects of the article use as support for their opinions.
- Use the My Notes section to describe any similarities or differences this article has with the previous two articles you have read about the homework debate.
- Circle unknown words and phrases. Try to determine the meaning of the words by using context clues, word parts, or a dictionary.

News Article

Texas Teacher Implements No-Homework Policy, the Internet Rejoices

by **Ashley May,** *USA Today,* **Aug. 24, 2016**

1   A second grade teacher's no-homework policy has gone viral, thanks to a student's mother posting about it on Facebook.

2   Last week, mom Samantha Gallagher posted a note on Facebook from her daughter's teacher reading: "After much research this summer, I'm trying something new. Homework will only consist of work that your student did not finish during the school day. There will be no formally assigned homework this year."

3   Godley Elementary School teacher Brandy Young told parents research doesn't prove homework improves performance. So, she said, time after school is best spent eating dinner as a family, reading together, playing outside and getting children to bed early.

4   It was a decision Young said she made with the support of her district.

5   "Our district, campus, and teaching teams are exactly the supportive environment you need if you're going to break the mold and try something new," Young said in an email. "We're never really afraid to voice new opinions and ideas because our leadership is always so supportive, and our coworkers want what's best for educating our students."

KNOWLEDGE QUEST

Knowledge Question:

What are some intended goals of homework, and how can homework policy be changed to better align with these goals?

My Notes

6 Gallagher said her daughter is "loving her new teacher already!" The post has more than 67,400 shares on Facebook and started a healthy conversation on Reddit: I wish this was the homework policy when I was in school.

7 The response has been overwhelmingly "supportive and positive," Gallagher said. "Many who have responded are educators themselves wanting info from Mrs. Young on how to go about implementing the policy themselves."

8 Hosburgh said her daughter had about an hour of homework each night in first grade. "We plan on spending more time as a family unwinding and catching up in the evenings," she said. "Also Brooke is interested in gymnastics and this will allow more time for that."

9 The National PTA and the National Education Association recommends the maximum amount of homework (all subjects combined) should be 10 minutes or less per grade level per night. So, second grade students should have 20 minutes of homework per night.

10 Duke University Professor Harris M. Cooper, author of *The Battle over Homework: Common Ground for Administrators, Teachers, and Parents*, said short and simple homework assignments are necessary.

11 "A creative and thoughtful teacher can make reading with parents the homework assignment or go out and play, keep track of your batting average," Cooper said.

12 No homework is a "bad idea," he said, because homework creates good study habits and self-discipline.

13 He said it also allows parents to monitor their children's progress.

14 "Homework is a lot like medication," he said. "If you're taking too much, it can kill you. If you take too little, it has no effect."

🚫 Knowledge Quest
- What surprises you most about what you just read?
- What details in this article stand out to you?

My Notes

☑ **Focus on the Sentence**

Complete the following sentences about the article you just read.

Brandy Young stopped formally assigning homework because _____

_____

Brandy Young stopped formally assigning homework, but _____

_____

Returning to the Text

- Return to the text as you respond to the following questions. Use text evidence to support your responses.
- Write other questions you have in your Reader/Writer Notebook.

8. How did Brandy Young arrive at the decision to change the homework policy? Use text evidence to support your response.

_____

_____

_____

_____

9. In paragraph 5, why does the author include quotation marks?

_____

_____

_____

_____

10. KQ What does the word *policy* mean in paragraph 6? Use a dictionary along with context clues from paragraphs 1 through 6 to help you decide. Then summarize Young's *policy* in your own word and tell whose support she needed in order to set it in place.

_____

_____

_____

_____

11. Why does the author include paragraphs 9 and 10 in the article?

_____

_____

_____

_____

12. What is the author's purpose for writing this article?

_____

_____

_____

_____

13. **KQ** Based on what you know from reading all three articles, what can you infer about why many parents and teachers might support Young's idea? Why might a high school student's parent be less supportive?

_____

_____

_____

_____

⊘ Knowledge Quest

After reading these three articles about homework, jot down your own ideas on the purpose of homework in your class. Write about how you would change the homework policy to better align with your goals.

① INDEPENDENT READING LINK

You can continue to build your knowledge about homework and other academic considerations by reading related articles at ZINC Reading Labs. Search for keywords such as *homework* or *school policies*.

 ZINC

Working from the Text

14. Return to the Revisiting an Argument graphic organizer and identify the components of the argument you read in this activity.

15. Take a side in the homework argument, using the evidence you found in the texts. In the My Notes space, write why that evidence provides the most convincing support for your position. Then brainstorm other reasons and/or evidence that might strengthen either side of the argument.

☑ Check Your Understanding

Quickwrite: Why is it important to identify reasons and evidence in an argumentative text? Why is it also necessary to analyze how the reasons and evidence support claims?

_____

_____

_____

_____

Debating the Issue

> **Should students be assigned homework?**

Writing to Sources: Argument

In preparation for the class debate, you will now formulate a written response about your opinion on the previous question. Read the question carefully and decide whether to answer yes or no. Then write about your opinion. Be sure to:

- Clearly state your opinion in your writing.
- Provide reasons and cite evidence from the three argumentative texts you have read on the issue to support your opinion.
- Use words, phrases, and clauses to clearly connect reasons and evidence to claims.
- Write in a formal style.

Rules for Debate

For your debate, you will use a process called "Philosophical Chairs." This process organizes the debate and does the following:

- Helps you become aware of your own position on a topic
- Helps you practice using reasons and evidence to support your position
- Exposes you to alternative perspectives (others' positions) on a topic

Listen as your teacher describes how the debate will be done.

Rules of Engagement

- Listen carefully when others speak; seek to understand their position even if you don't agree.
- Wait for the mediator to recognize you before you speak; only one person speaks at a time. Speak clearly and loudly enough to be heard by the audience. Explicitly refer to evidence from the texts as you offer new support or elaborate on a previous point.
- If you have spoken for a side, you must wait until three other people on your side speak before you speak again.
- If you are undecided, you may sit in the available "hot seats," but for no longer than 4 minutes.
- Since this is not a team game, don't cheer or jeer your classmates as they move.

Your Final Argument

16. Complete the graphic organizer to show your final argument.

Issue: Should students be assigned homework?	
Claim:	
Reason 1:	**Evidence** (facts, statistics, examples, observations, quotations, expert opinion): **Source:**
Reason 2:	**Evidence** (facts, statistics, examples, observations, quotations, expert opinion): **Source:**
Reason 3:	**Evidence** (facts, statistics, examples, observations, quotations, expert opinion): **Source:**

☑ Check Your Understanding

How did you do in the debate? Complete the self-assessment and set at least one goal for improvement.

	Sometimes	Always	Never
I explicitly referred to evidence from the texts.			
I offered new support or elaborated on previous points.			
I spoke clearly, slowly, and loudly enough to be heard by the audience.			

Do Your Research: Sources, Citation, and Credibility

Learning Strategies

Quickwrite
Graphic Organizer
Note-taking

VOCABULARY

ACADEMIC

When you **research** (verb), you locate reliable information from a variety of sources. The word *research* (noun) also describes the information found from the search. Research is a process that involves planning, reading, asking questions, finding answers, synthesizing information, and drawing conclusions.

Learning Targets

- Learn to examine sources for reliability, credibility, and bias.
- Learn how to paraphrase and cite source materials to avoid plagiarism.
- Apply understanding of sources, citation, and credibility through discussion, note-taking, and research.

Preview

In this activity, you will learn how to cite sources ethically and evaluate a source's credibility by looking for bias.

1. Read and think about the following quotes by Bernard M. Baruch, American financial expert and presidential advisor (1870–1965):

"Every man has a right to his own opinion, but no man has a right to be wrong in his facts."

"If you get all the facts, your judgment can be right; if you don't get all the facts, it can't be right."

Quickwrite: Based on the quotations, what is the role of **research** in presenting an argument?

_____

_____

_____

_____

_____

_____

_____

2. Use the graphic organizer to review the research process and decide how comfortable you are with each step.

The Research Process	Self-Assessment		
	Very Comfortable	**Somewhat Comfortable**	**Not Comfortable**
Step 1: Identify the topic, issue, or problem.			
Step 2: Form a set of questions that can be answered through research.			
Step 3: Gather evidence and refocus when necessary.			
Step 4: Evaluate sources.			
Step 5: Draw conclusions.			
Step 6: Communicate findings.			

Sources, Citation, and Credibility

3. Take notes about *sources*, *citation*, and *credibility* in the boxes that follow. Above each term, write what you already know about it. Then below each term, write words or phrases from your reading and discussion that relate to the term.

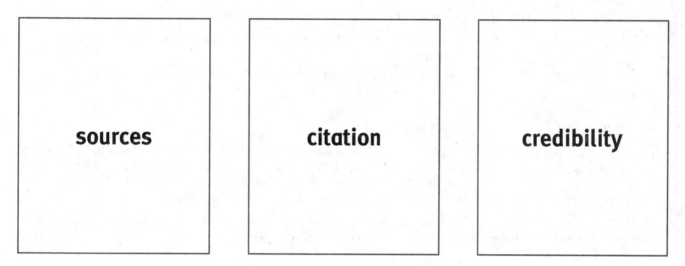

| sources | citation | credibility |

Sources

A source is any place you get valid information for your research. A source can be a document, a person, a film, a historical text, and so on. Sources are generally classified as primary or secondary.

- **Primary Source:** An account or document created by someone with firsthand knowledge or experience of an event. Letters, journal entries, **blogs**, eyewitness accounts, speeches, and interviews can all be all primary sources.

- **Secondary Source:** Documents supplied and compiled by people who do not have firsthand knowledge of an event. History textbooks, book reviews, documentary films, websites, and most magazine and newspaper articles are secondary sources.

4. Revisit the sources you have read in the unit. What kind of sources are they? When might it be effective to use primary sources to support your argument? When might it be effective to use secondary sources to support your argument?

_____

_____

_____

_____

_____

WORD CONNECTIONS

Etymology

The word **blog** was first used in the late 1990s as a shortened form of *weblog*, a website in the form of a journal. *Blog* combines the sound and meaning of two words, *web* and *log*, a system of word invention used by author Lewis Carroll in *Through the Looking-Glass*. The use of *blog* was picked up by Web companies and individual Internet users and led to other derivations such as the verb *blogging*, to write short, informal posts on a blog site.

VOCABULARY

ACADEMIC

By citing research, you avoid the mistake of **plagiarism**, which is using or imitating another person's words or ideas without giving proper credit. Whether intentional or accidental, plagiarism is not ethical and must be avoided in all writing.

When you **cite**, or provide a **citation**, you follow the practice of quoting or referring to sources of textual evidence. The word *cite* comes from the Latin word meaning "to set in motion." *Cite* has come to mean "to quote or refer to."

My Notes

Using Sources Ethically

When using someone else's ideas in your writing, it is critical that you give proper credit to the person who first stated the idea. **Plagiarism** occurs when you use someone else's writing in your own writing as if you came up with the idea. Properly **cite** your sources to help you avoid plagiarism.

To use sources ethically and avoid plagiarism, do the following:

- Properly quote and cite all language that is directly picked up from another source.
- Give proper credit to the originators of all ideas or concepts that you have paraphrased in your writing.

Citations

It is important to provide basic bibliographic information for sources. This practice helps you give credit to information that is not your own when you communicate your findings and thus avoid plagiarism. Basic bibliographic information includes the author, title, source, date, and medium of publication.

The following models show the MLA standard format for citing basic bibliographic information for common types of sources.

- **Book**

    Last name, First name of author. *Title of Book*. City of Publication: Publisher, Year of Publication. Medium of Publication.

    Example: Henley, Patricia. *The Hummingbird House*. Denver: MacMurray, 1999. Print.

- **Film or Video Recording (DVD)**

    Title of Film. Director. Distributor, Release year. Medium.

    Example: *Star Wars Episode IV: A New Hope*. Dir. George Lucas. Twentieth Century Fox, 2006. DVD.

- **Personal Interview (Conducted by Researcher)**

    Last Name, First Name Middle Name of Person Interviewed. Personal, Email, or Telephone interview. Day, Month (abbreviated), Year of Interview.

    Example: Jackson, Anne. Telephone interview. 6 Dec. 2012.

- **Internet Site**

    "Article or Specific Page Title." *Title of Website*. Name of Site Sponsor (if available), Date posted or last updated, if available. Medium of Publication. Day, Month (abbreviated), Year Accessed.

    Example: "Abraham Lincoln." *The White House*. Web. 16 Apr. 2013.

- **Magazine or Newspaper Article**

    Last name, First name of author. "Title of Article." *Title of Periodical*. Day Month Year: pages. Medium of publication.

    Example: Poniewozik, James. "TV Makes a Too-Close Call." *Time*. 20 Nov. 2000: 70–71. Print.

5. Imagine you are researching whether it is ethical to keep animals in zoos. You have used the following sources. Write basic bibliographic information for each.

Source	Bibliographic Information
You read a book on animal treatment in zoos called *Animal Attractions: Nature on Display in American Zoos,* by Elizabeth Hanson. It was published in 2002 in New York. The publishing company is Princeton University Press.	
You used information from a webpage titled *Classroom Magazine*. The copyright date is 2001. National Geographic hosts the site. The title of the article is "A Bear of a Job." You visited the site on 1/20/13.	
You conducted a phone interview with a zookeeper named Nancy Hawkes from Woodland Park Zoo in Seattle, Washington, on February 7, 2013.	

Reliability and Credibility

Any source you use must be reliable and **credible**. Evaluating a source's reliability and credibility will help you determine if you should use the information as part of your evidence when you communicate your findings. You can ask the following questions to determine if a source is reliable and credible:

- **Who is the author?** Can the author be trusted? Credible sources are written by authors respected in their fields of study. Reliable authors will cite their sources so that you can check the accuracy of and support for what they have written. (This is also a good way to find more sources for your own research.)

- **How recent is the source?** The choice to seek recent sources depends on your topic. While sources on the American Civil War may be decades old and still contain accurate information, sources on information technologies or other areas that are experiencing rapid changes need to be much more current.

- **What is the author's purpose, and who is the intended audience?** Is the author presenting an objective view of a topic, or does the author have a bias toward a certain point of view? Who is funding the research or writing of this source? What types of reader is the author trying to reach? When a source is written with a particular bias, its credibility could be called into question. The source may be credible; however, you need to be careful that your sources don't limit your coverage of a topic to one side of a debate. When a source has a particular bias, you must find research from the opposing viewpoint in order to gain a whole picture of the topic.

> **ACADEMIC VOCABULARY**
>
> To be **credible** is to be believable and trustworthy. Evidence must be credible in order to be convincing. The credibility of research information and of the researchers is enhanced when sources of evidence are properly evaluated and cited.

My Notes

Internet Sites

Be especially careful when evaluating Internet sources! Be critical of websites for which an author cannot be determined unless the site is associated with a reputable institution such as a respected university, a credible media outlet, a government program or department, or a well-known organization. Beware of using sites such as Wikipedia, which are collaboratively developed by users. Because anyone can add or change content, the validity of information on such sites may not meet the standards for academic research.

Some Internet sites may contain more reliable and credible information than others. A credible Internet source is one that contains information that is well researched, a bibliography or list of resources, and a statement of the site's purpose. One way to know whether a website is credible is through its domain suffix. The domain name is the web address, or Internet identity. The domain suffix, typically the three letters that follow the "dot," is the category in which that website falls.

Domain Suffix	Definition/Description
.com	Stands for "commercial." Websites with this suffix are created to make a profit from their Internet services. Typically these websites sell goods or services.
.org	Stands for "organization." Primarily used by nonprofit groups but available to any organization.
.net	Stands for "network." Used by Internet service providers or Web-hosting companies.
.edu	Stands for "education." Used by major universities or educational organizations and institutions.
.gov	Stands for "government." Used by local, state, and federal government sites.

6. Which of the domain suffixes in the chart would provide the most reliable and credible information for research on whether it is ethical to keep animals in a zoo? Why?

7. Which suffixes might provide the least reliable and credible information? Why?

☑ Check Your Understanding

Go back to the Internet source for which you recorded basic bibliographic information. Based only on the information you are given for the website, would you consider information from this Internet source to be reliable and credible? Why or why not?

Conducting Research

Think about the controversial topic you felt strongly about at the beginning of the unit or one you feel strongly about now. Apply what you have learned about sources, citation, and credibility as you plan for and conduct initial research on the topic. Follow the prompts in the graphic organizer as a guide.

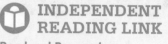

INDEPENDENT READING LINK

Read and Research

In your Reader/Writer Notebook, identify which sources have been quoted or paraphrased in your independent reading texts. Use one of the citations to find the original source for the information. Read the original source and compare the source to the material in your independent reading text.

Topic:

My current position:

Type of source:	Basic bibliographic information:	Is the source reliable and credible? Does the source have a bias? Explain.

Interesting information/Notes:

The Formality of It All: Style and Tone

Learning Strategies

Graphic Organizer
Substituting/Replacing
Self-Editing/Peer Editing
Quickwrite

Learning Targets

- Analyze the purpose of formal style and tone.
- Write letters using both formal and informal tone.

Preview

In this activity, you will learn about tone and practice using a formal style versus an informal style of writing.

VOCABULARY

LITERARY

Tone is the attitude that a writer or speaker displays toward his or her subject.

Formal style is a style of writing or speaking that is appropriate for formal communication, such as in academics or business.

Identifying Tone

1. Authors of argumentative texts use **tone** as a way of convincing you, the reader or listener, to adopt their viewpoint, or agree with their claim. Listen to your teacher read a line of dialogue and choose a word from the Tone Word Bank to describe the attitude, or tone.

Tone Word Bank

angry	sad	sentimental
sharp	cold	upset
urgent	complimentary	condescending
bored	poignant	sympathetic
afraid	happy	confused
apologetic	childish	humorous
joyful	calm	mocking
sarcastic	sweet	bitter
tired	shocked	proud
giddy	serious	dramatic

2. When you are writing an argumentative text, you need to select a tone that is appropriate for your audience. Look back at the arguments you read in Activities 3.3 and 3.4. Who do you think was the intended audience for each argument? Why do you think so?

My Notes

3. Think about the audience and purpose for each of the situations in the graphic organizer. Which style of writing would be most appropriate for each situation—formal style or informal style?

Audience/Purpose	Appropriate Style
You are writing an essay for a school exam.	
You are writing a caption for a picture you are posting on social media.	
You are writing a letter to your principal to convince him or her to fund a new sports team.	

Formal Style Versus Informal Style

4. Look at the following examples of formal style and informal style. What are the differences you notice? Try to write your own definitions of *formal style* and *informal style* and check them against a dictionary or glossary. Then complete the chart by translating each sentence into its opposite style.

Formal Style:

Informal Style:

Formal	Informal
Please refrain from talking.	Hey, quit talking.
Will you be attending the dance this evening?	Are you gonna go to the dance later?
Hello. How are you today?	
	Too much homework stinks.
	That lunch made me gag.
He launched his bicycle off the ramp and flew through the air.	

LANGUAGE & WRITER'S CRAFT: Formal Style

It is important to maintain consistency in style and tone so readers can follow your ideas. Readers will be confused if your writing jumps back and forth between formal and informal style.

Consistent Formal Style: *You must adhere to the guidelines. Your cooperation will be noted and appreciated.*

Inconsistent Formal Style: *You must adhere to the guidelines. It would be totally awesome if you'd do that.*

Consistent Informal Style: *The speaker says we should stop using plastic bags. She gave some good reasons for this.*

Inconsistent Informal Style: *The speaker suggests discontinuing the use of plastic bags. Her reasons were totally bogus.*

Use the following list of characteristics of formal style to keep your writing style consistently formal.

Formal Style

DO:	DO NOT:
• **Adhere to the rules of proper grammar and mechanics.**	• **Do not use contractions.** They indicate an informal style. **Example:** Don't be late.
• **Use precise, specific diction:** Use diction that is specific to the topic and precise for the audience. **Example:** During the debate, the opponent provided several pieces of **evidence** to support her **claim** and refute her opponent's **argument**. (The words *evidence*, *claim*, *refute*, and *argument* are specific words used when writing about argumentative tasks.)	• **Do not use slang words.** They indicate an informal style. **Example:** During the debate, the opponent was off the wall and said totally bogus things.
	• **Avoid non sequiturs.** Non sequiturs are sentences that do not flow with the ideas being communicated by the rest of the paragraph. **Example:** Too much homework puts extra stress on students. It impacts them in all aspects of life. **I like watching television.** The stress will counteract any benefits gained from doing the homework.
• **Establish your tone and utilize it throughout your writing.**	• **Avoid using texting and social media shorthand.** **Example:** Id luv 2 go 2 the game. LOL!

PRACTICE In your Reader/Writer Notebook, rewrite the following paragraph to be consistent in formal style and tone.

Last month, this crazy guest speaker came to school. She presented several ideas for ways we could save water at home and at school. To be honest, I thought her ideas were way off the wall, and I didn't think they would fly, anyway. But she asked us to implement at least two of her suggestions for one month, to journal about what we were doing, and then to ping her. My family okayed my proposal, so for one month we all took shorter showers, and we only ran the dishwasher and washing machine when they were full. We also cut the water when brushing our teeth. My dad recorded the water meter reading at the beginning and the end of the month and compared them to the previous month. The results blew me away! We saved tons of water. I dropped her a note, and she got right back to me. Now I'm telling all of my friends to check out her website and get on her water-saving wagon.

Working from the Text

5. Use the graphic organizer to help you analyze the tone and style of "A Teacher's Defense of Homework" in Activity 3.3. Provide evidence from the text of Townsend's specific diction and use of precise nouns and verbs.

Purpose	Examples of Formal Style

6. What is Townsend's tone? Is her tone appropriate for the audience and purpose? Why?

☑ Check Your Understanding

Quickwrite: Why is it important to use a formal style and tone in argumentative writing? What happens to your argument when you don't maintain a consistent formal style and tone? Use the My Notes section to jot down your thoughts.

📝 Argumentative Writing Prompt

You are trying to convince your principal to change a school rule or policy (e.g., cell phone usage, school starting time). Work collaboratively to write two letters to experiment with tone and formal style. For Letter 1, write a short letter to your principal using informal style and a friendly tone. For Letter 2, transform your first letter to use formal style and a businesslike tone. Be sure to:

- State a clear claim and support it with clear reasons and relevant evidence using reliable and credible sources.

- Pay attention to style and tone.

- Provide a concluding statement that wraps up your argument.

Be prepared to share both letters with your peers.

📦 INDEPENDENT READING LINK

Read and Connect

Look for examples of formal and informal style used in your independent reading. In what context is each style used? Who is the speaker? Who is the audience? What is the subject under discussion? Record some examples of tone in your Reader/Writer Notebook and log your responses to the questions for each.

Learning Strategies

Graphic Organizer
Drafting
Self-Editing/Peer Editing

My Notes

Learning Targets
- Evaluate the purpose of visual displays for communicating information.
- Create a visual display to support a claim.

Preview

In this activity, you will read data about the use of technology and use the information to create a graphic of your own.

Types of Graphics

Graphics can make arguments more persuasive and help viewers understand the evidence in a new way. They can provide data, show images, or illustrate a process. Every graphic tells its own story:

Line graphs show change in quantities over time.

Bar graphs often compare quantities within categories.

Pie graphs or **circle graphs** show proportions by dividing a circle into different sections.

Flowcharts show a sequence or steps.

Timelines list events in chronological order.

Tables use columns to present information in categories that are easy to compare.

Diagrams are drawings that explain or show the parts of something.

1. Use the preceding descriptions to identify what type of graphic each of these is.

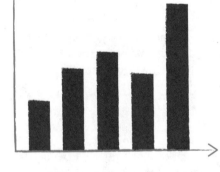

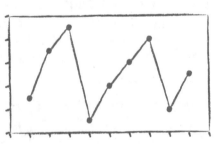

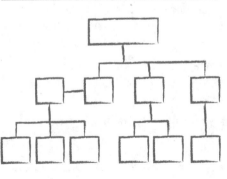

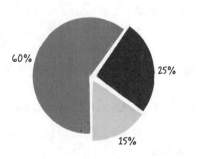

Reading Graphics

Graphics need to be read as closely as print texts. Here are some tips for reading graphics:

- **Read the title.** It tells you what the graphic is about.
- **Read the labels.** Headings, subheadings, and numbers tell you what the graphic is about and describe the specific information given for each category of the graphic.
- **Analyze other features.** Follow arrows and lines to understand the direction or order of events or steps. Read numbers carefully, noting how amounts or intervals of time increase or decrease. If there is a key, pay attention to why different colors are used.

Setting a Purpose for Reading

- Highlight statistics that surprise or interest you.
- Use the My Notes section to briefly summarize the information in each graphic.
- Circle unknown words and phrases. Try to determine the meaning of the words by using context clues, word parts, or a dictionary.

Circle Graph

Figure 7. Proportion of daily computer, tablet, and smartphone use devoted to various activities, among U.S. teens. *by Common Sense Media*

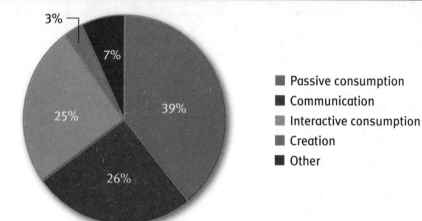

- Passive consumption
- Communication
- Interactive consumption
- Creation
- Other

Making Observations

- What are your first thoughts about the graphic?
- Are you surprised by any of the data presented in this graphic?

Returning to the Text

- Return to the graphic as you respond to the following questions. Use evidence to support your responses.
- Write any additional questions you have about the circle graph in your Reader/Writer Notebook.

2. What does this graphic show? Do not quote the title exactly.

_____

_____

_____

_____

3. What does the whole circle represent? What do the slices represent?

_____

_____

_____

_____

4. Why did the author choose to present this information in a circle graph?

_____

_____

_____

_____

5. How is the information arranged in the circle graph when compared to the key? Why do you think the author chose to organize the information this way?

_____

_____

_____

_____

6. Make a prediction about what each category means. What does the author mean by _passive consumption, communication, interactive consumption_, and _creation?_

_____

_____

_____

_____

Table

Consumption, communication, and creation: Time spent using digital media daily, by activity. *by Common Sense Media*		
Activity	Among Tweens	Among Teens
Passive consumption	**1:02 (41%)**	**2:06 (39%)**
• Watching online videos	:25	:35
• Watching TV	:18	:22
• Reading	:01	:05
• Listening to music	:18	1:04
Interactive consumption	**:56 (37%)**	**1:19 (25%)**
• Playing games	:44	:44
• Browsing websites	:12	:36
Communication	**:22 (14%)**	**1:24 (26%)**
• Using social media	:16	1:11
• Video-chatting	:06	:13
Creation	**:05 (3%)**	**:09 (3%)**
• Making art or music	:04	:06
• Writing	:01	:04
Other	**:08 (5%)**	**:23 (7%)**
Total	**2:33**	**5:21**

Making Observations
- Based on your own experience, do you think the data in the graphic is accurate?
- What data surprised you in this graphic?

Returning to the Text

- Return to the graphic as you respond to the following questions. Use evidence to support your responses.
- Write any additional questions you have about the table in your Reader/Writer Notebook.

7. What does this graphic show? Do not quote the title exactly.

_____

_____

_____

_____

8. What do the numbers with colons represent? What do the percentages represent?

_____

_____

_____

_____

9. Who spends more time on devices each day, tweens or teens? How much time do they spend?

_____

_____

_____

_____

10. What two major things are being compared in this table? Why did the author choose to use a table?

_____

_____

_____

_____

11. What does the row at the bottom show? Why did the author include the last row?

_____

_____

_____

_____

12. Look back at the prediction you made for question 6. Was your prediction confirmed? If not, how can you revise your prediction?

_____

_____

_____

Working from the Text

13. How is the content of the two graphics alike?

_____

_____

_____

14. How is the content of the two graphics different?

_____

_____

_____

_____

15. What is the purpose of each graphic?

_____

_____

_____

_____

16. How does the information in the second graphic help you better understand the information in the first graphic?

_____

_____

_____

_____

17. Your teacher will now show you a video clip. What are the visuals used? Why are they used?

_____

_____

_____

_____

My Notes

Writing to Sources: Argument

Work collaboratively to write a short argument supporting the following claim: *Teens spend too much time being passive consumers on their devices.* Be sure to:

- State your claim clearly at the beginning of your argument.
- Provide clear reasons and evidence from texts you've read to support your claim.
- Maintain a consistent formal style and tone.

Adding a Visual

After you write your argument, create a visual display to support the claim. Be creative but purposeful. Use one of the types of graphics described in this activity or create your own type of graphic. Make sure the visual display is clear and supports your argument.

Consider other visual or multimedia components (images, music, sound) that might be helpful for your display.

Presenting Your Argument

- State your claim clearly and speak at an appropriate rate with good volume and proper enunciation.
- Check that your reasons and evidence are researched properly and clearly support the claim.
- Use your visual to help the class understand your information in a new way.
- Use a formal style and a tone appropriate for the purpose.
- Maintain eye contact and use natural gestures.

☑ Check Your Understanding

Why are visual displays, such as charts or graphs, helpful in trying to convince an audience? Which of the visual displays that you viewed was most effective? Why?

INDEPENDENT READING LINK

Read and Research

Find two graphics that relate to the controversy you are reading about for your independent reading. In your Reader/Writer Notebook, briefly summarize the information presented in each and keep notes about how you might use the information in a debate.

Debate It: Organizing and Communicating an Argument

Learning Strategies

Marking the Text
Metacognitive Markers
Graphic Organizer
Debate
Paraphrasing

Learning Targets

- Summarize the key ideas of an article about the pros and cons of social networking.
- Plan an argument about social networking by writing reasons and evidence that support a position.
- Present a position on the controversy in a debate using evidence from research and contributing ideas clearly and responding to others' ideas.
- Integrate ideas from multiple texts to build knowledge and vocabulary about technology and communication.

Preview

In this activity, you will read an article about the impacts of social media on kids and discuss and debate the positives and negatives of social media.

Setting a Purpose for Reading

- As you read the following news article, use the metacognitive markers "?" and "!" (e.g., wow, surprising, I can relate, etc.).
- Circle unknown words and phrases. Try to determine the meaning of the words by using context clues, word parts, or a dictionary.

Introducing the Strategy: Metacognitive Markers

Using metacognitive markers involves marking the text with symbols to reflect the thinking you are doing as you read. After reading, you can scan the text and use your markers to quickly find evidence when you are talking or writing about a text. Here are the markers:

? Use a question mark for questions you have about the text.

! Use an exclamation point for a reaction to what you are reading.

* Use an asterisk for a comment about the text.

_ Use an underline to identify a key idea or detail in the text.

About the Author

As a bureau chief, writer, reporter, and author, Katy Steinmetz has covered topics from technology to culture and language. Steinmetz is a graduate of Columbia University and the University of Missouri, where she studied English and journalism. Her work adds insight to the growing debate about the pros and cons of social media.

KNOWLEDGE QUEST

Knowledge Question:

Over time, how has technology changed the way we communicate with friends and family?

In Activity 3.8, you will read two texts about the positive and negative effects of social media. While you read and build knowledge about the topic, think about your answer to the Knowledge Question.

My Notes

proportions: groups or percentages

phubbing: ignoring a friend in favor of looking at a smartphone or other device

Article

Teens Are Over Face-to-Face Communication, Study Says

from **TIME Magazine**
by **Katy Steinmetz**

1   When Common Sense surveyed roughly a thousand teenagers about their habits back in 2012, most of them said that their favorite way to communicate with friends was "in person." Fast forward six years, and face-to-face communication has apparently lost its youthful sheen.

2   Most teens now say their favorite mode of communication is texting (35%), according to a new survey released Monday from Common Sense, a children's and media advocacy organization. Compared to 2012, much higher **proportions** selected social media (16%) and video chatting (10%), while less than one third said they prefer chatting with friends face-to-face.

3   Researcher Vicky Rideout, who worked on both reports, suggests that the findings could mean that Americans are "beginning to see some kind of fundamental shift in how we interact with each other." While that might raise red flags—particularly for anyone born before the founding of Google— Rideout also notes that teenagers reported that technology is having positive effects on their lives.

4   The main focus of the report, which is based on responses from 1,141 13- to 17-year-olds, was social media usage. When asked about how using social media makes them feel, around one in five teens said that it had effects like making them feel more popular and more confident, as well as less lonely and less depressed. A very small percentage said the opposite. "Even the most depressed teens are likely to say that social media makes them feel better," Rideout says.

5   The report also suggests that young people see downsides. Many struggle to tear themselves away from their devices, even if they're aware that "**phubbing**" can be bad for relationships. Nearly half (44%) say they get frustrated with their friends for being on their phones when they're hanging out together, yet an even greater proportion (54%) admit that they get distracted by social media when they should be paying more attention to the people that they're with.

6   About one-third of respondents said that they never, or hardly ever, put their phones away when visiting family, doing homework, or having a meal with someone. An even higher proportion (55%) say that their phones are almost always out when they're spending time with friends.

7   Today's teenagers report using social media more frequently than teens did six years ago. Back then, about one-third said they used it more than once a day; now more than two-thirds do. That shift has no doubt been aided by the increased rate of smartphone ownership among the younger set. Nearly 90% of teenagers now say they have a smartphone, compared to 41% who said so in 2012. Many young people (72%) also believe that tech companies **manipulate** users in order to get them to spend more time on their devices, according to the survey.

8   The report also provides hard numbers to back up the observation that teenagers are pretty over Facebook. Nearly 70% said that **platform** was their "main social media site" in 2012. Now just 15% do. Instead, more than 40% say their go-to platform is Snapchat, which was launching around the same time the last survey was put in the field.

9   Technology continues to be a rapidly evolving landscape, and Rideout says more work needs to be done to understand the **net effect** technology is having on kids' well-being. For now, she recommends encouraging teenagers to use media in "**mindful**" ways, so that they are capable of putting their devices down when circumstances demand it.

✺ Knowledge Quest
- What are your first thoughts about the article?
- What captures your attention most about the way teen communication is described in this article?

manipulate: covertly or negatively

platform: technology's operating system

net effect: final effect or result influence

mindful: aware

Returning to the Text

- Return to the text as you respond to the following questions. Use text evidence to support your responses.
- Write any additional questions you have about the news article in your Reader/Writer Notebook.

1. **KQ** What does the word *sheen* mean in the first paragraph? Use context clues and a dictionary to help you decide. Then tell why you think the author used the words "youthful sheen" to describe something that face-to-face communication has lost due to teens' use of social media.

   _____

   _____

   _____

   _____

2. **KQ** Who is most likely to be alarmed by teens' shift away from using face-to-face communication, and what might be the cause for their alarm?

   _____

   _____

   _____

   _____

3. What do teens admit are some pitfalls of social media? What is the author's purpose in paragraphs 1–6, and why is it important to know the pitfalls of social media?

   _____

   _____

   _____

   _____

4. What do teens believe when it comes to pressure and manipulation from tech companies? How does this affect their use of cell phones?

   _____

   _____

   _____

   _____

5. **KQ** In paragraph 8, it says that teens who used to use Facebook as their "main social media site" now use Snapchat instead. What do you infer is the reason for this?

   _____

   _____

   _____

6. How does the concept of well-being and mindfulness in paragraph 9 tell you if a person is "in control of" or "being controlled by" technology and social media?

_____

_____

_____

_____

Working from the Text

7. Work collaboratively to examine the main idea of the news article. Use a graphic organizer similar to the one that follows. Write the positive effects of social networking according to the article on the left side and the negative effects on the right.

Positive	Negative

8. **Group Discussion:** Do you agree or disagree with the statement that *social media usage has a negative impact on kids*? Use the following protocol to discuss your ideas with your peers.

- One participant shares.
- The other participants take turns responding directly to the person who shared.
- The first participant responds to or builds on his or her peers' comments (through reflecting and paraphrasing) and has "the last word."

Follow the same pattern until all participants have shared. As you share and respond to the discussion, keep these points in mind:

- Listen actively to each speaker's specific position and claims.
- Determine whether the speaker fully supports his or her claims with reasons and evidence.
- Ask questions if you need to clarify a point.
- Remember to support your own argument and claim with both reasons and clear, relevant evidence.
- Respond appropriately to any questions you are asked.

My Notes

☑ **Focus on the Sentence**

Write two statements based on information your peers shared during your discussion and then write two follow-up questions you asked or would like to ask.

Statement 1: _____

_____

Statement 2: _____

_____

Question 1: _____

_____

Question 2: _____

_____

Setting a Purpose for Reading

- As you read the following informational text, continue to use metacognitive markers to engage with the text and, as you gain more information, to support a position on the value of social networking.
- Circle unknown words and phrases. Try to determine the meaning of the words by using context clues, word parts, or a dictionary.

Informational Text

Are Social Networking Sites Good for Our Society?

by **ProCon.org**

Introduction: 76% of American adults online use social networking sites such as Facebook, Instagram, Twitter, LinkedIn, and Pinterest, as of July 2015, up from 26% in 2008. [26][189]. On social media sites like these, users may develop biographical profiles, communicate with friends and strangers, do research, and share thoughts, photos, music, links, and more.

KNOWLEDGE QUEST

Knowledge Question:

Over time, how has technology changed the way we communicate with friends and family?

Social Media and the Spread of Information

Pro: Social media spreads information faster than any other media.

Evidence

- 78.5% of traditional media reporters polled used social media to check for breaking news. [190]

- 59% of Twitter users and 31% of Facebook users polled followed breaking news on these sites. [191]

- Social media sites are one of the top news sources for 46% of Americans, compared to 66% for television, 26% for printed newspapers, and 23% for radio. [192]

- President Donald Trump said that the immediacy that Twitter affords him is the reason why he tweets, noting that press conferences and press releases take too long to reach the public. [271]

Con: Social media enables the spread of unreliable and false information.

Evidence

- 64% of people who use Twitter for news say that they have encountered something they "later discovered wasn't true," and 16% of Twitter news users say that "they had retweeted or posted a tweet they later discovered to be false." [227]

- In the three months prior to the 2016 US presidential election, false news stories about the two candidates were shared a total of 37.6 million times on Facebook. [269]

- A University of Michigan study found that even when false information is corrected, the numbers of people who see or share the correction via social media is lower than number who saw or shared the false information in the first place. [272]

Social Media and Education

Pro: Social media sites help students do better at school.

Evidence

- 59% of students with access to the Internet report that they use social media to discuss educational topics and 50% use the sites to talk about school assignments. [9]

- After George Middle School in Portland, Oregon, introduced a social media program to engage students, grades went up by 50%, chronic absenteeism went down by 33%, and 20% of students school-wide voluntarily completed extra-credit assignments.[10] [11]

Con: Students who are heavy social media users tend to have lower grades.

Evidence

- 31% of teens say that using social media during homework reduces the quality of their work. [235]

- Students who used social media while studying scored 20% lower on tests. [84]

- One study found that in schools which introduced a ban on cell phones, student performance improved 6.41%. [234]

- Another found that grades began a steady decline after secondary school students reached 30 minutes of daily screen time. After four hours, average GPAs dropped one full grade. [184]

Social Media and Relationships

Pro: Social media allows people to improve their relationships and make new friends.

Evidence

- 72% of all teens connect with friends via social media. [200]

- 83% of these teens report that social media helps them feel more connected to information about their friends' lives, 70% report feeling more connected to their friends' feelings, and 57% make new friends. [200]

Con: Social media can lead to stress and offline relationship problems.

Evidence

- 31% of teens who use social media have fought with a friend because of something that happened online. [236]

- One study found that the more Facebook friends a person has, the more stressful Facebook is to use. [87]

Social Media and Social Interaction

Pro: Social media facilitates face-to-face interaction.

Evidence

- People use social media to network at in-person events and get to know people before personal, business, and other meetings. [23]

- Pew Research Center's Internet and American Life Project found that messaging on social media leads to face-to-face interactions when plans are made via the sites and social media users messaged close friends an average of 39 days each year while seeing close friends in person 210 days each year. [24]

Con: Social media causes people to spend less time interacting face-to-face.

Evidence

- A USC Annenberg School study found that the percentage of people reporting less face-to-face time with family in their homes rose from 8% in 2000 to 34% in 2011. [98]

- 32% reported using social media or texting during meals (47% of 18-34 year olds) [99] instead of talking with family and friends.

My Notes

_____
_____
_____
_____
_____
_____
_____
_____
_____
_____
_____
_____
_____

Footnotes & Sources

The background and pro and con arguments were written by ProCon.org staff based upon input from the following footnotes (directly referenced) and sources (used for general research and not directly referenced). To find the complete directory of sources, visit the ProCon.org website and search for Social Networking.

9. National School Boards Association, "Creating and Connecting: Research and Guidelines on Online Social—and Educational—Networking," nsba.org, July 2007

10. Sarah Kessler, "The Case for Social Media in Schools," mashable.com, Sep. 29, 2010

11. Elizabeth Delmatoff, "How Social Media Transformed Our School Community," oregoned.org, Apr. 2010

23. Morgan, "5 Ways Social Media Can Facilitate Offline Networking," sociableboost.com, May 8, 2012

24. Annalisa Rodriguez, "Social Media Doesn't Mean Social Isolation," usatodayeducate.com, Oct. 16, 2012

Knowledge Quest

- What are some ideas from this informational text that seemed contradictory?
- What statistic about social media use surprised you the most?

Returning to the Text

- Return to the text as you respond to the following questions. Use text evidence to support your responses.
- Write any additional questions you have about the news article in your Reader/Writer Notebook.

9. Based on what you read in the "Social Media and the Spread of Information" table, what suggestion would you make to people who rely on social media for breaking news?

_____

_____

_____

_____

10. Why does social media help some students do better at school but not others?

_____

_____

_____

_____

11. **KQ** What does the word *offline* mean in the "Social Media and Relationships" table? Use context clues and a dictionary to help you decide. Then think about what the article "Teens Are Over Face-to-Face Communication, Study Says" has to say about the effects of social media on *offline* relationships. What frustrations do teens describe, and how might these frustrations lead to the kinds of conflict described in the table?

_____

_____

_____

_____

12. **KQ** What evidence in the "Social Media and Social Interaction" table is supported by statistics about in-person interaction in the article "Teens Are Over Face-to-Face Communication, Study Says"?

_____

_____

_____

_____

13. **KQ** How can synthesizing information from "Are Social Networking Sites Good for Our Society?" and "Teens Are Over Face-to-Face Communication, Study Says" help you understand how to use social media to foster in-person interactions?

_____

_____

_____

_____

14. **KQ** Why is data helpful when providing an argument or claim? How do the multiple sources in "Are Social Networking Sites Good for Our Society?" help you form arguments about the pros and cons of social media?

_____

_____

_____

_____

INDEPENDENT READING LINK

You can continue to build your knowledge about the ways technology has changed how we communicate by reading other articles at ZINC Reading Labs. Search for *communication technology*.

◯ Knowledge Quest

After reading the article and informational text on the pros and cons of social media, what has changed about your understanding of how technology has affected our communication with friends and family over time? Do you think the effect has been more positive or negative? Discuss your ideas with a partner and then write a summary of your discussion.

Working from the Text

15. What are the four categories of pros and cons presented in the article?

_____

_____

_____

_____

16. How is the evidence organized and presented?

_____

_____

_____

17. How does the organization of the evidence help readers?

_____

_____

_____

_____

18. Which evidence did you find most interesting? Why was the evidence interesting?

_____

_____

_____

_____

19. Summarize three or four key ideas from the preceding text that support your position on whether social media and networking are good for society.

_____

_____

_____

_____

_____

_____

_____

_____

_____

20. Use the following KWHL graphic organizer to record information as you continue researching the topic of social media and networking. After reading the texts in this activity, what additional questions do you have? What reasons and evidence do you need to support your position?

Claim:

K	W	H	L
Paraphrase the ideas that stand out to you in relationship to your assigned side of the issue.	What further questions do you have?	Where could you find answers? What other reliable and credible resources could you access?	Add notes from your research.

✅ **Check Your Understanding**

Quickwrite: Summarize the findings of your research.

_____

_____

_____

_____

Gaining Perspectives

Think about other forms of media, such as radio, television, fliers, newspapers, and magazines. Do other media have the same type of influence over people and communities as social media? Why or why not? With a partner, imagine you are trying to encourage people to develop good habits, like exercising or eating healthy foods. Choose a good habit you would like to promote and then think about how you could use social media to promote it. Which form of media would reach the most people in your network? Which forms of media would have the most staying power and credibility? What could happen if you used more than one form of media to network? Discuss your ideas with classmates. Then summarize the outcome of your discussion in your Reader/Writer Notebook.

Preparing to Debate

21. Consider all of the research you have done and complete the graphic organizer to prepare for the debate. Remember that the statement you are arguing is whether you agree or disagree that social media and networking has a negative impact on kids.

Preparing an Argument		
Claim:		
Reason 1:	**Reason 2:**	**Reason 3:**
Evidence (*facts, statistics, examples, observations, quotations, and expert opinion*)	**Evidence** (*facts, statistics, examples, observations, quotations, and expert opinion*)	**Evidence** (*facts, statistics, examples, observations, quotations, and expert opinion*)
Source Citation:	**Source Citation:**	**Source Citation:**
Tone:		
Language (words/phrases) to use to create a formal style:		

22. After completing your research, create a visual display (e.g., a graph or chart) that will help support your claim.

Debating the Topic

During the debate, be sure to:

- State a clear claim.
- Support your claim with reasons and evidence; when necessary, offer new support or elaborate on a previous point.
- Maintain a formal style and appropriate tone that adheres to the conventions of language.
- Speak clearly, slowly, and loudly enough to be heard by the audience.
- Maintain comfortable eye contact with your audience and use natural gestures.
- Listen to other speakers' claims, reasons, and evidence and distinguish between claims that are supported by credible evidence and those that are not.

Try using the following types of sentence starters when you respond to the ideas of others:

- You claim that ... , but have you considered ... ?
- Even though you just said that ... , I believe that ...
- I agree with what you said about ... , but I think that ...
- You make a good point about ... , and I would add that ...

When you are in the outer circle, create and use a chart such as the one that follows to take notes on the comments made by the inner circle. Be prepared to share your observations.

Argument FOR	Supported by evidence? yes/no	Argument AGAINST	Supported by evidence? yes/no
	_____ _____		_____ _____
	yes/no _____ _____		yes/no _____ _____
	yes/no _____ _____		yes/no _____ _____

After the debate: Was your position strengthened, weakened, or changed completely as a result of the evidence for or against each argument? Explain.

☑ Check Your Understanding

Respond to the Essential Question: How do you effectively communicate in order to convince someone? Add your response to your Portfolio.

🎲 Independent Reading Checkpoint

In your Reader/Writer Notebook, write a few paragraphs describing a controversy at the center of your Independent Reading texts. Summarize the various sides of the argument. Then write a claim you would be able to support with reasons and evidence.

Researching and Debating a Controversy

📝 ASSIGNMENT

Work collaboratively to research one side of a controversy that is affecting your school, community, or society. Then participate in a modified debate in which you argue your position and incorporate a visual display with appropriate headings and labels and/or multimedia for support.

Planning and Prewriting: Take time to make a plan for generating ideas and research questions.	▪ What is your issue, who does this issue affect, and what side will you be arguing? ▪ How can you state your position clearly as a claim? ▪ What questions will guide your research?
Researching: Gather information from a variety of credible sources.	▪ Where can you find sources, and how can you tell that the sources are reliable, credible, and useful? ▪ Which strategies will you use to help you understand informational texts? ▪ How will you take notes by paraphrasing reasons and evidence and recording bibliographic information?
Preparing and Creating: Plan talking points and create a visual display.	▪ What kind of graphic organizer could help you select the best reasons and evidence from your research? ▪ How will you select talking points and create index cards for each point to support your claim? How can you ensure you are using your sources ethically? How can your notes help you use formal, conventional language? ▪ How will you create a visual that will enhance your talking points? ▪ How can the Scoring Guide help you evaluate how well you are prepared to meet the requirements of the assignment?
Speaking and Listening: Actively participate in and observe the class debates.	▪ How will you ensure you use elements of good public speaking, such as speaking at an appropriate rate and volume with clear enunciation and using eye contact and natural gestures? ▪ How will you be sure that you and the other speakers all have the opportunity to voice your opinions? ▪ How will you use your visual display to support your argument? ▪ How will you complete a viewing guide to ensure active listening as an audience member?

Reflection

After completing this Embedded Assessment, think about how you went about accomplishing this task and respond to the following:

- Did your position on the issue remain the same or change after the discussion? Explain your position and what caused it to remain the same or change.
- What part of preparing for the debate was your strongest (e.g., researching, organizing the argument, collaboration, creating the visual display)? Explain.
- What part of the debate was your strongest (e.g., explaining ideas, using formal language, speaking, listening)? Explain.

SCORING GUIDE

Scoring Criteria	Exemplary	Proficient	Emerging	Incomplete
Ideas	The argument • shows extensive evidence of the student's ability to gather evidence, form questions to refocus inquiry, and evaluate the credibility of a variety of sources. • avoids plagiarism by including properly cited bibliographic information.	The argument • provides sufficient evidence of the student's ability to gather evidence, form questions to refocus inquiry, and evaluate the credibility of multiple sources. • avoids plagiarism by including basic bibliographic information.	The argument • provides insufficient evidence of the student's ability to gather evidence, form questions to refocus inquiry, and evaluate the credibility of multiple sources. • includes partial or inaccurate bibliographic information.	The argument • provides little or no evidence of the student's use of a research process. • lacks bibliographic information or contains information that appears to have been plagiarized.
Structure	The debater • sequences reasons and evidence to support a claim effectively. • integrates visual or multimedia displays to enhance and clarify information. • transitions smoothly between talking points; responds to others' ideas by contributing relevant new support and elaboration.	The debater • sequences reasons and evidence to support a claim logically. • uses an appropriate visual or multimedia display to clarify information. • follows protocol to transition between talking points; avoids repetition when contributing new support or elaboration.	The debater • uses flawed sequencing; supports the claim ineffectively. • uses a weak or unclear visual or multimedia display. • transitions between talking points inconsistently; contributes primarily unrelated and/or repetitive support and elaboration to the discussion.	The debater • does not support the claim. • lacks a visual or multimedia display. • does not follow rules for group discussion.
Use of Language	The debater • uses effective eye contact, gestures, volume, pacing, and enunciation. • demonstrates command of the conventions of standard English grammar, usage, and language. • maintains a consistently appropriate style and tone.	The debater • uses sufficient eye contact, gestures, volume, pacing, and enunciation. • demonstrates adequate command of the conventions of standard English grammar, usage, and language. • maintains a generally appropriate style and tone.	The debater • uses eye contact, gestures, volume, pacing, and enunciation unevenly. • demonstrates partial command of the conventions of standard English grammar, usage, and language. • maintains an inconsistently appropriate style and/or tone.	The debater • uses flawed or ineffective speaking skills. • commits frequent errors in standard English grammar, usage, and language. • uses an inappropriate style and/or tone.

Unpacking Embedded Assessment 2

Learning Strategies

Think-Pair-Share
Graphic Organizer
Previewing

My Notes

Learning Targets

- Analyze and summarize the skills and knowledge needed to complete Embedded Assessment 2 successfully.

Preview

In this activity, you will unpack Embedded Assessment 2 and preview the next half of the unit.

Making Connections

In the first part of this unit, you learned about elements essential to argumentative writing: claims, reasons, and evidence. In this part of the unit, you will expand on your writing skills by writing an argumentative letter to persuade an audience to agree with your position on an issue.

Essential Questions

Reflect on your increased understanding of the Essential Questions. Based on your current understanding, how would you answer these questions now?

- Why do we have controversy in society?
- How do we communicate in order to convince others?

Developing Vocabulary

In your Reader/Writer Notebook, look at the new vocabulary you learned as you were introduced to argumentative writing in the first half of this unit. Re-sort the words in the graphic organizer, once again using the QHT strategy. Notice which words have moved from one column to another.

Academic Vocabulary	Literary Terms
controversy	tone
argument	formal style
claim	
reasons	
evidence	
research	
citation	
plagiarism	
credible	

Q	H	T

Unpacking Embedded Assessment 2

Read the assignment for Embedded Assessment 2: Writing an Argumentative Letter.

Think about a topic (subject, event, idea, or controversy) that you truly care about and take a position on it. Write an argumentative letter to convince an audience to support your position on the topic.

In your own words, summarize what you will need to know to complete this assessment successfully. With your class, create a graphic organizer to represent the skills and knowledge you will need to complete the tasks identified in the Embedded Assessment.

INDEPENDENT READING LINK

Reading Plan

To support your learning in the second half of the unit, continue reading books, magazine articles, or news articles that explore a current "hot topic" or controversial issue.

My Notes

Learning Targets

- Explore rhetorical appeals used in argumentative writing.
- Read closely to identify claim, reasons, and evidence and how they support an author's purpose.
- Generate ideas and apply an organizational pattern to write an argumentative paragraph that supports a claim with sound reasons and evidence.

Preview

In this activity, you will explore argument and persuasion by reading an argumentative letter and doing research to draft an argumentative paragraph of your own.

Thinking About Persuasion

1. Think about times in the past when you tried to convince someone to believe or do something. Were you successful? Write at least four examples of times you tried to be persuasive and what the outcome was of each.

Times I Was Persuasive	Outcome

2. For each successful outcome listed in the preceding chart, write down the reasons you gave that persuaded the other person. Try to list four or five supporting reasons for each example.

3. Which of the examples given in step 2 were appeals to the emotions of your listener? Which were appeals to your listener's logic, or intelletual appeals?

4. With a group of classmates, discuss the reasons you each recorded and whether they were appeals to emotion or logic. Based on the reasons you used, were emotional appeals or logical appeals more effective?

Setting a Purpose for Reading

- As you read, pause after each paragraph to think about what new arguments or information the paragraph added.
- Circle unknown words and phrases. Try to determine the meaning of the words by using context clues, word parts, or a dictionary.

Letter

Student Draft Letter

Dear **Legislator,**

1   We live in the 21st century and see technology all around us. Americans have access to the Internet almost everywhere, at home, on cell phones, and even at school. For some students, school is the only access they have to the Internet. The web also provides many more learning opportunities and prepares us students for high school and the real world. Internet access for students in school libraries is crucial for our success.

My Notes

My Notes

2   Students need school access to the Internet because computers and the price for Internet service can sometimes be too costly for a family. Internet service providers, such as Quest, charge an average of fifty dollars a month. Many times teachers assign projects that students need access to computers to complete. Internet access in the school library is sometimes the only option for numerous pupils. If that only option is taken away, innocent students will be penalized for not being able to fulfill a school project.

3   When we get to high school, we will be getting prepared for the real-world that is coming to us sooner than we think. In the technology filled society that we are about to embark on, we will have to know many skills on how to best utilize a computer and the Internet. My cousin is a good example of someone who is utilizing the technology skills he learned as a teenager. He is in college and takes courses online. Taking online courses allows him to have a job and go to college at the same time. He says he spends close to 10 hours a week studying, mostly at night after his job. Knowing how to use the Internet is helping build a successful future. Students spend most of their time in school around adults that are here to teach them life skills. I believe that we can learn the most in preparation for the real world in school!

4   In conclusion, the best solution is to continue allowing school libraries to provide Internet access for students. For many, that provides the only access they have. It not only provides gateways for better learning experiences, but also readies us for the big journey that is ahead of us once we leave the comfort of middle and high school. Can you even imagine what kind of struggles would come our way if state legislators choose to terminate school Internet access?

Sincerely,

A Concerned Student

Making Observations
- What details from the letter made an impression on you?
- Which words or phrases jumped out to you?
- What opinions did you form as you read the letter?

Returning to the Text

- Return to the text as you respond to the following questions. Use text evidence to support your responses.
- Write any additional questions you have about the draft letter in your Reader/Writer Notebook.

5. What is the author's main argument? Identify details from paragraphs 1 and 2 that help you determine the main idea.

_____

_____

_____

_____

6. What does paragraph 2 say about students having access to the Internet from home instead of school?

_____

_____

_____

_____

7. How is the "real world" similar to school where the Internet is concerned? Use evidence from the text in your response.

_____

_____

_____

_____

8. How does the author use paragraphs 3 and 4 to develop and strengthen the argument? Use evidence from the text in your response.

_____

_____

_____

_____

Working from the Text

9. What is the author's purpose in writing the letter? Identify claims in the letter and explain how they relate to the author's purpose.

_____

_____

_____

_____

10. Return to the letter to mark the text for formal style. Annotate the text to identify the author's tone. In My Notes, write how the author's formal style and tone help make the argument convincing or not. Support your response with examples from the letter.

11. With the guidance of your teacher, conduct research as needed and draft another body paragraph for this letter. You will return to this body paragraph to practice revision strategies and refine your writing skills. Follow the steps to research and draft a paragraph.

Prewriting

Brainstorm evidence for the main idea (reason) of your new paragraph.

Research

- What questions will guide your research?
- Where will you gather evidence?
- What sources will you consult?

Drafting

After conducting initial research, generate an outline for the body paragraph and then write your draft. Remember that each body paragraph should consist of:

- **A topic sentence:** a sentence that includes a subject and an opinion that relates directly the claim (thesis)
- **Transitions:** words used to connect ideas (e.g., *for example, for instance*)
- **Supporting information:** specific evidence and details (What facts and details are most appropriate? Do you accurately synthesize information from a variety of sources?)
- **Reflective commentary:** sentences that explain how the information is relevant to the claim/thesis. (Also, use reflective commentary to bring a sense of closure to the paragraph.)

12. Draft your body paragraph in the space that follows.

_____

_____

_____

_____

_____

_____

_____

_____

_____

_____

_____

_____

_____

_____

_____

_____

☑ Check Your Understanding

Create a Writer's Checklist based on what you already know you should "be sure to" do to create a successful argument.

Facts and Feelings: Rhetorical Appeals in Argumentative Writing

VOCABULARY

LITERARY

Rhetorical appeals, or persuasive strategies, are used in arguments to support claims.
Logos is a rhetorical appeal that uses logical reasoning and evidence.
Pathos is a rhetorical appeal to feelings.
Logical fallacies are errors in reasoning that are commonly introduced when writers or speakers try to use pathos.

My Notes

_____
_____
_____
_____
_____
_____
_____
_____
_____
_____
_____
_____
_____
_____
_____
_____
_____
_____

Learning Targets

- Identify logos and pathos used in an argument.
- Examine evidence and explain how it is relevant and sufficient to support a claim.
- Integrate ideas from multiple texts to build knowledge and vocabulary about the culture and perspectives of American Indians.

Preview

In this activity, you will learn about appealing to a reader's reason and emotion by reading and analyzing a persuasive letter.

Rhetoric and Rhetorical Appeals

Rhetoric is the art of using words to persuade in writing and speaking. Writers use different types of rhetoric depending on their audience and purpose. Good arguments include sound reasoning and evidence and spur an audience to action or a change of mind. Writers who use logic that is backed up with evidence such as statistics and proven examples are using the **rhetorical appeal** known as **logos**. Writers sometimes use language and examples that are meant to appeal to the audience's emotions and feelings. This rhetorical appeal is known as **pathos**. Though it is a powerful and often necessary tool, pathos should be used sparingly in an argument because it typically does not include the relevant evidence that is required to support a claim. This can easily lead to **logical fallacies**. Logical fallacies are errors in reasoning, usually illegitimate arguments or irrelevant points. Some common logical fallacies include *slippery slope* (taking the cause-and-effect chain too far and concluding that if A happens, Z will happen too), *either/or* (oversimplifying the argument by making it only two sides or choices), and *circular reasoning* (restating the argument rather than actually proving it).

Setting a Purpose for Reading

- As you read, use two different highlighters: one for highlighting appeals to logic and one for highlighting appeals to emotion.
- Circle unknown words and phrases. Try to determine the meaning of the words by using context clues, word parts, or a dictionary.

About the Author

Scott H. Peters (of the Chippewa Tribe) was the president of the Grand Council Fire of American Indians, an organization that worked for better treatment of and policies toward American Indian populations and Native American tribes.

About the Letter

In 1927, William Hale Thompson, a political campaigner, used a slogan of "America First" to claim that history textbooks were biased in favor of the British. Thompson won reelection as the mayor of Chicago and demanded that the city's textbooks be replaced with books that focused on the accomplishments of groups in the United States. Scott H. Peters wrote to the mayor on behalf of the Grand Council Fire of American Indians to describe how Native Americans, like other ethnic groups, were misrepresented in textbooks.

Letter

The First Americans

by **Scott H. Peters,** Grand Council Fire of American Indians

December 1, 1927

To the mayor of Chicago:

1   You tell all white men "America First." We believe in that. We are the only ones, truly, that are one hundred percent. We therefore ask you, while you are teaching schoolchildren about America First, teach them truth about the First Americans.

2   We do not know if school histories are pro-British, but we do know that they are unjust to the life of our people—the American Indian. They call all white victories battles and all Indian victories massacres. The battle with Custer has been taught to schoolchildren as a fearful massacre on our part. We ask that this, as well as other incidents, be told fairly. If the Custer battle was a massacre, what was Wounded Knee?

3   History books teach that Indians were murderers—is it murder to fight in self-defense? Indians killed white men because white men took their lands, ruined their hunting grounds, burned their forests, destroyed their buffalo. White men penned our people on **reservations**, then took away the reservations. White men who rise to protect their property are called patriots—Indians who do the same are called murderers.

4   White men call Indians **treacherous**—but no mention is made of broken treaties on the part of the white man. White men say that Indians were always fighting. It was only our lack of skill in white man's warfare that led to our defeat. An Indian mother prayed that her boy be a great medicine man rather than a great warrior. It is true that we had our own small battles, but in the main we were peace loving and home loving.

5   White men called Indians thieves—and yet we lived in frail skin lodges and needed no locks or iron bars. White men call Indians savages. What is civilization? Its marks are a noble religion and philosophy, original arts, stirring music, rich story and legend. We had these. Then we were not savages, but a civilized race.

6   We made blankets that were beautiful, that the white man with all his machinery has never been able to duplicate. We made baskets that were beautiful. We wove in beads and colored quills designs that were not just decorative motifs but were the outward expression of our very thoughts. We made pottery—pottery that was useful, and beautiful as well. Why not make schoolchildren acquainted with the beautiful handicrafts in which we were skilled? Put in every school Indian blankets, baskets, pottery.

KNOWLEDGE QUEST

Knowledge Question:
What is unique about the culture and perspectives of American Indians?
In Activity 3.11, you will read a text about the juxtaposition of the "American dream" and the experiences of American Indian individuals and view photographs of their art. While you read and build knowledge about American Indian culture and perspectives, think about your answer to the Knowledge Question.

My Notes

reservations: lands in the United States set aside for use by Native Americans

treacherous: not to be trusted

7 We sang songs that carried in their melodies all the sounds of nature—the running of waters, the sighing of winds, and the calls of the animals. Teach these to your children that they may come to love nature as we love it.

8 We had our statesmen—and their oratory has never been equaled. Teach the children some of these speeches of our people, remarkable for their brilliant oratory.

9 We played games—games that brought good health and sound bodies. Why not put these in your schools? We told stories. Why not teach schoolchildren more of the wholesome proverbs and legends of our people? Tell them how we loved all that was beautiful. That we killed game only for food, not for fun. Indians think white men who kill for fun are murderers.

10 Tell your children of the friendly acts of Indians to the white people who first settled here. Tell them of our leaders and heroes and their deeds. Tell them of Indians such as Black Partridge, Shabbona, and others who many times saved the people of Chicago at great danger to themselves. Put in your history books the Indian's part in the World War. Tell how the Indian fought for a country of which he was not a citizen, for a flag to which he had no claim, and for a people that have treated him unjustly.

11 The Indian has long been hurt by these unfair books. We ask only that our story be told in fairness. We do not ask you to overlook what we did, but we do ask you to understand it. A true program of America First will give a generous place to the culture and history of the American Indian.

12 We ask this, Chief, to keep sacred the memory of our people.

⊘ Knowledge Quest

- What are your first thoughts about this letter?
- What details capture your attention the most?

In this photograph, a Navajo weaver kneels at a loom, skillfully creating a geometrically patterned rug while a young boy watches and admires the artistry. This is an example of the beautiful handicrafts that Scott H. Peters appeals to the mayor of Chicago to include in history textbooks.

Woven Figurine from the Tohono O'odham culture, circa 1970.

 Knowledge Quest

- What is most striking to you about the Navajo weaver photograph?
- What about the image of the figurine captures your interest?

KNOWLEDGE QUEST

Knowledge Question:
What is unique about the culture and perspectives of American Indians?

Returning to the Text

- Return to the text as you respond to the following questions. Use text evidence to support your responses.
- Write any additional questions you have about the letter in your Reader/Writer Notebook.

1. **KQ** Who were the *First Americans*? Use context clues to find out. Then make an inference about why Peters uses the name *First Americans* in his letter.

   _____

   _____

   _____

   _____

2. **KQ** What perspective is presented in paragraph 2? Use text evidence in your response.

   _____

   _____

   _____

   _____

3. What mood does the speaker set with his tone? What words or phrases in the opening paragraphs reflect this mood?

_____

_____

_____

_____

4. How are the words *murderer* and *savage* used to appeal to the reader? Are they a rhetorical device or a logical fallacy? Provide text evidence in your response.

_____

_____

_____

_____

5. In paragraphs 3–5, how does the author respond to negative perceptions of Native Americans?

_____

_____

_____

_____

6. **KQ** What do the photographs that follow the letter show? How do they support the letter's content?

_____

_____

_____

_____

7. What is the purpose of Peters's letter, and how is it conveyed in the text?

_____

_____

_____

_____

Knowledge Quest

After reading this text about American Indians, how has your understanding developed about the ways American Indian culture and perspectives are unique?

INDEPENDENT READING LINK

You can continue to build your knowledge about American Indian culture and perspectives by reading other articles at ZINC Reading Labs. Search for keywords such as *Native-Americans* or *American Indians*.

Working from the Text

8. Reread the letter. Use the graphic organizer to record examples of the writer's use of rhetorical appeals.

Title: *The First Americans*
Appeals to Reason: logos *(facts, statistics, examples, observations, quotations, and expert opinions)*
Examples:
Appeals to Feelings: pathos *(emotional language; mention of basic values)*
Examples:

ACADEMIC

In order to be convincing, evidence must be both **relevant**, or closely connected to the matter at hand, and **sufficient**, or enough for the purpose of supporting a claim or reason. Judging whether evidence is relevant and sufficient is a skill that takes practice.

9. **Group Discussion:** Choose one piece of evidence and discuss how it is **relevant**. Record your group's responses.

_____

_____

_____

10. Look at the author's appeals to feelings. Are these appeals supported by relevant evidence, or are they possibly logical fallacies?

_____

_____

_____

11. Look at all of the evidence together. Is it **sufficient** to support the claim of the letter? Explain your answer.

_____

_____

_____

12. Revisit and reread another text you have previously read in this unit. Analyze that text for rhetorical appeals. Then complete the graphic organizer.

Title:

Appeals to Reason: logos *(facts, statistics, examples, observations, quotations, and expert opinions)*

Examples:

Appeals to Feelings: pathos *(emotional language; mention of basic values)*

Examples:

☑ Check Your Understanding

Quickwrite: Which text do you find most convincing? How did that author incorporate rhetorical appeals to create the argument? Did the argument of that text use one kind of appeal—logos or pathos—more than the other? Did the argument seem to include any logical fallacies?

_____

_____

_____

_____

_____

_____

_____

Gaining Perspectives

You've been reading about the portrayal of Native Americans in the United States. Now think about the United States' system of democracy (a system whose principles originated in ancient Greece). With a partner, discuss how this system can help people stand up for what they believe in and fight for what is right. When you are done, summarize the outcome of the discussion in your Reader/Writer Notebook.

Learning Targets

- Identify which elements are essential to a sentence and which elements are not.
- Use commas, parentheses, and dashes to set off nonrestrictive/parenthetical elements.
- Use punctuation correctly when writing and editing.

Identifying Necessary Information and Extra Information

Sentences are made up of many pieces of information. Some information is necessary for understanding the meaning of a sentence. Pieces of information that are necessary to a sentence are called restrictive (or essential) elements. For example, *The term* logos *names a rhetorical appeal that uses logical reasoning*.

Pieces of information that add extra (but unnecessary) detail to a sentence are called nonrestrictive (or nonessential) elements. Nonrestrictive elements need to be set off with punctuation. For example, *Logos, a term that comes from the ancient Greek language, names a rhetorical appeal that uses logical reasoning*.

1. Read the following sentences. Decide whether the bolded information is necessary to the sentence. If it is necessary, write "restrictive" on the line. If it is extra information, write "nonrestrictive."

   a. Scott H. Peters, **a Chippewa**, was president of the council. _____

   b. The Chippewa Indian **Scott H. Peters** was president of the council. _____

2. Explain your answers to step 1.

Punctuating Nonrestrictive Elements

Nonrestrictive elements are set off from a sentence by punctuation: commas, parentheses, or dashes. Each punctuation mark suggests something a little different.

Most of the time, a comma or a pair of commas sets off nonrestrictive elements.

> Example: **Using rhetorical appeals,** Peters makes his case for inclusion.

> Example: Peters's letter, **which was written in 1927,** discusses Native American culture.

Parentheses suggest that the information inside them is less important than the information in the rest of the sentence. Parentheses are always used in pairs.

> Example: The term *logos* (**from the Greek for "word" or "reason"**) names a rhetorical appeal that uses logical reasoning.

A dash or pair of dashes can be used to emphasize nonrestrictive elements.

> Example: We played games—**games that brought good health and sound bodies.**

> Example: The sounds of nature—**the running of water, the sighing of winds, and the calls of the animals**—were in Native American songs.

Remember that restrictive elements do not have to be set off with punctuation. Extra punctuation can make your sentences confusing.

3. For each of the following sentences, underline the nonrestrictive element and insert a comma or pair of commas to set it off.

   a. We ask that this as well as other incidents be told fairly.

   b. Teach the children some of these speeches remarkable for their brilliant oratory.

4. For each of the following sentences, underline the nonrestrictive element and insert parentheses to set it off.

   a. The Chippewa also called Ojibwe or Ojibwa live in North America.

   b. The "dreamcatcher" a handmade object with a wooden hoop and a loose net or web originated with the Objibwe.

5. For each of the following sentences, underline the nonrestrictive element and insert a dash or pair of dashes to set it off.

   a. Wounded Knee the site of a massacre of Lakota men, women, and children is in South Dakota.

   b. I have read several novels by the author Louise Erdrich one of many notable Ojibwe.

6. For each of the following sentences, delete any unnecessary punctuation around restrictive elements.

   a. In history class yesterday, we learned that the word, wigwam, may come from the Objibwe word for "a dwelling."

   b. Some Chippewa prefer to call themselves anishinaabe, a word, meaning "original people."

Editing

Read this student summary of part of "The First Americans." Work with a partner to check whether restrictive and nonrestrictive elements are punctuated correctly. Mark the text to correct the mistakes.

[1] The letter "The First Americans" was written in 1927. [2] Scott H. Peters the president of the Grand Council Fire of American Indians sent it to the mayor of Chicago William Hale Thompson. [3] In the letter, Peters uses rhetorical appeals both logos and pathos to make his case. [4] He asks that, textbook makers acknowledge Native American arts and teachings woven blankets and baskets, pottery, songs, oratory, and games.

☑ Check Your Understanding

Imagine you are editing a classmate's writing and you notice this sentence:

The purpose of this letter which was written in 1927 was to tell the mayor, of Chicago, that the history and culture of Native Americans should be taught better.

Write a note to the writer describing why the original sentence was confusing. Then add a question to your Editor's Checklist that will remind you to check for correct punctuation of nonrestrictive elements in your own writing.

Practice

Return to the answers you wrote in Activity 3.11 and check them for correct punctuation of restrictive elements. Be sure to:

- Underline any nonrestrictive elements and punctuate them correctly, using commas, parentheses, or dashes.
- Look at other points where you used commas, parentheses, or dashes and check to see whether they are used correctly.

Citing Evidence

Learning Strategies

Metacognitive Markers

My Notes

Learning Targets

- Record information about credible sources, cite them accurately, and paraphrase relevant information.
- Use appositives to give specific information about sources.

Preview

In this activity, you will learn how to cite sources and make use of appositives, both of which are tools you can use when adding appeals to your argumentative letter.

Giving Credit Where Credit Is Due

What does it mean to "give credit" when writing an argumentative text? How does this help writers avoid plagiarism? What does "giving credit" have to do with logos?

Citing Sources

When using information gained from research, it is important to cite the sources of that information to avoid plagiarism. Remember that plagiarism is using someone else's work without giving them credit. It is also important to represent sources accurately, without introducing any errors or misinterpretations.

For argumentative writing, citing sources also builds credibility with an audience and adds authority to evidence.

You can incorporate research material into your writing in two ways:

- **Direct quotations** are word-for-word quotes from the source. The source must be named. Direct quotations are usually short.
- **Paraphrasing** involves putting a passage from source material into your own words while maintaining its meaning. A paraphrase must also be attributed to the original source. Paraphrased material is usually shorter than the original passage; it takes a somewhat broader portion of the source and condenses it slightly.

Tips for Citing Sources

Follow these tips for citing sources to avoid plagiarism and improve the organization of your writing:

- Use a statement that credits the source (e.g., "According to Jonas Salk, ___").
- Put quotation marks around any unique words or phrases that you cannot or do not want to change (e.g., "savage inequalities exist throughout our educational system").
- If you are having trouble paraphrasing, try writing your version of a text without looking at the original, relying only on your memory and notes.

- Check your paraphrase against the original text. Correct any errors in content accuracy and be sure to use quotation marks to set off any exact phrases from the original text. Also, make sure you didn't repeat the original text's sentence and paragraph structure, as copying these is also considered plagiarism.

LANGUAGE & WRITER'S CRAFT: Using Appositives

An appositive is a noun or noun phrase that gives more information about or explains another noun in the same sentence. An appositive can be a single word or a phrase. Appositives are usually set off by commas, parentheses, or dashes.

> **Single word with comma:** *My best friend, **Sean**, is an expert on baseball.*

> **Phrase with comma:** *Mary Southard, **director of volunteers at the children's hospital**, reports that over fifty new volunteers signed up this year.*

> **Phrase with parentheses:** *Louis (a forward on last year' s team) is coaching the junior varsity team this year.*

> **Phrase with dashes:** *I asked Sara—the only person in the class that I know—to be my lab partner.*

When you cite sources in an argument, use appositives to give more precise information about a source. This information strengthens your appeal to logos.

PRACTICE Combine the following parts to create a sentence with an appositive phrase. Pay attention to your punctuation.

- president and publisher of HarperCollins Children's books
- Susan Katz
- explains that teen fiction is "hot" right now to people who read e-books

---

☑ Focus on the Sentence

Add appositives to the following sentences about "The First Americans."

Scott H. Peters, _____ ,

wrote a letter to the mayor of Chicago to urge him to include fair and accurate information about

Native Americans.

William Hale Thompson, _____ ,

claimed that textbooks were biased in favor of the British.

My Notes

1. Imagine you were the author of the letter "The First Americans" and you wanted to add some evidence of Native Americans' contribution to World War I. Find a credible digital or print source of this information and paraphrase the information you find most relevant to include in the letter.

2. **Revising to Add Appeals:** Return to the body paragraph you wrote for the model argumentative letter in Activity 3.10. Mark the text for appeals to logos (or logic) that you used. Revise the paragraph as needed to add appeals to logos and strengthen your reasons and evidence. Be sure to:

   - Support your claim with valid evidence (statistics, examples, quotations).
   - Cite sources from your research as needed to strengthen the logic of your argument.
   - Use at least one appositive phrase to give more precise information about a source.

Add this writing piece to your Portfolio.

☑ Check Your Understanding

Explain the relationship between citing sources and appealing to logos. Then describe one revision you made to your body paragraph for the "Student Draft Letter" and why you made it.

INDEPENDENT READING LINK

Read and Research

Discuss with a partner how the author of your independent reading book gives credit to his or her sources. If you wanted more information on one of the sources cited, discuss how would you know where to look. Record answers in your Reader/Writer Notebook.

Playing with Persuasive Diction: Appealing to Pathos

Learning Targets

- Analyze the figurative, connotative, and technical meanings of words and phrases used in a text.
- Identify and analyze examples of persuasive diction
- Match style and purpose in writing by applying looping and persuasive diction to add pathos.

Preview

In this activity, you will learn to harness the power of persuasive language to appeal to a reader's emotions.

Learning Strategies

Skimming/Scanning
Marking the Text
Looping

My Notes

What's in a Word?

Consider how similar words can make you feel different ways. Would you rather be called *youthful* or *immature*? Would you rather be considered *curious* or *nosy*? Word choice, or diction, is an important aspect of argumentative writing. Because words can carry an emotional impact, each one represents an opportunity for the writer to convince his or her audience.

Learning from Advertisements

1. As you skim through ads, record words that stand out for their emotional meaning (strong connotative diction).

2. Sort the adjectives and verbs you find by adding them to the following lists:

Power Adjective List

amazing, authentic

best

dependable, diagnosed

easy

free

guaranteed

healthy

important, improved, instant

limited, lucky

mixed

new

powerful

secure

tested

uneven, unique, unreal, unsurpassed

vital

wonderful

My Notes

Power Verb List

abolish, achieve, act, adopt, anticipate, apply, assess

boost, break, bridge, build

capture, change, choose, clarify, comprehend, create

decide, define, deliver, design, develop, discover, drive

eliminate, ensure, estimate, evaluate, exploit, explore

filter, finalize, focus, foresee

gain, gather, generate, grasp

identify, improve, increase, innovate, inspire, intensify

lead, learn

manage, master, maximize, measure, mobilize, motivate

overcome

penetrate, persuade, plan, prepare, prevent

realize, reconsider, reduce, replace, resist, respond

save, sift, solve, stop, succeed

train, transfer, transform

understand, unleash

win

Introducing the Strategy: Adding by Looping

Looping helps you add to your thoughts, clarify your thinking, or generate new ideas. With looping, you underline an important sentence or a particular word or phrase in your writing. You then write a few more sentences to add new ideas. Repeat this process with the new sentences you wrote to help you keep adding ideas to your writing.

3. Imagine you have drafted the following note to your family trying to convince them where to go on vacation. Use looping to add an emotional appeal by underlining an important sentence, phrase, or word and then writing two more sentences in the space that follows. Be sure to use power adjectives and verbs in your new sentences.

Dear Family,

   I would like to go to Colorado for our family vacation. We could go on a rafting trip there! I have heard that rafting is an exhilarating experience. My friend's family went last summer, and she described plunging down rapids and paddling against intense currents. Going rafting together would be exciting and would probably make our family bond even stronger.

Thank you for considering it.

Your daughter

Your two new sentences:

a.

_____

_____

_____

_____

_____

b.

_____

_____

_____

_____

_____

☑ Check Your Understanding

Respond to the following questions about the note you just revised.

- What is the relationship between persuasive diction and appealing to pathos?
- What power adjectives and verbs did you add that were especially effective?
- If you were going to improve the practice paragraph even more, what would you do? What do you notice is missing? Explain.

Revising for Persuasive Diction: Return to the body paragraph you wrote and revised for the model argumentative letter (Activity 3.11). Revise the paragraph for persuasive diction. To properly add pathos to the development of your argument, be sure to:

- Mark the text for appeals to pathos you may have already used.
- Add emotional appeals that support your logical appeals for a balance that fits your purpose and audience. Avoid accidentally creating a logical fallacy.
- Use looping to revise by adding new ideas and persuasive diction (power verbs and adjectives).

My Notes

_____

_____

_____

_____

_____

_____

_____

_____

_____

_____

_____

_____

_____

_____

_____

_____

_____

_____

_____

_____

_____

_____

_____

_____

_____

INDEPENDENT READING LINK

Read and Respond

Find at least five words or phrases that carry strong emotional meaning in your independent reading. Write them in your Reader/Writer Notebook and set a goal to use them in your own writing.

Writing an Introduction and a Conclusion

© 2021 College Board. All rights reserved.

Learning Strategies

Metacognitive Markers

My Notes

Learning Targets

- Write an argument to support a claim with clear reasons and evidence.
- Write effective introductions and conclusions to an argument.

Preview

In this activity, you will write an argumentative letter and revise it to strengthen its persuasiveness.

Timed Writing

On a separate piece of paper, write a response to one of the following prompts or to one your teacher provides. Consider audience and purpose as you plan your draft. Remember to apply your knowledge of how to write a claim and support it with relevant reasons and evidence. If possible, use a word-processing program to create your draft and develop your keyboarding skills. If writing by hand, double-space your draft to provide room for revision.

Argumentative Writing Prompt: Write a letter to do one of the following:

- Convince a family member of something you would like to do over the summer.
- Convince your principal or a teacher to change a school rule or policy.
- Convince a friend of something you would like to do together over the weekend.

1. Now that you have drafted your letter, analyze the beginning and ending of your text. Explain how you started and ended your letter.

Introductions and Conclusions

Review the following guidelines about writing an introduction and a conclusion. Mark the text for new or important information as you read.

An **introduction** contains the following:

- **A hook.** Can you think of an event, a question, or a real-life story (called an anecdote) to hook your reader?
- **A connection between the hook and the claim.** How does your hook relate to your claim?
- **The claim.** Your viewpoint on an issue is important to you; what is it?

Introduction

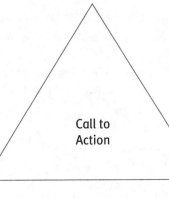

Hook

Connection

Claim

A **conclusion** contains the following:

- A **summary** of the most important reason for the argument
- A **call to action** restating what you want the reader to believe or do

It is important to end an argument in a convincing way. You might conclude your argument by summarizing your most important reason. However, an especially effective conclusion is a call to action in which you state for the last time what the reader should believe or do. It is also interesting and effective to revisit the idea in your hook at some point in your conclusion.

Call to
Action

Conclusion

2. Return to the sample argumentative letter in Activity 3.10 and reread its introduction and conclusion. Mark the text for the components of an effective introduction and conclusion. Make notes about any revisions that you would consider to improve the beginning and ending of the letter.

My Notes

 Focus on the Sentence

Change the sentence fragments into complete sentences. Use correct capitalization and punctuation.

introduction includes

_____

_____

an event, a question, or a real-life story

_____

_____

includes a summary and

_____

_____

Revising Your Letter: Return to the letter you drafted for the timed writing in this activity and revise by looping, adding, deleting, and replacing to improve its introduction, body paragraphs, and conclusion. Be sure to:

• Inform your audience of the purpose and introduce your claim clearly in the introduction.

• Revise the body paragraphs to make your reasons and evidence stronger.

• Revise the ending to make sure your letter connects to the claim, reasons, and evidence in the argument you have presented.

• Check that words are spelled correctly and that you are using correct grammar and punctuation, specifically the correct use of commas, parentheses, and dashes.

Saying Too Much or Too Little?

Learning Targets

- Identify and use transitions to improve the coherence of writing.
- Revise writing by using transitions, deleting, and creating complex sentences to clarify claims, reasons, and evidence.

Preview

In this activity, you and a partner will experiment with giving coherent directions, and you will learn new strategies to improve these skills. Then you will revise your argumentative letter to make it more coherent.

Learning Strategies

Visualizing
Rereading
Marking the Text
Adding
Substituting/Replacing
Deleting

My Notes

Giving and Interpreting Directions

Work with a partner to draw a picture. One person will give the directions for drawing the picture while the other person follows them.

1. As the person giving directions, think about what you will say and the best way to communicate what is to be drawn by your partner. Write notes to yourself in the following space.

2. As the person following the directions, was your drawing successful? What did your partner say that helped you draw correctly? What additional information would have been helpful?

Revising for Coherence

As you learned in the preceding exercise, explaining clearly makes a difference in how well your audience understands your meaning. In Unit 1, you learned that the term *coherence* refers to the logical organization of an essay. A coherent essay ties ideas together to flow smoothly from one sentence to the next and from one paragraph to the next, making the essay easy to follow for the reader.

An effective way to revise for coherence is to use transitions, both within and between paragraphs. Transitions help you move from one sentence or thought to another.

Certain words and phrases in the English language are typical transitions. These transitions are outlined in the following table. Read the information in the table and place a star (*) next to the words or phrases you used or heard in the drawing activity.

Transitions That ...	Transitional Signal Words and Phrases
Add ideas	*in addition, furthermore, moreover, further, besides, too, also, and then, then too, again, next, secondly, equally important*
Compare or contrast	*similarly, likewise, in comparison, in a like manner, however, in contrast, conversely, on the other hand, but, nevertheless, and yet, even so, still*
Show examples	*for example, for instance*
Reinforce an idea	*indeed, in fact, as a matter of fact, to be sure, of course, in any event, by all means*
Indicate results	*as a result, as a consequence, consequently, therefore, thus, hence, accordingly*
Express a sequence of ideas	*first, second, soon after, then, previously, meanwhile, in the meantime, later, at length, after a while, immediately, next*
Show proximity	*here, nearby, at this spot, near at hand, in this area, on the opposite side, across from, not far from*
Conclude	*finally, in short, in other words, to sum up, in conclusion, in the end*

3. Return to the "Student Draft Letter" in Activity 3.10 and read it for organization and coherence. Mark the text for transitional words and phrases. Make notes about any revisions that you think would improve coherence.

Revising for Coherence: Return to the letter you drafted and revised for the timed writing prompt in Activity 3.14. Revise to improve its coherence. Be sure to:

- Use adding or replacing to incorporate transitional words and phrases that link ideas within each of your paragraphs and help the reader move from one paragraph to the next.
- Use words and/or phrases to clarify the relationships between your ideas, specifically your claims, reasons, and evidence.
- Read your revised piece to a peer for feedback on its coherence.

My Notes

Introducing the Strategy: Deleting

When you revise by **deleting**, you identify irrelevant, repetitive, or meaningless words and remove them from your writing. When you delete a word, phrase, or sentence, reread the section aloud to make sure that it still makes sense after your deletion. Deleting sentences or parts of sentences can improve overall coherence in your writing.

Revising by Deleting

4. Revise the following paragraph. Identify words and sentences that are irrelevant, repetitive, or meaningless and delete them by drawing a line through them. Then write your new paragraph in the space that follows.

   My family and I had a great time on our fun rafting trip. We went to Colorado. Colorado is called the Rocky Mountain State. The rafting was really very exciting and scary. The weather was a little cold, so we all got sick on our way home.

5. Why did you delete the words and/or sentences you did?

6. Return to the "Student Draft Letter" from Activity 3.10. Reread it to see if any part is irrelevant, repetitive, or meaningless. Make notes about any sentences that you would consider deleting and tell why you think the deletion is needed.

7. Return to the letter you revised for the timed writing in Activity 3.14. Read it for coherence and for possible sentences or ideas to delete. Be sure to:

   - Read for coherence to help you decide whether deleting (or adding) ideas would improve the flow of the letter.
   - Identify and remove irrelevant, repetitive, or meaningless ideas.
   - Check your letter for correct spelling, grammar, and punctuation.
   - Select a part of your letter that you revised by deleting. Read the "before" and "after" versions to a peer to get feedback.

LANGUAGE & WRITER'S CRAFT: Using Complex Sentences

Varying the types of sentences you use in your writing helps keep your audience interested, and it helps your writing to flow well. One way to create sentence variety is to use complex sentences.

A complex sentence is made up of a dependent clause and an independent clause. These two clauses show a close relationship between two ideas. Read this complex sentence: *I think we should help clean up the park on Saturday because we want a clean, safe place to hang out.* The first part of the sentence states an opinion, while the second part gives a reason.

Independent Clause: The independent clause can stand alone as a sentence. *I think we should help clean up the park on Saturday* is an independent clause.

Dependent Clause: A dependent clause cannot stand alone as a sentence. *Because we want a clean, safe place to hang out* cannot stand alone as a sentence.

A dependent clause usually starts with a "dependent marker," such as *after, although, as if, as though, because, before, in order that, provided that, since, unless, whereas,* or *while.*

When writing a complex sentence, either clause can come first. Use a comma at the end of the dependent clause if it appears first in the sentence.

Independent Clause First: *Tickets may sell out quickly because the movie is so popular.*

Dependent Clause First: *Because the movie is so popular, tickets may sell out quickly.*

PRACTICE Add a dependent clause to this independent clause to create a complex sentence.

I would like our family to take a trip to the beach this summer

Add an independent clause to this dependent clause to create a complete sentence.

before we all get too busy to spend time together

Revising by Creating Complex Sentences

8. Revise the following paragraph by combining sentences to create complex sentences. Use a dependent marker to connect the dependent and independent clauses.

We should go to the movies on Saturday. The weather will be lousy. The test we had today was tough. A movie will be a good way to unwind. The *new Hunger* Games installment is out. I know you're a big fan of the books. This will convince you to see all the films in the series, too. I may be able get my brother to drive us. He wants to see it anyway.

☑ Check Your Understanding

Explain three ways you can revise your writing to improve its coherence.

Preparing to Write an Argument

Learning Strategies

Graphic Organizer
Paraphrasing

Learning Targets

- Reflect on personal argumentative writing skills.
- Assess strengths and weaknesses and plan how to address them in future writing.

Preview

In this activity, you will assess your argumentative writing strengths and weaknesses and make a plan for improving weak points.

Final Preparations

1. Use the graphic organizer to help you reflect on what you have learned about argumentative writing and revising and how you will use your knowledge to complete Embedded Assessment 2.

Argumentative Letter Reflection and Planning		
Scoring Criteria Paraphrase the specific evaluation criteria from the Scoring Guide.	**Reflection** Self-assess by describing an area of strength and an area of weakness for you.	**Planning** How can you use this information to help you write your argumentative letter? What do you plan to do? Be specific.
Ideas	Strength: Weakness:	
Structure	Strength: Weakness:	
Use of Language (including conventions)	Strength: Weakness:	

2. Now that you have drafted your letter, analyze the beginning and ending of your text. Explain how you started and ended your letter.

_____

_____

_____

Independent Reading Checkpoint

Take a position in the controversy you have been reading about independently and prepare an organized oral presentation about it. Use reasons and evidence to support your position and convince the class that your side is the correct side to be on.

Writing an Argumentative Letter

ASSIGNMENT

Think about a topic (subject, event, idea, or controversy) that you truly care about and take a position on it. Write an argumentative letter to convince an audience to support your position on the topic.

Planning and Prewriting: Take time to make a plan for generating ideas and research questions.	■ What is a relevant topic that you care about and can take a position on? ■ How can you use a prewriting strategy such as prewriting or webbing to explore your ideas? ■ What questions will guide your research?
Researching: Gather information from a variety of credible sources.	■ Where can you find sources, and how can you tell that the sources are credible and useful? ■ Which strategies will you use to help you understand informational texts? ■ How will you take notes by paraphrasing reasons and evidence and recording bibliographic information?
Drafting: Write an argumentative letter that is appropriate for your task, purpose, and audience.	■ How will you select the best reasons and evidence from your research? ■ Who is the audience for your letter, and what would be an appropriate tone and style for this audience?
Evaluating and Revising the Draft: Create opportunities to review and revise your work.	■ During the process of writing, when can you pause to share with and respond to others? ■ What is your plan to add suggestions and revision ideas into your draft? ■ How can you revise your draft to improve your diction and syntax? ■ How can the Scoring Guide help you evaluate how well your draft meets the requirements of the assignment?
Checking and Editing for Publication: Confirm that your final draft is ready for publication.	■ How will you check for grammatical and technical accuracy? ■ How will you use technology to format and publish your writing?

Reflection

After completing this Embedded Assessment, think about how you went about accomplishing this task and respond to the following:

- What were the strongest elements of your argument?
- How did you use emotional appeals to connect with your audience?

SCORING GUIDE

Scoring Criteria	Exemplary	Proficient	Emerging	Incomplete
Ideas	The letter • supports a claim with compelling reasons, evidence, and commentary, including relevant facts, details, quotes, paraphrases, and rhetorical appeals (pathos, logos). • avoids plagiarism by including proper and thorough citations.	The letter • supports a claim with sufficient reasons, evidence, and commentary, including adequate facts, details, quotes, paraphrases, and rhetorical appeals (pathos, logos). • avoids plagiarism by including basic citations.	The letter • has an unclear or unfocused claim and/or insufficient support, such as unrelated, weak, or inadequate facts, details, quotes, paraphrases, and rhetorical appeals (pathos, logos). • includes partial or inaccurate citations.	The letter • has no obvious claim or provides minimal or inaccurate support. • lacks citations and/or appears plagiarized.
Structure	The letter • follows an effective organizational structure, including an engaging introduction and a thoughtful conclusion. • uses a variety of effective transitional strategies to create coherence.	The letter • follows a logical organizational structure, including an introduction with a hook and a conclusion that follows from the argument presented. • uses transitional strategies to clarify and link ideas.	The letter • follows a flawed or uneven organizational structure and may have a weak introduction and/or conclusion. • uses basic transitional strategies ineffectively or inconsistently.	The letter • has little or no organizational structure. • uses few or no transitional strategies.
Use of Language	The letter • uses persuasive and connotative diction. • demonstrates command of the conventions of standard English capitalization, punctuation, spelling, grammar, and usage. • maintains an engaging and appropriate style and tone.	The letter • uses some persuasive and/or connotative diction. • demonstrates adequate command of the conventions of standard English capitalization, punctuation, spelling, grammar, and usage. • maintains an appropriate style and tone.	The letter • uses basic or weak diction. • demonstrates partial command of the conventions of standard English capitalization, punctuation, spelling, grammar, and usage. • maintains an inconsistently appropriate style and/or tone.	The letter • uses confusing or vague diction. • lacks command of the conventions of standard English capitalization, punctuation, spelling, grammar, and usage; frequent errors obscure meaning. • has an inappropriate style and/or tone.

UNIT 4

VISUAL PROMPT
A change of scene on the stage can involve a new set, new lighting, and new characters. How does that compare to a change of scene you might undergo in your own life?

A CHANGE OF SCENE

Have you ever been at sea in a dense fog, when it seemed as if a tangible white darkness shut you in, and the great ship, tense and anxious, groped her way toward the shore with plummet and sounding-line, and you waited with beating heart for something to happen? I was like that ship before my education began, only I was without compass or sounding-line, and had no way of knowing how near the harbour was.

—from *The Story of My Life* by Helen Keller

CONTENTS

Texts not included in these materials.

My Independent Reading List

Learning Strategies

Think-Pair-Share
QHT
Close Reading
Paraphrasing
Graphic Organizer

My Notes

Learning Targets

- Preview the big ideas and vocabulary for the unit.
- Identify and analyze the skills and knowledge needed to complete Embedded Assessment 1 successfully.

Preview

In this activity, you will think about what you already know about research as well as the differences between reading texts and seeing them performed.

Making Connections

Over the course of this year, you've read a wide range of texts—from personal narratives and novels to news articles and historical documents. In this unit, you will explore two more narrative genres—poetry and plays. Reading, researching, writing, and performing the poems and plays will strengthen your literary analysis skills and build your confidence to speak in front of your peers.

Essential Questions

Based on your current knowledge, how would you answer these questions?

1. How can research inform an understanding of a literary text?
2. How is reading a text similar to and different from viewing and performing a text?

Developing Vocabulary

Use a QHT chart to sort the Academic Vocabulary and Literary Terms from the Contents page into the columns *Q, H,* and *T*. Remember that *Q* means that you have questions about the meaning of the word because it is unfamiliar; *H* means that you have heard of the word, so it is familiar; and *T* means that you can teach the word to your classmates because you know it so well. One academic goal is to move all words to the *T* column by the end of the unit.

INDEPENDENT READING LINK

Reading Plan

The first half of this unit focuses on poems, a diverse and interesting literary genre. Find a poet that interests you and collect things they've written (poems, letters, autobiographies) as well as things that have been written about them (biographies, reviews, news articles). Create a reading schedule for yourself and keep track of what you read in your Independent Reading List.

Unpacking Embedded Assessment 1

Read the assignment and Scoring Guide for Embedded Assessment 1.

Work collaboratively to conduct research, synthesize findings, and present a poet's life journey. Your presentation should be five minutes in length, and speaking parts should be divided equally. If possible, incorporate a poem written by the poet and multimedia elements, including video and sound, into your presentation.

With your class, paraphrase the expectations from the Scoring Guide and create a graphic organizer to use as a visual reminder of the required concepts (what you need to know) and skills (what you need to do). After each activity, use this graphic organizer to guide reflection about what you have learned and what you still need to learn in order to be successful on the Embedded Assessment.

Playing with Rhythm and Rhyme

Learning Targets

- Analyze how the parts of a limerick fit into its overall structure and work together to develop theme.
- Rehearse a limerick and present a practiced oral interpretation of the poem, demonstrating command of rhyme, rhythm, inflection, and rate.

Preview

In this activity, you will explore the work of famous limerick writer Edward Lear and present an interpretation of one of the limericks to the class.

Introducing the Strategy: Oral Interpretation

An oral interpretation of text involves reading aloud the text expressively in order to share personal insights into the text's meaning with an audience. In order to read expressively, one might change the loudness of his or her voice and express emotions that match the purpose and tone of the text. Also, delivering a good oral interpretation involves reading the text fluently while also using an appropriate reading **rate** and proper **inflection**.

Poetic Form: Limerick

Limericks are poems that have a specific rhyme scheme. Limericks usually have three long lines that end in words that have one end rhyme and two shorter lines that end in words that have another end rhyme. The **meter** of a limerick is created by stressing the rhyming words.

Setting a Purpose for Reading

- As you read, underline words and phrases that show rhyme and rhythm.
- Circle unknown words and phrases. Try to determine the meaning of the words by using context clues, word parts, or a dictionary.

About the Author

Edward Lear (1812–1888) was the second youngest of 21 children. Born in England, he traveled the world despite suffering from epilepsy his entire life. His main love was being an artist, but he is better remembered for being a writer. In addition to writing structured limericks, he wrote a unique kind of nonsense poetry. He created drawings to accompany many of his poems.

Learning Strategies

Graphic Organizer
Oral Reading
Marking the Text
Note-taking

VOCABULARY

LITERARY

Rate is the speed at which a speaker delivers words.

Inflection is the emphasis a speaker places on words through changes in pitch or volume.

A **limerick** is a light, humorous, nonsensical verse of five lines, usually with a rhyme scheme, or rhyming pattern, of a-a-b-b-a.

A poem's rhythm, or **meter**, is the pattern or flow of sound created by the poet's arrangement of stressed and unstressed syllables. Many types of poems, including limericks, have a specific rhythm.

My Notes

GRAMMAR & USAGE

Punctuation Conventions

Writers use punctuation to help readers read with the appropriate inflection and pauses.

Commas (,) and **semicolons** (;) signal a brief pause, so slow down the rate of speaking.

The **dash** (—) is used to emphasize the content that follows, so read the content with emphasis.

Exclamation points (!) indicate that the speaker feels strong emotion (e.g., excitement, concern, or surprise), so read the content with louder volume, a faster rate, and a higher inflection.

Here are some examples from the poem: Line 1, *beard*, (comma); Line 2, *feared!*— (exclamation point, dash); Line 12, *still*; (semicolon). As you read the poem, look for additional examples of these kinds of punctuation. Use the punctuation to read the poem with the appropriate inflection and pauses.

My Notes

_____

_____

_____

_____

_____

_____

_____

_____

_____

_____

_____

There was an Old Man with a beard, who said, "It is just as I feared!—
Two Owls and a Hen, four Larks and a Wren,
Have all built their nests in my beard!"

Limericks

from

A Book of Nonsense

by **Edward Lear**

1

There was an Old Man with a beard,
Who said, "It is just as I feared!—
Two Owls and a Hen,
Four Larks and a Wren,
Have all built their nests in my beard!"

2

There was an Old Man with a nose,
Who said, "If you choose to suppose
That my nose is too long,
You are certainly wrong!"
That remarkable Man with a nose.

3

There was an Old Man on a hill,
Who seldom, if ever, stood still;
He ran up and down,
In his Grandmother's gown,
Which adorned that Old Man on a hill.

4

There was a Young Lady whose chin
Resembled the point of a pin;

So she had it made sharp,
And purchased a harp,
And played several tunes with her chin.

5

There was an Old Man of Kilkenny,
Who never had more than a penny;
He spent all that money
In onions and honey,
That wayward Old Man of Kilkenny.

6

There was an Old Man in a boat,
Who said, "I'm afloat! I'm afloat!"
When they said, "No! you ain't!"
He was ready to faint,
That unhappy Old Man in a boat.

7

There was an old man from Nantucket,
Who kept all his cash in a bucket.
His daughter named Nan
Ran away with a man.
And as for the bucket, Nantucket.

There was a Young Lady whose chin resembled the point of a pin;
So she had it made sharp, and purchased a harp,
And played several tunes with her chin.

Making Observations

• What reaction do you have to these limericks?
• Which limerick stands out to you as the funniest?

My Notes

Returning to the Text

- Return to the limericks as you respond to the following questions. Use text evidence to support your responses.
- Write any additional questions you have about the limericks in your Reader/Writer Notebook.

1. What does the title of the collection tell you about the theme of the limericks? Which details in the limericks relate to the title?

2. How do meter and rhythm affect the mood of these limericks?

3. Read the seventh limerick. Who took the bucket? How do context clues help you figure out the play on words in the last line?

4. After reading all seven limericks, would you call their writing style formal or informal? Also, what is the writer's attitude toward the subject of each limerick? Do all the limericks have the same tone? Explain your answer.

Working from the Text

5. You will perform an assigned limerick for your group or class. Copy your poem onto a separate piece of paper or large index card. This will become your cue card during your performance. Mark the text to help you perform it by doing the following:

   • Use one color to highlight the three end words that rhyme with one another. Use a second color for the other two end words that rhyme.

   • Look at the punctuation to help guide your inflection and rate for your oral delivery. Highlight or note places where you should go slower or faster.

   • Count and record the number of syllables per line. Consider using a dictionary or other resource to ensure your syllable count is correct. Then circle the stressed syllables or mark them with a third color.

6. Read your limerick aloud to yourself and follow your markings for rate, inflection, and tone. Make adjustments as needed.

7. Memorize your limerick and rehearse your oral interpretation. Practice delivering your poem. Be sure to use effective rate, inflection, and tone.

8. When it is your turn, perform your oral interpretation of a limerick.

☑ Check Your Understanding

Listen to your classmates' performances. What do you notice about the rate, inflection, and tone of each performance? Decide which performances were best and write an explanation for the elements of performance used and how they affected the oral interpretation.

INDEPENDENT READING LINK

Read and Discuss

Select a poem by your poet that has an interesting rhyme scheme or meter. Analyze it and speak it out loud to yourself. In a small group, read your poem aloud and listen as others do the same. What was challenging about reading the poem aloud? What part of it was fun?

Learning Strategies

Choral Reading
Marking the Text
Rereading
Read Aloud

VOCABULARY

LITERARY

Free verse is poetry that does not follow any regular pattern, meter, or rhyme. Poems written in free verse can use a wide range of literary devices and techniques to play with meaning and language.

Prose is a more ordinary form of writing than free verse. Articles and stories are forms of prose. Sometimes, free verse poetry can sound or look like prose because of its loose structure and absence of pattern, meter, or rhyme. However, line breaks and special uses of capitalization and punctuation set free verse poetry apart from prose and create a unique structure that some readers prefer over traditional poetry.

My Notes

Learning Targets

- Analyze a poem for details, theme, and meaning.
- Creatively present a poem to the class using the appropriate rate, inflection, and tone.

Preview

In this activity, you will read a series of poems and analyze the details and structure of each. Then you will perform one of the poems aloud.

Poetic Form: Free Verse

A **free verse** poem is a poem that does not have a formal structure. It does not have a rhyme scheme or a regular meter, nor does it have a set number of lines. When reading a free verse poem, use the punctuation marks to help guide your expression, rate, and intonation.

Setting a Purpose for Reading

- Underline punctuation that shows when to slow down or pause during oral delivery.
- Create an image in your mind of the sights, smells, and sounds that the poet describes.
- Circle unknown words and phrases. Try to determine the meaning of the words by using context clues, word parts, or a dictionary.

Poem

Oranges

by **Gary Soto**

The first time I walked
With a girl, I was twelve,
Cold, and weighted down
With two oranges in my jacket.
5 December. Frost cracking
Beneath my steps, my breath
Before me, then gone,
As I walked toward
Her house, the one whose
10 Porch light burned yellow
Night and day, in any weather.
A dog barked at me, until

My Notes

She came out pulling
At her gloves, face bright
15 With rouge. I smiled,
Touched her shoulder, and led
Her down the street, across
A used car lot and a line
Of newly planted trees,
20 Until we were breathing
Before a drugstore. We
Entered, the tiny bell
Bringing a saleslady
Down a narrow aisle of goods.
25 I turned to the candies
Tiered like bleachers,
And asked what she wanted—
Light in her eyes, a smile
Starting at the corners
30 Of her mouth. I fingered
A nickel in my pocket,
And when she lifted a chocolate
That cost a dime,
I didn't say anything.
35 I took the nickel from
My pocket, then an orange,
And set them quietly on
The counter. When I looked up,
The lady's eyes met mine,
40 And held them, knowing
Very well what it was all
About.
        Outside,
A few cars hissing past,
Fog hanging like old

45 Coats between the trees.
   I took my girl's hand
   In mine for two blocks,
   Then released it to let
   Her unwrap the chocolate.
50 I peeled my orange
   That was so bright against
   The gray of December
   That, from some distance,
   Someone might have thought
55 I was making a fire in my hands.

My Notes

Making Observations

- Who is the speaker in this poem?
- What details do you notice about the characters and setting?
- What figures of speech do you notice in the poem? How do you know they are figures of speech?

☑ Focus on the Sentence

Identify whether the following phrases are complete sentences (S) or fragments (F). Copy the complete sentences on the line beneath the text, adding correct capitalization and punctuation. Turn the fragments into complete sentences with capitalization and punctuation by using details from the text.

a cold gray day in december

_____

the boy has a nickel but

_____

understands the situation

_____

they hold hands

_____

Returning to the Text

- Return to the poem as you respond to the following questions. Use text evidence to support your responses.
- Write any additional questions you have about the poem in your Reader/Writer Notebook.

1. From what point of view is the poem written? How does this point of view affect the poem?

_____

_____

_____

_____

2. There is a stanza break between lines 42 and 43. What effect does this stanza break have on the poem?

_____

_____

_____

_____

3. Read lines 43 through 45 of the poem. What two examples of figurative language do you see in these lines? What things are compared in each example?

_____

_____

_____

_____

4. To what does the author compare the orange in lines 50 through 55? What does the orange symbolize?

_____

_____

_____

_____

5. What are some of the themes of the poem? Support your answer with details from the poem.

_____

_____

_____

_____

Setting a Purpose for Reading

- Underline punctuation that shows when to slow down or pause during oral delivery.
- Create a mental image of the sights, smells, tastes, and sounds that the poet describes.
- Circle unknown words and phrases. Try to determine the meaning of the words by using context clues, word parts, or a dictionary.

My Notes

About the Author

Naomi Shihab Nye (1952–) was born in St. Louis, Missouri, but she spent her formative years in Jerusalem, Israel, and San Antonio, Texas. Her father was a Palestinian refugee, and her mother was an American of Swiss and German descent. She uses this diverse background in her poems, once saying, "The primary source of poetry has always been local life, random characters met on the streets, our own ancestry sifting down to us through small essential daily tasks." She still lives and works in San Antonio.

Poem

Trying to Name What Doesn't Change

by **Naomi Shihab Nye**

Roselva says the only thing that doesn't change
is train tracks. She's sure of it.
The train changes, or the weeds that grow up spidery
by the side, but not the tracks.
5 I've watched one for three years, she says,
and it doesn't curve, doesn't break, doesn't grow.

Peter isn't sure. He saw an abandoned track
near Sabinas, Mexico, and says a track without a train
is a changed track. The metal wasn't shiny anymore.
10 The wood was split and some of the ties were gone.

Every Tuesday on Morales Street
butchers crack the necks of a hundred hens.
The widow in the tilted house
spices her soup with cinnamon.
15 Ask her what doesn't change.

Stars explode.
The rose curls up as if there is fire in the petals.
The cat who knew me is buried under the bush.

The train whistle still wails its ancient sound
20 but when it goes away, shrinking back
from the walls of the brain,
it takes something different with it every time.

Making Observations

- What images in the poem struck you?
- Which of your senses did the details in the poem activate?

Returning to the Text

- Return to the poem as you respond to the following questions. Use text evidence to support your responses.
- Write any additional questions you have about the poem in your Reader/Writer Notebook.

6. What is Roselva's opinion about the topic posed in the title? What is Peter's response?

_____

_____

_____

_____

7. How does the widow represent both changing and not changing?

_____

_____

_____

_____

8. What conclusion does the speaker reach at the end of the poem?

_____

_____

_____

_____

Setting a Purpose for Reading

- Underline words and phrases that show **alliteration**.
- Create an image in your mind from the descriptive words the author uses.
- Circle unknown words and phrases. Try to determine the meaning of the words by using context clues, word parts, or a dictionary.

About the Author

Paul Fleischman (1952–) writes historical fiction and drama as well as poetry. He loves to make a connection between writing and music, as he does in "Fireflies." He won the Newbery Medal in 1989 for *Joyful Noise*: *Poems for Two Voices*.

LITERARY

Alliteration is the repetition of consonant sounds at the beginnings of words that are close together. For example:

Lucie loves lions and lollipops.

Kind-hearted Kate helped Henry with his homework.

VOCABULARY

WORD CONNECTIONS

Word Relationships
Looking for the relationships among words can help you make meaning. For example, **fly**, **flying**, and **flight** have similar meanings. Other relationships may be shown with different words that have similar meanings. What do **copying**, **scribblers**, and **signing** have in common?

My Notes

Poem

Fireflies
A Poem for Two Voices

by **Paul Fleischman**

Light	Light
	is the ink we use
Night	Night
is our parchment	
5	We're fireflies
fireflies	flickering
flitting	
	flashing
fireflies	
10 glimmering	fireflies
	gleaming
glowing	
Insect calligraphers	Insect calligraphers
practicing penmanship	
15	copying sentences
Six-legged scribblers	Six-legged scribblers
of vanishing messages,	
	fleeting graffiti
Fine artists in flight	Fine artists in flight
20 adding dabs of light	
	bright brush strokes
Signing the June nights	Signing the June nights
as if they were paintings	as if they were paintings
	We're
25 flickering	fireflies
fireflies	flickering
fireflies.	fireflies.

Making Observations
- What words stood out to you?
- What image did the poem leave you with?

Returning to the Text

- Return to the poem as you respond to the following questions. Use text evidence to support your responses.
- Write any additional questions you have about the poem in your Reader/Writer Notebook.

9. What is one example of a variation from standard English in this poem? Why do you think the poet did not use standard English in this instance?

_____

_____

_____

_____

10. What are some examples of figurative language in the poem? What purpose does this figurative language achieve?

_____

_____

_____

_____

11. What are two different ways that fireflies are "fine artists in flight"?

_____

_____

_____

_____

12. What are some examples of alliteration in the poem?

_____

_____

_____

_____

Working from the Text

13. What are the differences between fixed form poetry (such as limericks) and free verse poetry? How does each type of poetry affect how the author expresses ideas? What are the benefits of each type of poetry?

14. How might alliteration strengthen a poem or performance?

☑ Check Your Understanding

Explain what guided your reading pace and inflection when you read this free verse poem. How did you know where to insert pauses?

Introducing the Strategy: Choral Reading

Choral reading is reading text aloud in groups to present an interpretation of a text. This strategy can be used to develop reading fluency; to practice phrasing, pacing, and reading dialogue; and to show how a character's emotions are captured through vocal emphasis and tone.

---

15. Your teacher will assign one of the three poems to your group for choral reading. For your poem:

- Copy the poem onto a separate piece of paper or large index cards that will become your cue cards during your performance.

- Work to make meaning of your poem by diffusing the text. Summarize the poem on the back of the cards and state the main idea.

- Analyze the structure of the poem and plan your choral reading. Mark the text, deciding how you could divide up the poem for two to three voices. You may also want some lines to be read by more than one speaker at the same time. Why should you emphasize these words in the poem?

- Highlight the punctuation to show when to slow down or pause during your oral delivery.

- Highlight alliteration in the poem. Decide how you will use this feature in your oral delivery.

- Remember that a performance requires careful analysis to determine appropriate rate (speed), inflection (emphasis on specific words for effect), and tone (speaker's attitude toward the subject). It also requires appropriate eye contact and facial expressions, which should be consistent with the other elements. Reread the text and record your analysis of these five elements of performance next to your poem.

- Props can be used to clarify ideas and add interest. Brainstorm creative yet simple ideas for props. Record your ideas for props next to appropriate lines in the poem. Any movements you create with the props should be natural, purposeful, and meaningful.

- Parts of "Fireflies" can be read by two voices at the same time. Words in blue can be spoken by the two speakers together. Mark the rest of the poem to decide how you would have two people read lines at the same time.

16. Prepare to deliver your choral reading. Reread your lines aloud multiple times to improve your fluency.

17. Rehearse your performance with your partner or group. As you rehearse:

- Deliver a choral reading of your poem until it is smooth and effective.
- Practice your lines with an effective rate, inflection, and tone.
- Use facial expressions and eye contact appropriate for your lines.
- Practice delivering your poem with props.

When it is your turn, perform your poem.

Reflection

As your classmates deliver their choral readings, listen closely to comprehend the tone and meaning of each poem. Also evaluate each speaker's rate and inflection for how they added to your understanding. Use the graphic organizer that follows to compare and contrast the experience of reading the poems to hearing and seeing them performed. Be sure to include responses to these questions in your comparison:

- What was your understanding of the poem from reading it alone?
- How did your understanding change during group discussions and preparing for a choral reading?
- How did listening to a live performance change how you visualized the scene from the poem?

INDEPENDENT READING LINK

Read and Respond

Compare the structure of one of the poems read in class with the structure of a poem written by the poet you are studying independently. Write about how the structures are alike and how they affect the meaning of the poems.

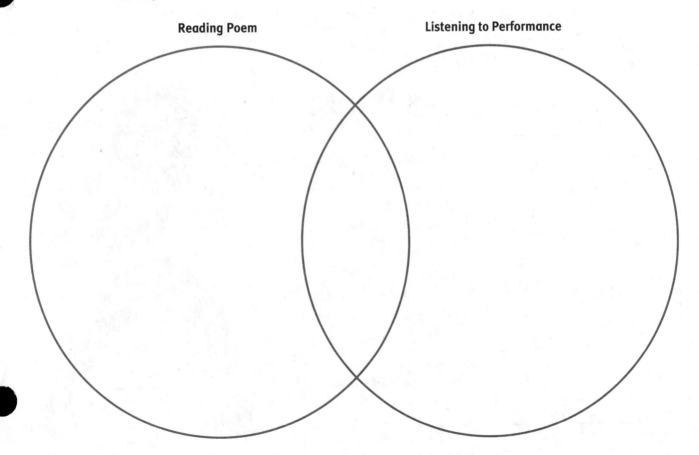

Reading Poem | Listening to Performance

One Poet's Voice, Many Poetic Forms

Learning Strategies

Close Reading
Marking the Text

My Notes

Learning Targets

- Examine multiple forms of poetry written by the same poet and analyze the effect of poetic structures on a reader.
- Compose an original poem in a chosen form.

Preview

In this activity, you will read and analyze several poems written by Pat Mora and compose a poem of your own.

About the Author

Pat Mora (1942–) is originally from El Paso, Texas. She has degrees from the University of Texas, El Paso. She has received numerous awards and fellowships, including a fellowship in poetry from the National Endowment for the Arts.

Setting a Purpose for Reading

- Underline the rhyming words and highlight figures of speech.
- Circle punctuation that shows when to pause during an oral reading.
- Circle unknown words and phrases. Try to determine the meaning of the words by using context clues, word parts, or a dictionary.

Poem

I Can Dance

by **Pat Mora**

I can dance,
moving muscles and knees,
shoulders and hips,
smart as you please.

5   I can dance,

like the guys on TV,
like the dudes on the street,
feeling free and at ease.

I can dance,

10 the old and the new,
baby, I've got the beat.
Watch my step. It's a breeze—
in my room alone
with the door closed.

Making Observations

- What stands out most to you about this text?
- What questions does this text help you answer?

Returning to the Text

- Return to the poem as you respond to the following questions. Use text evidence to support your responses.
- Write any additional questions you have about the poem in your Reader/Writer Notebook.

1. What does it mean when the speaker feels "free and at ease"?

_____

_____

_____

_____

2. How does the speaker feel about his or her dancing in front of other people? Use evidence from the text to support your inference.

_____

_____

_____

_____

3. Which two similes does the speaker use to compare his or her dancing? What purpose do these comparisons serve?

_____

_____

_____

_____

4. Why do the last two lines of the poem break from the rhythm, structure, and format of the first three stanzas? How does this break tie in with the meaning of the poem?

_____

_____

_____

_____

My Notes

Poetic Forms: Ode and Pantoum

Poetry is a diverse genre of literature. You've read limericks and free verse poems, and now you will have the chance to explore two more unique forms of poetry: *ode* and *pantoum*.

Ode: This form of poetry often celebrates a person, place, thing, or idea. Many cultures have versions of odes, and the stanza forms differ from poem to poem. Some famous odes include "Ode on a Grecian Urn" by John Keats, "Ode to Beauty" by Ralph Waldo Emerson, and "Ode to a Large Tuna in the Market" by Pablo Neruda.

Pantoum: This form of poetry consists of four-line stanzas in which the second and fourth lines of each stanza inspire the first and third lines of the next stanza. The format allows poets to establish repetition while they play with sentence types, punctuation, and new ideas.

Setting a Purpose for Reading

- Underline the words or phrases that can be seen as complimentary to teachers.
- Highlight figures of speech.
- Circle unknown words and phrases. Try to determine the meaning of the words by using context clues, word parts, or a dictionary.

Poem (Ode)

Ode to Teachers

by **Pat Mora**

I remember
the first day,
how I looked down,
hoping you wouldn't see
5 me,
and when I glanced up,
I saw your smile
shining like a soft light
from deep inside you.
10 "I'm listening," you encourage us.
"Come on!
Join our conversation,
let us hear your neon certainties,
thorny doubts, tangled angers,"
15 but for weeks I hid inside.
I read and reread your notes
praising
my writing,

and you whispered,
20 "We need you
and your stories
and questions
that like a fresh path
will take us to new vistas."
25 Slowly, your faith grew
into my courage
and for you—
instead of handing you
a note or apple or flowers—
30 I raised my hand.
I carry your smile
and faith inside like I carry
my dog's face,
my sister's laugh,
35 creamy melodies,
the softness of sunrise,
steady blessings of stars,
autumn smell of gingerbread,
the security of a sweater on a chilly day.

Making Observations
- How would you describe the speaker in this poem?
- What descriptive words and phrases struck you?
- What impressions do you have of the speaker and the teacher?

Returning to the Text

- Return to the poem as you respond to the following questions. Use text evidence to support your responses.
- Write any additional questions you have about the poem in your Reader/Writer Notebook.

5. In what way did the teacher encourage the speaker of the poem?

_____

_____

_____

_____

6. How did the speaker's confidence grow?

_____

_____

_____

_____

7. Why did the author write this poem?

_____

_____

_____

_____

8. How does the meter in the first four lines of the final stanza draw the reader's attention?

_____

_____

_____

_____

Setting a Purpose for Reading

- Mark lines that are similar with a unique symbol for each pair of lines.
- Use the My Notes section to write any questions you have about the poem's structure.
- Circle unknown words and phrases. Try to determine the meaning of the words by using context clues, word parts, or a dictionary.

Poem (Pantoum)

Dumped

by **Pat Mora**

> I can't believe you dumped me.
> > For months, I felt so happy inside.
> What a catastrophe!
> > Now I feel ugly and just want to hide.
> 5 All those months, I felt so happy inside.
> > Was everything you said untrue?
> Now I just want to hide
> > and try to forget I loved you. Still do.
> Was everything you said untrue?
> 10 "Let's just be friends." I hate those words.
> I'm trying to forget I loved you and still do.
> > I ache at the mean rumors I've heard.
> "Let's just be friends." Haunting words.
> > Me, a lump you dumped, casually.
> 15 How I ache at the rumors I've heard.
> > My heart broke, my private catastrophe.

Making Observations
- How is the speaker in this poem feeling?
- What words stood out to you the most?

My Notes

Returning to the Text

- Return to the poem as you respond to the following questions. Use text evidence to support your responses.
- Write any additional questions you have about the poem in your Reader/Writer Notebook.

9. What reaction does the speaker have to being dumped? Use text evidence to support your answer.

_____

_____

_____

_____

10. What inference can you make about the rumors that the speaker has heard?

_____

_____

_____

_____

11. How do the repeated phrases affect the meaning of the poem?

_____

_____

_____

_____

12. What does the author mean by "haunting words" in line 13? Are words really haunting the author? How is this phrase an example of figurative language?

_____

_____

_____

_____

13. Why did the author choose the pantoum form for this poem?

_____

_____

_____

_____

© 2021 College Board. All rights reserved.

🌱 Gaining Perspectives

In the poem "Dumped," the speaker has a broken heart after a relationship ends. Imagine you are a friend of the speaker. You want to cheer this person up by suggesting that he or she stay busy with school and extracurricular activities. What could you do to help this person? Make a list of ideas and mark each as "verbal" or "nonverbal." Then share your ideas with a partner. Then switch roles. When finished, summarize the outcome of the role play in your Reader/Writer Notebook.

Working from the Text

14. Looking at the three poems by Pat Mora, what kinds of experiences does she write about? What themes are present in all three poems? Use evidence from the poems to support your inference.

_____

_____

_____

_____

15. How might Mora's real-life experiences influence her writing? How does this make readers relate to her writing?

_____

_____

_____

_____

16. Following are types of figurative language. Your teacher will assign a word to you. Create a Word Wall card for your assigned word. Your examples should incorporate figurative language from the poems you have read in this unit as well as original sentences. You will be able to use the Word Wall as a reminder of these terms as you study more literature.

Language Type	Definition
Types of Figurative Language	**Imaginative language that is not meant to be interpreted literally**
Hyperbole	extreme exaggeration used for emphasis, often used for comic effect
Simile	a comparison between two unlike things using the word *like* or *as* (X is *like* Y)
Metaphor	a comparison between two unlike things in which one thing is said to be another (X = Y)
Personification	a kind of metaphor that gives objects or abstract ideas human characteristics
Pun	the humorous use of a word or words to suggest another word with the same sound but a different meaning

Sample Word Wall card:

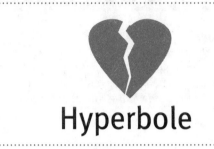

Hyperbole

an exaggeration for effect (Definition)

I could sleep for days. (Example 1)

I can't live without you. (Example 2)

You are breaking my heart. (Example 3)

17. You will now present your Word Wall card. Remember these presenting tips:

When you are the speaker:

- Come to the presentation prepared.
- Use appropriate eye contact, adequate volume, good speaking rate, natural gestures, and clear enunciation.
- Form and respond to specific questions relating to the topic under discussion.

When you are the listener:

- Understand ideas by taking notes and asking questions for clarification after each speaker presents.
- Explore ideas by challenging your group to think about the topic on a deeper level.

☑ Check Your Understanding

"I Can Dance," "Ode to Teachers," and "Dumped" all were published in the same book. What do the poems have in common? How are they different? Think in terms of theme, language, message, and form. Use evidence from the poems to support your response.

✏ Narrative Writing Prompt

Look back at the poetic forms you have explored in this unit. Choose one for your own original poem or choose the form of a poem you have read before. Choose a topic that is appropriate to the form and start your composition. Be sure to:

- Use your genre knowledge to remain true to the poetic form you chose or bend the rules purposefully.
- Include some figurative language to create a distinctive voice and be prepared to identify what type of figurative language it is.
- Read your poem aloud to yourself or someone else as you revise it.
- Follow the conventions of English unless you disregard a convention purposefully.

The Work of a Poet

Learning Targets

- Analyze primary and secondary sources about Pat Mora and generate research questions.
- Provide basic bibliographic information about sources.
- Integrate ideas from multiple texts to build knowledge and vocabulary about how personal stories inspire others to challenge themselves.

Preview

In this activity, you will analyze primary and secondary sources about Pat Mora's life and use them to generate research questions.

Primary and Secondary Sources

Researchers use a variety of **sources** to learn about their subjects. In Unit 3, you learned that primary sources are original documents, such as letters and speeches. Secondary sources are not original documents—they are written about the subject and often synthesize information from several other sources.

Setting a Purpose for Reading

- As you read, draw a star next to any advice you find interesting.
- Circle unknown words and phrases. Try to determine the meaning of the words by using context clues, word parts, or a dictionary.

Letter

from

A Letter to Gabriela, A Young Writer

by **Pat Mora**

Dear Gabriela,

1   Your mother tells me that you have begun writing poems and that you wonder exactly how I do it. Do you perhaps wonder why I do it? Why would anyone sit alone and write when she could be talking to friends on the telephone, eating mint chocolate chip ice-cream in front of the television, or buying a new red sweater at the mall?

2   And, as you know, I like people. I like long, slow lunches with my friends. I like to dance. I'm no **hermit**, and I'm not shy. So why do I sit with my tablet and pen and mutter to myself?

3   There are many answers. I write because I'm a reader. I want to give to others what writers have given me, a chance to hear the voices of people I will never meet. Alone, in private. And even if I meet these authors, I wouldn't hear

Learning Strategies

Collaborative Discussion
Generating Questions
Marking the Text
Graphic Organizer

ACADEMIC

When you cite **sources** in research, you are referring to a place from which information comes or is obtained. Sources must be evaluated and cited to avoid plagiarism. Using and citing good sources makes your research more credible.

VOCABULARY

KNOWLEDGE QUEST

Knowledge Question:

How do personal stories inspire others to challenge themselves?

In Activity 4.5, you will read two texts about author Pat Mora. While you read and build knowledge about the theme, think about your answer to the Knowledge Question.

hermit: person who doesn't go out much

My Notes

what I hear along with the page, words carefully chosen, woven into a piece unlike any other, enjoyed by me in a way no other person will, in quite the same way, enjoy them. I suppose I'm saying that I love the privateness of writing and reading. It's delicious to curl into a book.

4   I write because I'm curious. I'm curious about me. Writing is a way of finding out how I feel about anything and everything. Now that I've left the desert where I grew up, for example, I'm discovering how it feels to walk on spongy fall leaves and to watch snow drifting up on a strong wind. I notice what's around me in a special way because I'm a writer. It's like radar, like the **keen** listening and looking of Indiana Jones when he walks into the jungle loud with parrots and monkeys. So I notice my world more, and then I talk to myself about it on paper. Writing is my way of saving my feelings.

5   I write because I believe that Mexican Americans need to take their rightful place in American literature. We need to be published and to be studied in schools and colleges so that the stories and ideas of our people won't quietly disappear. Although I'm happy when I finish the draft of a poem or story, deep inside I always wish I wrote better, that I could bring more honor and attention to, for example, the *abuelitas* I write about. The mix of sadness and pleasure occurs often in life, doesn't it, Gabriela?

6   I know that the society we live in and the shows and ads we see all affect us. It's not easy to learn to judge others fairly, not because of the car they drive, the house they live in, the church they attend, the color of their skin, the language they speak at home. It takes courage to face the fact that we all have ten toes, get sleepy at night, get scared in the dark. Some families, some cities, some states, and even some countries foolishly convince themselves that they're better than others. And then they teach their children this ugly lie. It's like a weed with burrs and stickers that pricks people.

7   How are young women who are Afro American, Asian American, Native American, Hispanics, or members of all the other ethnic groups supposed to feel about themselves? Some are proud of their cultural roots. But commercials are also busy trying to convince us that our car, clothes, and maybe even our family aren't good enough. It's so hard in 1990 to be yourself, your many interesting selves, because billboards and magazine ads tell you that beautiful is being thin, maybe blonde, and rich, rich, rich. No wonder we don't always like ourselves when we look in the mirror.

8   There are no secrets to good writing. Read. Listen. Write. Read. Listen. Write. You learn to write well by reading wonderful writing and by letting those words and ideas become part of your blood and bones. But life is not all books. You become a better writer by listening—to yourself and to all the colors, shapes, and sounds around you. Listen with all of your senses. Listen to the wrinkles on your *tía's* face.

9   Writers write. They don't just talk about writing just as dancers don't just talk about dancing. They do it because they love it and because they want to get better and better. They practice and practice to loosen up just as you practiced

WORD CONNECTIONS

Content Connections
Burrs are parts of a plant that contain seeds. Burrs have little hooks on the outside, so if you brush up against one, it will literally stick to you when it hooks onto your hair or clothes.

keen: sharp, focused

and practiced when you were learning to talk. And because you practiced, you don't talk the way you did when you were three.

10 … Usually I like to start [writing] in a sunny spot with a yellow, lined tablet and a pen. I have a number of **false starts**. I'm working but having fun … Alone. The first line of a poem is sometimes a hard one because I want it to be an interesting line. It may be the only line a reader will glance at to decide whether to read the whole piece. I'm searching for the right beginning. I play a little game with myself. (This game works with any kind of writing.) I tell myself to write any line no matter how bad or dull, since I can later throw it away. If I sit waiting for the perfect line, I might never write the poem. I'm willing to make a fool of myself. So I start, usually slowly. I write a few lines, read them aloud, and often start again. I keep sections I like and **discard** the uninteresting parts. The next day I read my work and try to improve it. I'm trying to pull out of myself the poem or story that's deep inside.

11 It's important, Gabriela, not to fall in love with the words you write. Pick your words or phrases, and then stand back and look at your work. Read it out loud.

12 You and I are lucky to be writers. So many women in history and even today who could be much better writers than I am have not had that private pleasure of creating with words. Maybe their families think writing is a waste of time, maybe they don't believe in themselves, maybe they have to work hard all day and then have to cook and clean and take care of their children at night, maybe they've never been taught to read and write.

13 I hope that you develop pride in being Mexican American and that you discover what you have to say that no one else can say. I hope that you continue writing, Gabriela.

© 2021 College Board. All rights reserved.

Knowledge Quest

- What stands out most for you about this letter?
- How do you feel after reading the letter?

false starts: starts that result in having to start again

discard: throw away

Returning to the Text

- Return to the letter as you respond to the following questions. Use text evidence to support your responses.
- Write any additional questions you have about the letter in your Reader/Writer Notebook.

1. Is this a primary or secondary source? Explain your answer.

_____

_____

_____

_____

2. Why does the author repeat the line "I write because ..."?

_____

_____

_____

_____

3. In paragraph 9, what does the author compare writing to? What is the purpose of this simile?

_____

_____

_____

_____

4. **KQ** In paragraph 7, Mora says that some people find it hard to be themselves despite the fact that they are "proud of their cultural roots." What are cultural roots, and what do they have to do with Mora's reason for writing? Also, what do they have to do with the hopes she expresses for Gabriela in paragraph 13?

_____

_____

_____

_____

5. **KQ** What does Mora want Gabriela to learn from her letter? What is the letter's theme?

_____

_____

_____

_____

Setting a Purpose for Reading

- Underline words and phrases that compliment Pat Mora's writing.
- Circle unknown words and phrases. Try to determine the meaning of the words by using context clues, word parts, or a dictionary.

News Article

Pat Mora's love for words spreads a river of literacy

by **Julie L. Ortiz,** *Borderzine,* **September 30, 2010**

1   EL PASO, Texas—Award-winning writer Pat Mora is a jack-of-all-trades. She writes poetry, books for adult readers, inspirational books for children and young adults, and is a dedicated **advocate** for reading and literacy.

2   Open any of her works and you are taken on a journey that flows like water, bringing freshness to a reader's mind. Her works are important to the border community. They paint a picture of the region's Hispanic culture for those who are not familiar with the border. Mora is a pioneer in Chicano Literature and her numerous awards and **fellowships** are **testament** to her talent.

3   A perfect example is her short poem entitled *Unrefined.* "The desert is no lady. / She screams at the spring sky, / dances with her skirts high, / kicks sand, flings tumbleweeds, / digs her nails into all flesh. / Her unveiled lust fascinates the sun."

4   Mora's work reflects her homegrown El Paso roots and the Hispanic culture that infuses the U.S. Mexico border region. Now a resident of Santa Fe, N. M., she is a former teacher and administrator and an alumnus of Texas Western College and the University of Texas at El Paso.

5   The pieces she chooses to read on tour reflect her emotions, her heritage, and her love of words. Mora chose to come back to her alma mater, the University of Texas at El Paso in September to promote her body of work and to spread her idea of "Bookjoy"—what she says readers feel when they read. She hopes she can inspire everyone to enjoy reading and writing.

6   In an excerpt from *Adobe Odes*, she reads about her uncle not being able to afford college. She explains to her audiences that many people are in similar situations. Her goal is to illuminate her readers to the power of reading—that reading is just as powerful as paying for a formal education.

7   "I need to be alone when I write," Mora said. Most of her work comes to mind through periods of **solitude** frequently in the vast deserts of the southwest. That environment is important to her art, almost always a catalyst for some of her work, mostly her poetry, but she says that she can gain inspiration from anything, or anyone.

KNOWLEDGE QUEST

Knowledge Question:
How do personal stories inspire others to challenge themselves?

GRAMMAR & USAGE

Quoting Lines of Poetry
When quoting lines of poetry in another piece of writing, use **slashes** to show the line breaks of the poem. This is done so that line breaks can be maintained in a flowing piece of text without having to waste space. See paragraph 3 for an example of how slashes are used to show line breaks.

WORD CONNECTIONS

Multiple-Meaning Words
The word **reflect** is a multiple-meaning word. Among its definitions are "to give back an image of," "to bend or to fold back light," "to express an emotion," "to bring to show," or "to think quietly." Which of these meanings fits the context of the word in paragraph 5?

advocate: supporter
fellowships: grants given to someone to continue work in a field of study
testament: evidence or proof
solitude: aloneness

My Notes

8 Not only is she an inspiration to adults, but Mora's children's works have **garnered** many adolescent fans. Children excitedly line up to have their books autographed by the author on her book tours. One of her popular works is *Dizzy in Your Eyes: Love Poems*—a series of poems meant to inspire teenagers in a positive light.

9 Mora is currently on a book tour promoting her latest work *Zing: Seven Creativity Practices for Educators and Students*. Mora hopes that teachers and students can implement this work in the classroom. It is a guidebook that encourages creativity through Mora's own creative experiences. She wants to share her creativity with others to inspire them to write.

10 Along with promoting her writing, she is also a national advocate for reading and literacy for children of all ages, adults, and aspiring teachers. She established April 30 as "El día del los niños, el día de los libros" (Children's Day, Book Day), in which children and literacy are celebrated. April 30, 2011, marks the 15th anniversary for this event.

Cover of Book Fiesta!, a Pura Belpré Award–winning picture book published in 2016

garnered: gained

Ø Knowledge Quest

- What is your impression of the kind of person Mora is?
- What is something interesting you learned about Mora?

Returning to the Text

- Return to the article as you respond to the following questions. Use text evidence to support your responses.
- Write any additional questions you have about the article in your Reader/Writer Notebook.

6. Where did Mora grow up? Why is this important in her writing?

_____

_____

_____

_____

7. Is this a primary or secondary source? Explain your answer.

_____

_____

_____

_____

8. Why did the author write this article?

_____

_____

_____

_____

9. What is the author's claim about Mora? How does she support it?

_____

_____

_____

_____

10. **KQ** The author of this article uses the word *inspirational* to describe Mora. What does it mean to be *inspirational*? Use a dictionary to find out. Then list some qualities that make Mora inspirational.

_____

_____

_____

_____

11. How does the poem in paragraph 3 fit into the rest of the article? Why do you think the author chose to include the poem?

_____

_____

_____

12. KQ Think about what you learned about Mora from her letter and this article. How does Mora use her own experiences to inspire future writers?

_____

_____

_____

_____

INDEPENDENT READING LINK

You can continue to build your knowledge about how personal stories inspire others to challenge themselves by reading other articles at ZINC Reading Labs. Search for keywords such as *inspiration* or *challenges*.

Knowledge Quest

After reading these two texts about Pat Mora, think about the ways personal stories can inspire, challenge, and ultimately change a person. Think about a time when you felt inspired by someone's story. Write a paragraph that briefly summarizes the story and tells why you felt challenged by it and what it led you to do.

Working from the Text

13. Skim through the two texts again, this time taking notes using a graphic organizer like the one that follows.

    • **Left Column:** Paraphrase, summarize, and quote information that answers the following research questions: *Who* is Pat Mora? *When* did she live? *What* has she accomplished? *What* has been her journey to success? *Where* is she from? *What* has she written? *Why* does she write? *How* does she get her ideas?

    • **Middle Column:** Categorize or classify the information as it relates to Pat Mora. Possible categories include "Life," "Childhood," "Culture," "Personality," and "Work."

    • **Right Column:** Generate some new secondary questions from the information and refine the original question as necessary.

	Information	Categories of Information	New Research Questions
1			
2			

14. Think about the source of the two texts. Are these sources reliable and credible? Why do you think so?

    _____

    _____

    _____

    _____

15. Brainstorm how you could use multimedia to clarify ideas and add interest to a presentation of this information (e.g., graphics, images, music, sound).

    _____

    _____

    _____

    _____

VOCABULARY

ACADEMIC

Creating a **bibliography**, or a list of source materials used to prepare a research paper or presentation, is an important part of a researcher's responsibility. Many formats exist to create a bibliography. Use style guides to be sure you are formatting yours properly.

My Notes

INDEPENDENT READING LINK

Read and Respond

Find an informational text about the poet whose work you are reading independently. Ask yourself the following questions about the source: *Is this source reliable? How do you know? Does the source show any bias toward or against the person?* If you decide the text is reliable, use it to answer existing research questions and generate new ones.

16. Writers create a **bibliography** to give full credit to the sources from which they cite information. Record basic bibliographic information for the texts you read in this activity. Note that online information may not have a publication date, in which case you should use the date on which you accessed the information from the Internet.

Source 1:

> **Author:**
>
> **Title:**
>
> **Source:**
>
> **Date of Publication:**

Source 2:

> **Author:**
>
> **Title:**
>
> **Source:**
>
> **Date of Publication:**

☑ Focus on the Sentence

Write a statement and a question about Pat Mora's life or work.

Statement: _____

_____

_____

Question: _____

_____

_____

Deepening Understanding: Research

Learning Targets

- Research the life journey of one poet using multiple print and digital sources that have been evaluated for their credibility.
- Write an informational text integrating information gained through research.

Preview

In this activity, you will plan and conduct a research project about a famous poet that will include gathering and evaluating sources.

Conducting Research

1. Use notes from the previous activity to help you brainstorm ideas for research.
   Topics or Poets to Research:

2. Select a research topic and work collaboratively in your research team to develop thoughtful questions to guide your research.
   Research Questions:

3. Assign each team member a category or subtopic to research. That person will be responsible for gathering information related to that category and generating additional research questions. Revisit your major research question to see if it needs to be revised based on your findings.

4. Identify potential sources (print and/or online).
   - Which sources are best for your topic?
   - Where can you find them?

5. **Evaluate** your sources by determining their reliability, credibility, and usefulness.
   - Can you trust the source of information? Why or why not?
   - How does the source address your research question(s)?
   - Does the source have a bias toward or against a person or topic?

6. Use reading strategies to make meaning of the informational texts.
   - Which strategies work best for you when you read informational texts?
   - What will you do if you do not understand the text?

7. **Annotate** your sources as you read to make sure that you understand what you are reading. For paper sources, mark the text with pencil and highlighters. If you are working digitally, use the tools available in PDF or word-processing software. Your annotations will help you set up your double-entry journal.

Learning Strategies

Graphic Organizer
Paraphrasing
Prewriting
Generating Questions
Collaborative Discussion
Note-taking

INDEPENDENT READING LINK

Read and Research

To practice generating questions and identifying sources, plan a research project about the poet whose work you are reading independently. Think of some research questions about your poet. Find several sources that contain information about the poet. Evaluate each source for reliability and credibility and write several sentences about why each source would be appropriate for your research project.

ACADEMIC

When you **evaluate**, you examine and judge carefully in order to determine the value of something, such as an idea, a comment, or a source.

When you **annotate**, you write notes to capture or explain ideas that help you and others understand a text.

VOCABULARY

My Notes

8. Take notes using a double-entry journal. In the left column, paraphrase, summarize, and quote information that answers your research questions. In the right column, form a response to the information (statements and/or questions). Think about the following:

   • When should you paraphrase or summarize?

   • When should you directly quote?

   • What makes a response effective?

9. Print, copy, and/or record multimedia sources to clarify ideas and add interest to your presentation (e.g., graphics, images, music/sound).

   • Where can you find effective multimedia sources?

   • How will the selected multimedia sources support your audience's understanding of key information about your topic?

10. Record basic bibliographic information for each of your sources (author, title, source, date of publication, type: print or online) on note cards or in your Reader/Writer Notebook.

   Source #:

Author:
Title:
Source:
Date of Publication:
Type (print or online):

11. Continue to research until you thoroughly answer your research questions, revising your plan as needed.

   • Have you learned enough about your topic to create a presentation and communicate your ideas to an audience?

   • Do you feel confident answering questions about your topic?

Writing to Sources: Informational Text

Explain what you have learned about your selected poet through research. Be sure to:

• Answer your research questions by drawing on several sources.

• Assess the credibility of your sources and provide bibliographic information for each of the sources you choose.

• Provide relevant information and examples from multiple sources, making sure to quote or paraphrase information to avoid plagiarism.

• Use academic vocabulary, literary terms, and a formal style and tone.

• Revise as needed to improve the organization of ideas and to add transitions and/or to use a variety of sentence types.

Planning to Present Research

Learning Targets
- Synthesize research about a poet.
- Use technology to create a multimedia presentation on a poet.

Preview
In this activity, you will work with your research team to synthesize information and create a multimedia presentation.

Synthesizing Research

1. You will now present your research to the rest of your research team. You can use your notes or your response to the writing prompt in Activity 4.6 to guide your presentation.

   When you are the speaker:
   - Come to the discussion prepared.
   - Use appropriate eye contact, adequate volume, and clear enunciation.
   - Form and respond to specific questions relating to the topic under discussion.

   When you are the listener:
   - Take notes and ask questions for clarification after each speaker presents in order to understand their ideas.
   - Challenge your group to explore ideas and think about the topic on a deeper level.
   - Evaluate the strength of ideas to provide constructive feedback and offer suggestions to strengthen ideas when necessary.

2. Collaborate with your research team to synthesize information by putting different pieces of your research together to form a coherent whole. Use the following questions to guide the process:
   - What conclusion(s) can you draw about the poet and his or her life?
   - How can you organize and sequence (order) your information to make your conclusions clear to others (e.g., use headings and transitions)? Use the mapping strategy to show your thinking.
   - How can you use technology to create multimedia and/or visual displays to clarify ideas and add interest?
   - Which of the poet's poems might add to your presentation? Could you read it orally or present it visually?

Learning Strategies
Collaborative Discussion
Note-taking
Mapping
Generating Questions

WORD CONNECTIONS

Roots and Affixes
The word **collaborate** contains the Latin root *labor,* meaning "work," and the prefix *co-* or *col-,* meaning "together" or "with." Knowing the Latin root *labor* can also help you understand the meaning of the word *elaboration* ("the process of working something out in detail"). Knowing the Latin prefix *col-* can also help you understand the meaning of *collect* ("to gather together").

My Notes

3. Identify areas where you might need to do more research. Your combined information might leave a question unanswered or need transitional details.

4. Collaboratively generate secondary research questions and assign one to each team member for further research.

🔲 Independent Reading Checkpoint

Gather and organize your research and prepare to give a short, informal presentation to a small group of students about your poet. In your presentation, discuss the kinds of poetry your poet writes as well as key details about your poet's life. Explain what makes your poet unique and provide evidence from your research to support your position. Even though the presentation should be informal, use your presentation skills: maintain good eye contact, speak at a good rate and volume, enunciate words clearly, use natural gestures and conventional English, and organize your ideas so they are easy to follow.

Researching and Presenting a Poet

✍ ASSIGNMENT

Work collaboratively to conduct research, synthesize findings, and present a poet's life journey. Your presentation should be five minutes in length, and speaking parts should be divided equally. If possible, incorporate a poem written by the poet as well as multimedia elements, including video and sound, into your presentation.

Planning and Prewriting: Take time to make a plan for generating ideas and research questions.	▪ How will you select a poet that your group is interested in? ▪ What questions will guide your research? How will you refine them over time if needed? ▪ How will you ensure that each group member is researching a different aspect of your topic?
Researching: information from a variety of relevant sources.	▪ Where can you find sources, and how can you tell that the sources are relevant and useful? ▪ How will you take notes by paraphrasing information and recording bibliographic information? ▪ How will you use research to gather visuals and other multimedia?
Preparing and Creating: Organize talking points and create a multimedia presentation.	▪ What strategy will you use to organize information? ▪ How will you be sure that ideas are presented clearly with an introduction, transitions, and a conclusion? ▪ How will you integrate multimedia and visuals to clarify and add interest?
Evaluating and Rehearsing: Create opportunities to review and rehearse your presentations.	▪ When can you present to a group of your peers to get feedback and suggestions for improvement? ▪ How can the Scoring Guide help you evaluate how well prepared you are to meet the requirements of the assignment?
Speaking and Listening: Participate effectively as both a presenter and audience member.	▪ How will you use volume, eye contact, and enunciation to engage your audience? ▪ How will you take notes during the other students' presentations?

Reflection

After completing this Embedded Assessment, think about how you went about accomplishing this task. Then respond to the following questions:

• How did researching a poet help you understand that poet's work more deeply?
• Which of the class presentations were the most engaging, and why?

SCORING GUIDE

Scoring Criteria	Exemplary	Proficient	Emerging	Incomplete
Ideas	The presentation • supports a clearly focused main idea with relevant descriptions, facts, and details synthesized from a variety of sources. • includes a correct and complete bibliography or works cited page.	The presentation • supports a main idea with sufficient descriptions, facts, and details synthesized from multiple sources. • includes a bibliography or works cited page that follows a standard format.	The presentation • has an unclear, unfocused, or insufficiently supported main idea; may rely too heavily on a single source for information. • includes a partial or inaccurate bibliography or works cited page.	The presentation • does not include a main idea or shows little or no evidence of research. • lacks a bibliography or works cited page.
Structure	The presentation • demonstrates strong evidence of collaboration. • sequences ideas effectively, including an engaging introduction, clear headings, smooth transitions, and a logical conclusion. • integrates a variety of multimedia to enhance ideas.	The presentation • demonstrates adequate evidence of collaboration. • sequences ideas logically, including an introduction, headings, transitions, and a concluding section/statement. • uses multimedia to clarify ideas and add interest.	The presentation • demonstrates uneven or ineffective collaboration. • uses flawed sequencing; may lack one or more of the following: an introduction, headings, transitions, and a concluding section/statement. • uses multimedia ineffectively.	The presentation • demonstrates a failure to collaborate. • has little or no discernible structure. • lacks multimedia support.
Use of Language	The presenter • uses effective eye contact, gestures, volume, pacing, and enunciation. • demonstrates command of the conventions of standard English grammar, usage, and language, including a variety of syntax. • maintains a consistently formal style and tone, including the consistent use of academic vocabulary and literary terms.	The presenter • uses appropriate eye contact, gestures, volume, and enunciation. • demonstrates adequate command of the conventions of standard English grammar, usage, and language, including a variety of syntax. • maintains a generally formal style and tone, including the use of some academic vocabulary or literary terms.	The presenter • uses eye contact, gestures, volume, and enunciation unevenly. • demonstrates partial command of the conventions of standard English grammar, usage, and language; uses little variety of syntax. • maintains an inconsistently formal style and/or tone and uses limited academic vocabulary or literary terms.	The presenter • uses flawed or ineffective speaking skills. • makes frequent errors in standard English grammar, usage, and language. • uses an inappropriate style and/or tone.

Unpacking Embedded Assessment 2

Learning Targets

- Identify the knowledge, skills, and vocabulary needed to complete Embedded Assessment 2 successfully.
- Preview and practice the skills needed for a class performance.

Preview

In this activity, you will unpack Embedded Assessment 2 and preview the next half of the unit.

Making Connections

In the first part of this unit, you learned how to do research, and you presented your research on a topic related to a poet. In the second part of the unit, you will learn how to perform a scene from a classic play.

Essential Questions

Reflect on your understanding of the first Essential Question. How can research inform an understanding of a literary text? How would you answer that question at this point in the unit?

Developing Vocabulary

1. Resort the following Academic Vocabulary and Literary Terms using the QHT strategy.

Academic Vocabulary	Literary Terms
source	rate
bibliography	inflection
evaluate	meter
annotate	alliteration

Q (unfamiliar)	H (familiar)	T (very familiar)

My Notes

INDEPENDENT READING LINK

Reading Plan

To support your learning in the second half of the unit, find a fiction or nonfiction text about someone (a character or a real person) who struggled with physical or mental challenges and changed in some way.

Create a reading plan for the text you have chosen.

My Notes

2. Compare this sort with your original sort. How many words have changed category? How many have stayed the same?

3. Select a word from the chart and write a concise statement about your learning. How has your understanding of the word changed over the course of this unit?

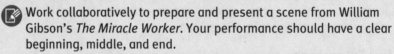

Unpacking Embedded Assessment 2

Read the assignment for Embedded Assessment 2: Performing a Scene.

Work collaboratively to prepare and present a scene from William Gibson's *The Miracle Worker*. Your performance should have a clear beginning, middle, and end.

Work with your class to paraphrase the expectations and create a graphic organizer to use as a visual reminder of the required concepts (what you need to know) and skills (what you need to do). Copy the graphic organizer for future reference. After each activity, use this graphic to guide reflection about what you have learned and what you still need to learn in order to be successful on the Embedded Assessment.

Play Ball: Analyzing a Game of Life

Learning Targets

- Explain how a text's structure contributes to the development of a theme.
- Analyze an author's use of diction to create meaning and tone.

Preview

In this activity, you will read a story about baseball and friendship and write about the story's theme.

Learning Strategies

Predicting
Marking the Text
Summarizing
Collaborative Discussion
Close Reading
Brainstorming
Drafting

Setting a Purpose for Reading

- Underline words and phrases that suggest emotion.
- Pause after each "inning" to think about how the section builds on what came before it or shows a change in the characters' feelings.
- Circle unknown words and phrases. Try to determine the meaning of the words by using context clues, word parts, or a dictionary.

Short Story

The Southpaw

by **Judith Viorst**

WORD CONNECTIONS

Etymology
The word **southpaw** is baseball slang for a left-handed pitcher. Originally baseball diamonds were laid out with home plate to the west, so left-handed pitchers' pitching arms would be facing south when they stood on the pitching mound.

Inning 1

Dear Richard,
Don't invite me to your birthday party because I'm not coming. And give back the Disneyland sweatshirt I said you could wear. If I'm not good enough to play on your team, I'm not good enough to be friends with.

Your former friend,

Janet

P.S. I hope when you go to the dentist he finds 20 cavities.

Dear Janet,
Here is your stupid Disneyland sweatshirt, if that's how you're going to be. I want my comic books now—finished or not. No girl has ever played on the Mapes Street baseball team, and as long as I'm captain, no girl ever will.

Your former friend,

Richard

P.S. I hope when you go for your checkup you need a tetanus shot.

My Notes

My Notes

Inning 2

Dear Richard,
I'm changing my goldfish's name from Richard to Stanley. Don't count on my vote for class president next year. Just because I'm a member of the ballet club doesn't mean I'm not a terrific ballplayer.

> Your former friend,
> Janet

P.S. I see you lost your first game 28–0.

Dear Janet,
I'm not saving any more seats for you on the bus. For all I care you can stand the whole way to school. Why don't you just forget about baseball and learn something nice like knitting?

> Your former friend,
> Richard

P.S. Wait until Wednesday.

Inning 3

Dear Richard,
My father said I could call someone to go with us for a ride and hot-fudge sundaes. In case you didn't notice, I didn't call you.

> Your former friend,
> Janet

P.S. I see you lost your second game, 34–0.

Dear Janet,
Remember when I took the laces out of my blue-and-white sneakers and gave them to you? I want them back.

> Your former friend,
> Richard

P.S. Wait until Friday.

Inning 4

Dear Richard,
Congratulations on your unbroken record. Eight straight losses, wow! I understand you're the laughing stock of New Jersey.

> Your former friend,
> Janet

P.S. Why don't you and your team forget about baseball and learn something nice like knitting maybe?

Dear Janet,
Here's the silver horseback riding trophy that you gave me. I don't think I want to keep it anymore.

> Your former friend,
> Richard

P.S. I didn't think you'd be the kind who'd kick a man when he's down.

Inning 5

Dear Richard,
I wasn't kicking exactly. I was kicking back.

> Your former friend,
> Janet

P.S. In case you were wondering, my batting average is .345.

Dear Janet,
Alfie is having his tonsils out tomorrow. We might be able to let you catch next week.

> Richard

Inning 6

Dear Richard,
I pitch.

> Janet

Dear Janet,
Joel is moving to Kansas and Danny sprained his wrist. How about a permanent place in the outfield?

> Richard

Inning 7

Dear Richard,
I pitch.

> Janet

GRAMMAR & USAGE

Adverbs
An **adverb** answers the question *how* or *in what way*. The suffix *-ly* may be added to adjectives to form adverbs. Look for the adverb *exactly* in Inning 5 of "The Southpaw." It tells in what way Janet was kicking. Adverbs can also be used to help set a desired tone in writing. Notice how the author uses adverbs with verbs to help communicate the attitude with which a character performs the action of the verb or even to add a note of sarcasm, as in Janet's "Inning 5" retort that she was "kicking back."

Adjectives and Predicate Adjectives

An **adjective** describes a noun or a pronoun and answers the question *what kind, which one, how many,* or *how much.* Using adjectives with different levels of intensity can change the tone of writing. In Inning 4 of "The Southpaw," the author's use of the adjective *unbroken* strengthens the mocking tone of the note. **Predicate adjectives** are adjectives that follow the verb *to be* or linking verbs, as in this sentence in Inning 9: *Nobody ever said that I was unreasonable. Unreasonable* is a predicate adjective, following the linking verb *was.* When reading, notice the way the author uses adjectives and predicate adjectives that have the appropriate intensity for the tone he or she is trying to set.

My Notes

_____

_____

_____

_____

_____

_____

_____

_____

_____

_____

_____

_____

_____

_____

_____

_____

Dear Janet,

Ronnie caught the chicken pox and Leo broke his toe and Elwood has these stupid violin lessons. I'll give you first base, and that's my final offer.

> Richard

Inning 8

Dear Richard,

Susan Reilly plays first base, Marilyn Jackson catches, Ethel Kahn plays center field, I pitch. It's a package deal.

> Janet

P.S. Sorry about your 12-game losing streak.

Dear Janet,

Please! Not Marilyn Jackson.

> Richard

Inning 9

Dear Richard,

Nobody ever said that I was unreasonable. How about Lizzie Martindale instead?

> Janet

Dear Janet,

At least could you call your goldfish Richard again?

> Your friend,
> Richard

Making Observations

- What opinions did you form as you read the letters?
- What personal connections did you make with the story?
- What do the two characters sound like?

Returning to the Text

- Return to the short story as you respond to the following questions. Use text evidence to support your responses.
- Write any additional questions you have about the short story in your Reader/Writer Notebook.

1. What is the main idea of the Inning 2 section? Which details in this section support the main idea?

_____

_____

_____

_____

2. How is Richard's baseball team doing in Inning 4? Support your answer with text evidence.

_____

_____

_____

_____

3. Which sentence in Inning 5 shows that Richard may be changing his mind?

_____

_____

_____

_____

4. In Inning 9, how can you tell that Richard's attitude has changed since the beginning of the story?

_____

_____

_____

_____

5. How does the author develop point of view in this story?

_____

_____

_____

_____

6. How does the way the story is organized by sections help the author tell the story?

_____

_____

_____

_____

Literacy Center Reading

For this activity, you will analyze the story and participate in collaborative work and discussion.

First Base

Use precise adjectives to describe tone.

You might say that the two characters in "The Southpaw" express a *mad* or *angry* tone in the first half of the story, but these words are not precise. Reread your assigned letters (see following list) and discuss each letter's tone with your group members. Using classroom resources such as a thesaurus, tone list, and Word Wall, brainstorm a list of synonyms for the identified tone and order them from least intense to most intense. Then agree upon and record a precise adjective in the My Notes section next to each assigned letter. Leave your brainstorming notes for other groups to use as a resource.

Group 1: Letters 1–4   Group 3: Letters 9–12
Group 2: Letters 13–18   Group 4: Letters 5–8

Note: Groups 1, 3, and 4 should first review the previous responses and revise to identify a more accurate or precise tone.

Second Base

Use adverbs to communicate tone.

Adverbs can also show a character's tone. Next to each character's name in your assigned letters, record a verb and precise adverb that capture the writer's emotions. For example, a character could <u>state</u> *proudly*, <u>demand</u> *angrily*, or <u>explain</u> *regretfully*. Use classroom resources such as a dictionary, adverb list, or Word Wall to expand your options.

Group 1: Letters 5–8   Group 3: Letters 13–18
Group 2: Letters 1–4   Group 4: Letters 9–12

Third Base

Summarize the point of view.

Reread your assigned letters (see following list). In the My Notes section, concisely summarize each set of letters by explaining each character's point of view and how it is created.

Group 1: Letters 9–12   Group 3: Letters 1–4
Group 2: Letters 5–8   Group 4: Letters 13–18

Note: Groups 2, 3, and 4 should first review the previous responses and revise if they can write a more accurate or concise summary.

Home Base

Make a connection between conflict and plot.

Think of the exchange of letters in the story as a baseball scoreboard. The first two letters between Janet and Richard are Inning 1, letters 3 and 4 are Inning 2, and so on. For each pair of assigned letters, decide who "wins" the argument. Write a "1" in his or her box and a "0" in the other character's box. Explain your thinking in the My Notes section and discuss the connection between conflict and plot.

	Inning 1 (1–2)	Inning 2 (3–4)	Inning 3 (5–6)	Inning 4 (7–8)	Inning 5 (9–10)	Inning 6 (11–12)	Inning 7 (13–14)	Inning 8 (15–16)	Inning 9 (17–18)
Janet									
Richard									

Group 1: Letters 13–18
Group 2: Letters 9–12

Group 3: Letters 5–8
Group 4: Letters 1–4

☑ Check Your Understanding

Write a final set of letters to end the story, one by Janet and one by Richard. Be sure to maintain a friendly tone to reflect the characters' changed attitudes.

_____

_____

_____

_____

_____

_____

_____

_____

_____

_____

_____

_____

_____

_____

_____

_____

_____

_____

LANGUAGE & WRITER'S CRAFT: Pronouns

Correct language use is just as important in speaking as in writing. As you complete writing and speaking assignments in this unit, be aware of how you are using pronouns and follow these rules:

- Recognize and correct inappropriate shifts in noun/pronoun agreement in both number and person.

  Correct: *Alfie is having his tonsils out tomorrow. They have been bothering him.*

  Incorrect: *Alfie is having his tonsils out tomorrow. It has been bothering him.*

- Avoid vague pronouns when referring to characters or to actions. Make sure the antecedent is clear and easy to recognize.

  Correct: *Remember when I took the laces out of my blue-and-white sneakers and gave the laces to you? I want the laces back.*

  Incorrect: *Remember when I took the laces out of my blue-and-white sneakers and gave them to you? I want them back.*

  Correct: *Joel is moving to Kansas and Danny sprained his wrist. We don't know when Danny will be back.*

  Incorrect: *Joel is moving to Kansas and Danny sprained his wrist. We don't know when he will be back.*

PRACTICE Revise the following sentences to show correct pronoun usage.

The teacher moved their desk to the back of the room.

Tiffany and Nicole usually play basketball after school, but she had to go home early.

The coaches wanted the players to study. They wanted them all to pass the exam.

Use classroom texts to find examples of pronouns and antecedents.

- Write an example of text that includes both a pronoun and its antecedent.

- Write an example of text that includes nouns and pronouns that agree in both number and gender.

Writing to Sources: Informational Text

Think about the characters, conflict, and plot of this story. Explain one theme of the story and identify the details that show the theme. Be sure to:

- Establish a central idea.
- Support the central idea with textual evidence from the story and thoughtful analysis.
- Use precise diction (e.g., specific literary terms) to create a formal tone and check all pronouns for clarity.
- Check your spelling, especially words that are frequently confused with each other like *its/it's, there/their/they're,* and *to/two/too.*

Language Checkpoint:
Using Subordinating Conjunctions

Learning Targets

- Identify subordinating conjunctions that commonly appear in text.
- Understand the proper function of subordinating conjunctions.
- Revise sentences for proper use of subordinating conjunctions.

Preview

In this activity, you will learn how subordinating conjunctions are used in writing to bring together different but related ideas. Then you will practice editing your own writing, along with that of your peers, to make sure you can use subordinating conjunctions correctly.

Identifying Subordinating Conjunctions

Sentences are made up of **clauses**. An **independent clause** can be a complete sentence on its own: *The dog barked. He was hungry.* A **dependent clause** cannot be a complete sentence on its own. The dependent clause depends on an independent clause to make a complete sentence.

When two independent clauses are related, they can be combined into one sentence. One way to do this is by turning one of the clauses into a dependent clause by using a **subordinating conjunction**. It needs to be combined with an independent clause to be a complete sentence.

> *The dog barked <u>because</u> he was hungry.*

While there are many words that can work as subordinating conjunctions, some of the most common include: **after, although, as, because, before, if, since, until, when,** and **while.**

1. In the sentences that follow, circle the subordinating conjunctions.

    a. Don't invite me to your birthday party because I'm not coming.

    b. If we don't score 10 runs this inning, we are going to lose this game.

    c. I was excited to pitch until my elbow started to hurt during class.

    d. The crowd was ecstatic after the batter crushed a home run on the first pitch.

Practice with Subordinating Conjunctions

Common Subordinating Conjunctions				
after	although	as	because	before
if	since	until	when	while

2. In the sentences that follow, fill in the blank with one of the subordinating conjunctions from the preceding list. Try not to use the same subordinating conjunction more than once. Check to make sure each conjunction you choose makes the sentence complete and sounds correct when you read it aloud.

    a. Jessika was exhausted _____ she didn't get enough sleep the night before.

    b. Richard managed to get himself up for school _____ his parents were away for a few days.

    c. _____ he was tired of losing game after game, Danny made sure to always put in a strong effort.

Revising

Read the following piece of writing about "The Southpaw." There are several short, choppy sentences that could be combined using subordinating conjunctions. Revise the text to include more complex sentences. You might need to rearrange the sentences a little to make them flow.

The short story "The Southpaw" has an unusual structure. It is a series of letters written by the two main characters, Richard and Janet. They start off mad at each other. Richard won't let Janet play on his team. Janet writes the first letter. Richard tells her that she cannot play. He says she must not be a good player. She is in the ballet club. Richard decides to let Janet play. His players start to get sick and injured.

☑ Check Your Understanding

Add at least two items to your Editor's Checklist to help you remember to use subordinating conjunctions in your own writing.

Practice

Return to the piece of informational writing you completed at the end of Activity 4.9. Reread your draft and circle any subordinating conjunctions you used. Identify whether the conjunctions you used make your writing clear and find two more sentences to combine using a subordinating conjunction.

Drama Games

ACTIVITY

4.10

Learning Targets

- Collaborate and perform a series of drama games to explore how tone, facial expressions, eye contact, and other elements contribute to the overall success of a performance.

Preview

In this activity, you will learn some drama games that actors use to explore their characters and warm up before rehearsals and performances.

Introducing the Strategy: Drama Games

Games can be a fun way to learn. **Drama games** are a form of role playing. Performing a role helps you make meaning of a text and understand it from the viewpoint of both a reader and a performer. Drama games require imagination, teamwork, and rehearsal. They also require an exchange of ideas in order to make a text come alive visually.

Game 1: Accept-Change-Pass

1. Stand up and form a circle of four to six students.
2. The student whose birthday is closest to today's date becomes the first actor. He or she holds up an imaginary box and pulls out an imaginary object.
3. After setting the box down, the actor pretends to use the object without speaking or making a sound. Each person in the group gets a chance to try to identify the object.
4. Once someone correctly identifies the object, the actor places the object back in the box, picks up the box, and passes it to his or her left.
5. Repeat the process until all group members have had a chance to play the actor's role.

Game 2: Shadowing

1. Stand up, form pairs, and label yourselves *Y* and *Z*.
2. After your teacher calls out an action, the Y students begin to silently pantomime the action while the Z students copy them. Students Y and Z should look like reflections in a mirror.
3. At the teacher's signal, switch roles. This time the Z students choose their own actions to pantomime as the Y students copy their actions.

Game 3: The Cycle of Life

1. Stand up and form a circle of four to five students.
2. Plan a tableau and then brainstorm ways to role-play the five stages of humans: infancy, childhood, adolescence, adulthood, and old age. Use sounds—but no words—and imaginative props to enhance your performance.
3. After planning and rehearsing, return to your seat.
4. When it is your group's turn, form a tableau of ages, mixing up the order. Freeze for a count of ten and then come to life, one by one, with sounds and props. After you perform your role, the rest of the class guesses which age you represented.

Learning Strategies

Drama Games
Rehearsal
Brainstorming
Role Playing

WORD CONNECTIONS

Roots and Affixes
Pantomime contains the Greek root *mime*, meaning "mimic," and the prefix *pan-*, meaning "all" or "entirely." Knowing the Greek root *mime* can also help you understand the meaning of the word *mimetic* ("characterized by imitation"). Knowing the Greek prefix *pan-* can also help you understand the meaning of the word *panacea* ("a remedy for all disease or illness").

LITERARY

A **tableau** is a purposeful arrangement of characters frozen as if in a painting or a photograph. The arrangement should convey information about the characters and their relationships.

VOCABULARY

Game 4: The Tone Game

In order to effectively deliver lines in a drama, you must accurately express your character's tone of voice. As you know, delivery rate, inflection, and facial expressions help to communicate tone. Because this is such a key part of a performance, it is important to practice speaking with different tones to get feedback from an audience.

1. When it is your turn, select a line and one of the tones from the following options. Do your best to deliver the line effectively to others in your group. They should be able to identify the tone right away. Remember that facial expressions and eye contact help to communicate tone.

2. If your audience cannot guess your intended tone, revise your approach and try again.

I am going home now! **Tone: angry**	**I need to eat something!** **Tone: urgent**	**I need a break.** **Tone: playful**
I am going home now. **Tone: sad**	**I need to eat something!** **Tone: joyful**	**I need a break!** **Tone: angry**
I am going home now! **Tone: excited**	**I need to eat something.** **Tone: depressed**	**I need a break.** **Tone: sarcastic**
I am going home now. **Tone: indifferent**	**I need to eat something.** **Tone: nervous**	**I need a break.** **Tone: indifferent**
I am going home now. **Tone: bored**	**I need to eat something.** **Tone: indifferent**	**I need a break.** **Tone: bored**

☑ Check Your Understanding

Quickwrite: Why is teamwork a necessary part of any dramatic performance? Why is it important to plan and rehearse facial expressions and movement prior to a performance?

_____

_____

_____

_____

Introducing *The Miracle Worker*

Learning Targets

- Analyze visual texts and make predictions about the characters, plot, and conflict of a play.
- Analyze how conflicts in a play establish the play's exposition and introduce complications.

Preview

In this activity, you will begin your analysis of a play by meeting its characters, observing its historical setting in film, and examining its first major conflicts.

Introducing the Play

The Miracle Worker is a **play** written by American playwright William Gibson, based on Helen Keller's autobiography, *The Story of My Life*. It was first performed as a teleplay in 1957 and then as a Broadway production starring Anne Bancroft as Annie Sullivan and Patty Duke as Helen Keller in 1959. The two women went on to lead the cast of a 1962 film version of the story, winning Academy Awards for their performances ("Best Actress" for Bancroft and "Best Supporting Actress" for Duke).

About the Author

William Gibson (1914–2008) was an American playwright whose writing career spanned 70 years. *The Miracle Worker* was Gibson's most critically acclaimed piece both on stage and on film. His screenplay for the 1962 movie received an Oscar nomination. Gibson was born in New York City, and he died at age 94 in Massachusetts.

Cast of Characters

    DOCTOR

    KATE, Helen's mother

    KELLER, Helen's father

    HELEN

    MARTHA

    PERCY, child of servants

    AUNT EV

    JAMES, Captain Keller's son by his first marriage

    ANAGNOS, Director of the Perkins Institution for the Blind

    ANNIE SULLIVAN

    VINEY, a servant

    BLIND GIRLS

Learning Strategies

Graphic Organizer
Double-Entry Journal
Close Reading
Brainstorming

VOCABULARY

LITERARY

A **play** is a story that is told through the dialogue and actions of actors on a stage. Some plays have a narrator, but many do not—the burden is on the actors and props to provide all the necessary details of the story.

WORD CONNECTIONS

Word Parts

The word **teleplay** is a combination of the words *television* and *screenplay*. A screenplay is a script written for film. A teleplay is a script written for television.

My Notes

A SERVANT

OFFSTAGE VOICES

Time: The 1880s

Place: *In and around the Keller homestead in Tuscumbia, Alabama; also, briefly, the Perkins Institute for the Blind, in Boston.*

☑ Focus on the Sentence

Look at the image from the film *The Miracle Worker*. It depicts the characters of Annie Sullivan and Helen Keller. Write two statements about the image and two questions that the image raises for you.

Statement 1: _____

_____

Statement 2: _____

_____

Question 1: _____

_____

Question 2: _____

_____

The Miracle Worker, Act I

1. As you watch the film *The Miracle Worker* over the next several activities, use a double-entry journal to record your thoughts, comments, and connections in response to the elements of a play (or, in this case, film). Be sure your notes are thorough, since you will need to remember details of the film without rewatching it.

Elements of a Play	Thoughts, Comments, and Connections
Plot	
Setting (Time, Era, Location, Culture)	
Characters	
Action	
Conflict	

2. View the beginning of the film. Use the following table to keep track of how the characters and conflicts are introduced through dialogue.

Character	Character Point of View (Opinions and Ideas)	Textual Evidence
Doctor		
Kate		
Keller		
Helen		
Aunt Ev		
James		
Annie		

My Notes

Working from the Film

3. What is the setting of this story in terms of location, culture, and historical time period? What are some details that show this setting?

4. What events create a conflict in the story? How do the members of the Keller family respond to the conflict?

5. What words and phrases give you insight into the kind of person Annie Sullivan is?

6. What can you infer about the central conflict in the story? How is it both internal and external?

☑ Check Your Understanding

In a few sentences, summarize what characters, setting, and plot were established in this part of the film.

✍ Writing to Sources: Informational Text

Write a paragraph that explains the conflict that is introduced, the reaction of the Keller family members, and the complications that you believe will result from this event. Be sure to:

- Include a topic sentence that states how the conflict is introduced.
- Use supporting details that connect the Kellers' reactions.
- Add commentary about how you believe the characters will change as a result of this conflict.

One Event, Two Genres

Learning Targets

- Read accounts of one event in two genres to deepen understanding.
- Analyze how an author's purpose influences the way an event is portrayed.
- Describe how a conflict is introduced in both drama and literary nonfiction.
- Integrate ideas from multiple texts to build knowledge and vocabulary about roles one person might have in improving the life of another person.

Preview

In this activity, you will examine an event that is described in both a play and an autobiography to see how genre and author's purpose shape the way it is told.

Plays on the Page

Plays are meant to be performed, but actors have to read them before they can perform them. The way the playwright communicates important ideas about **staging** to the director and actors is through the use of stage directions and implied stage actions.

- **Stage Directions:** explicit instructions about movement on the stage and the tone of lines
- **Implied Stage Actions:** actions that are implied in the dialogue

Setting a Purpose for Reading

- Underline words and phrases that vividly describe emotions.
- Highlight words and phrases in the dialogue that imply an action the actors must take.
- Draw a star next to text where a conflict is being introduced.
- Circle unknown words and phrases. Try to determine the meaning of the words by using context clues, word parts, or a dictionary.

Play

from
The Miracle Worker, Act I

by **William Gibson**

Meanwhile, inside, ANNIE *has given* HELEN *a key; while* ANNIE *removes her bonnet,* HELEN *unlocks and opens the suitcase. The first thing she pulls out is a voluminous shawl. She fingers it until she perceives what it is; then she wraps it around her, and acquiring* ANNIE'S *bonnet and smoked glasses as*
5 *well, dons the lot: the shawl swamps her, and the bonnet settles down upon the glasses, but she stands before a mirror cocking her head to one side, then to the other, in a mockery of adult action.* ANNIE *is amused, and talks to her as one might to a kitten, with no trace of company manners.*

Learning Strategies

Marking the Text
Close Reading
Collaborative Discussion

VOCABULARY

ACADEMIC
Staging is the method of arranging the actors, props, and scenery on stage. It describes how these objects are placed in relation to one another. It can also refer to the way a scene is set up in a movie.

INDEPENDENT READING LINK

Read and Discuss
Consider the first obstacle that the subject in your independent reading has faced. How is it similar to Helen Keller's struggle? How is it different? Discuss your response with a partner and listen to their response. Briefly compare and contrast what each of you presented.

KNOWLEDGE QUEST

Knowledge Question:
What roles might one person have in improving the life of another person?

In Activity 4.12, you will read two texts about the life of Helen Keller. While you read and build knowledge about the theme, think about your answer to the Knowledge Question.

My Notes

ANNIE: All the troubles I went to and that's how I look?

10 (HELEN *then comes back to the suitcase, gropes for more, lifts out a pair of female drawers.*)

Oh, no. Not the drawers!

(*But* HELEN *discarding them comes to the elegant doll. Her fingers explore its features, and when she raises it and finds its eyes open and close, she is at first*
15 *startled, then delighted. She picks it up, taps its head vigorously, taps her own chest, and nods questioningly.* ANNIE *takes her finger, points it to the doll, points it to* HELEN*, and touching it to her own face, also nods.* HELEN *sits back on her heels, clasps the doll to herself, and rocks it.* ANNIE *studies her, still in bonnet and smoked glasses like a caricature of herself, and addresses her humorously.*)

20 All right, Miss O'Sullivan. Let's begin with doll.

(*She takes* HELEN'S *hand; in her palm* ANNIE'S *forefinger points, thumb holding her other fingers clenched.*)

D.

(*Her thumb next holds all her fingers clenched, touching* HELEN'S *palm.*)

25 O.

(*Her thumb and forefinger extend.*)

L.

(*Same contact repeated.*)

L.

30 (*She puts* HELEN'S *hand to the doll.*)

Doll.

JAMES: You spell pretty well.

(ANNIE *in one hurried move gets the drawers swiftly back into the suitcase, the lid banged shut, and her head turned, to see* JAMES *leaning in the doorway.*)

35 Finding out if she's ticklish? She is.

(ANNIE *regards him* **stonily**, *but* HELEN *after a scowling moment tugs at her hand again, imperious.* ANNIE *repeats the letters, and* HELEN *interrupts her fingers in the middle, feeling each of them, puzzled.* ANNIE *touches* HELEN'S *hand to the doll, and begins spelling into it again.*)

40 What is it, a game?

ANNIE [**CURTLY**]: An alphabet.

JAMES: Alphabet?

ANNIE: For the deaf.

(HELEN *now repeats the finger movements in air, exactly, her head cocked to*
45 *her own hand, and* ANNIE'S *eyes suddenly gleam.*)

stonily: coldly or in an unfriendly way
curtly: in a clipped or harsh way

Ho. How bright she is!

JAMES: You think she knows what she's doing?

(He takes HELEN'S hand, to throw a meaningless gesture into it; she repeats this one too.)

50 She imitates everything, she's a monkey.

ANNIE [VERY PLEASED]: Yes, she's a bright little monkey, all right.

(She takes the doll from HELEN and reaches for her hand; HELEN instantly grabs the doll back. ANNIE takes it again, and HELEN'S hand next, but HELEN is incensed now; when ANNIE draws her hand to her face to shake her 55 *head no, then tries to spell to her, HELEN slaps at ANNIE'S face. ANNIE grasps HELEN by both arms and swings her into a chair, holding her pinned there, kicking, while glasses, doll, bonnet fly in various directions. JAMES laughs.)*

JAMES: She wants her doll back.

ANNIE: When she spells it.

60 **JAMES:** Spell, she doesn't know the thing has a name, even.

ANNIE: Of course not, who expects her to, now? All I want is her fingers to learn the letters.

JAMES: Won't mean anything to her.

(ANNIE gives him a look. She then tries to form HELEN'S fingers into the 65 *letters, but HELEN swings a **haymaker** instead, which ANNIE barely ducks, at once pinning her down again.)*

Doesn't like that alphabet, Miss Sullivan. You invent it yourself?

(HELEN is now in a rage, fighting tooth and nail to get out of the chair, and ANNIE answers while struggling and dodging her kicks.)

70 **ANNIE:** Spanish monks under a—vow of silence. Which I wish you'd take!

(And suddenly releasing HELEN'S hands, she comes and shuts the door in JAMES'S face. HELEN drops to the floor, groping around for the doll. ANNIE looks around desperately, sees her purse on the bed, rummages in it, and comes up with a battered piece of cake wrapped in newspaper; with her foot 75 *she moves the doll deftly out of the way of HELEN'S groping, and going on her knee she lets HELEN smell the cake. When HELEN grabs for it, ANNIE removes the cake and spells quickly into the reaching hand.)*

Cake. From Washington up north, it's the best I can do.

(HELEN'S hand waits, baffled. ANNIE repeats it.)

80 C, a, k, e. Do what my fingers do, never mind what it means.

(She touches the cake briefly to HELEN'S nose, pats her hand, presents her own hand. HELEN spells the letters rapidly back. ANNIE pats her hand enthusiastically and gives her the cake; HELEN crams it into her mouth with both hands. ANNIE watches her, with humor.)

WORD CONNECTIONS

Etymology
The word **imitate** comes from the Latin root *imitat*, which means "to copy," and *imago*, which means "image." The word is used today to mean that one thing looks or acts like another.

GRAMMAR & USAGE

Verb Tenses
Writers use verbs to show what happened and when it happened. When reading about an action, pay attention to which tense the verb takes.

The first sentence of this excerpt says "has given," indicating that the giving already happened in the past. Then it says, "ANNIE removes her bonnet." This form of the verb *remove* shows that it is happening right now, while we watch. Near the end of the passage, Annie says, "Get it down fast, maybe I'll steal that back too." In this sentence, the "I'll" stands for "I will" and shows that an action will happen in the future.

Find additional examples of past, present, and future tense verbs in the rest of the passage.

---

haymaker: punch with the fist

My Notes

_____

_____

_____

_____

_____

_____

_____

_____

_____

_____

_____

_____

_____

_____

wretch: unfortunate or unhappy person

85 Get it down fast, maybe I'll steal that back too. Now.

(She takes the doll, touches it to HELEN'S nose, and spells again into her hand.)

D, o, l, l. Think it over.

(HELEN thinks it over, while ANNIE presents her own hand. Then HELEN spells three letters. ANNIE waits a second, then completes the word for HELEN
90 *in her palm.)*

L.

(She hands over the doll, and HELEN gets a good grip on its leg.)

Imitate now, understand later. End of the first les—

(She never finishes, because HELEN swings the doll with a furious energy,
95 *it hits ANNIE squarely in the face, and she falls back with a cry of pain, her knuckles up to her mouth. HELEN waits, tensed for further combat. When ANNIE lowers her knuckles she looks at blood on them; she works her lips, gets to her feet, finds the mirror, and bares her teeth at herself. Now she is furious herself.)*

100 You little **wretch**, no one's taught you any manners? I'll—

(But rounding from the mirror she sees the door slam, HELEN and the doll are on the outside, and HELEN is turning the key in the lock. ANNIE darts over, to pull the knob; the door is locked fast. She yanks it again.)

Helen! Helen, let me out of—

This photo of Helen Keller (left) and Anne Sullivan (right) illustrates the way Keller read Sullivan's lips. Keller used this method of lip reading with everyone, including presidents of the United States and Hollywood celebrities.

⊘ Knowledge Quest

- What happens in this scene?
- What is most interesting to you about the way that Annie relates to Helen?

Returning to the Text

- Return to the text as you respond to the following questions. Use text evidence to support your responses.
- Write any additional questions you have about the play in your Reader/Writer Notebook.

1. How does Helen react to conflict in the scene?

_____

_____

_____

_____

2. What do you learn about Helen and Annie from the scene's staging?

_____

_____

_____

_____

3. What do you learn about Annie from her reaction to Helen?

_____

_____

_____

_____

4. **KQ** Annie's actions show that she empathizes with Helen. How does Annie show empathy toward Helen, and how does this make her a good teacher for Helen?

_____

_____

_____

_____

5. **KQ** The term *miracle worker* is used to refer to the character of Annie in this play. What is a *miracle worker*, and in what ways does Annie exemplify one?

_____

_____

_____

_____

Gaining Perspectives

In *The Miracle Worker*, Act 1, Annie Sullivan is teaching sign language to Helen Keller for the first time when Helen's brother, James, enters the room. Think about how James reacts to Helen. Then think about how Annie reacts to Helen. Who demonstrates effective conflict-management strategies, and who does not? For example, where does Annie practice assertiveness? What does James do to make the situation worse, and how could Annie have redirected him to be more supportive? With a partner, imagine you are teaching Helen to communicate. Role-play a positive conversation with Annie and James as they work with Helen. Write down three negotiation strategies or plans to communicate effectively, such as the use of assertiveness, compromise, or open discussion about what each person needs and how each person feels. When you are finished, summarize the outcome of the discussion in your Reader/Writer Notebook.

Setting a Purpose for Reading

- As you read the excerpt, underline words and phrases that vividly describe emotions.
- Circle unknown words and phrases. Try to determine the meaning of the words by using context clues, word parts, or a dictionary.

About the Author

Helen Keller (1880–1968) was a college graduate who helped found Helen Keller International and the American Civil Liberties Union (ACLU) despite an illness that left her both blind and deaf at the age of two. During Keller's troubled childhood, some family members thought that she should be institutionalized due to her wild behavior. Instead, her parents sought a teacher who could educate their daughter. Keller grew up to be a famous activist who worked to improve the lives of blind people.

Autobiography

from The Story of My Life, Chapter 4

by **Helen Keller**

1   The most important day I remember in all my life is the one on which my teacher, Anne Mansfield Sullivan, came to me. I am filled with wonder when I consider the immeasurable contrasts between the two lives which it connects. It was the third of March, 1887, three months before I was seven years old.

2   On the afternoon of that eventful day, I stood on the porch, dumb, expectant. I guessed vaguely from my mother's signs and from the hurrying to and fro in the house that something unusual was about to happen, so I went to the door and waited on the steps. The afternoon sun **penetrated** the mass of honeysuckle that covered the porch, and fell on my upturned face. My fingers lingered almost unconsciously on the familiar leaves and blossoms which had just come forth to greet the sweet southern spring. I did not know what the future held of **marvel** or surprise for me. Anger and bitterness had preyed upon me continually for weeks and a deep **languor** had succeeded this passionate struggle.

3   Have you ever been at sea in a dense fog, when it seemed as if a **tangible** white darkness shut you in, and the great ship, tense and anxious, groped her way toward the shore with **plummet and sounding-line**, and you waited with beating heart for something to happen? I was like that ship before my education began, only I was without compass or sounding-line, and had no way of knowing how near the harbour was. "Light! give me light!" was the wordless cry of my soul, and the light of love shone on me in that very hour.

WORD CONNECTIONS

Multiple-Meaning Words

In the past, the word **dumb** meant "unable to speak." When Keller writes, "I stood on the porch, dumb," she refers to her severe speech impairment. It is still used to mean that someone is temporarily unable to speak, such as in the sentence *She watched the sunset in silence, struck dumb by the beauty of the sky.* However, in its newer sense, *dumb* means lacking in intelligence or common sense. The newer meaning has become more widespread, and as a result, calling someone dumb is offensive.

KNOWLEDGE QUEST

Knowledge Question:

What roles might one person have in improving the life of another person?

penetrated: entered into
marvel: wonder
languor: state of being tired
tangible: touchable
plummet and sounding-line: a weighted line used for finding the depth of water

My Notes

4   I felt approaching footsteps, I stretched out my hand as I supposed to my mother. Someone took it, and I was caught up and held close in the arms of her who had come to reveal all things to me, and, more than all things else, to love me.

5   The morning after my teacher came she led me into her room and gave me a doll. The little blind children at the Perkins Institution had sent it and Laura Bridgman had dressed it; but I did not know this until afterward. When I had played with it a little while, Miss Sullivan slowly spelled into my hand the word "d-o-l-l." I was at once interested in this finger play and tried to imitate it. When I finally succeeded in making the letters correctly I was flushed with childish pleasure and pride. Running downstairs to my mother I held up my hand and made the letters for *doll*. I did not know that I was spelling a word or even that words existed; I was simply making my fingers go in monkey-like imitation. In the days that followed I learned to spell in this **uncomprehending** way a great many words, among them pin, hat, cup, and a few verbs like sit, stand, and walk. But my teacher had been with me several weeks before I understood that everything has a name.

6   One day, while I was playing with my new doll, Miss Sullivan put my big rag doll into my lap also, spelled "d-o-l-l" and tried to make me understand that "d-o-l-l" applied to both. Earlier in the day we had had a tussle over the words "m-u-g" and "w-a-t-e-r." Miss Sullivan had tried to impress it upon me that "m-u-g" is mug and that "w-a-t-e-r" is water, but I persisted in confounding the two. In despair she had dropped the subject for the time, only to renew it at the first opportunity. I became impatient at her repeated attempts and, seizing the new doll, I **dashed** it upon the floor. I was **keenly** delighted when I felt the fragments of the broken doll at my feet. Neither sorrow nor regret followed my passionate outburst. I had not loved the doll. In the still, dark world in which I lived there was no strong **sentiment** or tenderness. I felt my teacher sweep the **fragments** to one side of the **hearth**, and I had a sense of satisfaction that the cause of my discomfort was removed. She brought me my hat, and I knew I was going out into the warm sunshine. This thought, if a wordless **sensation** may be called a thought, made me hop and skip with pleasure.

⊘ Knowledge Quest

- What happens in this story?
- What is your impression of Helen after reading this story?

uncomprehending: not grasping or understanding

dashed: hit or smashed

keenly: eagerly or enthusiastically

sentiment: emotional attachment

fragments: pieces

hearth: floor of a fireplace

sensation: feeling

Returning to the Text

- Return to the text as you respond to the following questions. Use text evidence to support your responses.
- Write any additional questions you have about the autobiography in your Reader/Writer Notebook.

6. How was this account of Miss Sullivan bringing Helen a doll different from the scene depicted in the play?

_____

_____

_____

_____

7. What are some emotions Helen experienced over the course of this story?

_____

_____

_____

_____

8. KQ In paragraph 6, Helen says she "persisted" in confounding the spellings for *mug* and *water*. *Persisted* is the past tense form of *persist*. What does it mean to *persist*? Also, what does Miss Sullivan *persist* in doing for Helen so Helen can have a better life?

_____

_____

_____

_____

9. What is the meaning of the word *passionate* in the final paragraph? Explain how context clues help you answer.

_____

_____

_____

_____

10. KQ What are some character traits that Miss Sullivan shows through her actions in this story and *The Miracle Worker* that enable her to improve Helen's life?

_____

_____

_____

_____

11. How is the point of view in this autobiography used to build a deeper understanding of Helen's life experiences?

_____

_____

_____

_____

_____

12. How does the structure of a personal narrative differ from a play?

_____

_____

_____

_____

_____

INDEPENDENT READING LINK

You can continue to build your knowledge about roles one person might have in improving the life of another person by reading other articles at ZINC Reading Labs. Search for keywords such as *mentors* or *helping others*.

Knowledge Quest

After reading these two texts about the life of Helen Keller, talk with a partner about the roles one person might have in improving the life of another person. Then answer *who, what, where, when,* and *why* questions to tell about one person you know who has changed someone else's life.

Working from the Text

13. In a small group, discuss the following questions:

- What is Helen's purpose for writing this personal narrative in her autobiography? How does this purpose shape the way the information is presented?

- What is Gibson's purpose for writing the play? How does this purpose shape the way the information is presented?

☑ Check Your Understanding

How was reading the scene from the play similar to reading the excerpt from the autobiography? How was it different?

📝 Narrative Writing Prompt

Choose one of the following prompts to respond to.

- Revisit the scene from the play and write Helen's internal monologue about the events. Be sure to incorporate both the stage directions Gibson wrote and the information you learned about Helen's childhood thoughts from the personal narrative.

- Draw the scene described in the play and the autobiography in one frame, like a painting, or several frames, like a comic strip.

Learning Strategies

Chunking the Text
Close Reading
Collaborative Discussion

INDEPENDENT READING LINK

Read and Respond

Think about the historical and cultural setting that the subject of your independent reading text lives in. Where and when is it? What impact does this setting have on the person's struggle? How would the struggle have been different at another time in history or in some other place? Respond to these questions in your Reader/Writer Notebook.

My Notes

Learning Targets

- Analyze how the historical and cultural settings of the play influence the characters and plot.
- Describe and analyze how the author's use of language contributes to the mood of the play and the voices of characters.
- Analyze how a playwright uses metaphor to achieve a specific purpose.
- Analyze how printed versions of a story, drama, or poem are the same and different from audio, video, or live versions.

Preview

In this activity, you will begin Act II of *The Miracle Worker* by watching the first scene and reading the second scene. You will then analyze the time and place of the play to see what impact this setting has on the story.

Setting a Purpose for Viewing

- Jot down words that describe the characters' actions and emotions during the scene.
- Record clues that indicate the setting of the scene, both in terms of era and location.
- Circle unknown words and phrases. Try to determine the meaning of the words by using context clues, word parts, or a dictionary.

Working from the Film

1. What are some props the actors use in this scene that show it takes place in the past?

2. What does Kate's unfamiliarity with sign language show about the historical and cultural setting she lives in? How will this setting drive the plot?

3. What other aspects of this scene show the historical setting? Why is the historical setting important to the plot of the play?

4. How would you describe each of the characters based on words they use (dialogue) and their movements (staging)?

ANNIE:

HELEN:

KATE:

Setting a Purpose for Reading

- Create an image in your mind of the scene as you read.
- Underline words that the playwright uses to describe Annie in stage directions and dialogue.
- Use the My Notes section to write one- or two-word descriptions of the characters at different parts of the scene.
- Circle any words or phrases you are unfamiliar with. Some may be difficult vocabulary you can look up in a dictionary. Others may be historical or cultural references you can research.

Play

from The Miracle Worker, Act II

by **William Gibson**

Chunk 1

VINEY: Breakfast ready!

(VINEY *comes down into the sunlight beam and pumps a pitcherful of water. While the pitcher is brimming we hear conversation from the dark; the light grows to the family room of the house where all are either entering or already*
5 *seated at breakfast, with* KELLER *and* JAMES *arguing the war.* HELEN *is wandering around the table to explore the contents of the other plates. When* ANNIE *is in her chair, she watches* HELEN. VINEY *reenters, sets the pitcher on the table;* KATE *lifts the almost empty biscuit plate with an inquiring look,* VINEY *nods and bears it off back, neither of them interrupting the men.*
10 ANNIE *meanwhile sits with fork quiet, watching* HELEN, *who at her mother's plate pokes her hand among some scrambled eggs.* KATE *catches* ANNIE'S *eyes on her, smiles with a wry gesture.* HELEN *moves on to* JAMES'S *plate, the male talk continuing,* JAMES *deferential and* KELLER *overriding.)*

JAMES: —no, but shouldn't we give the devil his due, Father? The fact is we
15 lost the South two years earlier when he **outthought** us behind Vicksburg.

KELLER: Outthought is a peculiar word for a butcher.

JAMES: Harness maker, wasn't he?

KELLER: I said butcher, his only virtue as a soldier was numbers and he led them to slaughter with no more regard than for so many sheep.

20 **JAMES:** But even if in that sense he was a butcher, the fact is he—

outthought: thought faster or in a superior way

My Notes

KELLER: And a drunken one, half the war.

JAMES: Agreed, Father. If his own people said he was I can't argue he—

KELLER: Well, what is it you find to admire in such a man, Jimmie, the butchery or the drunkenness?

25 JAMES: Neither, Father, only the fact that he beat us.

KELLER: He didn't.

JAMES: Is it your **contention** we won the war, sir?

KELLER: He didn't beat us at Vicksburg, we lost Vicksburg because Pemberton gave Bragg five thousand of his cavalry, and Loring, whom

30 I knew personally for a nincompoop before you were born, marched away from Champion's Hill with enough men to have held them. We lost Vicksburg by stupidity **verging on** treason.

JAMES: I would have said we lost Vicksburg because Grant was one thing no Yankee general was before him—

35 KELLER: Drunk? I doubt it.

JAMES: **Obstinate**.

KELLER: Obstinate. Could any of them compare even in that with old Stonewall? If he'd been there we would still have Vicksburg.

JAMES: Well, the butcher simply wouldn't give up; he tried four ways of

40 getting around Vicksburg and on the fifth try he got around. Anyone else would have pulled north and—

KELLER: He wouldn't have got around if we'd had a Southerner in command, instead of a half-breed Yankee traitor like Pemberton—

Chunk 2

45 *(While this background talk is in progress, HELEN is working around the table, ultimately toward ANNIE'S plate. She messes with her hands in JAMES'S plate, then in KELLER'S, both men taking it so for granted they hardly notice. Then HELEN comes groping with soiled hands past her own plate, to ANNIE'S; her hand goes to it, and ANNIE, who has been waiting,*

50 *deliberately lifts and removes her hand. HELEN gropes again, ANNIE firmly pins her by the wrist and removes her hand from the table. HELEN thrusts her hands again, ANNIE catches them, and HELEN begins to flail and make noises; the interruption brings KELLER'S gaze upon them.)*

What's the matter there?

55 KATE: Miss Annie. You see, she's **accustomed** to helping herself from our plates to anything she—

ANNIE (EVENLY): Yes, but I'm not accustomed to it.

KELLER: No, of course not. Viney!

KATE: Give her something, Jimmie, to quiet her.

60 JAMES (BLANDLY): But her table manners are the best she has. Well.

(He pokes across with a chunk of bacon at HELEN'S hand, which ANNIE releases; but HELEN knocks the bacon away and stubbornly thrusts at ANNIE'S plate. ANNIE grips her wrists again, the struggle mounts.)

KELLER: Let her this time, Miss Sullivan, it's the only way we get any adult

contention: claim
verging on: which was almost
obstinate: stubborn
accustomed: used to

My Notes

65 conversation. If my son's half **merits** that description.

(He rises.)

I'll get you another plate.

ANNIE (GRIPPING HELEN): I have a plate, thank you.

KATE (CALLING): Viney! I'm afraid what Captain Keller says is only too
70 true, she'll **persist** in this until she gets her own way.

KELLER (AT THE DOOR): Viney, bring Miss Sullivan another plate—

ANNIE (STONILY): I have a plate, nothing's wrong with the plate, I
intend to keep it.

(Silence for a moment, except for HELEN'S noises as she struggles to get
75 *loose; the KELLERS are a bit nonplused, and ANNIE is too darkly intent on*
HELEN'S *manners to have any thoughts now of her own.)*

JAMES: Ha. You see why they took Vicksburg?

KELLER (UNCERTAINLY): Miss Sullivan. One plate or another is hardly
a matter to struggle with a deprived child about.

80 **ANNIE:** Oh, I'd sooner have a more—

(HELEN begins to kick, ANNIE moves her ankles to the opposite side of the
chair)

—heroic issue myself, I—

KELLER: No, I really must insist you—

85 *(HELEN bangs her toe on the chair and sinks to the floor, crying with rage*
and feigned injury; ANNIE keeps hold of her wrists, gazing down, while
KATE *rises.)*

Now she's hurt herself.

ANNIE (GRIMLY): No, she hasn't.

90 **KELLER:** Will you please let her hands go?

KATE: Miss Annie, you don't know the child well enough yet, she'll
keep—

ANNIE: I know an ordinary tantrum well enough, when I see one, and a
badly spoiled child—

95 **JAMES:** Hear, hear.

KELLER (VERY ANNOYED): Miss Sullivan! You would have more
understanding of your pupil if you had some pity in you. Now kindly do
as I—

ANNIE: Pity?

100 *(She releases HELEN to turn equally annoyed on KELLER across the*
table; instantly HELEN scrambles up and dives at ANNIE'S plate. This
time ANNIE intercepts her by pouncing on her wrists like a hawk, and her
temper boils.)

For this **tyrant**? The whole house turns on her whims, is there anything
105 she wants she doesn't get? I'll tell you what I pity, that the sun won't
rise and set for her all her life, and every day you're telling her it will.
What good will your pity do her when you're under the strawberries,
Captain Keller?

---

merits: is worthy of
persist: keep going
intent: focused
feigned: faked
tyrant: cruel ruler

My Notes

KELLER (OUTRAGED): Kate, for the love of heaven will you—

110 **KATE:** Miss Annie, please, I don't think it serves to lose our—

ANNIE: It does you good, that's all. It's less trouble to feel sorry for her than to teach her anything better, isn't it?

KELLER: I fail to see where you have taught her anything yet, Miss Sullivan!

115 **ANNIE:** I'll begin this minute, if you'll leave the room, Captain Keller!

Chunk 3

KELLER (ASTONISHED): Leave the—

ANNIE: Everyone, please.

(She struggles with HELEN, while KELLER endeavors to control his voice.)

120 **KELLER:** Miss Sullivan, you are here only as a paid teacher. Nothing more, and not to lecture—

ANNIE: I can't unteach her six years of pity if you can't stand up to one tantrum! Old Stonewall, indeed. Mrs. Keller, you promised me help.

KATE: Indeed I did, we truly want to—

125 **ANNIE:** Then leave me alone with her. Now!

KELLER (IN A WRATH): Katie, will you come outside with me? At once, please.

(He marches to the front door. KATE and JAMES follow him. Simultaneously ANNIE releases HELEN'S wrists, and the child again sinks
130 *to the floor, kicking and crying her weird noises. ANNIE steps over her to meet VINEY coming in the rear doorway with biscuits and a clean plate, surprised at the general commotion.)*

VINEY: Heaven sakes—

ANNIE: Out, please.

135 *(She backs VINEY out with one hand, closes the door on her astonished mouth, locks it, and removes the key. KELLER meanwhile snatches his hat from a rack, and KATE follows him down the porch steps. JAMES lingers in the doorway to address ANNIE across the room with a bow.)*

JAMES: If it takes all summer, general.

140 *(ANNIE comes over to his door in turn, removing her glasses grimly; as KELLER outside begins speaking, ANNIE closes the door on JAMES, locks it, removes the key, and turns with her back against the door to stare ominously at HELEN, kicking on the floor. JAMES takes his hat from the rack and, going down the porch steps, joins KATE and KELLER talking in*
145 *the yard, KELLER in a sputter of ire.)*

KELLER: This girl, this—cub of a girl—presumes! I tell you, I'm of half a mind to ship her back to Boston before the week is out. You can inform her so from me!

KATE (EYEBROWS UP): I, Captain?

150 **KELLER:** She's a **hireling**. Now I want it clear, unless there's an apology and complete change of manner, she goes back on the next train! Will you make that quite clear?

endeavors: tries
simultaneously: at the same time
ominously: in a threatening way
hireling: someone hired to do work

KATE: Where will you be, Captain, while I am making it quite—

KELLER: At the office!

155 *(He begins off left, finds his napkin still in his **irate** hand, is uncertain with it, dabs his lips with dignity, gets rid of it in a toss to* JAMES, *and marches off.* JAMES *turns to eye* KATE.*)*

JAMES: Will you?

(KATE'S mouth is set, and JAMES studies it lightly.)

160 I thought what she said was **exceptionally** intelligent. I've been saying it for years.

KATE (NOT WITHOUT SCORN): To his face?

(She comes to relieve him of the white napkin, but reverts again with it.)

Or will you take it, Jimmie? As a flag?

Making Observations

- What is the main action happening at the beginning of this scene?
- What questions do you have about this scene?
- What is your impression of the Keller household now?

☑ Focus on the Sentence

For each character in this scene, write a complete sentence about the character that uses one of the appositives that follow. Write your sentence in present tense and use correct capitalization and punctuation.

a veteran of the Civil War

_____

_____

a young man who enjoys goading his father

_____

_____

a loving mother

_____

_____

a strong-willed young woman hired to teach Helen

_____

_____

a blind and deaf girl

_____

_____

My Notes

irate: very angry
exceptionally: unusually

Returning to the Text

- Return to the text as you respond to the following questions. Use text evidence to support your responses.
- Write any additional questions you have about the play in your Reader/Writer Notebook.

5. What arguments come up in this scene? Who is in conflict with whom?

_____

_____

_____

_____

6. What do you think Annie is thinking as she watches Helen stealing food? Use text evidence in your response.

_____

_____

_____

_____

7. What do we learn about James, Captain Keller, Kate, and Annie from the dialogue and staging in this scene?

_____

_____

_____

_____

8. How does James calling Annie "general" contribute to the mood in this scene? What metaphor does this begin to establish?

_____

_____

_____

_____

9. What is the impact of James's point of view in this scene?

_____

_____

_____

_____

Setting a Purpose for Viewing

- Note similarities and differences between the film and the play in how the story's plot unfolds.
- Think about how your perceptions of the story's characters and setting are both similar to and different from how the film depicts them.

The breakfast scene from *The Miracle Worker*, directed by Arthur Penn, 1962

Making Observations

- How is what you "saw" and "heard" when reading the play different from what you saw and heard when you watched the film?
- What did you notice about the actors' choices in the scene?
- What physical and visual elements stuck out to you?

Working from the Text

10. In small groups, conduct some research into the American Civil War. To begin this research, revisit the scene and note people and battles that are mentioned. Once you have collected some information, use the following questions to guide your discussion:

    - How does cultural background affect the relationship between Annie and Keller?
    - Why did the playwright choose to use the metaphor of war in this play? What effect does this metaphor have on the play?

11. You will now act out chunk 1 three times. The first time, act out only the conversation between the "grown-ups." The second time, act out only the action between Helen and Annie. The third time, put both parts together. Be sure to:

    - Use punctuation as a guide in reading the lines fluently.
    - Use the stage directions to inform your tone of voice and facial expressions.

☑ Check Your Understanding

Quickwrite: How did the scene change each time it was performed?

Meaning in the Silence

Learning Strategies

Chunking the Text
Close Reading
Collaborative Discussion

My Notes

Learning Targets

- Analyze how stage directions fit into the overall structure of a play and develop theme.
- Work collaboratively to make meaning of a scene.
- Demonstrate an understanding of a scene and characters.
- Identify and analyze internal and external conflict.

Preview

In this activity, you will read and watch a scene from Act II of *The Miracle Worker* that relies on staging alone to advance a theme and develop the plot. You will then illustrate the scene using your analyses of the text as a guide.

Setting a Purpose for Reading

- Use two highlighters to mark vivid verbs and adverbs.
- Create a mental image of the action being described.
- Circle unknown words and phrases. Try to determine the meaning of the words by using context clues, word parts, or a dictionary.

Play

from # The Miracle Worker, Act II

by **William Gibson**

My Notes

> ANNIE *meanwhile has begun by slapping both keys down on a shelf out of* HELEN'S *reach; she returns to the table, upstage.* HELEN'S *kicking has subsided, and when from the floor her hand finds* ANNIE'S *chair empty she pauses.* ANNIE *clears the table of* KATE'S, JAMES'S, *and* KELLER'S *plates; she*
> 5 *gets back to her own across the table just in time to slide it* **deftly** *away from* HELEN'S *pouncing hand. She lifts the hand and moves it to* HELEN'S *plate, and after an instant's exploration,* HELEN *sits again on the floor and* **drums** *her heels.* ANNIE *comes around the table and resumes her chair. When* HELEN *feels her skirt again, she ceases kicking, waits for whatever is to come, renews*
> 10 *some kicking, waits again.* ANNIE, *retrieving her plate takes up a forkful of food, stops it halfway to her mouth, gazes at it* **devoid** *of appetite, and half-lowers it; but after a look at* HELEN *she sighs, dips the forkful toward* HELEN *in a for-your-sake toast, and puts it in her own mouth to chew, not without an effort.*
>
> …
>
> 15 ANNIE *now reaches over to spell into her hand but* HELEN *yanks it away; she gropes to the front door, tries the knob, and finds the door locked, with no key. She gropes to the rear door and finds it locked, with no key. She commences to bang on it.* ANNIE *rises, crosses, takes her wrists, draws her resisting back to the table, seats her, and releases her hands upon her plate; as* ANNIE *herself*
> 20 *begins to sit,* HELEN *writhes out of her chair, runs to the front door, and tugs and kicks at it.* ANNIE *rises again, crosses, draws her by one wrist back to the table, seats her, and sits;* HELEN *escapes back to the door, knocking over her mother's chair en route.* ANNIE *rises again in pursuit, and this time lifts* HELEN **bodily** *from behind and bears her kicking to her chair. She deposits her and*
> 25 *once more turns to sit.* HELEN *scrambles out, but as she passes,* ANNIE *catches her up again from behind and deposits her in the chair;* HELEN *scrambles out on the other side, for the rear door, but* ANNIE, *at her heels, catches her up and deposits her again in the chair. She stands behind it.* HELEN *scrambles out to her right, and the instant her feet hit the floor* ANNIE *lifts and deposits*
> 30 *her back; she scrambles out to her left and is at once lifted and deposited back. She tries right again and is deposited back, and tries left again and is deposited back, and now* **feints** ANNIE *to the right but is off to her left, and is promptly deposited back. She sits a moment and then starts straight over the tabletop, dishware* **notwithstanding**; ANNIE *hauls her in and deposits her back, with*
> 35 *her plate spilling in her lap, and she melts to the floor and crawls under the table,* **laborious** *among its legs and chairs; but* ANNIE *is swift around the table and waiting on the other side when she surfaces, immediately* **bearing her aloft**; HELEN *clutches at* JAMES'S *chair for* **anchorage**, *but it comes with her, and halfway back she abandons it to the floor.* ANNIE *deposits her in her chair, and*
> 40 *waits.* HELEN *sits tensed, motionless. Then she tentatively puts out her left foot*

---

deftly: quickly and skillfully
drums: taps
devoid: with no trace of
bodily: by the whole body
feints: makes a fake movement intending to distract
notwithstanding: regardless of
laborious: with a lot of effort
bearing her aloft: lifting her up
anchorage: stability

My Notes

and hand, ANNIE **interposes** *her own hand, and at the contact HELEN jerks hers in. She tries her right foot, ANNIE blocks it with her own, and HELEN jerks hers in. Finally, leaning back, she slumps down in her chair, in a* **sullen biding.**

…

45 ANNIE *puts the spoon first into HELEN'S hand, then sets the plate down. HELEN discarding the spoon reaches with her hand, and ANNIE stops it by the wrist; she replaces the spoon in it. HELEN impatiently discards it again, and again ANNIE stops her hand, to replace the spoon in it. This time HELEN throws the spoon on the floor. ANNIE, after considering it, lifts HELEN bodily*
50 *out of the chair, and in a wrestling match on the floor, closes her fingers upon the spoon and returns her with it to the chair. HELEN again throws the spoon on the floor. ANNIE lifts her out of the chair again; but in the struggle over the spoon HELEN, with ANNIE on her back, sends her sliding over her head; HELEN flees back to her chair and scrambles into it. When ANNIE comes after*
55 *her she clutches it for dear life; ANNIE pries one hand loose, then the other, then the first again, then the other again, and then lifts HELEN by the waist, chair and all, and shakes the chair loose. HELEN wrestles to get free, but ANNIE pins her to the floor, closes her fingers upon the spoon, and lifts her kicking under one arm; with her other hand she gets the chair in place again and plunks HELEN*
60 *back on it. When she releases her hand, HELEN throws the spoon at her.*

ANNIE *now removes the plate of food. HELEN grabbing finds it missing and commences to bang with her fists on the table. ANNIE collects a fistful of spoons and descends with them and the plate on HELEN; she lets her smell the plate, at which HELEN ceases banging, and ANNIE puts the plate down and a*
65 *spoon in HELEN'S hand. HELEN throws it on the floor. ANNIE puts another spoon in her hand. HELEN throws it on the floor. ANNIE puts another spoon in her hand. HELEN throws it on the floor. When ANNIE comes to her last spoon she sits next to HELEN and gripping the spoon in HELEN'S hand compels her to take food in it up to her mouth. HELEN sits with lips shut. ANNIE waits*
70 *a stolid moment, then lowers HELEN'S hand. She tries again; HELEN'S lips remain shut. ANNIE waits, lowers HELEN'S hand. She tries again; this time HELEN suddenly opens her mouth and accepts the food. ANNIE lowers the spoon with a sigh of relief, and HELEN spews the mouthful out at her face. ANNIE sits a moment with eyes closed, then takes the pitcher and dashes its*
75 *water into HELEN'S face, who gasps astonished. ANNIE, with HELEN'S hand, takes up another spoonful and shoves it into her open mouth. HELEN swallows involuntarily, and while she is catching her breath ANNIE forces her palm open, throws four swift letters into it, then another four, and bows toward her with* **devastating** *pleasantness.*

80 **ANNIE:** *Good girl.*

(ANNIE lifts HELEN'S hand to feel her face nodding; HELEN grabs a fistful of her hair, and yanks. The pain brings ANNIE to her knees, and HELEN pummels her; they roll under the table, and the lights commence to dim out on them.)

---

interposes: inserts
sullen biding: sulky waiting
devastating: fierce

Making Observations

- What did you notice about this text that was different from previous scenes?
- Which details struck you as particularly important?
- How did your impression of Helen or Annie change as you read?

Returning to the Text

- Return to the text as you respond to the following questions. Use text evidence to support your responses.
- Write any additional questions you have about the play in your Reader/Writer Notebook.

1. What actions are repeated over and over during the scene as Annie reacts to Helen?

_____

_____

_____

_____

2. Look at the specific words used to explain Helen's repeated actions. What are the words? What meaning do they add to the scene?

_____

_____

_____

_____

3. What is causing Helen's wild behavior?

_____

_____

_____

_____

4. How does the staging reveal more about Annie's character?

_____

_____

_____

_____

Setting a Purpose for Viewing

- As you view the performance of the scene, follow along in the script.
- Jot down words that summarize the external conflict of the scene.

Making Observations

- How did the actors reflect the stage directions you read?
- What was different about viewing this scene from reading the stage directions?

☑ Focus on the Sentence

Now that you have read the stage directions for a scene and watched it being performed by actors, complete the following sentences to summarize why stage directions are important.

Stage directions are important because _____

_____

Stage directions are important, but _____

_____

Stage directions are important, so _____

_____

Setting the Scene

5. With your class, brainstorm a list of topics or one-word themes that were introduced in this passage. You should have evidence from the passage to support your words. Choose one topic and write a sentence summarizing what the author says about it in the passage. Share your sentence with a partner and either choose one of the two sentences or combine them into one sentence. Revise that sentence to become a theme statement.

6. With your partner, go back into the text or the notes you took about the film to find evidence that supports your theme statement. Then join another pair and share your theme statements and textual evidence.

7. Illustrate the action of this event using a six-frame comic strip. Choose six of the most significant events in the passage and fill each frame with one of them. Beneath each frame, explain in words what is happening in the image (who is in it, what the person is doing, and why this event is significant to the play).

8. Work in small groups to combine your comic strips. First, identify the central conflict in this scene and choose six frames that explain how that conflict is introduced, how it builds, how it resolves, and how it will carry over into the rest of the play. Edit any frames and explanations that might need to be revised. Then put the frames in order.

9. Imagine that you will perform this scene for an audience. What information would the audience need to know about what happened previously to make sense of the action? Who are the characters? How do the characters relate to one another? What has happened to get the action to this point? Draft an introduction to your comic strip to ensure your audience understands the action.

10. Revisit your sixth frame. Think about what will happen next, using paragraph 4 and the single line of dialogue to inform your conclusion. Which characters will change as a result of this scene? What conflicts will be complicated? Write a concluding paragraph that supplies your audience with a sense of closure.

Memories, Decisions, and Compromises

Learning Targets

- Analyze how conflicts in a drama advance the plot's rising action and climax as well as how playwrights develop characters through dialogue and staging.
- Create a thematic statement about a scene using textual evidence.
- Perform a scene using punctuation to inform delivery.
- Analyze how the printed version of a play is the same as and different from the film version.

Preview

In this activity, you will view scenes from Act II of *The Miracle Worker* to analyze character and plot development as well as practice delivering lines.

Setting a Purpose for Viewing

- Keep notes about how the different characters' points of view change throughout the scene.
- Keep track of words and images that make you respond to the scene emotionally—sadness, sympathy, outrage, disappointment, disbelief, and so on.

Making Observations

- What did you learn about Annie from the flashback in the film?
- How did your impressions of Keller, Kate, and Annie change?
- What emotional reaction did you have to the scene? Why?

Working from the Film

1. What decision(s) does Keller make in this scene? What decision(s) does Annie make? Which of these decisions are most significant to the plot? Support your answer with evidence from the film.

2. Which characters make compromises in this scene? What do they give up? What do they get in return?

3. How do the decisions and compromises in this scene develop the characters and move the plot forward?

Learning Strategies

Summarizing
Marking the Text

My Notes

My Notes

4. How did the author use a flashback to help develop Annie's character and point of view?

5. In this scene, Annie is reading a factual report in the present and remembering an emotional event from her past. In the following chart, summarize what the report is saying in the left column; in the right column, summarize what Annie is remembering as she reads the report.

The Perkins report says ...	Annie remembers ...

6. In groups, compare and contrast the ideas in these two columns. How does the author's choice to include a factual report and emotional memories in the same scene advance the plot of the play?

Setting a Purpose for Reading
- Highlight all the stage directions.
- Underline words, phrases, and punctuation that give the actors direction.
- Circle unknown words and phrases. Try to determine the meaning of the words by using context clues, word parts, or a dictionary.

Play

from
The Miracle Worker, Act II
by **William Gibson**

(In the darkness down left a hand strikes a match and lights a hanging oil lamp. It is KELLER'S hand, and his voice accompanies it, very angry; the lights rising here before they fade on ANNIE show KELLER and KATE inside a suggestion of a garden house, with a bay-window seat towards center and a
5 *door at back.)*

KELLER: *Katie, I will not have it! Now you did not see when that girl after supper tonight went to look for Helen in her room—*

KATE: *No.*

KELLER: *The child practically climbed out of her window to escape from*
10 *her! What kind of teacher is she? I thought I had seen her at her worse this morning, shouting at me, but I come home to find the entire house*

My Notes

disorganized by her—Helen won't stay one second in the same room, won't come to the table with her, won't let herself be bathed or undressed or put to bed by her, or even by Viney now, and the end result is that you have to do

15 more for the child than before we hired this girl's services! From the moment she stepped off the train she's been nothing but a burden, **incompetent**, **impertinent**, **ineffectual**, **immodest**—

KATE: *She folded her napkin, Captain.*

KELLER: *What?*

20 **KATE:** *Not ineffectual. Helen did fold her napkin.*

KELLER: *What in heaven's name is so extraordinary about folding a napkin?*

KATE (*WITH SOME HUMOR*): *Well. It's more than you did, Captain.*

KELLER: *Katie. I did not bring you all the way out here to the garden house*

25 *to be **frivolous**. Now, how does Miss Sullivan propose to teach a deaf-blind pupil who won't let her even touch her?*

KATE (*A PAUSE*): *I don't know.*

KELLER: *The fact is, today she **scuttled** any chance she ever had of getting along with the child. If you can see any point or purpose to her staying on here*

30 *longer, it's more than—*

KATE: *What do you wish me to do?*

KELLER: *I want you to give her **notice**.*

KATE: *I can't.*

KELLER: *Then if you won't, I must. I simply will not—*

35 (*He is interrupted by a knock at the back door. KELLER after a glance at KATE moves to open the door; ANNIE in her smoked glasses is standing outside. KELLER contemplates her, heavily.*)

Miss Sullivan.

ANNIE: *Captain Keller.*

40 (*She is nervous, keyed up to seizing the bull by the horns again, and she assumes a cheeriness which is not unshaky.*)

Viney said I'd find you both over here in the garden house. I thought we should—have a talk?

KELLER (*RELUCTANTLY*): *Yes. I—Well, come in.*

45 (*ANNIE enters and is interested in this room; she **rounds** on her heel, anxiously, studying it. KELLER turns the matter over to KATE, **sotto voce**.*)

Katie.

KATE (*TURNING IT BACK, COURTEOUSLY*): *Captain.*

(*KELLER clears his throat, makes ready.*)

incompetent: unable to do things well or successfully

impertinent: rude or poorly mannered

ineffectual: not effective

immodest: lacking humility or decency

frivolous: taking things lightly or in a joking manner

scuttled: ruined

notice: word that employment will end

rounds: turns

sotto voce: in a quiet voice, as though to avoid being overheard

My Notes

50 **KELLER:** *I, ah—wanted first to make my position clear to Mrs. Keller, in private. I have decided I—am not satisfied—in fact, am deeply dissatisfied— with the manner in which—*

ANNIE *(INTENT): Excuse me, is this little house ever in use?*

KELLER *(WITH PATIENCE): In the hunting season. If you will give me your*
55 *attention, Miss Sullivan.*

(ANNIE turns her smoked glasses upon him; they hold his unwilling stare.)

I have tried to make allowances for you because you come from a part of the country where people are—women, I should say—come from who—well, for whom—

60 *(It begins to elude him.)*

—allowances must—be made. I have decided, nevertheless, to—that is, decided I—

(Vexedly)

Miss Sullivan, I find it difficult to talk through those glasses.

65 **ANNIE** *(EAGERLY, REMOVING THEM): Oh, of course.*

KELLER *(DOURLY): Why do you wear them? The sun has been down for an hour.*

ANNIE *(PLEASANTLY, AT THE LAMP): Any kind of light hurts my eyes.*

(A silence; KELLER ponders her, heavily.)

70 **KELLER:** *Put them on. Miss Sullivan, I have decided to—give you another chance.*

ANNIE *(CHEERFULLY): To do what?*

KELLER: *To—remain in our employ.*

(ANNIE'S eyes widen.)

75 *But on two conditions. I am not accustomed to rudeness in servants or women, and that is the first. If you are to stay, there must be a* radical *change of manner.*

ANNIE *(A PAUSE): Whose?*

KELLER *(EXPLODING): Yours, young lady, isn't it obvious? And the second*
80 *is that you persuade me there's the slightest hope of your teaching a child who flees from you now like the plague, to anyone else she can find in this house.*

ANNIE *(A PAUSE): There isn't.*

Making Observations

- Did any major difference between the film and the play stand out to you?
- How would you describe both Annie and Keller after reading this scene?

vexedly: in a frustrated or annoyed way
radical: big, dramatic

Returning to the Text

- Return to the text as you respond to the following questions. Use text evidence to support your responses.
- Write any additional questions you have about the play in your Reader/Writer Notebook.

7. What new information is given about Annie in this passage? How does this new information complicate the central conflict?

_____

_____

_____

_____

8. How does the cultural setting of the play influence Keller's conflict with Annie? How does it influence their characters? Use evidence from the text in your answer.

_____

_____

_____

_____

9. What mood is created in this scene? Which words show this mood?

_____

_____

_____

_____

10. How do the film and the play show conflict? How do actors in a film or play know which emotions to show?

_____

_____

_____

_____

11. How do the dialogue and staging in the passage reinforce the idea that Keller and Annie have different understandings of the situation?

_____

_____

_____

_____

Working from the Text

12. Now you will work with your groups to rehearse and perform this scene. Use the analysis you have done, the stage directions, the implied staging, and the punctuation marks to guide your performance. Carefully consider your inflection, facial expressions, and gestures. To ensure that you pronounce all of the words correctly, use a dictionary to determine the pronunciation and syllabication of any words that are unfamiliar to you.

13. **Quickwrite:** How would these scenes change if they were being recounted by Annie in an autobiography? Consider how the ideas, organization, and language would be different.

_____

_____

_____

_____

✍ Writing to Sources: Informational Text

Think about the theme of memory in this scene. What do you think the author is saying about the way that memories and experiences can cause or complicate conflicts or motivate a character's decisions and compromises? Choose details from the text (e.g. experiences/ memories, decisions, and compromises) and explain how they contribute to the development of theme. Be sure to:

- Include a strong thesis statement that structures your writing.
- Use complex sentences when possible.
- Use details to support your claims.
- Provide a strong conclusion.

🗊 Independent Reading Checkpoint

Organize and present a short presentation about the central figure in your Independent Reading text. Explain what the person's struggles entailed and how these struggles made life difficult. Include information about how the person overcame the struggle.

Performing a Scene

ASSIGNMENT

Work collaboratively to prepare and present a scene from William Gibson's play *The Miracle Worker*. Your performance should have a clear beginning, middle, and end.

Planning: Take time to make a plan for your performance.	■ How will you structure your performance group? What roles (beyond acting and directing) will each person perform to prepare the performance? ■ How will you choose a director and divide the parts fairly among the actors?
Analyzing: Read your script carefully for understanding and character analysis.	■ How can you work collaboratively to make meaning of the text? ■ How will you (as an actor) work independently to further analyze your character? ■ How will you (as the director) support the actors in their character analysis? ■ What resources can you use to determine the meaning and pronunciation/syllabication of words you don't know?
Preparing and Rehearsing: Create and revise a performance plan.	■ How will you (as an actor) learn your lines and create cue cards to aid memorization and performance? ■ How will you (as the director) draft an introduction and conclusion and help the actors to prepare? ■ How will you work collaboratively to revise and polish your performance plan?
Evaluating and Performing: Create opportunities to review and rehearse your presentations.	■ How can the Scoring Guide help you evaluate how well you are prepared to meet the requirements of the assignment? ■ How will you use oral, physical, and visual elements to engage your audience? ■ How will you take notes during the other students' presentations to compare and contrast their interpretations with your own?

Reflection

After completing this Embedded Assessment, think about how you went about accomplishing this task. Then respond to the following:

- How did students perform the same characters differently? Which choices did you think were most effective and engaging?

- How was your own interpretation of your role different from the film actor's interpretation?

SCORING GUIDE

Scoring Criteria	Exemplary	Proficient	Emerging	Incomplete
Ideas	The performance • demonstrates a deep understanding of a scene and characters. • uses a variety of physical and visual elements (facial expressions, movement, props or background sounds/images) effectively. • shows evidence of extensive planning, rehearsal, and reflection.	The performance • demonstrates an adequate understanding of a scene and characters. • uses some physical and visual elements (facial expressions, movement, props or background sounds/images) to convey meaning. • shows evidence of sufficient planning, rehearsal, and reflection.	The performance • demonstrates a partial or flawed understanding of a scene and characters. • uses distracting or basic physical and visual elements (facial expressions, movement, props or background sounds/images). • shows evidence of ineffective or insufficient planning, rehearsal, and reflection.	The performance • demonstrates little or no understanding of a scene and characters. • lacks physical and/or visual elements. • does not show evidence of planning, rehearsal, and reflection.
Structure	The performance • demonstrates strong evidence of collaboration. • depicts a significant scene with a clear beginning, middle, and end. • provides an engaging introduction and conclusion.	The performance • demonstrates adequate evidence of collaboration. • depicts a scene with a beginning, middle, and end. • provides an introduction and conclusion.	The performance • demonstrates uneven or ineffective collaboration. • depicts a scene with an unclear beginning, middle, and/or end. • provides a weak introduction and/or conclusion.	The performance • demonstrates a failure to collaborate. • depicts a scene that is too short. • lacks an introduction and/or conclusion.
Use of Language	The performer • demonstrates effective oral interpretation skills, including eye contact, volume, rate, inflection, tone, and rhythm. • uses punctuation cues (periods, commas, semicolons, dashes, exclamation points) accurately and consistently to inform vocal delivery.	The performer • demonstrates adequate oral interpretation skills, including eye contact, volume, rate, inflection, tone, and rhythm. • uses some punctuation cues (periods, commas, semicolons, dashes, exclamation points) to inform vocal delivery.	The performer • demonstrates inadequate oral interpretation skills. • uses punctuation cues (periods, commas, semicolons, dashes, exclamation points) unevenly or inconsistently.	The performer • demonstrates flawed or ineffective oral interpretation skills. • does not recognize punctuation cues or uses them incorrectly.

Group 1
ACT II, SCENE 7

(The lights dim into a cool silhouette scene around her, the lamp paling out, and now, in formal entrances, persons appear around ANNIE *with furniture for the room:* PERCY *crosses the stage with a rocking chair and waits;* MARTHA, *from another direction, bears in a stool,* VINEY *bears in a small*
5 *table, and the other servant rolls in a bed partway from left; and* ANNIE, *opening her eyes to put her glasses back on, sees them. She turns around in the room once and goes into action, pointing out locations for each article; the servants place them and leave, and* ANNIE *then darts around, interchanging them. In the midst of this—while* PERCY *and* MARTHA *reappear with a*
10 *tray of food and a chair, respectively—*JAMES *comes down from the house with* ANNIE'S *suitcase and stands viewing the room and her quizzically;* ANNIE *halts abruptly under his eyes, embarrassed, then seizes the suitcase from his hand, explaining herself brightly.)*

ANNIE: I always wanted to live in a doll's house!

15 *(She sets the suitcase out of the way, and continues;* VINEY *at left appears to position a rod with drapes for a doorway, and the other servant at center pushes in a wheelbarrow loaded with a couple of boxes of* HELEN'S *toys and clothes.* ANNIE *helps lift them into the room, and the servant pushes the wheelbarrow off. In none of this is any heed taken of the imaginary walls of*
20 *the garden house, the furniture is moved in from every side and itself defines the walls.)*

ANNIE *now drags the box of toys into center, props up the doll conspicuously on top; with the people melted away, except for* JAMES, *all is again still. The lights turn again without pause, rising warmer.)*

25 **JAMES:** You don't let go of things easily, do you? How will you—win her hand now, in this place?

ANNIE (CURTLY): Do I know? I lost my temper, and here we are!

JAMES (LIGHTLY): No touching, no teaching. Of course, you are bigger—

ANNIE: I'm not counting on force, I'm counting on her. That little imp is
30 dying to know.

JAMES: Know what?

ANNIE: Anything. Any and every crumb in God's creation. I'll have to use that appetite too.

(She gives the room a final survey, straightens the bed, arranges the curtains.)

35 **JAMES** (a pause): Maybe she'll teach you.

ANNIE: Of course.

JAMES: That she isn't. That there's such a thing as—dullness of heart. Acceptance. And letting go. Sooner or later we all give up, don't we?

ANNIE: Maybe you all do. It's my idea of the original sin.

My Notes

40 **JAMES:** What is?

ANNIE (WITHERINGLY): Giving up.

JAMES (NETTLED): You won't open her. Why can't you let her be? Have some—pity on her, for being what she is—

ANNIE: If I'd ever once thought like that, I'd be dead!

45 **JAMES** (PLEASANTLY): You will be. Why trouble?

(ANNIE *turns to glare at him; he is mocking.*)

Or will you teach me?

(*And with a bow, he drifts off.*

Now in the distance there comes the clopping of hoofs, drawing near, and
50 *nearer, up to the door; and they halt. ANNIE wheels to face the door. When*
it opens this time, the KELLERS—KATE in traveling bonnet, KELLER also
hatted—are standing there with HELEN between them; she is in a cloak.
KATE gently cues her into the room. HELEN comes in groping, baffled, but
interested in the new surroundings; ANNIE evades her exploring hand, her
55 *gaze not leaving the child.*)

ANNIE: Does she know where she is?

KATE (SHAKES HER HEAD): We rode her out in the country for two hours.

KELLER: For all she knows, she could be in another town—

(HELEN *stumbles over the box on the floor and in it discovers her doll*
60 *and other battered toys, is pleased, sits to them, then becomes puzzled and*
suddenly very wary. She scrambles up and back to her mother's thighs, but
ANNIE *steps in, and it is hers that* HELEN *embraces.* HELEN *recoils, gropes,*
and touches her cheek instantly.)

KATE: That's her sign for me.

65 **ANNIE:** I know.

(HELEN *waits, then recommences her groping, more urgently.* KATE
stands indecisive and takes an abrupt step toward her, but ANNIE'S *hand is*
a barrier.)

In two weeks.

70 **KATE:** Miss ANNIE, I—Please be good to her. These two weeks, try to be
very good to her—

ANNIE: I will.

(KATE, *turning then, hurries out. The* KELLERS *cross back of the main*
house. ANNIE *closes the door.* HELEN *starts at the door jar and rushes it.*
75 ANNIE *holds her off.* HELEN *kicks her, breaks free, and careens around*
the room like an imprisoned bird, colliding with furniture, groping wildly,
repeatedly touching her cheek in a growing panic. When she has covered the
room, she commences her weird screaming. ANNIE *moves to comfort her, but*
her touch sends HELEN *into a paroxysm of rage: she tears away, falls over her*

80 *box of toys, flings the box too, reels to her feet, rips curtains from the window, bangs and kicks at the door, sweeps objects off the mantelpiece and shelf, a little tornado incarnate, all destruction, until she comes upon her doll and, in the act of hurling it, freezes. Then she clutches it to herself, and in exhaustion sinks sobbing to the floor. ANNIE stands contemplating her, in some awe.)*

85 Two weeks.

(She shakes her head, not without a touch of disgusted bewilderment.)

What did I get into now?

(The lights have been dimming throughout, and the garden house is lit only by moonlight now, with ANNIE lost in the patches of dark.)

Group 2
ACT II, SCENE 8

90 *(KATE, now hatless and coatless, enters the family room by the rear door, carrying a lamp. KELLER, also hatless, wanders simultaneously around the back of the main house to where JAMES has been waiting, in the rising moonlight, on the porch.)*

KELLER: I can't understand it. I had every intention of dismissing that girl, 95 not setting her up like an empress.

JAMES: Yes, what's her secret, sir?

KELLER: Secret?

JAMES (pleasantly): That enables her to get anything she wants out of you? When I can't.

100 *(JAMES turns to go into the house, but KELLER grasps his wrist, twisting him half to his knees. KATE comes from the porch.)*

KELLER (angrily): She does not get anything she—

JAMES (IN PAIN): Don't—don't—

KATE: Captain.

105 **KELLER:** He's afraid.

(He throws JAMES away from him, with contempt.)

What *does* he want out of me?

JAMES (an outcry): My God, don't you know?

(He gazes from KELLER to KATE.)

110 Everything you forgot, when you forgot my mother.

KELLER: What!

(JAMES wheels into the house. KELLER takes a stride to the porch, to roar after him.)

One thing that girl's secret is not, she doesn't fire one shot and disappear!

My Notes

My Notes

115 (KATE *stands rigid, and* KELLER *comes back to her.*)

Katie. Don't mind what he—

KATE: Captain, I am proud of you.

KELLER: For what?

KATE: For letting this girl have what she needs.

120 **KELLER:** Why can't my son be? He can't bear me, you'd think I treat him as hard as this girl does Helen—

(*He breaks off, as it dawns on him.*)

KATE (GENTLY): Perhaps you do.

KELLER: But he has to learn some respect!

125 **KATE** (A PAUSE, WRYLY): Do you like the child?

(*She turns again to the porch, but pauses, reluctant.*)

How empty the house is, tonight.

(*After a moment she continues on in,* KELLER *stands moveless, as the moonlight dies on him.*)

Group 3
ACT II, SCENE 9

130 (*The distant belfry chimes toll, two o'clock, and with them, a moment later, comes the boy's voice on the wind, in a whisper:*)

Boy's Voice. Annie. Annie.

(*In her patch of dark* ANNIE, *now in her nightgown, hurls a cup into a corner as though it were her grief, getting rid of its taste through her teeth.*)

135 **ANNIE:** No! No pity, I won't have it.

(*She comes to* HELEN, *prone on the floor.*)

On either of us.

(*She goes to her knees, but when she touches* HELEN'S *hand the child starts up awake, recoils, and scrambles away from her under the bed.* ANNIE *stares*
140 *after her. She strikes her palm on the floor, with passion.*)

I will touch you!

(*She gets to her feet, and paces in a kind of anger around the bed, her hand in her hair, and confronting* HELEN *at each turn.*)

How, how? How do I—

145 (ANNIE *stops. Then she calls out urgently, loudly.*)

Percy! Percy!

(*She moves swiftly to the drapes, at left.*)

Percy, wake up!

(PERCY'S voice comes in a thick sleepy mumble, unintelligible.)

150 Get out of bed and come in here, I need you.

(ANNIE darts away, finds and strikes a match, and touches it to the hanging lamp; the lights come up dimly in the room, and PERCY stands bare to the waist in torn overalls between the drapes, with eyes closed, swaying. ANNIE goes to him, pats his cheeks vigorously.)

155 **ANNIE:** You awake?

Percy. No'm.

ANNIE: How would you like to play a nice game?

Percy. Whah?

ANNIE: With Helen. She's under the bed. Touch her hand.

160 *(She kneels PERCY down at the bed, thrusting his hand under it to contact HELEN'S; HELEN emits an animal sound and crawls to the opposite side, but commences sniffing. ANNIE rounds the bed with PERCY and thrusts his hand again at HELEN; this time HELEN clutches it, sniffs in recognition, and comes scrambling out after PERCY, to hug him with delight. PERCY,*
165 *alarmed, struggles, and HELEN'S fingers go to his mouth.)*

Percy. Lemme go. Lemme go—

(HELEN fingers her own lips, as before, moving them in dumb imitation.)

She tryin' talk. She gonna hit me—

ANNIE (GRIMLY): She can talk. If she only knew, I'll show you how. She
170 makes letters.

(She opens PERCY'S other hand, and spells into it.)

This one is C. C.

(She hits his palm with it a couple of times, her eyes upon HELEN across him; HELEN gropes to feel what PERCY'S hand is doing, and when she
175 *encounters ANNIE'S she falls back from them.)*

She's mad at me now, though, she won't play. But she knows lots of letters. Here's another, A. C, a. C, a.

(But she is watching HELEN, who comes groping, consumed with curiosity; ANNIE makes the letters in PERCY'S hand, and HELEN pokes to question
180 *what they are up to. Then HELEN snatches PERCY'S other hand, and quickly spells four letters into it. ANNIE follows them aloud.)*

C, a, k, e! She spells cake, she gets cake.

(She is swiftly over to the tray of food, to fetch cake and a jug of milk.)

She doesn't know yet it means this. Isn't it funny she knows how to spell it
185 and doesn't know she knows?

My Notes

(She breaks the cake into two pieces, and extends one to each; HELEN rolls away from her offer.)

Well, if she won't play it with me, I'll play it with you. Would you like to learn one she doesn't know?

190 **Percy**. No'm.

(But ANNIE seizes his wrist and spells to him.)

ANNIE: M, i, l, k. M is this. I, that's an easy one, just the little finger. L is this—

(And HELEN comes back with her hand, to feel the new word. ANNIE
195 *brushes her away and continues spelling aloud to PERCY. HELEN'S hand comes back again, and tries to get in; ANNIE brushes it away again. HELEN'S hand insists, and ANNIE puts it away rudely.)*

No, why should I talk to you? I'm teaching Percy a new word. L. K is this—

(HELEN now yanks their hands apart; she butts PERCY away and thrusts
200 *her palm out insistently. ANNIE'S eyes are bright, with glee.)*

Ho, you're jealous, are you!

(HELEN'S hand waits, intractably waits.)

All right.

(ANNIE spells into it, milk; and HELEN after a moment spells it back to
205 *ANNIE. ANNIE takes her hand, with her whole face shining. She gives a great sigh.)*

Good! So I'm finally back to where I can touch you, hm? Touch and go! No love lost, but here we go.

(She puts the jug of milk into HELEN'S hand and squeezes PERCY'S shoulder.)

210 You can go to bed now, you've earned your sleep. Thank you.

(PERCY, stumbling up, weaves his way out through the drapes. HELEN finishes drinking and holds the jug out for ANNIE; when ANNIE takes it, HELEN crawls onto the bed and makes for sleep. ANNIE stands, looks down at her.)

Now all I have to teach you is—one word. Everything.

215 *(She sets the jug down. On the floor now ANNIE spies the doll, stoops to pick it up, and with it dangling in her hand, turns off the lamp. A shaft of moonlight is left on HELEN in the bed, and a second shaft on the rocking chair; and ANNIE, after putting off her smoked glasses, sits in the rocker with the doll. She is rather happy and dangles the doll on her knee, and it makes its*
220 *momma sound. ANNIE whispers to it in mock solicitude.)*

Hush, little baby. Don't—say a word—

(She lays it against her shoulder and begins rocking with it, patting its diminutive behind; she talks the lullaby to it humorously at first.)

Momma's gonna buy you—a mockingbird:

225 If that—mockingbird don't sing—

(The rhythm of the rocking takes her into the tune, softly, and more tenderly.)

Momma's gonna buy you a diamond ring:

If that diamond ring turns to brass—

230 *(A third shaft of moonlight outside now rises to pick out* JAMES *at the main house, with one foot on the porch step; he turns his body, as if hearing the song.)*

Momma's gonna buy you a looking-glass:

If that looking-glass gets broke—

(In the family room a fourth shaft picks out KELLER *seated at the table, in thought; and he, too, lifts his head, as if hearing.)*

235 Momma's gonna buy you a billy goat:

If that billy goat don't pull—

(The fifth shaft is upstairs in ANNIE'S *room and picks out* KATE, *pacing there; and she halts, turning her head, too, as if hearing.)*

Momma's gonna buy you a cart and bull:

240 If that cart and bull turns over,

Momma's gonna buy you a dog named Rover.

If that dog named Rover won't bark—

*(With the shafts of moonlight
on* HELEN, *and* JAMES, *and* KELLER, *and* KATE, *all moveless,*
245 *and* ANNIE *rocking the doll, the curtain ends the act.)*

Group 4
ACT III, SCENE 1, Part 1

(The stage is totally dark, until we see ANNIE *and* HELEN *silhouetted on the bed in the garden house.* ANNIE'S *voice is audible, very patient, and worn; it has been saying this for a long time.)*

ANNIE: Water, Helen. This is water. W, a, t, e, r. It has a name.

250 *(A silence. Then:)*

Egg, e, g, g. It has a name, the name stands for the thing. Oh, it's so simple, simple as birth, to explain.

(The lights have commenced to rise, not on the garden house but on the homestead. Then:)

255 Helen, Helen, the chick has to come out of its shell, sometime. You come out, too.

(In the bedroom upstairs, we see VINEY *unhurriedly washing the window,*

My Notes

_____

_____

_____

_____

_____

_____

_____

_____

_____

_____

_____

_____

_____

_____

_____

_____

_____

_____

_____

_____

_____

_____

_____

_____

_____

_____

_____

_____

_____

_____

_____

_____

_____

My Notes

_____
_____
_____
_____
_____
_____
_____
_____
_____
_____
_____
_____
_____
_____
_____
_____
_____
_____
_____
_____
_____
_____
_____
_____
_____
_____
_____
_____
_____
_____
_____
_____
_____
_____
_____

dusting, turning the mattress, readying the room for use again; then in the family room a diminished group at one end of the table—KATE, KELLER,

260 JAMES—*finishing up a quiet breakfast; then outside, down right, the other servant on his knees, assisted by* MARTHA, *working with a trowel around a new trellis and wheelbarrow. The scene is one of everyday calm, and all are oblivious to* ANNIE'S *voice.)*

There's only one way out, for you, and it's language. To learn that your

265 fingers can talk. And say anything, anything you can name. This is mug. Mug, m, u, g. Helen, it has a name. It—has—a—name.

(KATE rises from the table.)

KELLER (GENTLY): You haven't eaten, Katie.

KATE (SMILES, SHAKES HER HEAD): I haven't the appetite. I'm too—

270 restless, I can't sit to it.

KELLER: You should eat, my dear. It will be a long day, waiting.

JAMES (LIGHTLY): But it's been a short two weeks. I never thought life could be so—noiseless, went much too quickly for me.

(KATE and KELLER gaze at him, in silence. JAMES becomes uncomfortable.)

275 **ANNIE**: C, a, r, d. Card. C, a—

JAMES: Well, the house has been practically normal, hasn't it?

KELLER (HARSHLY): Jimmie.

JAMES: Is it wrong to enjoy a quiet breakfast, after five years? And you two even seem to enjoy each other—

280 **KELLER**: It could be even more noiseless, Jimmie, without your tongue running every minute. Haven't you enough feeling to imagine what Katie has been undergoing, ever since—

(KATE stops him, with her hand on his arm.)

KATE: Captain.

285 *(To JAMES)*

It's true. The two weeks have been normal, quiet, all you say. But not short. Interminable.

(She rises and wanders out; she pauses on the porch steps, gazing toward the garden house.)

290 **ANNIE** (FADING): W, a, t, e, r. But it means this. W, a, t, e, r. This. W, a, t—

JAMES: I only meant that Miss Sullivan is a boon. Of contention, though, it seems.

KELLER (HEAVILY): If and when you're a parent, Jimmie, you will understand what separation means. A mother loses a—protector.

295 **JAMES** (BAFFLED): Hm?

KELLER: You'll learn, we don't just keep our children safe. They keep us safe.

(He rises, with his empty coffee cup and saucer.)

There are of course all kinds of separation. Katie has lived with one kind for five years. And another is disappointment. In a child.

300 *(He goes with the cup out the rear door. JAMES sits for a long moment of stillness. In the garden house the lights commence to come up; ANNIE, haggard at the table, is writing a letter, her face again almost in contact with the stationery; HELEN, apart on the stool, and for the first time as clean and neat as a button, is quietly crocheting an endless chain of wool, which snakes*
305 *all around the room.)*

ANNIE: "I, feel, every, day, more, and, more, in—"

(She pauses, and turns the pages of a dictionary open before her; her finger descends the words to a full stop. She elevates her eyebrows, then copies the word.)

310 "—adequate."

(In the main house JAMES pushes up and goes to the front doorway, after KATE.)

JAMES: Kate?

(KATE turns her glance. JAMES is rather weary.)

315 I'm sorry. Open my mouth, like that fairy tale, frogs jump out.

KATE: No. It has been better. For everyone.

(She starts away, up center.)

ANNIE (WRITING): "If, only, there, were, someone, to, help, me, I, need, a, teacher, as, much, as, Helen—"

320 **JAMES:** Kate.

(KATE halts, waits.)

What does he want from me?

KATE: That's not the question. Stand up to the world, Jimmie, that comes first.

JAMES (a pause, wryly): But the world is him.

325 **KATE:** Yes. And no one can do it for you.

JAMES: Kate. *(His voice is humble.)* At least we——Could you—be my friend?

KATE: I am.

(KATE turns to wander, up back of the garden house. ANNIE'S murmur comes at once; the lights begin to die on the main house.)

330 **ANNIE:** "—My, mind, is, undisiplined, full, of, skips, and, jumps, and—" *(She halts, rereads, frowns.)* Hm. *(ANNIE puts her nose again in the dictionary, flips back to an earlier page, and fingers down the words; KATE presently comes down toward the bay window with a trayful of food.)* Disinter—disinterested—disjoin—dis—*(She backtracks, indignant.)*
335 Disinterested, disjoin—Where's disipline? *(She goes a page or two back,*

My Notes

searching with her finger, muttering.) What a dictionary, have to know how to spell it before you can look up how to spell it, disciple, discipline! Diskipline. *(She corrects the word in her letter.)* Undisciplined.

(But her eyes are bothering her, she closes them in exhaustion and gently 340 *fingers the eyelids.* KATE *watches her through the window.)*

KATE: What are you doing to your eyes?

*(*ANNIE *glances around; she puts her smoked glasses on and gets up to come over, assuming a cheerful energy.)*

ANNIE: It's worse on my vanity! I'm learning to spell. It's like a surprise
345 party, the most unexpected characters turn up.

KATE: You're not to overwork your eyes, Miss Annie.

ANNIE: Well.

(She takes the tray, sets it on her chair, and carries chair and tray to HELEN.*)*

Whatever I spell to Helen I'd better spell right.

350 **KATE** (ALMOST WISTFUL): How—serene she is.

ANNIE: She learned this stitch yesterday. Now I can't get her to stop!

(She disentangles one foot from the wool chain and sets the chair before HELEN. HELEN, *at its contact with her knee, feels the plate, promptly sets her crocheting down, and tucks the napkin in at her neck, but* ANNIE
355 *withholds the spoon: when* HELEN *finds it missing, she folds her hands in her lap, and quietly waits.* ANNIE *twinkles at* KATE *with mock devoutness.)*

Such a little lady, she'd sooner starve than eat with her fingers.

(She gives HELEN *the spoon, and* HELEN *begins to eat, neatly.)*

KATE: You've taught her so much, these two weeks. I would never have—

360 **ANNIE:** Not enough.

(She is suddenly gloomy, shakes her head.)

Obedience isn't enough. Well, she learned two nouns this morning, key and water, brings her up to eighteen nouns and three verbs.

KATE: (HESITANT): But—not——

365 **ANNIE:** No. Not that they mean things. It's still a finger-game, no meaning.

(She turns to KATE, *abruptly.)*

Mrs. Keller—

(But she defers it; she comes back, to sit in the bay, and lifts her hand.)

Shall we play our finger-game?

370 **KATE:** How will she learn it?

ANNIE: It will come.

(She spells a word; KATE *does not respond.)*

KATE: How?

ANNIE (A PAUSE): How does a bird learn to fly?

375 *(She spells again.)*

We're born to use words, like wings, it has to come.

KATE: How?

ANNIE (ANOTHER PAUSE, WEARILY): All right. I don't know how.

(She pushes up her glasses, to rub her eyes.)

380 I've done everything I could think of. Whatever she's learned here—keeping herself clean, knitting, stringing beads, meals, setting-up exercises each morning, we climb trees, hunt eggs, yesterday a chick was born in her hands—all of it I spell, everything we do, we never stop spelling. I go to bed with—writer's cramp from talking so much!

385 **KATE:** I worry about you, Miss Annie. You must rest.

ANNIE: Now? She spells back in her sleep, her fingers make letters when she doesn't know! In her bones those five fingers know, that hand aches to—speak out, and something in her mind is asleep, how do I—nudge that awake? That's the one question.

390 **KATE:** With no answer.

ANNIE (LONG PAUSE): Except keep at it. Like this.

(She again begins spelling—I, need—and KATE'S brows gather, following the words.)

KATE: More—time?

395 *(She glances at ANNIE, who looks her in the eyes, silent.)*

Here?

ANNIE: Spell it.

(KATE spells a word—no—shaking her head; ANNIE spells two words—why, not—back, with an impatient question in her eyes; and KATE moves
400 *her head in pain to answer it.)*

KATE: Because I can't—

ANNIE: Spell it! If she ever learns, you'll have a lot to tell each other, start now.

(KATE painstakingly spells in air. In the midst of this the rear door opens,
405 *and KELLER enters with the setter BELLE in tow.)*

My Notes

Group 5
ACT III, SCENE 1, Part 2

KELLER: Miss Sullivan? On my way to the office, I brought Helen a playmate—

ANNIE: Outside please, Captain Keller.

KELLER: My dear child, the two weeks are up today, surely you don't object
410 to—

ANNIE (RISING): They're not up till six o'clock.

KELLER (INDULGENT): Oh, now. What difference can a fraction of one day—

ANNIE: An agreement is an agreement. Now you've been very good, I'm sure you can keep it up for a few more hours.

415 *(She escorts* KELLER *by the arm over the threshold; he obeys, leaving* BELLE.*)*

KELLER: Miss Sullivan, you are a tyrant.

ANNIE: Likewise, I'm sure. You can stand there, and close the door if she comes.

420 **KATE**: I don't think you know how eager we are to have her back in our arms—

ANNIE: I do know, it's my main worry.

KELLER: It's like expecting a new child in the house. Well, she is, so—composed, so—

425 *(Gently)*

Attractive. You've done wonders for her, Miss Sullivan.

ANNIE (NOT A QUESTION): Have I.

KELLER: If there's anything you want from us in repayment tell us, it will be a privilege to—

430 **ANNIE**: I just told Mrs. Keller. I want more time.

KATE: Miss Annie—

ANNIE: Another week.

(HELEN lifts her head, and begins to sniff.)

KELLER: We miss the child. I miss her, I'm glad to say, that's a different
435 debt I owe you—

ANNIE: Pay it to Helen. Give her another week.

KATE (GENTLY): Doesn't she miss us?

KELLER: Of course she does. What a wrench this unexplainable—exile must be to her, can you say it's not?

440 **ANNIE**: No. But I—

(HELEN *is off the stool, to grope about the room; when she encounters* BELLE, *she throws her arms around the dog's neck in delight.*)

KATE: Doesn't she need affection too, Miss Annie?

ANNIE (WAVERING): She—never shows me she needs it, she won't have
445 any—caressing or—

KATE: But you're not her mother.

KELLER: And what would another week accomplish? We are more than satisfied, you've done more than we ever thought possible, taught her constructive—

450 **ANNIE**: I can't promise anything. All I can—

KELLER (NO BREAK):—things to do, to behave like—even look like—a human child, so manageable, contented, cleaner, more—

ANNIE (WITHERING): Cleaner.

KELLER: Well. We say cleanliness is next to godliness, Miss—

455 **ANNIE**: Cleanliness is next to nothing, she has to learn that everything has its name! That words can be her eyes, to everything in the world outside her, and inside too, what is she without words? With them she can think, have ideas, be reached, there's not a thought or fact in the world that can't be hers. You publish a newspaper, Captain Keller, do I have to tell you what
460 words are? And she has them already—

KELLER: Miss Sullivan.

ANNIE: —eighteen nouns and three verbs, they're in her fingers now, I need only time to push one of them into her mind! One, and everything under the sun will follow. Don't you see what she's learned here is only
465 clearing the way for that? I can't risk her unlearning it, give me more time alone with her, another week to—

KELLER: Look.

(*He points, and* ANNIE *turns.* HELEN *is playing with* BELLE'S *claws; she makes letters with her fingers, shows them to* BELLE, *waits with her palm,*
470 *then manipulates the dog's claws.*)

What is she spelling?

(*A silence.*)

KATE: Water?

(ANNIE *nods.*)

475 **KELLER**: Teaching a dog to spell.

(*A pause*)

The dog doesn't know what she means, any more than she knows what you mean, Miss Sullivan. I think you ask too much, of her and yourself. God may not have meant Helen to have the—eyes you speak of.

My Notes

_____

_____

_____

_____

_____

_____

_____

_____

_____

_____

_____

_____

_____

_____

_____

_____

_____

_____

_____

_____

_____

_____

_____

_____

_____

_____

_____

_____

_____

_____

_____

_____

_____

My Notes

480 **ANNIE** (TONELESS): I mean her to.

KELLER (CURIOUSLY): What is it to you?

(ANNIE'S *head comes slowly up.*)

You make us see how we indulge her for our sake. Is the opposite true, for you?

485 **ANNIE** (THEN): Half a week?

KELLER: An agreement is an agreement.

ANNIE: Mrs. Keller?

KATE (SIMPLY): I want her back.

(*A wait;* ANNIE *then lets her hands drop in surrender, and nods.*)

490 **KELLER**: I'll send Viney over to help you pack.

ANNIE: Not until six o'clock. I have her till six o'clock.

KELLER (CONSENTING): Six o'clock. Come, Katie.

(KATE, *leaving the window, joins him around back, while* KELLER *closes the door; they are shut out. Only the garden house is daylit now, and the light on*
495 *it is narrowing down.* ANNIE *stands watching* HELEN *work* BELLE'S *claws. Then she settles beside them on her knees and stops* HELEN'S *hand.*)

ANNIE (GENTLY): No.

(*She shakes her head, with* HELEN'S *hand to her face, then spells.*)

Dog. D, o, g, dog.

500 (*She touches* HELEN'S *hand to* BELLE. HELEN *dutifully pats the dog's head and resumes spelling to its paw.*)

Not water.

(ANNIE *rolls to her feet, brings a tumbler of water back from the tray, and kneels with it, to seize* HELEN'S *hand and spell.*)

505 Here. Water. Water.

(*She thrusts* HELEN'S *hand into the tumbler.* HELEN *lifts her hand out dripping, wipes it daintily on* BELLE'S *hide, and taking the tumbler from* ANNIE, *endeavors to thrust* BELLE'S *paw into it.* ANNIE *sits watching, wearily.*)

510 I don't know how to tell you. Not a soul in the world knows how to tell you. Helen, Helen.

(*She bends in compassion to touch her lips to* HELEN'S *temple, and instantly* HELEN *pauses, her hands off the dog, her head slightly averted. The lights are still narrowing, and* BELLE *slinks off. After a moment* ANNIE *sits back.*)

515 Yes, what's it to me? They're satisfied. Give them back their child and dog, both housebroken, everyone's satisfied. But me, and you.

(HELEN'S *hand comes out into the light, groping.*)

Reach. Reach!

(ANNIE, *extending her own hand, grips* HELEN'S; *the two hands are*
520 *clasped, tense in the light, the rest of the room changing in shadow.*)

I wanted to teach you—oh, everything the earth is full of, Helen,
everything on it that's ours for a wink and it's gone, and what we are on it,
the—light we bring to it and leave behind in—words, why, you can see five
thousand years back in a light of words, everything we feel, think, know—
525 and share, in words, so not a soul is in darkness, or done with, even in the
grave. And I know, I know, one word and I can—put the world in your
hand—and whatever it is to me, I won't take less! How, how, how do I tell
you that this—

(*She spells.*)

530 —means a word, and the word means this thing, wool?

(*She thrusts the wool at* HELEN'S *hand;* HELEN *sits, puzzled.* ANNIE *puts
the crocheting aside.*)

Or this—s, t, o, o, l—means this thing, stool?

(*She claps* HELEN'S *palm to the stool.* HELEN *waits, uncomprehending.*
535 ANNIE *snatches up her napkin, spells:*)

Napkin!

(*She forces it on* HELEN'S *hand, waits, discards it, lifts a fold of the child's
dress, spells:*)

Dress!

540 (*She lets it drop, spells:*)

F, a, c, e, face!

(*She draws* HELEN'S *hand to her cheek, and pressing it there, staring into the
child's responseless eyes, hears the distant belfry begin to toll, slowly: one, two,
three, four, five, six.*)

Group 6
ACT III, SCENE 2

545 (*On the third stroke the lights stealing in around the garden house show us
figures waiting:* VINEY, *the other servant,* MARTHA, PERCY *at the drapes,
and* JAMES *on the dim porch.* ANNIE *and* HELEN *remain, frozen. The
chimes die away. Silently* PERCY *moves the drape-rod back out of sight;*
VINEY *steps into the room—not using the door—and unmakes the bed;*
550 *the other servant brings the wheelbarrow over, leaves it handy, rolls the bed
off;* VINEY *puts the bed linens on top of a waiting boxful of* HELEN'S *toys
and loads the box on the wheelbarrow;* MARTHA *and* PERCY *take out
the chairs, with the trayful, then the table; and* JAMES, *coming down and
into the room, lifts* ANNIE'S *suitcase from its corner.* VINEY *and the other*
555 *servant load the remaining odds and ends on the wheelbarrow, and the*

My Notes

servant wheels it off. VINEY *and the children, departing, leave only JAMES in the room with ANNIE and HELEN. JAMES studies the two of them, without mockery, and then, quietly going to the door and opening it, bears the suitcase out, and houseward. He leaves the door open.*

560 KATE *steps into the doorway, and stands.* ANNIE, *lifting her gaze from* HELEN, *sees her; she takes* HELEN'S *hand from her cheek and returns it to the child's own, stroking it there twice, in her mother-sign, before spelling slowly into it.)*

ANNIE: M, o, t, h, e, r. Mother.

565 (HELEN, *with her hand free, strokes her cheek, suddenly forlorn.* ANNIE *takes her hand again.)*

M, o, t, h——

(*But* KATE *is trembling with such impatience that her voice breaks from her, harsh.)*

570 **KATE:** Let her come!

(ANNIE *lifts* HELEN *to her feet, with a turn, and gives her a little push. Now* HELEN *begins groping, sensing something, trembling herself; and* KATE, *falling one step in onto her knees, clasps her, kissing her.* HELEN *clutches her, tight as she can.* KATE *is inarticulate, choked, repeating* HELEN'S *name* 575 *again and again. She wheels with her in her arms, to stumble away out the doorway;* ANNIE *stands unmoving, while* KATE *in a blind walk carries* HELEN *like a baby behind the main house, out of view.*

ANNIE *is now alone on the stage. She turns, gazing around at the stripped room, bidding it silently farewell, impassively, like a defeated general on the* 580 *deserted battlefield. All that remains is a stand with a basin of water; and here* ANNIE *takes up an eyecup, bathes each of her eyes, empties the eyecup, drops it in her purse, and tiredly locates her smoked glasses on the floor. The lights alter subtly; in the act of putting on her glasses,* ANNIE *hears something that stops her, with head lifted. We hear it too, the voices out of the past,* 585 *including her own now, in a whisper:)*

Boy's Voice. You said we'd be together, forever—You promised, forever and—Annie!

Anagnos's Voice. But that battle is dead and done with, why not let it stay buried?

590 **ANNIE'S Voice** (whispering): I think God must owe me a resurrection.

Anagnos's Voice. What?

(*A pause, and* ANNIE *answers it herself, heavily.)*

ANNIE: And I owe God one.

Boy's Voice. Forever and ever—

595 (ANNIE *shakes her head.)*

—forever, and ever, and—

(ANNIE covers her ears.)

— forever, and ever, and ever—

600 *(It pursues ANNIE; she flees to snatch up her purse, wheels to the doorway, and KELLER is standing in it. The lights have lost their special color.)*

KELLER: Miss—Annie.

(He has an envelope in his fingers.)

I've been waiting to give you this.

ANNIE (AFTER A BREATH): What?

605 **KELLER**: Your first month's salary.

(He puts it in her hand.)

With many more to come, I trust. It doesn't express what we feel, it doesn't pay our debt. For what you've done.

ANNIE: What have I done?

610 **KELLER**: Taken a wild thing, and given us back a child.

ANNIE (PRESENTLY): I taught her one thing, no. Don't do this, don't do that—

KELLER: It's more than all of us could, in all the years we—

ANNIE: I wanted to teach her what language is. I wanted to teach her yes.

615 **KELLER**: You will have time.

ANNIE: I don't know how. I know without it to do nothing but obey is—no gift, obedience without understanding is a—blindness, too. Is that all I've wished on her?

KELLER (GENTLY): No, no—

620 **ANNIE**: Maybe. I don't know what else to do. Simply go on, keep doing what I've done, and have—faith that inside she's—That inside it's waiting. Like water, underground. All I can do is keep on.

KELLER: It's enough. For us.

ANNIE: You can help, Captain Keller.

625 **KELLER**: How?

ANNIE: Even learning no has been at a cost. Of much trouble and pain. Don't undo it.

KELLER: Why should we wish to—

630 **ANNIE** (ABRUPTLY): The world isn't an easy place for anyone, I don't want her just to obey, but to let her have her way in everything is a lie, to her, I can't—

(Her eyes fill, it takes her by surprise, and she laughs through it.)

And I don't even love her, she's not my child! Well. You've got to stand between that lie and her.

635 **KELLER**: We'll try.

ANNIE: Because I will. As long as you let me stay, that's one promise I'll keep.

KELLER: Agreed. We've learned something too, I hope.

(A pause)

640 Won't you come now, to supper?

ANNIE: Yes.

(She wags the envelope, ruefully.)

Why doesn't God pay His debts each month?

KELLER: I beg your pardon?

645 **ANNIE**: Nothing. I used to wonder how I could—

(The lights are fading on them, simultaneously rising on the family room of the main house, where VINEY *is polishing glassware at the table set for dinner.)*

—earn a living.

650 **KELLER**: Oh, you do.

ANNIE: I really do. Now the question is, can I survive it!

(KELLER smiles, offers his arm.)

Keller. May I?

(ANNIE takes it, and the lights lose them as he escorts her out.)

Resources

Independent Reading

Learning Strategies

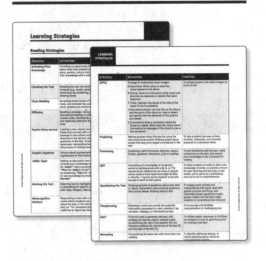

Graphic Organizers

English-Spanish Glossary

Index of Skills

Index of Authors and Titles

Suggestions for Independent Reading

These lists, divided into the categories of **Literature** and **Nonfiction/Informational Text**, include titles related to the themes and content of each unit. For your independent reading, you can select from this wide array of titles, which have been chosen based on complexity and interest. You can do your own research and select titles that intrigue you.

Unit 1 Independent Reading List: Stories of Change

Literature		
Author	**Title**	**Lexile**
Ada, Alma Flor	*My Name Is Maria Isabel*	860L
Avi	*The True Confessions of Charlotte Doyle*	740L
Black, Holly	*Geektastic: Stories from the Nerd Herd*	760L
Bradbury, Ray	*I Sing the Body Electric*	N/A
Bradbury, Ray	*R Is for Rocket*	N/A
Bunting, Eve	*One Green Apple*	450L
Crutcher, Chris	*Athletic Shorts: Six Short Stories*	1010L
Flake, Sharon	*The Skin I'm In*	670L
Guthrie, Peter	*Little Worlds: A Collection of Short Stories for the Middle School*	N/A
Hidier, Tanuja Desai	*Born Confused*	890L
Jimenez, Francisco	*La Mariposa (English)*	750L
Jimenez, Francisco	*La Mariposa (Spanish)*	N/A
Kadohata, Cynthia	*Kira-Kira*	740L
Keyes, Daniel	*Flowers for Algernon*	910L
Kroeber, Theodora	*The Inland Whale: Nine Stories Retold from California Indian Legends*	1170L
Lai, Thanhha	*Inside Out and Back Again*	800L
Levithan, David	*Friends: Stories About New Friends, Old Friends, and Unexpectedly True Friends*	930L
Lin, Grace	*Dumpling Days*	710L
Park, Linda Sue	*Project Mulberry*	690L
Philbrick, Rodman	*Freak the Mighty*	1000L
Philbrick, Rodman	*The Mostly True Adventures of Homer P. Figg*	950L
Rice, David	*Crazy Loco*	830L
Soto, Gary	*Baseball in April and Other Stories*	830L
Spinelli, Jerry	*Knots in My Yo-Yo String*	980L
Spinelli, Jerry	*Maniac Magee*	820L
Taylor, Mildred	*Roll of Thunder, Hear My Cry*	920L
Telgemeier, Raina	*Sisters*	GN290L
Telgemeier, Raina	*Hermanas*	GN290L
Telgemeier, Raina	*Smile*	GN410L
Telgemeier, Raina	*Sonríe*	N/A

| Yang, Gene Luen | *American Born Chinese* | 530L |
| Yep, Laurence | *Dragonwings* | 870L |

Nonfiction/Informational Text

Author	Title	Lexile
Agard, John	*Libro: una autobiografía*	940L
Ahmedi, Farah and Tamin Ansary	*The Story of My Life: An Afghan Girl on the Other Side of the Sky*	850L
Bode, Janet	*The Colors of Freedom: Immigrant Stories*	700L
Brown, Dinah	*¿Quién es Malala Yousafzai?*	680L
Jimenez, Francisco	*The Circuit: Stories from the Life of a Migrant Child*	880L
Myers, Walter Dean	*Bad Boy: A Memoir*	970L
Park, Linda Sue	*A Long Walk to Water: Based on a True Story*	720L
Paulsen, Gary	*Woodsong*	1090L
Pfetzer, Mark and Jack Galvin	*Within Reach: My Everest Story*	970L
Soto, Gary	*A Summer Life*	990L

Unit 2 Independent Reading List: The Power to Change

Literature

Author	Title	Lexile
Armstrong, William	*Sounder*	900L
Burnett, Frances Hodgson	*The Secret Garden*	710L
Burnett, Frances Hodgson	*El jardín secreto*	950L
Creech, Sharon	*Hate That Cat*	N/A
Creech, Sharon	*Love That Dog*	1010L
Creech, Sharon	*Ruby Holler*	660L
Creech, Sharon	*The Wanderer*	830L
Engle, Margarita	*¡Bravo! Poemas sobre hispanos extraordinarios*	N/A
Erdrich, Louise	*The Porcupine Year*	840L
DiCamillo, Kate	*Because of Winn Dixie*	610L
DiCamillo, Kate	*The Tiger Rising*	520L
Farley, Walter	*The Black Stallion*	680L
Funke, Cornelia	*Dragon Rider*	710L
George, Jean Craighead	*Julie of the Wolves*	860L
Gipson, Fred	*Old Yeller*	910L
Grogan, John	*Marley: A Dog Like No Other*	760L
Guest, Jacqueline	*Hat Trick*	710L
Hiaasen, Carl	*Hoot*	760L
Kadohata, Cynthia	*Cracker! The Best Dog in Vietnam*	730L
Korman, Gordon	*No More Dead Dogs*	610L
London, Jack	*The Call of the Wild*	1080L
London, Jack	*White Fang*	650L

Morey, Walt	Gentle Ben	740L
Mowat, Farley	Never Cry Wolf	1330L
O'Dell, Scott	Island of the Blue Dolphins	740L
O'Dell, Scott	La isla de los delfines azules	1090L
Naylor, Phyllis Reynolds	Shiloh	890L
Paulsen, Gary	Guts	1230L
Paulsen, Gary	My Life in Dog Years	1150L
Peterson, Shelley	Sundancer	N/A
Rawls, Wilson	Where the Red Fern Grows	790L
Ryan, Pam Munoz	Paint the Wind	780L
Ryan, Pam Muñoz	Esperanza Rising	750L
Ryan, Pam Muñoz	Esperanza renace	740L
Sewell, Anna	Black Beauty	650L
Sherlock, Patti	Letters from Wolfie	760L
Starr, Arigon	Super Indian (Series of 2)	N/A
Tamani, Liara	Calling My Name	N/A
Wedekind, Annie	A Horse of Her Own	1040L

Nonfiction/Informational Text

Author	Title	Lexile
Alifirenka, Caitlin and Martin Ganda with Liz Welch	I Will Always Write Back: How One Letter Changed Two Lives	790L
Chin-Lee, Cynthia	Akira to Zoltan: 26 Men Who Changed the World	1060L
Chin-Lee, Cynthia	Amelia to Zora: 26 Women Who Changed the World	1040L
Goodall, Jane	My Life with the Chimpanzees	910L
Grandin, Temple and Catherine Johnson	Animals in Translation	1130L
Guzman, Lila and Rick	Cesar Chavez: Fighting for Fairness	N/A
Halls, Kelly Milner	Wild Dogs: Past and Present	1010L
Hall, MH	King Arthur and the Knights of the Round Table	390L
Kehret, Peg	Shelter Dogs: Amazing Stories of Adopted Strays	940L
Lemke, Donald	Investigating the Scientific Method with Max Axiom, Super Scientist	760
Montgomery, Sy	Temple Grandin: How the Girl Who Loved Cows Embraced Autism and Changed the World	960L

Unit 3 Independent Reading List: Changing Perspectives

Literature		
Author	**Title**	**Lexile**
Alvarez, Julia	*Las historias de Tía Lola*	830L–850L
Alvarez, Julia	*The Tia Lola Stories Series*	830L–850L
Applegate, Katherine	*Home of the Brave*	N/A
Ellis, Deborah	*Jakeman*	N/A
Fullerton, Alma	*Libertad*	N/A
Howe, James	*The Misfits*	960L
Khan, Hena	*Night of the Moon*	780L
Khan, Rukhsana	*A New Life*	N/A
Krishnaswami, Uma	*The Grand Plan to Fix Everything*	770L
Na, An	*Wait for Me*	670L
Nye, Naomi Shihab	*19 Varieties of Gazelle: Poems of the Middle East*	970L
Smith, Greg Leitich	*Ninjas, Piranhas, and Galileo*	750L
Ursu, Anne	*Breadcrumbs*	720L

Nonfiction/Informational Text		
Author	**Title**	**Lexile**
Anderson, Judith	*Know the Facts About Personal Safety*	N/A
Beals, Melba Pattillo	*Warriors Don't Cry*	1000L
Fajardo, Anika	*The Debate about Homework*	850L
Halls, Kelly Milner	*Saving the Baghdad Zoo: A True Story of Hope and Heroes*	N/A
Hoose, Phillip	*Claudette Colvin: Twice Toward Justice*	1000L
Lewis, Barbara	*The Kid's Guide to Service Projects: Over 500 Service Ideas for Young People Who Want to Make a Difference*	850L
Marrin, Albert	*Black Gold: The Story of Oil in Our Lives*	1070L
McKee, Jonathan	*The Teen's Guide to Social Media & Mobile Devices*	N/A
Norgren, Jill	*Belva Lockwood: Equal Rights Pioneer*	N/A
O'Brien, Anne Ibley and Perry Edmond O'Brien	*After Gandhi: One Hundred Years of Nonviolent Resistance*	1080L
Pollan, Michael	*The Omnivore's Dilemma: The Secrets Behind What You Eat (Young Readers Edition)*	930L
Rockliff, Mara	*Get Real: What Kind of World Are You Buying?*	890L
Schlosser, Eric	*Chew on This: Everything You Don't Want to Know About Fast Food*	1110L
Stearman, Kaye	*Taking Action Against Homelessness*	N/A
Warren, Andrea	*Orphan Train Rider: One Boy's True Story*	960L

Unit 4 Independent Reading List: A Change of Scene

Literature		
Author	**Title**	**Lexile**
Alcorn, Stephen and Catherine Clinton	*I, Too, Sing America: Three Centuries of African American Poetry*	N/A
Algla, Jorge H.	*"Tardes"*	N/A
Barat, J.R.	*Poesía para gorriones*	N/A
Bruchac, Joseph	*Code Talker: A Novel About the Navajo Marines of World War Two*	910L
Dickens, Charles	*Oliver Twist*	970L
Janeczko, Paul B.	*A Poke in the I: A Collection of Concrete Poems*	N/A
Juster, Norton	*The Phantom Tollbooth*	1000L
Juster, Norton	*La caseta mágica*	N/A
Kipling, Rudyard	*Captains Courageous*	850L
London, Jack	*The Call of the Wild*	1080L
O'Connor, Barbara	*Wish*	850L
Palacio, R. J.	*Wonder*	790L
Palacio, R. J.	*La lección de August*	N/A
Rafter, Dan (adapted by)	*20,000 Leagues Under the Sea* (Graphic Novel)	N/A
Shelley, Mary	*Frankenstein*	810L
Shihab Nye, Naomi	*This Same Sky: A Collection of Poems from Around the World*	N/A
Smith, Betty	*A Tree Grows in Brooklyn*	810L
Stevenson, Robert Louis	*The Strange Case of Dr. Jekyll and Mr. Hyde*	1010L
Van Draanen, Wendelin	*The Running Dream*	HL650L
Verne, Jules	*20,000 Leagues Under the Sea*	1030L
Wagner, Lloyd (adapted by)	*The Call of the Wild* (Graphic Novel)	N/A

Nonfiction/Informational Text		
Author	**Title**	**Lexile**
Brown, Daniel James	*The Boys in the Boat: The True Story of an American Team's Epic Journey to Win Gold at the 1936 Olympics*	1000L
Cofer, Judith Ortiz	*Bailando en silencio*	1160L
Hodge, Robert	*Ugly*	890L
Prince, April Jones	*Who Was Mark Twain?*	910L
Stelson, Caren Barzelay	*Sachiko: A Nagasaki Bomb Survivor's Story*	850L
Webb, Brandon	*The Making of a Navy SEAL: My Story of Surviving the Toughest Challenge and Training the Best*	1020L
Zuckerman, Gregory	*Rising Above: How 11 Athletes Overcame Challenges in Their Youth to Become Stars*	1010L

Independent Reading Log

Directions: This log is a place to record your progress and thinking about your independent reading during each unit. Add your log pages to your Reader/Writer Notebook or keep them as a separate place to record your reading insights.

Unit _____

Independent Reading Title _____

Author(s) _____ Text Type _____

Pages read: from _____ to _____

_____
_____
_____
_____
_____
_____

Independent Reading Title _____

Author(s) _____ Text Type _____

Pages read: from _____ to _____

_____
_____
_____
_____
_____
_____
_____

Independent Reading Title _____

Author(s) _____ Text Type _____

Pages read: from _____ to _____

_____
_____
_____
_____
_____
_____
_____

Unit _____

Independent Reading Title _____

Author(s) _____ Text Type _____

Pages read: from _____ to _____

_____

_____

_____

_____

_____

Independent Reading Title _____

Author(s) _____ Text Type _____

Pages read: from _____ to _____

_____

_____

_____

_____

_____

_____

Independent Reading Title _____

Author(s) _____ Text Type _____

Pages read: from _____ to _____

_____

_____

_____

_____

_____

Independent Reading Title _____

Author(s) _____ Text Type _____

Pages read: from _____ to _____

_____

_____

_____

_____

_____

Learning Strategies

Reading Strategies

STRATEGY	DEFINITION	PURPOSE
Activating Prior Knowledge	Providing an opportunity for students to think about what they already know about a concept, place, person, culture, and so on, and share their knowledge with a wider audience	To prepare students to encounter new concepts, places, persons, cultures, and so on, prior to reading a text; an Anticipation Guide and a Quickwrite can be used to activate and assess prior knowledge
Chunking the Text	Breaking the text into smaller, manageable units of sense (e.g., words, sentences, paragraphs, whole text) by numbering, separating phrases, drawing boxes	To reduce the intimidation factor when encountering long words, sentences, or whole texts; to increase comprehension of difficult or challenging text
Close Reading	Accessing small chunks of text to read, reread, mark, and annotate key passages, word-for-word, sentence-by-sentence, and line-by-line	To develop comprehensive understanding by engaging in one or more focused readings of a text
Diffusing	Reading a passage, noting unfamiliar words, discovering meaning of unfamiliar words using context clues, dictionaries, and/or thesauruses, and replacing unfamiliar words with familiar ones	To facilitate a close reading of text, the use of resources, an understanding of synonyms, and increased comprehension of text
Double-Entry Journal	Creating a two-column journal (also called Dialectical Journal) with a student-selected passage in one column and the student's response in the second column (e.g., asking questions of the text, forming personal responses, interpreting the text, reflecting on the process of making meaning of the text)	To assist in note-taking and organizing key textual elements and responses noted during reading in order to generate textual support that can be incorporated into a piece of writing at a later time
Graphic Organizer	Using a visual representation for the organization of information from the text	To facilitate increased comprehension and discussion
KWHL Chart	Setting up discussion that allows students to activate prior knowledge by answering, "What do I **know**?"; sets a purpose by answering, "What do I **want** to know?"; helps preview a task by answering, "**How** will I learn it?"; and reflects on new knowledge by answering, "What have I **learned**?"	To organize thinking, access prior knowledge, and reflect on learning to increase comprehension and engagement
Marking the Text	Selecting text by highlighting, underlining, and/or annotating for specific components, such as main idea, imagery, literary devices, and so on	To focus reading for specific purposes, such as author's craft, and to organize information from selections; to facilitate reexamination of a text
Metacognitive Markers	Responding to text with a system of cueing marks where students use a ? for questions about the text; a ! for reactions related to the text; an * for comments about the text; and an underline to signal key ideas	To track responses to texts and use those responses as a point of departure for talking or writing about texts

STRATEGY	DEFINITION	PURPOSE
OPTIC	Strategy for evaluating visual images. **O** (Overview): Write notes on what the visual appears to be about. **P** (Parts): Zoom in on the parts of the visual and describe any elements or details that seem important. **T** (Title): Highlight the words of the title of the visual (if one is available). **I** (Interrelationships): Use the title as the theory and the parts of the visual as clues to detect and specify how the elements of the graphic are related. **C** (Conclusion); Draw a conclusion about the visual as a whole. What does the visual mean? Summarize the message of the visual in one or two sentences.	To analyze graphic and visual images as forms of text
Predicting	Making guesses about the text by using the title and pictures and/or thinking ahead about events that may occur based on evidence in the text	To help students become actively involved, interested, and mentally prepared to understand ideas
Previewing	Examining a text's structure, features, layout, format, questions, directions, prior to reading	To gain familiarity with the text, make connections to the text, and extend prior knowledge to set a purpose for reading
QHT	Expanding prior knowledge of vocabulary words by marking words with a **Q**, **H**, or **T** (Q signals words students do not know; H signals words students have heard and might be able to identify; T signals words students know well enough to teach to their peers)	To allow students to build on their prior knowledge of words, to provide a forum for peer teaching and learning of new words, and to serve as a prereading exercise to aid in comprehension
Questioning the Text	Developing levels of questions about text; that is, literal, interpretive, and universal questions that prompt deeper thinking about a text	To engage more actively and independently with texts, read with greater purpose and focus, and ultimately answer questions to gain greater insight into the text; helps students to comprehend and interpret
Paraphrasing	Restating in one's own words the essential information expressed in a text, whether it be narration, dialogue, or informational text	To encourage and facilitate comprehension of challenging text
RAFT	Primarily used to generate new text, this strategy can also be used to analyze a text by examining the role of the speaker (R), the intended audience (A), the format of the text (F), and the topic of the text (T).	To initiate reader response; to facilitate an analysis of a text to gain focus prior to creating a new text
Rereading	Encountering the same text with more than one reading	To identify additional details; to clarify meaning and/or reinforce comprehension of texts

STRATEGY	DEFINITION	PURPOSE
SIFT	Analyzing a fictional text by examining stylistic elements, especially symbol, imagery, and figures of speech in order to show how all work together to reveal tone and theme	To focus and facilitate an analysis of a fictional text by examining the title and text for symbolism, identifying images and sensory details, analyzing figurative language and identifying how all these elements reveal tone and theme
Skimming/Scanning	Skimming by rapid or superficial reading of a text to form an overall impression or to obtain a general understanding of the material; scanning focuses on key words, phrases, or specific details and provides speedy recognition of information	To quickly form an overall impression prior to an in-depth study of a text; to answer specific questions or quickly locate targeted information or detail in a text
SMELL	Analyzing a persuasive speech or essay by asking five essential questions: • **S**ender-receiver relationship—What is the sender-receiver relationship? Who are the images and language meant to attract? Describe the speaker of the text. • **M**essage—What is the message? Summarize the statement made in the text. • **E**motional Strategies—What is the desired effect? • **L**ogical Strategies—What logic is operating? How does it (or its absence) affect the message? Consider the logic of the images as well as the words. • **L**anguage—What does the language of the text describe? How does it affect the meaning and effectiveness of the writing? Consider the language of the images as well as the words.	To analyze a persuasive speech or essay by focusing on five essential questions
SOAPSTone	Analyzing text by discussing and identifying **S**peaker, **O**ccasion, **A**udience, **P**urpose, **S**ubject, and **Tone**	To facilitate the analysis of specific elements of nonfiction, literary, and informational texts, and show the relationship among the elements to an understanding of the whole
Summarizing	Giving a brief statement of the main points or essential information expressed in a text, whether it be narration, dialogue, or informational text	To facilitate comprehension and recall of a text
Think Aloud	Talking through a difficult passage or task by using a form of metacognition whereby the reader expresses how he/she has made sense of the text	To reflect on how readers make meaning of challenging texts and to facilitate discussion

STRATEGY	DEFINITION	PURPOSE
TP-CASTT	Analyzing a poetic text by identifying and discussing **T**itle, **P**araphrase, **C**onnotation, **A**ttitude, **S**hift, **T**heme, and **T**itle again	To facilitate the analysis of specific elements of a literary text, especially poetry. To show how the elements work together to create meaning
Visualizing	Forming a picture (mentally and/or literally) while reading a text	To increase reading comprehension and promote active engagement with text
Word Maps	Using a clearly defined graphic organizer such as concept circles or word webs to identify and reinforce word meanings	To provide a visual tool for identifying and remembering multiple aspects of words and word meanings

Writing Strategies

STRATEGY	DEFINITION	PURPOSE
Adding	Making conscious choices to enhance a text by adding additional words, phrases, sentences, or ideas	To refine and clarify the writer's thoughts during revision and/or drafting
Brainstorming	Using a flexible but deliberate process of listing multiple ideas in a short period of time without excluding any idea from the preliminary list	To generate ideas, concepts, or key words that provide a focus and/or establish organization as part of the prewriting or revision process
Deleting	Providing clarity and cohesiveness for a text by eliminating words, phrases, sentences, or ideas	To refine and clarify the writer's thoughts during revision and/or drafting
Drafting	Composing a text in its initial form	To incorporate brainstormed or initial ideas into a written format
Freewriting	Writing freely without constraints in order to capture thinking and convey the writer's purpose	To refine and clarify the writer's thoughts, spark new ideas, and/or generate content during revision and/or drafting
Generating Questions	Clarifying and developing ideas by asking questions of the draft. May be part of self-editing or peer editing	To clarify and develop ideas in a draft; used during drafting and as part of writer response
Graphic Organizer	Organizing ideas and information visually (e.g., Venn diagrams, flowcharts, cluster maps)	To provide a visual system for organizing multiple ideas, details, and/or textual support to be included in a piece of writing
Looping	After freewriting, one section of a text is circled to promote elaboration or the generation of new ideas for that section. This process is repeated to further develop ideas from the newly generated segments.	To refine and clarify the writer's thoughts, spark new ideas, and/or generate new content during revision and/or drafting

STRATEGY	DEFINITION	PURPOSE
Mapping	Creating a graphic organizer that serves as a visual representation of the organizational plan for a written text	To generate ideas, concepts, or key words that provide a focus and/or establish organization during the prewriting, drafting, or revision process
Marking the Draft	Interacting with the draft version of a piece of writing by highlighting, underlining, color-coding, and annotating to indicate revision ideas	To encourage focused, reflective thinking about revising drafts
Note-taking	Making notes about ideas in response to text or discussions; one form is the double-entry journal in which textual evidence is recorded on the left side and personal commentary about the meaning of the evidence on the other side	To assist in organizing key textual elements and responses noted during reading in order to generate textual support that can be incorporated into a piece of writing at a later time. Note-taking is also a reading and listening strategy.
Outlining	Using a system of numerals and letters in order to identify topics and supporting details and ensure an appropriate balance of ideas	To generate ideas, concepts, or key words that provide a focus and/or establish organization prior to writing an initial draft and/or during the revision process
Quickwrite	Writing for a short, specific amount of time in response to a prompt provided	To generate multiple ideas in a quick fashion that could be turned into longer pieces of writing at a later time (may be considered as part of the drafting process)
RAFT	Generating a new text and/or transforming a text by identifying and manipulating its component parts of Role, Audience, Format, and Topic	To generate a new text by identifying the main elements of a text during the prewriting and drafting stages of the writing process
Rearranging	Selecting components of a text and moving them to another place within the text and/or modifying the order in which the author's ideas are presented	To refine and clarify the writer's thoughts during revision and/or drafting
Self-Editing/Peer Editing	Working individually or with a partner to examine a text closely in order to identify areas that might need to be corrected for grammar, punctuation, spelling	To provide a systematic process for editing a written text to ensure correctness of identified components such as conventions of standard English
Sharing and Responding	Communicating with another person or a small group of peers who respond to a piece of writing as focused readers (not necessarily as evaluators)	To make suggestions for improvement to the work of others and/or to receive appropriate and relevant feedback on the writer's own work, used during the drafting and revision process
Sketching	Drawing or sketching ideas or ordering of ideas (includes storyboarding, visualizing)	To generate and/or clarify ideas by visualizing them (may be part of prewriting)
Substituting/ Replacing	Replacing original words or phrases in a text with new words or phrases that achieve the desired effect	To refine and clarify the writer's thoughts during revision and/or drafting

STRATEGY	DEFINITION	PURPOSE
TWIST	Arriving at a thesis statement that incorporates the following literary elements: **T**one, **W**ord choice (diction), **I**magery, **S**tyle, and **T**heme	To craft an interpretive thesis in response to a prompt about a text
Webbing	Developing a graphic organizer that consists of a series of circles connected with lines to indicate relationships among ideas	To generate ideas, concepts, or key words that provide a focus and/or establish organization prior to writing an initial draft and/or during the revision process
Writer's Checklist	Using a co-constructed checklist (that could be written on a bookmark and/or displayed on the wall) in order to look for specific features of a writing text and check for accuracy	To focus on key areas of the writing process so that the writer can effectively revise a draft and correct mistakes
Writing Groups	A type of discussion group devoted to sharing and responding to student work	To facilitate a collaborative approach to generating ideas for and revising writing

Speaking and Listening Strategies

STRATEGY	DEFINITION	PURPOSE
Choral Reading	Reading text lines aloud in student groups and/ or individually to present an interpretation	To develop fluency; differentiate between the reading of statements and questions; practice phrasing, pacing, and reading dialogue; show how a character's emotions are captured through vocal stress and intonation
Note-taking	Creating a record of information while listening to a speaker or reading a text	To facilitate active listening or close reading; to record and organize ideas that assist in processing information
Oral Reading	Reading aloud one's own text or the texts of others (e.g., echo reading, choral reading, paired readings)	To share one's own work or the work of others; build fluency and increase confidence in presenting to a group
Rehearsal	Encouraging multiple practices of a piece of text prior to a performance	To provide students with an opportunity to clarify the meaning of a text prior to a performance as they refine the use of dramatic conventions (e.g., gestures, vocal interpretations, facial expressions)
Role-Playing	Assuming the role or persona of a character	To develop the voice, emotions, and mannerisms of a character to facilitate improved comprehension of a text

Collaborative Strategies

STRATEGY	DEFINITION	PURPOSE
Discussion Groups	Engaging in an interactive, small-group discussion, often with an assigned role; to consider a topic, text, or question	To gain new understanding of or insight into a text from multiple perspectives
Think-Pair-Share	Pairing with a peer to share ideas before sharing ideas and discussion with a larger group	To construct meaning about a topic or question; to test thinking in relation to the ideas of others; to prepare for a discussion with a larger group

Graphic Organizer Directory

Contents

Active Listening Feedback

Presenter's name: _____

Content

What is the presenter's purpose? _____

What is the presenter's main point? _____

Do you agree with the presenter? Why or why not? _____

_____

_____

Form

Did the presenter use a clear, loud voice? ☐ yes ☐ no

Did the presenter make eye contact? ☐ yes ☐ no

One thing I really liked about the presentation:
_____
_____
_____
One question I still have:
_____
_____
_____

Other comments or notes:

Active Listening Notes

Title: _____

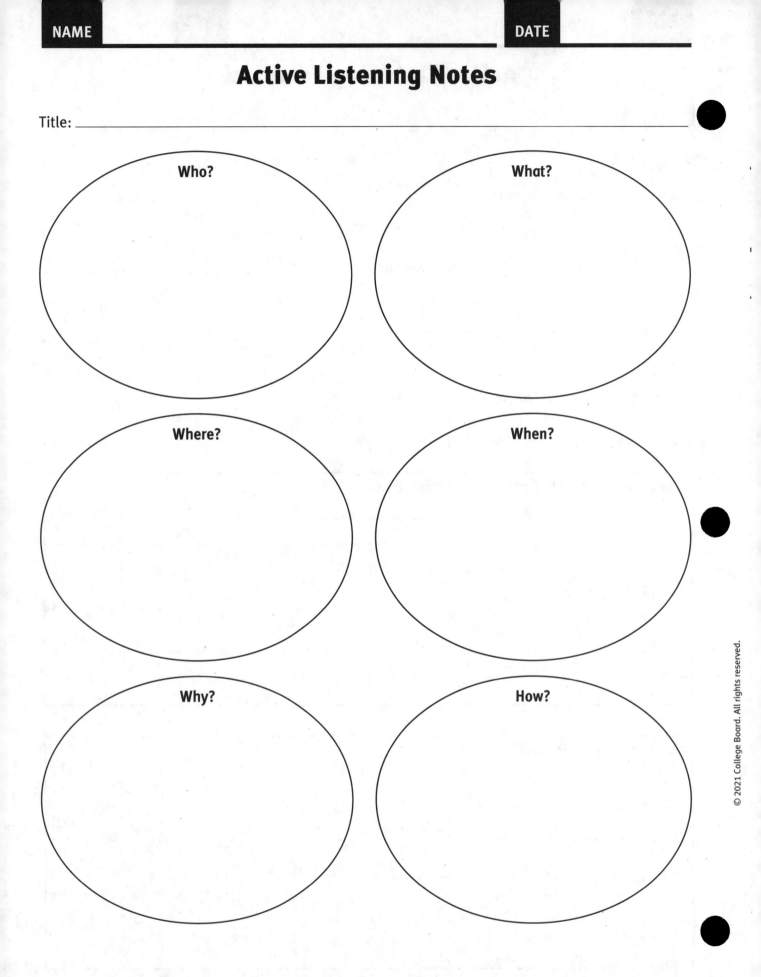

Who?

What?

Where?

When?

Why?

How?

Audience Notes and Feedback

Scoring Criteria	Notes/Feedback
Introduction/ Conclusion	
Timing	
Voice	
Eye Contact/ Gestures	
Use of Media, Visuals, Props	
Audience Engagement	

Cause and Effect

Title: _____

Cause: What happened?	→	**Effect:** An effect of this is
Cause: What happened?	→	**Effect:** An effect of this is
Cause: What happened?	→	**Effect:** An effect of this is
Cause: What happened?	→	**Effect:** An effect of this is

Character Map

Character name: _____

What does the character look like?

How does the character act and feel?

What do other characters say or think about the character?

Collaborative Dialogue

Topic: _____

Use the space below to record ideas.

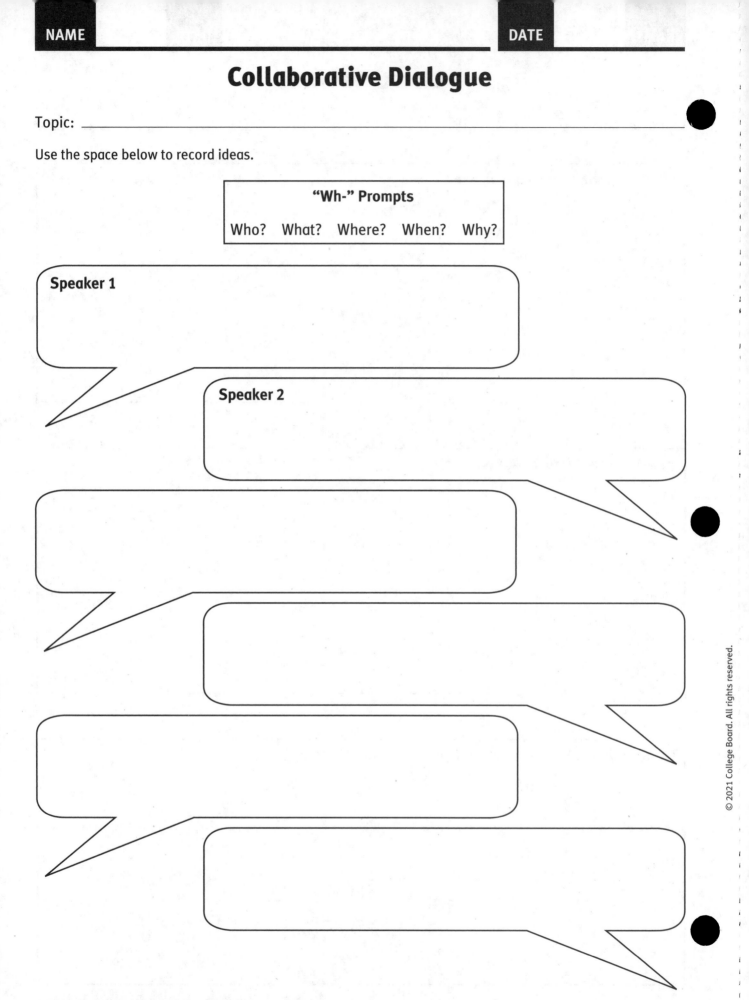

"Wh-" Prompts
Who?   What?   Where?   When?   Why?

Speaker 1

Speaker 2

Conclusion Builder

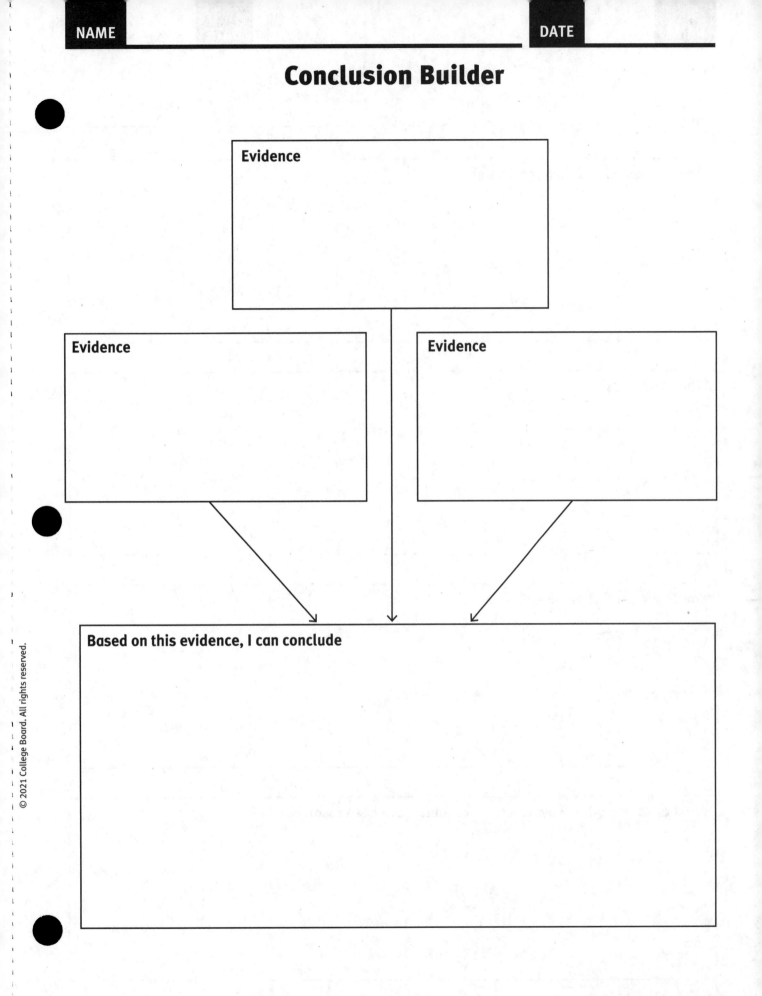

Evidence

Evidence

Evidence

Based on this evidence, I can conclude

Conflict Map

Title: _____

What is the main conflict in this story?

What causes this conflict?

How is the conflict resolved?

What are some other ways the conflict could have been resolved?

Conversation for Quickwrite

1. Turn to a partner and restate the prompt in your own words.

2. Brainstorm key words to use in your quickwrite response.

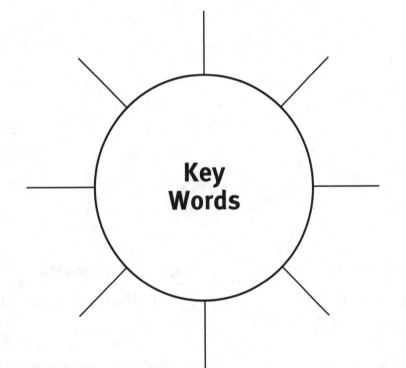

Key Words

3. Take turns explaining your ideas to your partner. Try using some of the key words you brainstormed.

4. On your own, write a response to the quickwrite.

Definition and Reflection

Academic Vocabulary Word
Definition in own words
Illustration (literal or symbolic)

My experiences with this concept:

- I haven't really thought about this concept.

  _____

- I have only thought about this concept in English Language Arts class.

  _____

- I have applied this concept in other classes.

  _____

- I have applied this concept outside of school.

  _____

My level of understanding:

- I am still trying to understand this concept.

  _____

- I am familiar with this concept, but I am not comfortable applying it.

  _____

- I am very comfortable with this concept and I know how to apply it.

  _____

- I could teach this concept to another classmate.

  _____

Discourse Starters

Questioning and Discussing a Text

One question I have is _____.

Could this mean _____?

Why do you think the author _____?

I understand _____, but I wonder _____.

I notice that _____.

I think this (word/sentence/paragraph) means _____.

I think _____ because the text says _____.

In paragraph _____, the author says _____.

According to the text, _____.

One way to interpret _____ is _____.

Summarizing

The main events that take place are _____.

The major points of the text are _____.

The main idea of _____ is _____.

One central idea of this text is _____.

Another central idea is _____.

All in all, the message is _____.

The author's main purpose is to _____.

Basically, the author is saying that _____.

Comparing and Contrasting

_____ and _____ are similar because _____.

_____ and _____ are similar in that they both _____.

_____ is _____. Similarly, _____ is _____.

One thing _____ and _____ have in common is _____.

_____ and _____ are different because _____.

_____ and _____ are different in that _____.

_____ is _____. On the other hand, _____ is _____.

One difference between _____ and _____ is _____.

Clarifying

I'm not sure I understand the instructions.

Could you repeat that please?

I have a question about _____.

I am having trouble with _____.

Will you explain that again?

Could you clarify _____?

Would you mind helping me with _____?

Which (page/paragraph/section) are we reading?

How do you spell/pronounce _____?

Discourse Starters

Agreeing and Disagreeing

I agree with the idea that _____ because _____.

I share your point of view because _____.

You made a good point when you said _____.

I agree with (a person) that _____.

Although I agree that _____, I also think _____.

I understand where you're coming from, but _____.

I disagree with the idea that _____ because _____.

I see it a different way because _____.

You have a point, but the evidence suggests _____.

Arguing and Persuading with Evidence

I believe that _____ because _____.

It is clear that _____ because _____.

One reason I think _____ is _____.

Based on evidence in the text, I think _____.

Evidence such as _____ suggests that _____.

An example to support my position is _____.

This is evident because _____.

What evidence supports the idea that _____?

Can you explain why you think _____?

Evaluating

This is effective because _____.

The evidence _____ is strong because _____.

This is convincing because _____.

I see why the author _____, but I think _____.

This is not very effective because _____.

The evidence _____ is weak because _____.

This would have been better if _____.

What do you think about the writer's choice to _____?

Why do you think _____ (is/isn't) effective?

Giving Feedback and Suggesting

The part where you _____ is strong because _____.

What impressed me the most is how you _____.

This is a good start. Maybe you should add _____.

I like how you _____, but I would try _____.

You might consider changing _____.

I would suggest revising _____ so that _____.

One suggestion would be to _____.

Why did you choose _____?

A better choice might be _____.

This would be clearer if _____.

Editor's Checklist

Over the course of the year with SpringBoard, customize this Editor's Checklist as your knowledge of language conventions grows. The three examples below show you how to write a good checklist item.

	Are all the sentences complete?
	Do the subject and verb of each sentence agree?
	Do all the sentences have correct punctuation?

Writer's Checklist

Ideas

	Does your first paragraph hook the reader?
	Is the purpose of your writing clear (to inform, to make an argument, etc.)?
	Is the genre of writing appropriate for your purpose?
	Is your main idea clear and easy to summarize?
	Does your text contain details and information that support your main idea?
	Are the ideas in the text well organized?
	Do you connect your ideas by using transitions?
	Do you use parallel structure to keep your ideas clear?
	Does each paragraph have a conclusion that transitions to the next paragraph?
	Does your writing end with a strong conclusion that restates the original purpose of the text?

Language

	Do you keep a consistent point of view throughout?
	Do you use the present tense when writing about a text?
	Are any shifts in verb tense easy to follow and necessary?
	Have you removed unnecessary or confusing words?
	Do you use vivid verbs and descriptive adjectives when appropriate?
	Do you use different styles of language (like figurative or sensory) when appropriate?
	Do you use a variety of sentence types?
	Do you vary the way you begin your sentences?
	Did you split up run-on sentences?
	Are your pronoun references clear?

Evaluating Online Sources

The URL
• What is its domain?
    • .com = a for-profit organization
    • .gov, .mil, .us (or other country code) = a government site
    • .edu = affiliated with an educational institution
    • .org = a nonprofit organization
• Is this URL someone's personal page?
• Do you recognize who is publishing this page?	

Sponsor: • Does the website give information about the organization or group that sponsors it? • Does it have a link (often called "About Us") that leads you to that information? • What do you learn?	
Timeliness: • When was the page last updated (usually this is posted at the top or bottom of the page)? • Is the topic something that changes frequently, like current events or technology?	
Purpose: • What is the purpose of the page? • What is its target audience? • Does it present information, opinion, or both? • Is it primarily objective or subjective? • How do you know?	
Author: • What credentials does the author have? • Is this person or group considered an authority on the topic?	
Links • Does the page provide links? • Do they work? • Are they helpful? • Are they objective or subjective?	

Idea and Argument Evaluator

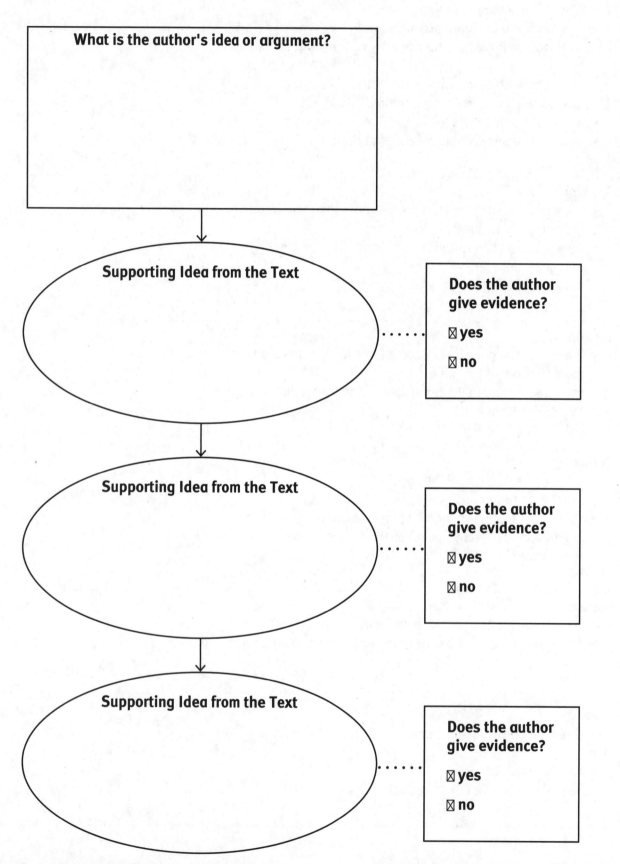

What is the author's idea or argument?

Supporting Idea from the Text

Does the author give evidence?

☒ yes

☒ no

Supporting Idea from the Text

Does the author give evidence?

☒ yes

☒ no

Supporting Idea from the Text

Does the author give evidence?

☒ yes

☒ no

Idea Connector

Directions: Write two simple sentences about the same topic. Next, write transition words around the Idea Connector. Then, choose an appropriate word to connect ideas in the two sentences. Write your combined sentence in the space below.

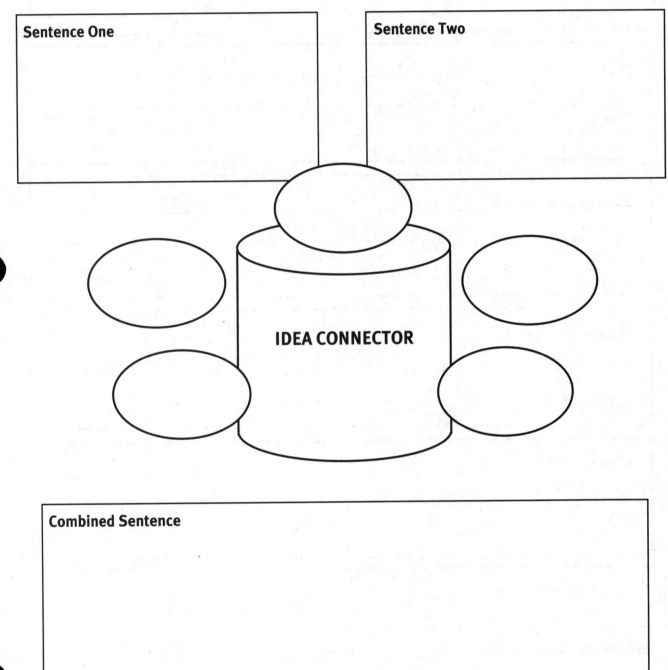

Sentence One

Sentence Two

IDEA CONNECTOR

Combined Sentence

Key Idea and Details Chart

Title/Topic _____

Key Idea _____
_____
_____

Supporting detail 1 _____
_____
_____

Supporting detail 2 _____
_____
_____

Supporting detail 3 _____
_____
_____

Supporting detail 4 _____
_____
_____

Restate topic sentence: _____
_____

Concluding sentence: _____
_____

Narrative Analysis and Writing

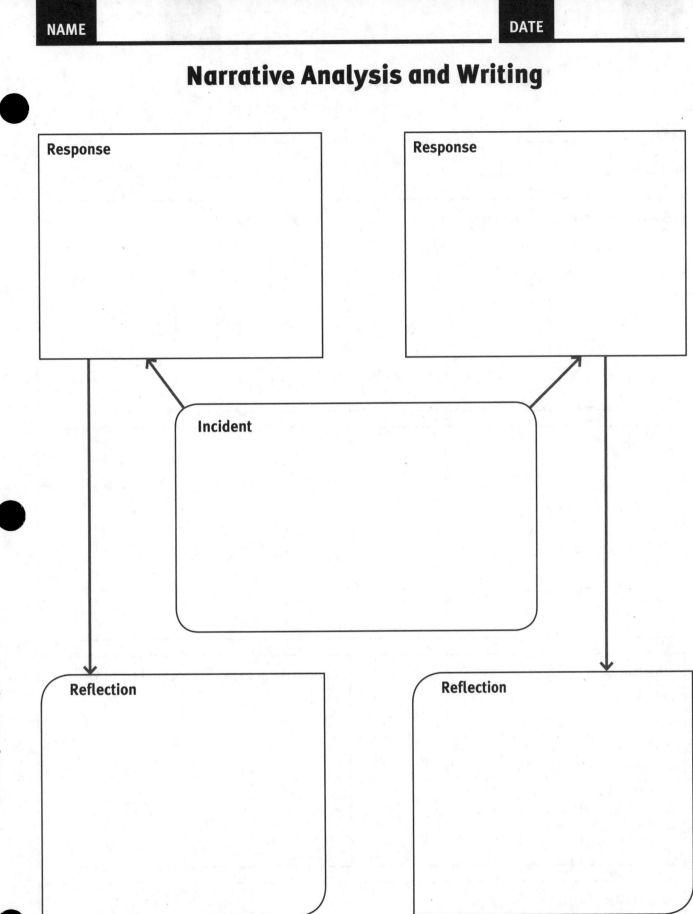

Response

Response

Incident

Reflection

Reflection

Notes for Reading Independently
Fiction

Title: _____

Author: _____

Something interesting I noticed:	A question I have:

Summary:

Illustration:

Connections to my life/other texts I've read:

How challenging this text was:

Easy   1   2   3   4   5   6   7   8   9   10   *Challenging*

Notes for Reading Independently
Nonfiction

Title: _____

Author: _____

Main idea:

Facts I learned:

Summary:

Questions I still have:

Connections to my life/other texts I've read:

How challenging this text was:										
Easy	1	2	3	4	5	6	7	8	9	10	Challenging

Opinion Builder

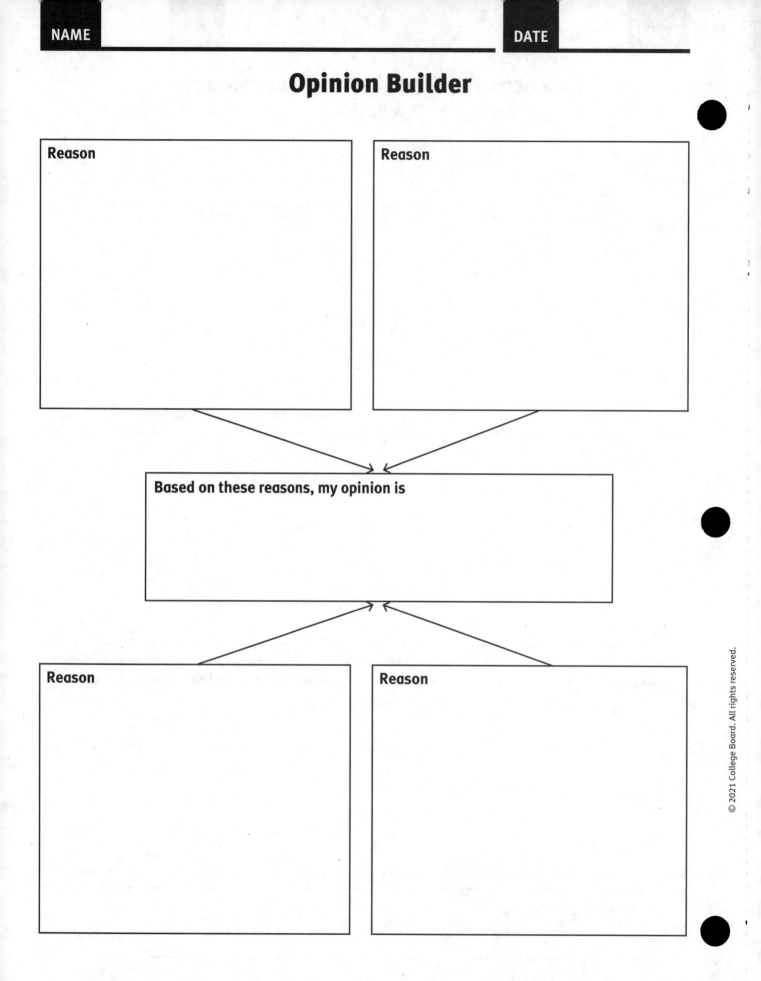

Reason

Reason

Based on these reasons, my opinion is

Reason

Reason

Paragraph Frame for Conclusions

Conclusion Words and Phrases

shows that

based on

suggests that

leads to

indicates that

influences

The _____ *(story, poem, play, passage, etc.)*
shows that *(helps us to conclude that)* _____
_____
_____

There are several reasons why. First, _____
_____
_____
_____
_____

A second reason is _____
_____
_____
_____
_____

Finally, _____
_____
_____
_____

In conclusion, _____
_____
_____
_____

Paragraph Frame for Sequencing

Sequence Words and Phrases

at the beginning

in the first place

as a result

later

eventually

in the end

lastly

In the _____ *(story, poem, play, passage, etc.)*

there are three important _____

(events, steps, directions, etc.)

First, _____

_____

_____

_____

_____

Second, _____

_____

_____

_____

_____

Third, _____

_____

_____

_____

_____

Finally, _____

_____

_____

_____

_____

Paraphrasing and Summarizing Map

What does the text say?	How can I say it in my own words?

How can I use my own words to summarize the text?

Peer Editing

Writer's name: _____

Did the writer answer the prompt? ☐ yes ☐ no

Did the writer use appropriate details or evidence to develop their writing? ☐ yes ☐ no

Is the writing organized in a way that makes sense? ☐ yes ☐ no

Did the writer use a variety of sentence types to make the writing more interesting? ☐ yes ☐ no

Are there any spelling or punctuation mistakes? ☐ yes ☐ no

Are there any grammar errors? ☐ yes ☐ no

Two things I really liked about the writer's story:

1. _____
   _____
   _____

2. _____
   _____
   _____

One thing I think the writer could do to improve the writing:

1. _____
   _____
   _____

Other comments or notes:

Persuasive/Argument Writing Map

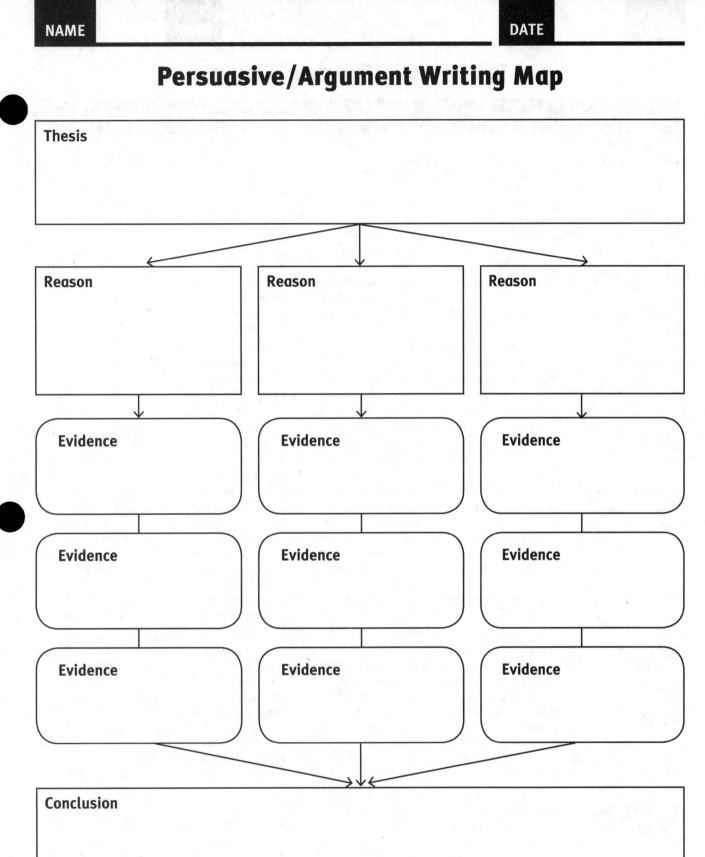

Thesis

Reason

Reason

Reason

Evidence

Evidence

Evidence

Evidence

Evidence

Evidence

Evidence

Evidence

Evidence

Conclusion

Presenting Scoring Guide

Scoring Criteria	Exemplary	Proficient	Emerging	Incomplete
Introduction / Conclusion	The presentation • provides a clear, engaging, and appropriate introduction to the topic or performance • provides a clear, engaging, and appropriate conclusion that closes, summarizes, draws connections to broader themes, or supports the ideas presented.	The presentation • provides a clear and appropriate introduction to the topic or performance • provides a clear and appropriate conclusion that closes, summarizes, draws connections to broader themes, or supports the ideas presented.	The presentation • provides an adequate introduction to the topic or performance • provides an adequate conclusion that closes, summarizes, draws connections to broader themes, or supports the ideas presented.	The presentation • does not provide an introduction to the topic or performance • does not provide a conclusion that closes, summarizes, draws connections to broader themes, or supports the ideas presented.
Timing	The presentation • thoroughly delivers its intended message within the allotted time • is thoughtfully and appropriately paced throughout.	The presentation • mostly delivers its intended message within the allotted time • is appropriately paced most of the time.	The presentation • delivers some of its intended message within the allotted time • is sometimes not paced appropriately.	The presentation • does not deliver its intended message within the allotted time • is not paced appropriately.
Voice (Volume, Enunciation, Rate)	The presentation • is delivered with adequate volume enabling audience members to fully comprehend what is said • is delivered with clear enunciation.	The presentation • is delivered with adequate volume enabling audience members to mostly comprehend what is said • is delivered with mostly clear enunciation.	The presentation • is delivered with somewhat adequate volume enabling audience members to comprehend some of what is said • is delivered with somewhat clear enunciation.	The presentation • is not delivered with adequate volume, so that audience members are unable to comprehend what is said • is delivered with unclear enunciation.
Eye Contact/ Gestures	The presentation • is delivered with appropriate eye contact that helps engage audience members • makes use of natural gestures and/or body language to convey meaning.	The presentation • is delivered with some appropriate eye contact that helps engage audience members • makes use of gestures and/or body language to convey meaning.	The presentation • is delivered with occasional eye contact that sometimes engages audience members • makes some use of gestures and/or body language to convey meaning.	The presentation • is not delivered with eye contact to engage audience members • makes little or no use of gestures and/or body language to convey meaning.
Use of Media, Visuals, Props	The presentation • makes use of highly engaging visuals, multimedia, and/or props that enhance delivery.	The presentation • makes use of visuals, multimedia, and/or props that enhance delivery.	The presentation • makes use of some visuals, multimedia, and/or props that somewhat enhance delivery.	The presentation • makes use of few or no visuals, multimedia, and/or props that enhance delivery.
Audience Engagement	The presentation • includes thoughtful and appropriate interactions with and responses to audience members.	The presentation • includes appropriate interactions with and responses to audience members.	The presentation • includes a few interactions with and responses to audience members.	The presentation • does not include interactions with and responses to audience members.

RAFT

Role	Who or what are you as a writer?
Audience	As a writer, to whom are you writing?
Format	As a writer, what format would be appropriate for your audience (essay, letter, speech, poem, etc.)?
Topic	As a writer, what is the subject of your writing? What points do you want to make?

Roots and Affixes Brainstorm

Directions: Write the root or affix in the circle. Brainstorm or use a dictionary to find the meaning of the root or affix and add it to the circle. Then, find words that use that root or affix. Write one word in each box. Write a sentence for each word.

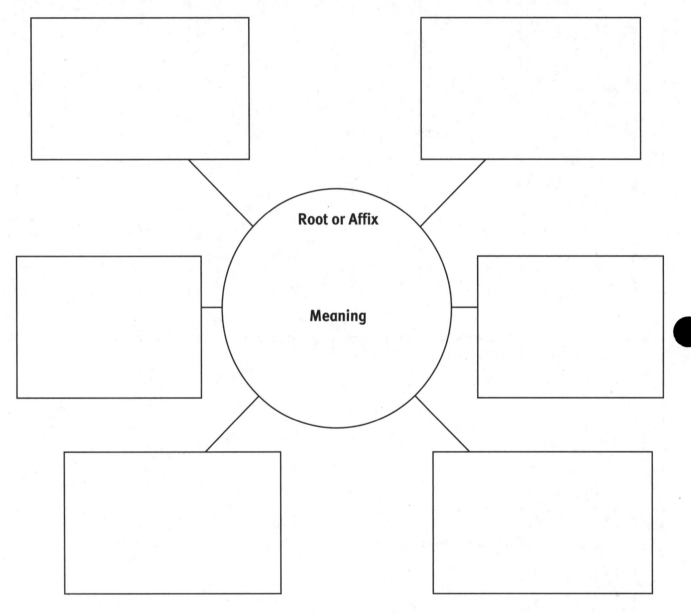

Root or Affix

Meaning

Round Table Discussion

Directions: Write the topic in the center box. One student begins by stating his or her ideas while the student to the left takes notes. Then the next student speaks while the student to his or her left takes notes, and so on.

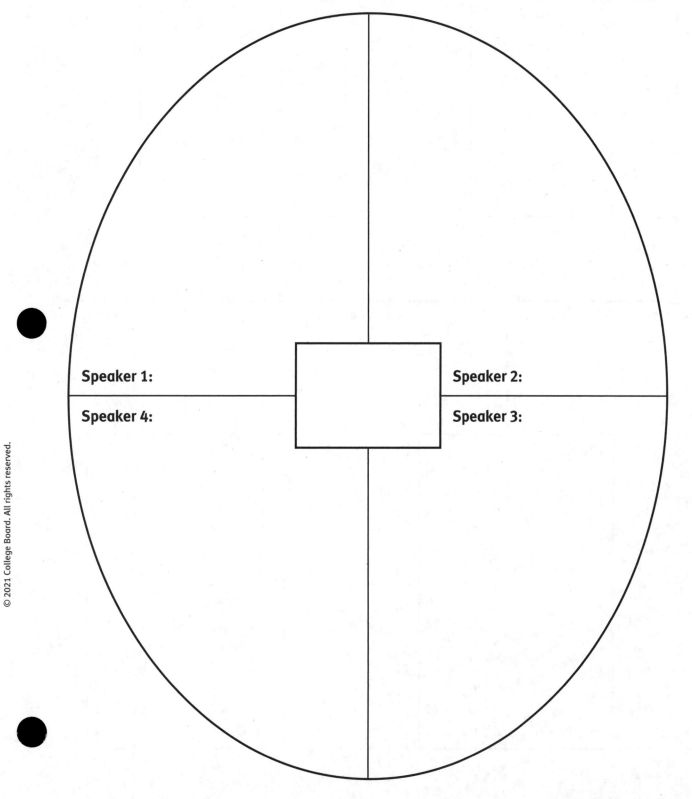

Speaker 1:

Speaker 2:

Speaker 4:

Speaker 3:

Sequence of Events Time Line

Title: _____

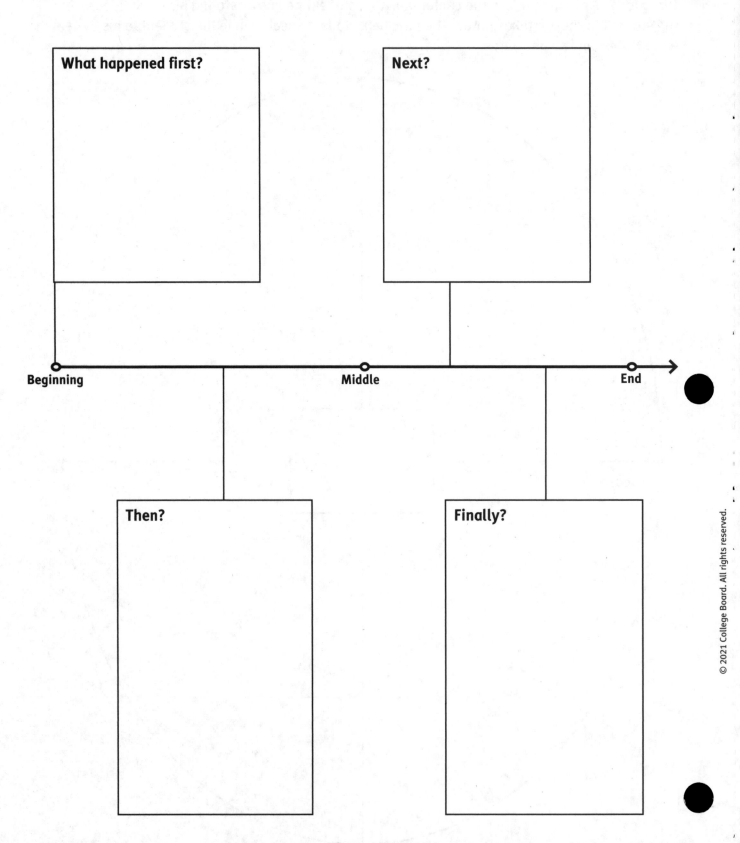

What happened first?

Next?

Beginning

Middle

End

Then?

Finally?

SMELL

Sender-Receiver Relationship—Who are the senders and receivers of the message, and what is their relationship (consider what different audiences the text may be addressing)?

Message—What is a literal summary of the content? What is the meaning/significance of this information?

Emotional Strategies—What emotional appeals (*pathos*) are included? What seems to be their desired effect?

Logical Strategies—What logical arguments/appeals (*logos*) are included? What is their effect?

Language—What specific language is used to support the message? How does it affect the text's effectiveness? Consider both images and actual words.

SOAPSTone

SOAPSTone	Analysis	Textual Support
Subject What does the reader know about the writer?		
Occasion What are the circumstances surrounding this text?		
Audience Who is the target audience?		
Purpose Why did the author write this text?		
Subject What is the topic?		
Tone What is the author's tone, or attitude?		

Text Structure Stairs

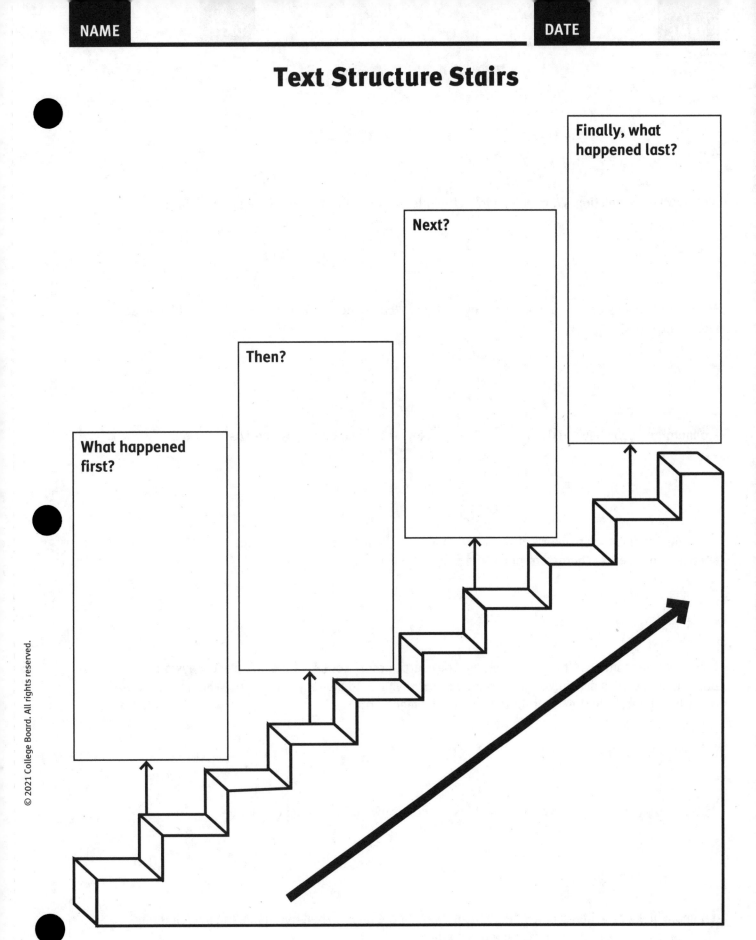

Finally, what happened last?

Next?

Then?

What happened first?

TP-CASTT Analysis

Poem Title:

Author:

Title: Make a Prediction. What do you think the title means before you read the poem?

Paraphrase: Translate the poem in your own words. What is the poem about? Rephrase difficult sections word for word.

Connotation: Look beyond the literal meaning of key words and images to their associations.

Attitude: What is the speaker's attitude? What is the author's attitude? How does the author feel about the speaker, about other characters, about the subject?

Shifts: Where do the shifts in tone, setting, voice, etc., occur? Look for time and place, keywords, punctuation, stanza divisions, changes in length or rhyme, and sentence structure. What is the purpose of each shift? How do they contribute to effect and meaning?

Title: Reexamine the title. What do you think it means now in the context of the poem?

Theme: Think of the literal and metaphorical layers of the poem. Then determine the overall theme. The theme must be written in a complete sentence.

TP-CASTT

● **Poem Title:**

Author:

Title		
Paraphrase		
Connotation		
Attitude		
Shifts		
Title		
Theme		

Unknown Word Solver

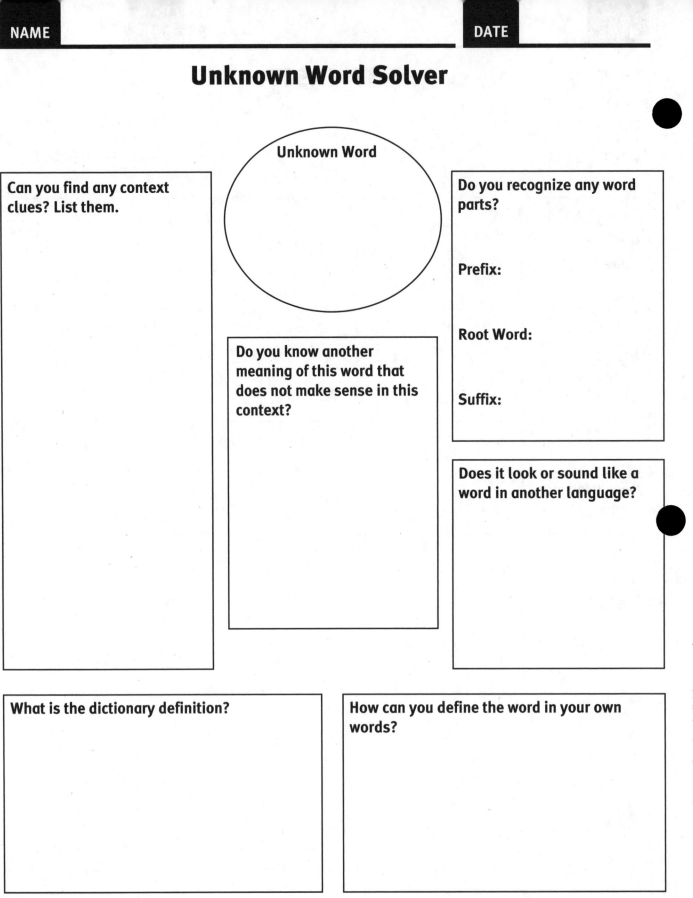

Unknown Word

Can you find any context clues? List them.

Do you recognize any word parts?

Prefix:

Root Word:

Suffix:

Do you know another meaning of this word that does not make sense in this context?

Does it look or sound like a word in another language?

What is the dictionary definition?

How can you define the word in your own words?

Venn Diagram for Writing a Comparison

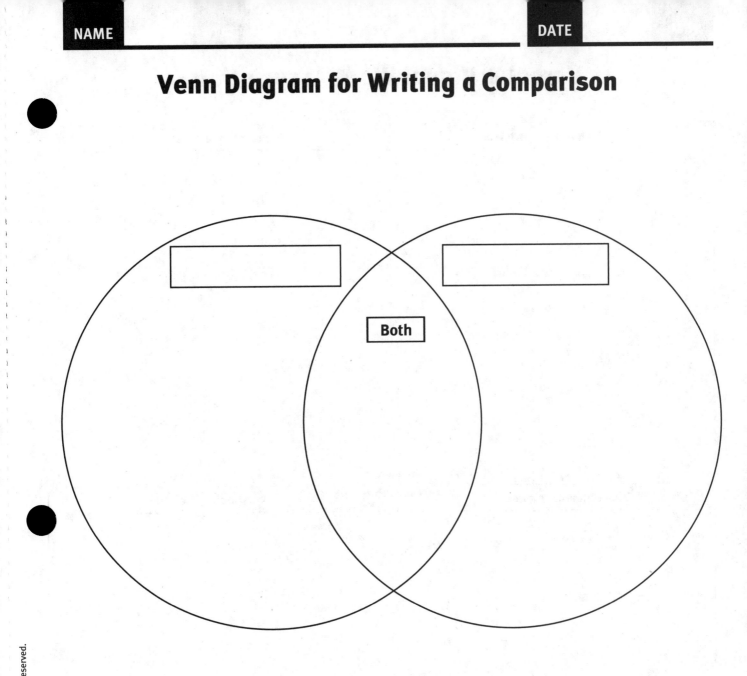

Both

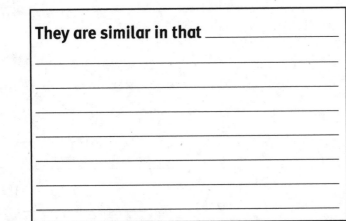

They are similar in that _____

_____

_____

_____

_____

_____

They are different in that _____

_____

_____

_____

_____

_____

Verbal & Visual Word Association

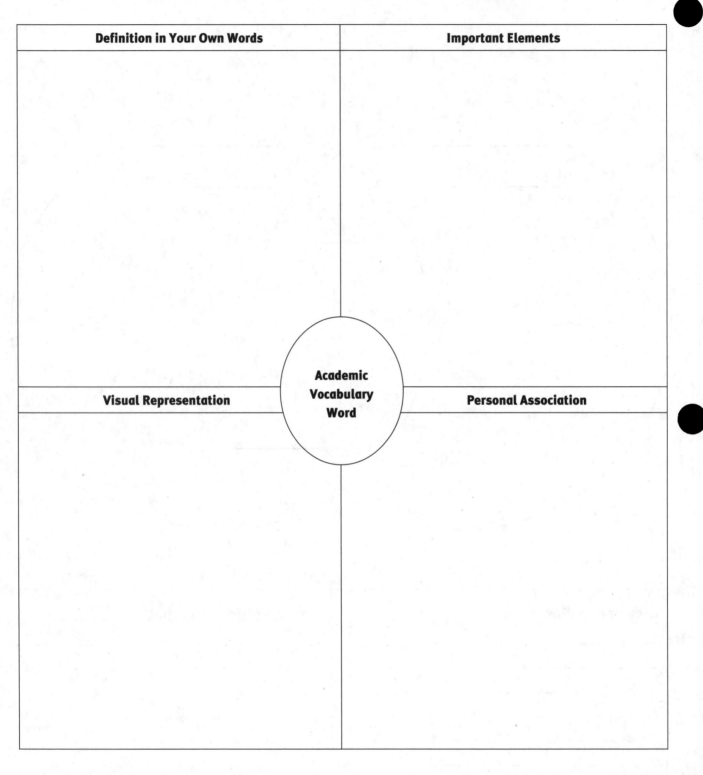

Definition in Your Own Words	Important Elements

Academic Vocabulary Word

Visual Representation	Personal Association

Web Organizer

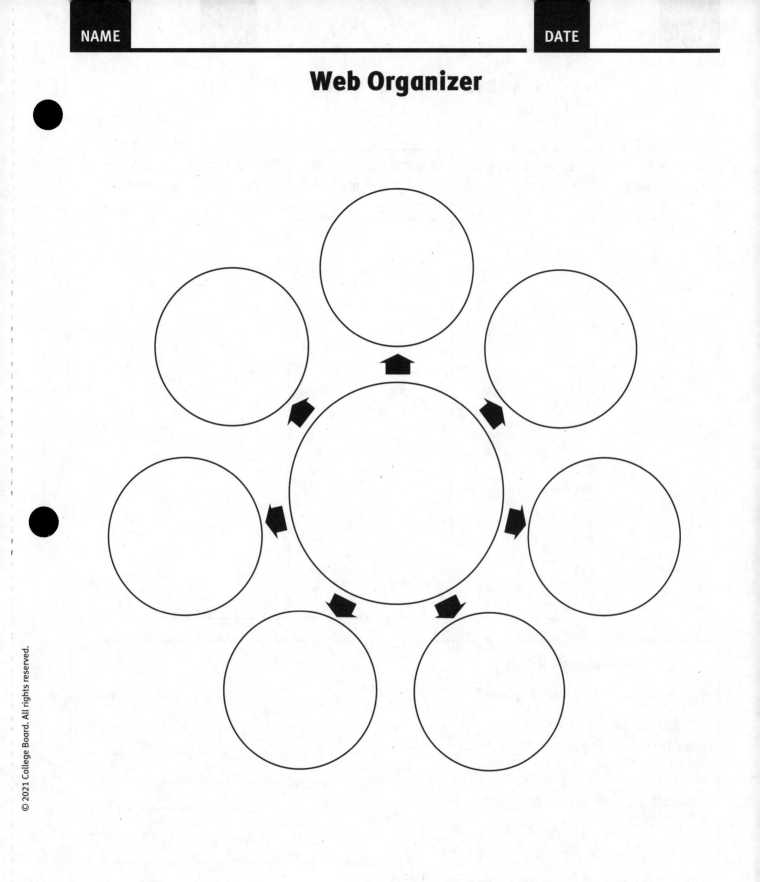

Word Choice Analyzer

Word or phrase from the text	Definition of word or phrase	How can I restate the definition in my own words?	What effect did the author produce by choosing these words?

Explain Your Analysis

The author uses the word or phrase _____ , which means

_____

Another way to say this is _____

_____

I think the author chose these words to _____

_____

_____

One way I can modify this sentence to add detail is to _____

_____

Word Map

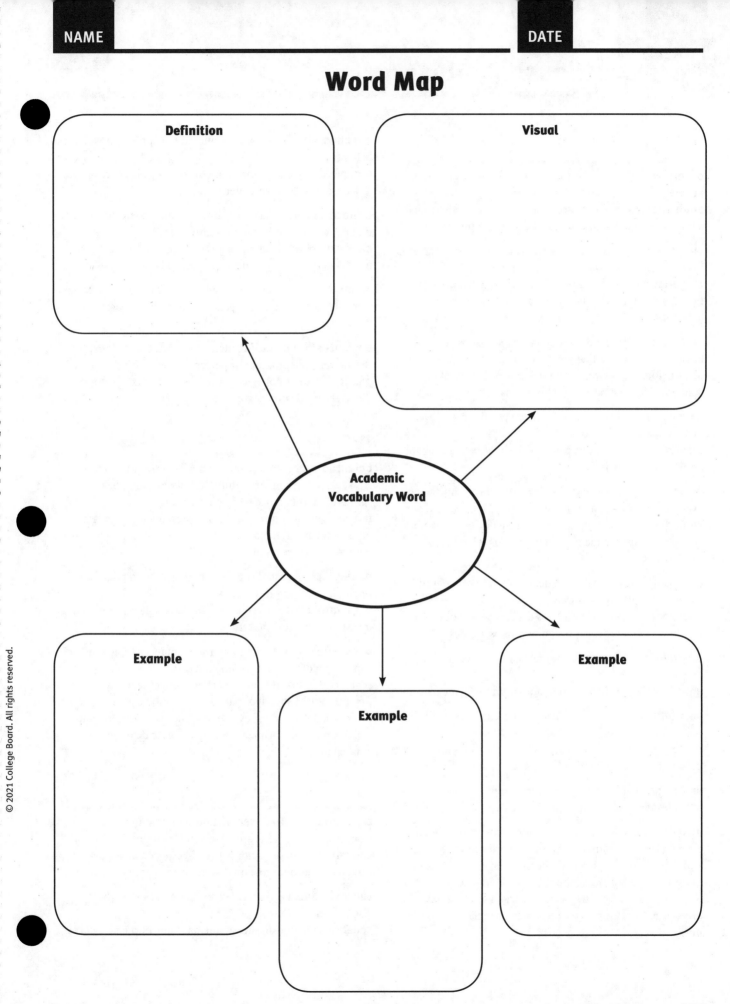

Definition

Visual

Academic Vocabulary Word

Example

Example

Example

Glossary/Glosario

A

advertising: the use of print, graphics, or videos to persuade people to buy a product or use a service
publicidad: uso de impresos, gráfica o videos para persuadir a las personas a comprar un producto o usar un servicio

allegory: a story in which the characters, objects, or actions have a meaning beyond the surface of the story
alegoría: cuento en el que los personajes, objetos o acciones tienen un significado que va más allá de la superficie de la historia

alliteration: the repetition of consonant sounds at the beginnings of words that are close together
aliteración: repetición de sonidos consonánticos al comienzo de palabras que están cercanas

allusion: a reference to a well-known person, place, event, literary work, or work of art
alusión: referencia a una persona, lugar, obra literaria u obra de arte muy conocidos

analogy: a comparison of the similarity of two things; for example, comparing a *part to a whole* or the *whole to a part*
analogía: comparación de la semejanza de dos cosas; por ejemplo, comparar una *parte con un todo* o el *todo con una parte*

analyze (literary): study the details of a work to identify essential features or meaning
analizar (literario): estudiar los detalles de una obra para identificar características o significados esenciales

anecdote: a brief, entertaining account of an incident or event
anécdota: breve relato entretenido de un incidente o suceso

annotate: write notes to explain or present ideas that help you analyze and understand a text
anotar: tomar notas para explicar o presentar las ideas que te ayuden a analizar y a entender un texto

antonyms: words with opposite meanings
antónimos: palabras con significados opuestos

archetype: a character, symbol, story pattern, or other element that is common to human experience across cultures and that occurs frequently in literature, myth, and folklore
arquetipo: personaje, símbolo, patrón de un cuento u otro elemento que es común a la experiencia humana a través de diversas culturas y que aparece con frecuencia en literatura, mitos y folclor

B

argument: facts or reasoning offered to support a position as being true
argumento: hechos o razonamiento entregados para apoyar una posición como verdadera

artifact: an object made by a human being, typically an item that has cultural or historical significance
artefacto: objeto hecho por un ser humano, habitualmente un objeto que tiene significación cultural o histórica

atmosphere: the feeling created by a literary work or passage
atmósfera: sentimiento creado por una obra o pasaje literario

audience: the intended readers of specific types of texts or the viewers of a program or performance
público: lectores objetivo de tipos específicos de textos o espectadores de un programa o actuación

B

balanced sentence: a sentence that presents ideas of equal weight in similar grammatical form to emphasize the similarity or difference between the ideas
oración balanceada: oración que presenta ideas de igual peso en forma gramatical similar para enfatizar la semejanza o diferencia entre las ideas

bibliography: a list of source materials used to prepare a research paper or presentation
bibliografía: lista de las fuentes utilizadas para preparar una investigación o una presentación

body paragraph: a paragraph that contains a topic sentence, supporting details and commentary, and a concluding sentence and that is usually part of a longer text
párrafo representativo: párrafo que contiene una oración principal, detalles de apoyo y comentarios, y una oración concluyente que normalmente forma parte de un texto más extenso

C

caricature: a visual or verbal representation in which characteristics or traits are distorted for emphasis
caricatura: representación visual o verbal en la que las características o rasgos son distorsionados para dar énfasis

cause: an initial action; an event that makes something else happen
causa: acción inicial; suceso que hace que otra cosa ocurra

character: a person or animal that takes part in the action of a literary work
personaje: persona o animal que participa en la acción de una obra literaria

characterization: the methods a writer uses to develop characters; for example, through description, actions, and dialogue
caracterización: métodos que usa un escritor para desarrollar personajes; por ejemplo, a través de descripción, acciones y diálogo

citation: giving credit to the authors of source information
cita: dar crédito a los autores de información usada como fuente

claim: a writer's statement of a position or opinion about a topic
afirmación: declaración de un escritor acerca de una posición u opinión sobre un tema

cliché: an overused expression or idea
cliché: expresión o idea usada en exceso

climax: the turning point or the high point of a story
clímax: punto de inflexión o momento culminante de un cuento

coherence: the clear and orderly presentation of ideas in a paragraph or essay
coherencia: presentación clara y ordenada de las ideas en un párrafo o ensayo

collaborate: work together with other members of a group
colaborar: trabajar en conjunto con otros miembros de un grupo

comedy: an entertainment that is amusing or humorous
comedia: espectáculo que es divertido o cómico

commentary: explanation of the way the facts, details, and/or examples in a paragraph or essay support the topic sentence
comentario: explicación de la manera en que los hechos, detalles y ejemplos de un párrafo o ensayo apoyan la oración principal

commercialism: an emphasis on gaining profits through advertising or sponsorship
mercantilismo: énfasis en obtener utilidades por medio de la publicidad o el auspicio

communication: the process of giving or exchanging information. **Verbal communication** involves the written or spoken word. **Nonverbal communication** involves movement, gestures, or facial expressions.
comunicación: proceso de dar o intercambiar información. La **comunicación verbal** involucra palabras escritas o habladas. La **comunicación no verbal** involucra movimientos, gestos o expresiones faciales.

compare: to identify similarities in two or more items; *see also* contrast
comparar: identificar semejanzas entre dos o más elementos; *ver también*, contrastar

concluding sentence: a final sentence that pulls together the ideas in a paragraph by restating the main idea or by summarizing or commenting on the ideas in the paragraph
oración concluyente: oración final que reúne las ideas de un párrafo, reformulando la idea principal o resumiendo o comentando las ideas del párrafo

conclusion: the ending of a paragraph or essay, which brings it to a close and leaves an impression with the reader
conclusión: fin de un párrafo o ensayo, que lo lleva a su término y deja una impresión en el lector

conflict: a struggle between opposing forces. In an **external conflict**, a character struggles with an outside force, such as another character or something in nature. In an **internal conflict**, the character struggles with his or her own needs, desires, or emotions.
conflicto: lucha entre fuerzas opuestas. En un **conflicto externo**, un personaje lucha contra una fuerza externa, como por ejemplo otro personaje o algo de la naturaleza. En un **conflicto interno**, el personaje lucha contra sus propias necesidades, deseos o emociones.

connotation: the suggested or implied meaning or emotion associated with a word—beyond its literal definition
connotación: significado o emoción sugerida o implícita que se asocia con una palabra—más allá de su definición literal

consumer: a buyer; a person who acquires goods and services
consumidor: comprador, persona que adquiere bienes y servicios

consumerism: the buying and consuming of goods and products; the belief that it is good to buy and consume goods and services
consumismo: compra y consumo de bienes y productos; creencia de que es bueno comprar y consumir bienes y servicios

context clue: information in words and phrases surrounding an unfamiliar word that hint at the meaning of the unfamiliar word.

clave de contexto: información en las palabras y frases que rodean una palabra no conocida y que dan una pista acerca del significado de esa palabra.

contrast: to identify differences in two or more items; *see also* compare

contrastar: identificar diferencias entre dos o más elementos; *ver también*, comparar

controversy: a public debate or dispute concerning a matter of opinion

controversia: debate público o disputa sobre una cuestión sujeta a opinión

copy: the actual text in an advertisement

texto publicitario: información actual en un anuncio publicitario

counter-argument: reasoning or facts given in opposition to an argument

contraargumento: razonamiento o hechos dados en oposición a un argumento

credible: to be trusted or believed

creíble: ser confiable o creíble

criteria: the facts, rules, or standards on which judgments are based.

criterios: hechos, reglas o estándares sobre las cuales están basadas las opiniones.

D

debate: *n.* a discussion involving opposing points of view; *v.* to present the sides of an argument by discussing opposing points

debate: *s.* discusión que involucra puntos de vista opuestos; *v.* presentar los lados de un argumento discutiendo puntos opuestos

definition: the process of making clear the meaning or nature of something

definición: proceso de aclarar el significado o naturaleza de algo

denotation: the exact, literal meaning of a word

denotación: significado exacto y literal de una palabra

detail: in writing, evidence (facts, statistics, examples) that supports the topic sentence

detalle: en la escritura, evidencia (hechos, estadística, ejemplos) que apoya la oracón principal

dialogue: conversation between characters

diálogo: conversación entre personajes

diction: a writer's or speaker's choice of words

dicción: selección de palabras por parte del escritor u orador

dissolve: the slow fading away of one image in a film as another fades in to take its place

desvanecimiento: desaparición lenta de una imagen en una película a medida que otra aparece progresivamente para tomar su lugar

drama: a genre of literature that is intended to be performed before an audience; a play

drama: género literario destinado a ser representado ante un público; obra teatral

dystopia: an imagined place or state in which the condition of life is imperfect or bad

distopía: lugar o estado imaginario en el que las condiciones de vida son imperfectas o malas

E

editorial: a short essay in which a publication, or someone speaking for a publication, expresses an opinion or takes a stand on an issue

editorial: ensayo corto en el que una publicación, o alguien que representa una publicación, expresa una opinión o toma partido acerca de un tema

effect: the result of an event or action

efecto: resultado de un suceso o acción

epic: a long narrative poem about the deeds of heroes or gods

épica: poema narrativo largo acerca de las proezas de héroes o dioses

epilogue: a section at the end of a book or play that extends or comments on the ending

epílogo: sección al final de un libro u obra teatral, que extiende o comenta el final

essay: a short literary composition on a single subject

ensayo: composición literaria corta acerca de un único tema

ethos: a rhetorical appeal that focuses on the character or qualifications of the speaker

ethos: recurso retórico centrado en el carácter o las capacidades del orador

euphemism: an inoffensive expression that is used in place of one that is considered harsh or blunt

eufemismo: expresión inofensiva usada en lugar de una considerada cruel o ruda

evaluate: to examine and judge carefully to determine the value of something, such as an idea, a comment, or a source
evaluar: estudiar y juzgar cuidadosamente para determinar el valor de algo, tal como una idea, un comentario, o una fuente

evidence: the information that supports or proves an idea or claim; forms of evidence include facts, statistics (numerical facts), expert opinions, examples, and anecdotes; see also, anecdotal, empirical, and logical evidence
evidencia: información que apoya o prueba una idea o afirmación; algunas formas de evidencia incluyen hechos, estadísticas (datos numéricos), opiniones de expertos, ejemplos y anécdotas; ver también evidencia anecdótica, empírica y lógica

explanatory essay: an essay that makes an assertion and explains it with details, reasons, textual evidence, and commentary
ensayo explicativo: ensayo que hace una afirmación y la explica con detalles, razones, evidencia textual y comentarios

explanatory paragraph: a paragraph that makes an assertion and supports it with details and commentary
párrafo explicativo: párrafo que hace una afirmación y la apoya con detalles y comentarios

exposition: events that give a reader background information needed to understand a story
exposición: sucesos que entregan al lector los antecedentes necesarios para comprender un cuento

F

fable: a brief story that teaches a lesson or moral, usually through animal characters that take on human qualities
fábula: cuento breve que enseña una lección o moraleja, normalmente por medio de personajes animales que asumen cualidades humanas

fact: a statement that can be proven
hecho: enunciado que puede demostrarse

fairy tale: a story that involves fantasy elements such as witches, goblins, and elves. These stories often involve princes and princesses and today are generally told to entertain children.
cuento de hadas: cuento que involucra elementos fantásticos como brujas, duendes y elfos. A menudo, estos cuentos involucran a príncipes y princesas y hoy se cuentan generalmente para entretener a los niños.

falling action: events after the climax of a story but before the resolution
acción descendente: sucesos posteriores al clímax de un cuento, pero antes de la resolución

fantasy: a story based on things that could not happen in real life
fantasía: cuento basado en cosas que no podrían ocurrir en la vida real

fiction: writing that consists of imagined events
ficción: escritura que consiste en acontecimientos imaginados

figurative language: imaginative language that is not meant to be interpreted literally
lenguaje figurativo: lenguaje imaginativo que no pretende ser interpretado literalmente

flashback: a sudden and vivid memory of an event in the past; also, an interruption in the sequence of events in the plot of a story to relate events that occurred in the past
narración retrospectiva: recuerdo repentino y vívido de un suceso del pasado; además, interrupción en la secuencia de los sucesos del argumento de un cuento para relatar sucesos ocurridos en el pasado

fluency: the ability to use language clearly and easily
fluidez: capacidad de usar el lenguaje fácilmente y de manera clara

folk literature: the traditional literature of a culture, consisting of a variety of myths and folk tales
literatura folclórica: literatura tradicional de una cultura, consistente en una variedad de mitos y cuentos folclóricos

folk tale: an anonymous traditional story passed on orally from one generation to another
cuento folclórico: cuento tradicional anónimo pasada oralmente de generación en generación

folklore: the stories, traditions, sayings, and customs of a culture or a society
folclor: historias, tradiciones, dichos y costumbres de una cultura o sociedad

foreshadowing: clues or hints signaling events that will occur later in the plot
presagio: claves o pistas que señalan sucesos que ocurrirán mas adelante en el argumento

formal style: a style of writing or speaking that is appropriate for formal communication such as in academics or business
estilo formal: estilo de escribir o hablar adecuado para la comunicación formal como la académica o comercial

free verse: a kind of poetry that does not follow any regular pattern, rhythm, or rhyme
verso libre: tipo de poesía que no sigue ningún patrón, ritmo o rima regular

G

genre: a category or type of literature, such as short story, folk tale, poem, novel, play
género: categoría o tipo de literatura, como el cuento corto, cuento folclórico, poema, novela, obra teatral

global revision: the process of deeply revising a text to improve organization, development of ideas, focus, and voice
revisión global: proceso de revisar en profundidad un texto para mejorar su organización, desarrollo de ideas, enfoque y voz

graphic novel: a narrative told through visuals and captions
novela gráfica: narrativa que se cuenta por medio de efectos visuales y leyendas

H

headline: a short piece of text at the top of an article, usually in larger type, designed to be the first words the audience reads
titular: trozo corto de texto en la parte superior de un artículo, habitualmente en letra más grande, diseñado para ser las primeras palabras que el público lear

humor: the quality of being comical or amusing
humor: cualidad de ser cómico o divertido

hook: *n.* a compelling idea or statement designed to get readers' attention in an introduction
gancho: *n.* idea o afirmación atractiva diseñada para captar la atención del lector en una introducción

hyperbole: extreme exaggeration used for emphasis, often used for comic effect
hypérbole: exageración extrema usada para dar énfasis, habitualmente usada para dar efecto cómico

I

iamb: a metrical foot that consists of an unstressed syllable followed by a stressed syllable
yambo: pie métrico que consta de una sílaba átona seguida de una sílaba tónica

iambic pentameter: a rhythmic pattern of five feet (or units) of one unstressed syllable followed by a stressed syllable
pentámetro yámbico: patrón rítmico de cinco pies (o unidades) de una sílaba átona seguida de una sílaba tónica

idiom: a figure of speech that cannot be defined literally
expresión idiomatica: figura del discurso que no puede definirse literalmente

image: a picture, drawing, photograph, illustration, chart, or other graphic that is designed to affect the audience in some purposeful way
imagen: pintura, dibujo, fotografía, ilustración, cuadro u otra gráfica diseñada para producir algún efecto intencional sobre el público

imagery: descriptive or figurative language used to create word pictures; imagery is created by details that appeal to one or more of the five senses
imaginería: lenguaje descriptivo o figurativo utilizado para crear imágenes verbales; la imaginería es creada por detalles que apelan a uno o más de los cinco sentidos

improvise: to respond or perform on the spur of the moment
improvisar: reaccionar o representar impulsivamente

incident: a distinct piece of action as in an episode in a story or a play. More than one incident may make up an event.
incidente: trozo de acción distintivo como un episodio de un cuento o de una obra teatral. Más de un incidente puede conformar un suceso.

inference: a logical guess or conclusion based on observation, prior experience, or textual evidence
inferencia: conjetura o conclusión lógica basada en la observación, experiencias anteriores o evidencia textual

inflection: the emphasis a speaker places on words through change in pitch or volume
inflexión: énfasis que pone un orador en las palabras por medio del cambio de tono o volumen

interpretation: a writer's or artist's representation of the meaning of a story or idea
interpretación: representación que hace un escritor o artista del significado de un cuento o idea

interview: a meeting between two people in which one, usually a reporter, asks the other questions to get that person's views on a subject
entrevista: reunión entre dos personas, en la que una, normalmente un reportero, hace preguntas a la otra para conocer sus opiniones acerca de un tema

introduction: the opening paragraph of an essay, which must get the reader's attention and indicate the topic
introducción: párrafo inicial de un ensayo, que debe captar la atención del lector e indicar el tema

L

legend: a traditional story believed to be based on actual people and events. Legends, which typically celebrate heroic individuals or significant achievements, tend to express the values of a culture.
leyenda: cuento tradicional que se considera basado en personas y sucesos reales. Las leyendas, que típicamente celebran a individuos heroicos o logros importantes, tienden a expresar los valores de una cultura.

limerick: a light, humorous, nonsensical verse of few lines, usually with a rhyme scheme of a-a-b-b-a
quintilla: verso liviano, humorístico, disparatado y de pocas líneas, normalmente con un esquema a-a-b-b-a

listening: the process of receiving a message and making meaning of it from verbal and nonverbal cues
escuchar: proceso de recibir el mensaje y comprender su significado a partir de claves verbales y no verbales

literary analysis: the process of examining closely and commenting on the elements of a literary work
análisis literario: proceso de examinar atentamente y comentar los elementos de una obra literaria

local revision: revising a text on a word or sentence level
revisión local: revisar un texto a nivel de palabras o de oraciones

logo: a unique design symbol used to identify a company visually
logotipo: símbolo único de diseño, utilizado para identificar visualmente una empresa

logos: a rhetorical appeal to reason or logic through statistics, facts, and reasonable examples
logos: apelación retórica a la razón o la lógica por medio de estadísticas, hechos y ejemplos razonables

M

media: the various means of mass communication, such as radio, television, newspapers, and magazines
medios de comunicación: los diversos medios de comunicación masiva, como radio, televisión, periódicos y revistas

media channel: a type of media, such as television or newspaper
canal mediático: tipo de medios de comunicación, como televisión o periódicos

metaphor: a comparison between two unlike things in which one thing becomes another
metáfora: comparación entre dos cosas diferentes en la que una cosa se convierte en otra

monologue: a speech or written expression of thoughts by a character
monólogo: discurso o expresión escrita de pensamientos por parte de un personaje

mood: the overall emotional quality of a work, which is created by the author's language and tone and the subject matter
carácter: la calidad emocional general de una obra, que es creada por el lenguaje y tono del autor y por el tema

motif: a recurring element, image, or idea in a work of literature
motivo: elemento, imagen o idea recurrente en una obra literaria

multimedia: the use of several media (for example, print, film, audio, and video) to communicate ideas
multimedia: uso de varios medios de comunicación (por ejemplo: impresos, cine, audio y video) para comunicar ideas

multiple intelligences: the variety of learning styles that everyone has in varying degrees. In each individual, different intelligences predominate.
inteligencias múltiples: diversidad de estilos de aprendizaje que todos tienen en diversos grados. En cada individuo predominan diferentes inteligencias.

myth: a traditional story that explains the actions of gods or heroes or the origins of the elements of nature
mito: cuento tradicional que explica las acciones de dioses o héroes o los orígenes de los elementos de la naturaleza

N

narrative: a type of writing that tells a story or describes a sequence of events in an incident
narrativa: tipo de escritura que cuenta un cuento o describe una secuencia de sucesos de un incidente

narrative poem: a story told in verse
poema narrativo: historia contada en verso

news article: an article in a news publication that objectively presents both sides of an issue
artículo noticioso: artículo de una publicación noticiosa que presenta objetivamente ambos lados de un asunto

nonfiction: writing that is based on facts and actual events
no ficción: escritura que se basa en hechos o acontecimientos reales

nonprint text: a text, such as film or graphics, that communicates ideas without print
texto no impreso: texto, como una película o gráfica, que comunica ideas sin imprimir

nonverbal communication: gestures, facial expressions, and inflection that form unspoken communication
comunicación no verbal: gestos, expresiones faciales e inflexión que forman la comunicación no hablada

novel: a type of literary genre that tells a fictional story
novela: tipo de género literario que cuenta una historia ficticia

O

objective: supported by facts and not influenced by personal opinion
objetivo: apoyado por hechos y no influenciado por la opinión personal

objective camera view: in film, when the camera takes a neutral point of view
visión objetiva de la cámara: en el cine, cuando la cámara toma un punto de vista neutro

omniscient: a third-person point of view in which the narrator is all-knowing
omnisciente: punto de vista de una tercera persona, en la que el narador lo sabe todo

onomatopoeia: the use of words that imitate the sounds of what they describe
onomatopeya: el uso de palabras que imitan los sonidos de lo que describen

one-liner: a short joke or witticism expressed in a single sentence
agudeza: chiste u comentario ingenioso que se expresa en una sola oración.

opinion: a perspective that can be debated
opinión: perspectiva que es debatible

oral interpretation: reading aloud a literary text with expression
interpretación oral: leer en voz alta un texto literario con expresión

oxymoron: a figure of speech in which the words seem to contradict each other; for example, "jumbo shrimp"
oxímoron: figura del discurso en la que las palabras parecen contradecirse mutuamente; por ejemplo, "audaz cobardía"

P

pantomime: a form of acting without words, in which motions, gestures, and expressions convey emotions or situations
pantomima: forma de actuación sin palabras, en la que los movimientos, gestos y expresiones transmiten emociones o situationes

paraphrase: to restate in one's own words
parafrasear: reformular en nuestras propias palabras

parody: a humorous imitation of a literary work
parodia: imitación humorística de una obra literaria

pathos: a rhetorical appeal to the reader's or listener's senses or emotions through connotative language and imagery
pathos: apelación retórica a los sentidos o emociones del lector u oyente por medio de un lenguaje connotativo y figurado

performance: presenting or staging a play
actuación: presentar o poner en escena una obra teatral

persona: the voice or character speaking or narrating a story
persona: voz o personaje que habla o narra una historia

personal letter: a written communication between friends, relatives, or acquaintances that shares news, thoughts, or feelings
carta personal: comunicación escrita entre amigos, parientes o conocidos, que comparte noticias, pensamientos o sentimientos

personal narrative: a piece of writing that describes an incident and includes a personal response to and reflection on the incident

narrativa personal: texto escrito que describe un incidente e incluye una reacción personal ante el incidente y una reflexión acerca de él

personification: a kind of metaphor that gives objects or abstract ideas human characteristics

personificación: tipo de metáfora que da características humanas a los objetos o ideas abstractas

perspective: the way a specific character views a situation or other characters

perspectiva: manera en que un personaje específico visualiza una situación o a otros personajes

persuasion: the act or skill of causing someone to do or believe something

persuasión: acto o destreza de hacer que alguien haga o crea algo

persuasive essay: an essay that attempts to convince the reader to take an action or believe an idea

ensayo persuasivo: ensayo que intenta convencer al lector de que realice una acción o crea una idea

phrasing: dividing a speech into smaller parts, adding pauses for emphasis

frasear: dividir un discurso en partes más pequeñas, añadiendo pausas para dar énfasis

pitch: the highness or lowness of a sound, particularly the voice in speaking

tono: altura de un sonido, especialmente de la voz al hablar

plagiarism: taking and using as your own the words and ideas of another

plagio: tomar y usar como propias las palabras e ideas de otro

plot: the sequence of related events that make up a story or novel

trama: secuencia de sucesos relacionados, que conforman un cuento o novela

point of view: the perspective from which a story is told. In **first-person** point of view, the teller is a character in the story telling what he or she sees or knows. In **third-person** point of view, the narrator is someone outside of the story.

punto de vista: perspectiva desde la cual se cuenta una historia. En el punto de vista de la **primera persona**, el relator es un personaje del cuento que narra lo que ve o sabe. En el punto de vista de la **tercera persona**, el narrador es alguien que está fuera del cuento.

prediction: a logical guess or assumption about something that has not yet happened

predicción: conjetura lógica o suposición acerca de algo que aún no ha ocurrido

presentation: delivery of a formal reading, talk, or performance

presentación: entrega de una lectura, charla o representación formal

prose: the ordinary form of written language, using sentences and paragraphs; writing that is not poetry, drama, or song

prosa: forma común del lenguaje escrito, usando oraciones y párrafos; escritura que no es poesía, drama ni canción

pun: the humorous use of a word or words to suggest another word with the same sound or a different meaning

retruécano: uso humorístico de una o varias palabras para sugerir otra palabra que tiene el mismo sonido o un significado diferente

purpose: the reason for writing; what the writer hopes to accomplish

propósito: razón para escribir; lo que el escritor espera lograr

Q

quatrain: a four-line stanza in poetry
cuarteta: en poesía, estrofa de cuatro versos

R

rate: the speed at which a speaker delivers words
rapidez: velocidad a la que el orador pronuncia las palabras

reasons: the points that explain why the author is making a certain claim

razones: los puntos que explican por qué un autor propone cierta afirmacón

reflection: a kind of thinking and writing that seriously explores the significance of an experience, idea, or observation

reflexión: tipo de pensamiento y escritura que explora seriamente la importancia de una experiencia, idea u observación

reflective essay: an essay in which the writer explores the significance of an experience or observation

ensayo reflexivo: ensayo en que el autor explora la importancia de una experiencia u observación

refrain: a regularly repeated word, phrase, line, or group of lines in a poem or song
estribillo: palabra, frase, verso o grupo de versos de un poema o canción que se repite con regularidad

relevant: closely connected to the matter at hand (for example, evidence supporting a claim)
relevante: relacionado estrechamente con el asunto en cuestión (por ejemplo, la evidencia que apoya una afirmación)

repetition: the use of the same words or structure over again
repetición: uso de las mismas palabras o estructura una y otra vez

research: (*v.*) to locate information from a variety of sources; (*n.*) the information found from investigating a variety of sources
investigar: (*v.*) proceso de buscar información en una variedad de fuentes; *también*, **investigación** (*n.*) información que se halla al investigar una variedad de fuentes

resolution: the outcome of the conflict of a story, when loose ends are wrapped up
resolución: resultado del conflicto de un cuento, cuando se atan los cabos sueltos

revision: a process of evaluating a written piece to improve coherence and use of language; *see also* local revision, global revision
revisión: proceso de evaluar un texto escrito para mejorar la coherencia y el uso del lenguaje; *ver también*, revisión local, revisión global

rhetorical appeals: the use of emotional, ethical, and logical arguments to persuade in writing or speaking
recursos retóricos: uso de argumentos emotivos, éticos y lógicos para persuadir al escribir o hablar

rhetorical question: a question asked to emphasize a point or create an effect; no answer is expected
pregunta retórica: pregunta que se hace para enfatizar un punto o crear un efecto; no se espera una respuesta

rhyme: the repetition of sounds at the ends of words
rima: repetición de sonidos al final de las palabras

rhyme scheme: a consistent pattern of end rhyme throughout a poem
esquema de la rima: patrón consistente de una rima final a lo largo de un poema

rhythm: the pattern of stressed and unstressed syllables in spoken or written language, especially in poetry
ritmo: patrón de sílabas acentuadas y no acentuadas en lenguaje hablado o escrito, especialmente en poesía

rising action: major events that develop the plot of a story and lead to the climax
acción ascendente: sucesos importantes que desarrollan la trama de un cuento y conducen al clímax

S

science fiction: a genre in which the imaginary elements of the story could be scientifically possible
ciencia ficción: género en que los elementos imaginarios del cuento podrían ser científicamente posibles

sensory language: words or information that appeal to the five senses
lenguaje sensorial: palabras o información que apelan a los cinco sentidos

sequence: the order in which events happen
secuencia: orden en que ocurren los sucesos

setting: the time and the place in which a narrative occurs
ambiente: tiempo y lugar en que ocurre un relato

short story: a work of fiction that presents a sequence of events, or plot, that deals with a conflict
cuento corto: obra de ficción que presenta una secuencia de sucesos, o trama, que tratan de un conflicto

simile: a comparison between two unlike things, using the words *like* or *as*
símil: comparación entre dos cosas diferentes usando las palabras como o *tan*

slogan: a catchphrase that evokes a particular feeling about a company and its product
eslogan: frase o consigna publicitaria que evoca un sentimiento en particular acerca de una empresa y su producto

source: a place from which information comes or is obtained
fuente: lugar de donde surge o se obtiene la información

speaker: the voice that communicates with the reader of a poem
hablante: la voz que se comunica con el lector de un poema

speaking: the process of sharing information, ideas, and emotions using verbal and nonverbal means communication
hablar: proceso de compartir información, ideas y emociones usando medios de comunicación verbales y no verbales

stanza: a group of lines, usually similar in length and pattern, that form a unit within a poem
estrofa: grupo de versos, normalmente similares en longitud y patrón, que forman una unidad dentro de un poema

stereotype: a fixed, oversimplified image of a person, group, or idea; something conforming to that image
estereotipo: imagen fija y demasiado simplificada de una persona, grupo o idea; algo que cumple esa imagen

subjective: influenced by personal opinions or ideas
subjectivo: influenciado por opiniones o ideas personales

subjective camera view: in film, when the camera seems to show the events through a character's eyes
visión subjetiva de la cámara: en el cine, cuando la cámara parece mostrar los sucesos a través de los ojos de un personaje

subplot: a secondary plot that occurs along with a main plot
trama secundaria: argumento secundario que ocurre conjuntamente con un argumento principal

sufficient: adequate for the purpose of supporting a claim or reason
suficiente: adecuado para cumplir con el propósito de apoyar una afirmación o razón

summarize: to briefly restate the main ideas of a piece of writing
resumir: reformular brevemente las ideas principales de un texto escrito

supporting details: in writing, evidence (facts, statistics, examples) that supports the topic sentence
detalles de apoyo: en la escritura, evidencia (hechos, estadísticas ejemplos) que apoya la oracon principal

symbol: an object, a person, or a place that stands for something else
símbolo: objeto, persona o lugar que representa otra cosa

symbolism: the use of symbols
simbolismo: el uso de símbolos

synonyms: words with similar meanings
sinónimos: palabras con significados semejantes

synthesize: to combine elements from different sources to create, express, or support a new idea
sintetizar: combinar elementos de diferentes fuentes para crear, expresar o apoyar una idea nueva

T

tableau: a purposeful arrangement of characters frozen as if in a painting or a photograph
cuadro: disposición intencional de personajes que permanecen inmóviles como en una pintura o foto

talking points: important points or concepts to be included in a presentation
puntos centrales: puntos o conceptos importantes a incluirse en una presentación

tall tale: a highly exaggerated and often humorous story about folk heroes in local settings
cuento increíble: cuento muy exagerado y normalmente humorístico acerca de héroes folclóricos en ambientes locales

target audience: the specific group of people that advertisers aim to persuade to buy
público objetivo: grupo específico de personas a quienes los publicistas desean persuadir de comprar

tempo: the speed or rate of speaking
ritmo: velocidad o rapidez al hablar

textual evidence: quotations, summaries, or paraphrases from text passages to support a position
evidencia textual: citas, resúmenes o paráfrasis de pasajes de texto para apoyar una position

theme: the central idea, message, or purpose of a literary work
tema: idea, mensaje o propósito central de una obra literaria

thesis statement: a sentence, in the introduction of an essay, that states the writer's position or opinion on the topic of the essay
enunciado de tesis: oración, en la introducción de un ensayo, que plantea el punto de vista u opinión del autor acerca del tema del ensayo

tone: a writer's or speaker's attitude toward a subject
tono: actitud de un escritor u orador hacia un tema

topic sentence: a sentence that states the main idea of a paragraph; in an essay, it also makes a point that supports the thesis statement
oración principal: oración que plantea la idea principal de un párrafo; en un ensayo, también plantea un punto que apoya el enunciado de tesis

transitions: words or phrases that connect ideas, details, or events in writing
transiciones: palabras o frases que conectan ideas, detalles o sucesos de un escrito

TV news story: a report on a news program about a specific event
documental de televisión: reportaje en un programa noticioso acerca de un suceso específico

U

utopia: an ideal or perfect place
utopía: lugar ideal o perfecto

V

verse: a unit of poetry, such as a line or a stanza
verso: unidad de la poesía, como un verso o una estrofa

voice: a writer's distinctive use of language
voz: uso distintivo del lenguaje por parte de un escritor

voice-over: the voice of an unseen character in film expressing his or her thoughts
voz en off: voz de un personaje de una película, que no se ve pero que expresa sus pensamientos

volume: the degree of loudness of a speaker's voice or other sound
volumen: grado de intensidad sonora de la voz de un orador o de otro sonido

W

wordplay: a witty or clever verbal exchange or a play on words
juego de palabras: intercambio verbal ingenioso u ocurrente o un juego con palabras

Index of Skills

Literary Skills

Action, 337, 355, 362

Alliteration, 291, 293, 294

Analyzing, 5, 11, 12, 18–19, 26, 66, 68, 70–71, 77, 82, 94, 96, 106, 116–118, 124, 126, 130, 140, 144–145, 146–147, 148, 149, 150, 256, 327, 356, 357, 363, 364, 368, 369

Argument, 189, 195, 197, 205, 208, 214, 245, 247, 257

Argumentative letter, 242, 245–246, 247, 262, 266, 267, 268, 274, 275, 276

Article, 226–227, 309–310

Audience, 195, 201, 211, 217

Author's purpose, 95, 195, 205, 211, 217, 220, 248, 254, 300, 308, 311, 312, 349

Autobiography, 22, 174, 176–177, 178, 181, 345–346, 348, 349, 368

Biography, 174, 179–180, 181

Blog, 209

Cause and effect, 25, 70, 250

Characterization, 26, 85, 94, 117, 168, 347, 361, 367

    actions, 11, 12, 33, 50, 98, 116, 117, 118, 143, 337, 339, 347, 350, 361

    appearance, 33, 50, 116, 117, 118

    attitudes, 33, 55, 325, 327, 329

    changes, 5, 11, 12, 13–14, 15, 18, 25, 47, 52–53, 57, 60, 65, 68, 79, 107, 121, 122, 136, 151, 156, 178, 338, 346, 362, 363

    feelings/emotions, 12, 32, 36, 122, 143, 323, 328, 343, 347, 350, 367

    graphic organizer, 25, 33, 34, 50, 53, 83, 97–98, 107, 109, 117, 121, 175

    words, 11, 32, 33, 36, 55, 94, 116, 118, 130, 143, 338, 343, 356

Character(s), 5, 60, 61, 68, 70, 77, 78, 85, 98, 100, 101, 111, 122.137, 138, 141, 143, 144, 147, 148, 288, 326, 337, 357, 361, 362, 370

    analysis of, 11, 12, 18–19, 26, 66, 68, 71, 82, 94, 116–118, 327, 356, 357, 363, 364, 368, 369

    emotions of, 11, 12, 32, 55, 122, 124, 136, 297, 301, 323, 328, 339, 347, 350, 367

    internal/external forces effecting, 96, 106, 109, 121, 122, 124, 135, 136, 139, 148, 178

    main, 5, 62, 68, 98, 117, 118

    point of view, 26, 32, 34, 36, 95, 101, 328, 337, 348, 356, 363, 364

Citations, 210–211

Comic strips, 362

Compare and contrast, 19–20, 117, 289, 297, 308

Conflict, 5, 36, 53, 60, 66, 70, 71, 72, 77, 78, 83, 84, 96, 98, 99, 100, 106, 111, 139, 147, 148, 149, 329, 337, 338, 339, 343, 344, 356, 362, 367

    external, 12, 13–14, 70, 82, 83, 139, 143, 338, 361

    internal, 12, 13–14, 70, 82, 83, 139, 143, 338

Connotation, 33, 36, 48, 98, 101, 263, 276

Context, 78, 96, 131

Correspondence, 209, 242, 245–246, 247, 251–252, 262, 266, 267, 268, 274, 275, 276, 305–307, 308, 328, 329, 332

Descriptive language, 39, 44, 45, 291, 298

Details, 11, 12, 22, 25, 32, 42, 52, 66, 76, 77, 79, 81, 83, 93, 94, 97, 116, 123, 124, 132, 141, 162, 163, 167, 171, 172, 181, 246, 284, 288, 289, 327, 330, 338, 361, 368

Dialogue, 5, 13–14, 26, 29, 36, 61, 67, 68, 78, 82, 337, 339, 351, 356, 362, 367

Diction (word choice), 33, 66, 67, 76, 93, 94, 130, 131, 141, 143, 217, 293, 302, 304, 311, 326, 344, 357, 361, 367

Drama, 132

Editorial, 4

Effect, 25, 45, 158, 163, 252, 289, 357

Essay, 21,269

Essential questions, 4, 45, 60, 106, 129, 136, 150, 188, 242, 280, 321

Fairy tale, 70, 71, 143

Fantasy, 60

Fiction, 21, 38, 62, 97, 111, 322

Figurative language, 11, 39, 52, 85, 95, 112, 131, 133, 134, 144, 288, 289, 293, 296, 297, 298, 302, 303, 304

Film, 107, 121, 137–138, 139, 209, 336, 337, 357, 367

Film biography, 174

Flashbacks, 122, 363, 364

Foreshadowing, 77

Hyperbole, 23, 43, 303

Images/imagery, 47, 75, 76, 93, 97, 134, 135, 291, 363

Informational text, 45, 109, 174, 181, 230–232, 233, 240, 275, 315, 316, 338, 368

Interpreting/interpretation, 151–152, 154–155, 157, 164

Key ideas, 124, 143, 147, 148, 149, 167, 178, 184, 235, 241, 247, 276, 294, 320, 327, 330

KWHL chart, 236

Letter, 209, 242, 245–246, 247, 251–252, 262, 266, 267, 268, 274, 275, 276, 305–307, 308, 328, 329, 332

Limerick, 264, 265, 281, 282–283

Literary analysis, 5, 12, 19, 70–71, 77, 96, 106, 124, 126, 130, 140, 144–145, 146–147, 148, 149, 150, 256

Literary terms, 2, 4, 5, 12, 22, 33, 39, 60, 62, 69, 70, 77, 85, 104, 106, 108, 111, 122, 133, 150, 154, 157, 174, 186, 214, 242, 250, 278, 280, 281, 286, 291, 316, 320, 321, 333, 335, 339

Logical fallacies, 250, 256, 257, 265

Marking the text, 281

Memoir, 163

Mental images, 39, 44, 66, 69, 85, 93, 286, 289, 292, 295, 351, 358

Metaphor, 39, 43, 45, 85, 95, 132, 133, 303, 356, 357

Meter, 281, 284, 300

Mood, 42, 44, 76, 82, 94, 123, 134, 254, 284, 356, 367

Mysteries, 97, 111

Myth, 73–75, 76, 77

Narrative, 5, 11, 12, 45, 47

    personal, 4, 6, 22–24, 25, 39–42, 61, 348, 349

Narrator, 5, 11–12–14, 18, 22, 25, 42, 43, 45, 48, 52–53, 57, 76, 335

News article, 226–227, 309–310

Nonfiction, 21, 322

Novel, 111, 112, 116–117, 121–122, 123–124, 126, 130–131, 139, 146–147, 148–149

Novel excerpt, 26, 27–31

Ode, 298

Opening sentence, 42, 52, 56

Opinion piece, 4, 8–10, 11, 14–16

Oral interpretation, 281, 294

Pantoum, 298, 301, 302

Personal narrative, 4, 6, 22–24, 25, 39–42, 61, 348, 349

Reading Skills

Writing Skills

Media Skills

Speaking and Listening Skills

Index of Authors and Titles

Credits

Unit 1

"The Circuit" by Francisco Jiménez from *The Circuit: Stories from the Life of a Migrant Child*. Copyright ©1997 by Francisco Jiménez. Reprinted by permission of University of New Mexico Press.

"Schools Hustle To Reach Kids Who Move With The Harvest, Not The School Year" by Peter Balonon-Rosen, copyright © 2016 Indiana Public Broadcasting Stations.

"My Superpowers" by Dan Greenburg as appeared in *Guys Write for Guys Read*, Jon Scieszka, editor. Copyright © 2014 by Dan Greenberg. Reprinted by permission of the author.

Excerpts from *Flipped* by Wendelin Van Draanen, copyright © 2001 by Wendelin Van Draanen Parsons. Used by permission of Alfred A. Knopf, an imprint of Random House Children's Books, a division of Random House LLC and Curtis Brown, Ltd. All rights reserved. Any third party use of this material, outside of this publication, is prohibited. Interested parties must apply directly to Random House LLC for permission.

"The Jacket" by Gary Soto from *The Effects of Knut Hamsun on a Fresno Boy: Recollections and Short Essays*. Copyright © 1983, 2000 by Gary Soto. Reprinted with the permission of The Permissions Company, Inc., on behalf of Persea Books, Inc. (New York), www. perseabooks.com.

"Thank You, M'am" from *Short Stories by Langston Hughes*. Copyright © 1996 by Ramona Bass and Arnold Rampersad. Reprinted by permission of Hill and Wang, a division of Farrar, Straus and Giroux, LLC.

Dover Children's Thrift Classics, *Favorite Greek Myths: In Easy-to-Read Type*, by Bob Blaisdell. © 1995 by Dover Publications, Inc. 978-0-486-28859-8

"Eleven" from *Woman Hollering Creek*. Copyright © 1991 by Sandra Cisneros. Published by Vintage Books, a division of Penguin Random House, New York and originally in hardcover by Random House. By permission of Susan Bergholz Literary Services, New York, NY and Lamy, NM. All rights reserved.

"The Treasure of Lemon Brown" by Walter Dean Myers, as appeared in *Boys Life* Magazine, March 1983. Copyright © 1983 by Walter Dean Myers. Reprinted by permission of Miriam Altshuler Literary Agency, on behalf of Walter Dean Myers.

Unit 2

From *Walk Two Moons* by Sharon Creech. Text copyright © 1994 by Sharon Creech. Used by permission of HarperCollins Publishers.

"Since Hanna Moved Away" from *If I Were in Charge of the World and Other Worries . . .*, published by Macmillan, 1981.

"Saying Farewell to a Faithful Pal" by John Grogan, as appeared in *Bad Dogs Have More Fun: Selected Writings on Family, Animals, and Life* from *The Philadelphia Inquirer*. Used with permission of The Philadelphia Inquirer. Copyright © 2014. All rights reserved.

"Dogs Make Us Human" reprinted with the permission of Scribner Publishing Group, a division of Simon & Schuster, Inc. and Dunow, Carlson & Lerner from *Animals in Translation* by Temple Grandin, Ph.D. and Catherine Johnson, Ph.D. Copyright © 2005 by Temple Grandin, Ph.D. and Catherine Johnson, Ph.D. All rights reserved.

"5 things you don't know about service dogs" by Morieka Johnson, copyright © 2012 by Mother Nature Network.

"My Story" reprinted with the permission of Scribner Publishing Group, a division of Simon & Schuster, Inc. and Dunow, Carlson & Lerner from *Animals in Translation* by Temple Grandin, Ph.D. and Catherine Johnson, Ph.D. Copyright © 2005 by Temple Grandin, Ph.D. and Catherine Johnson, Ph.D. All rights reserved.

Excerpt "Hampshire School for Wayward Wizards" from *Temple Grandin* by Sy Montgomery. Copyright © 2012 by Sy Montgomery. Reprinted by permission of Houghton Mifflin Harcourt Publishing Company and Blackstone Audio, Inc. All rights reserved.

Unit 3

"A Teacher's Defense of Homework," by Andrea Townsend, *The Atlantic*, September 25, 2013, https://www.theatlantic.com/education/archive/2013/09/a-teachers-defense-of-homework/279967/.

"A High School Student's Perspective on Homework," by Amedee Martella, ASCD, http://www.ascd.org/ascd-express/vol4/426-newvoices.aspx.

"Texas Teacher Implements No-Homework Policy, the Internet Rejoices," by Ashley May, from USA Today – (Academic Permission), www.usatoday.com, August 15, 2011, © 2011 Gannett-USA Today. All rights reserved. Used by permission and protected by the Copyright Laws of the United States. The printing, copying, redistribution, or retransmission of this Content without express written permission is prohibited.

"Teens Are Over Face-to-Face Communication, Study Says" by Katy Steinmetz, copyright September 10, 2018, Time, Inc.

"Pro and Con Arguments: 'Are social networking sites good for our society?'" by Procon.org. Copyright © 2012 Procon.org.

"The First Americans" by Scott H. Peters, Grand Council Fire of American Indians, 1927.

Unit 4

"The Jacket" by Gary Soto from *The Effects of Knut Hamsun on a Fresno Boy: Recollections and Short Essays.* Copyright © 1983, 2000 by Gary Soto. Reprinted with the permission of The Permissions Company, Inc., on behalf of Persea Books, Inc. (New York), www. perseabooks.com.

"Oranges" from *New and Selected Poems* by Gary Soto. © 1995 by Gary Soto. Used with permission of Chronicle Books LLC, San Francisco. Visit ChronicleBooks.com

"Trying to Name What Doesn't Change" by Naomi Shihab Nye from *Words Under the Words: Selected Poems.* Copyright © 1995 by Naomi Shihab Nye. Used with permission of Portland, Oregon: Far Corner Books.

"Fireflies" from *Joyful Noise* by Paul Fleischman. Text copyright © 1988 by Paul Fleischman. Used by permission of HarperCollins Publishers.

"The Southpaw" by Judith Viorst. Copyright © 1974 by Judith Viorst. From *Free to Be . . . You and Me.* This usage granted by permission of The Choate Agency, LLC. All rights reserved.

Image Credits

Cover: Tommy Daynjer/Shutterstock; 1 Kim Howell / Shutterstock; 6 © 2017 Francisco Jimenez; 7 Maryna Kriuchenko/Dreamstime.com; 17 inga spence / Alamy Stock Photo; 26 ZUMA Press, Inc. / Alamy Stock Photo; 29 mountain_inside/Deposit Photos; 39 Chris Felver/Contributor/Getty Images; 62 Photo by © CORBIS/Corbis via Getty Images; 66 The Miriam and Ira D. Wallach Division of Art, Prints and Photographs: Photography Collection, The New York Public Library. "Harlem Street: II. 422-424 Lenox Avenue, Manhattan." New York Public Library Digital Collections. Accessed October 27, 2016. http: 74 Basso CANNARSA/Agence Opale/Alamy Stock Photo; 75 Fine Art Photographic Library/SuperStock; 79 Agence Opale / Alamy Stock Photo; 80 zerbor/123RF; 81 Schalkwijk / Art Resource, NY; 85 Charles Sykes/AP Photo; 86 Bannister, Matt / Private Collection / Bridgeman Images; 92 LEOcrafts/iStock; 103 Nejron Photo/Shutterstock; 108 Moviestore collection Ltd / Alamy Stock Photo; 122 sevenMaps7/Shutterstock; 123 © Chad Mcdermott/Dreamstime.com; 133 Splash News / Alamy Stock Photo; 134 ASIFE/iStock; 137 Moviestore collection Ltd / Alamy Stock Photo; 142 SL_Photography/iStock; 160 Rick Smith/AP Images; 165 © 2017 Rosalie Winard; 166 Juniors Bildarchiv GmbH / Alamy Stock Photo; 177 ⊠ 2017 Jason Fulford; 180 © 2017 Rosalie Winard; 185 Copyright © 2017 by Jonathan Bartlett; 193 N/A 198 ⊠ 2017 Amadee Martella; 199 AP Photo/Matt Rourke; 203 bowdenimages/iStock; 218 N/A 218 N/A 218 N/A 218 N/A 227 PeopleImages/iStock; 253 "Female Figure." Photographed by Craig Smith. Copyright (C) 1970, Heard, Museum, Phoenix, Arizona; 253 "Navajo Wearver." Photographed by Fred Harvey Company. Copyright (C) 1920, Heard, Museum, Phoenix, Arizona; 277 Khakimullin Aleksandr/Shutterstock; 281 Hunt, William Holman (1827-1910) / Walker Art Gallery, National Museums Liverpool / Bridgeman Images 282 Chronicle / Alamy Stock Photo; 283 Lear, Edward (1812-88) / Private Collection / © Look and Learn / Bridgeman Images; 288 Martin Bustamante © 2018 College Board; 290 © 2017 Shevaun Williams; 296 © 2017 Cheron Bayna; 296 Martin Bustamante © 2018 College Board; 299 Lorelyn Medina/123RF; 299 Splash News / Alamy Stock Photo; 307 Ikon Images / Alamy Stock Photo; 310 Raphael Lopez 325 DusanVulic/iStock; 335 AP Photo/JWG; 336 Ronald Grant Archive / Alamy Stock; 342 Everett Collection/SuperStock; 345 Everett Collection/SuperStock; 357 United Archives GmbH / Alamy Stock Photo; 358 Photo 12 / Alamy Stock Photo.